TASK VARIABLES IN MATHEMATICAL PROBLEM SOLVING

Gerald A. Goldin and C. Edwin McClintock   Editors

THE FRANKLIN INSTITUTE PRESS℠

0302037X

MATH-STAT.

© 1984 by Gerald A. Goldin and C. Edwin McClintock

Published by THE FRANKLIN INSTITUTE PRESS^{SM}
Philadelphia, Pennsylvania

Current printing (last digit):
5 4 3 2 1

Printed in the United States of America

Library of Congress Cataloging in Publication Data
Main entry under title:

Task variables in mathematical problem solving.

  Reprint. Originally published: Columbus : ERIC
Clearinghouse for Science, Mathematics, and Environmental
Education, Ohio State University, College of Education,
1980. With new introd.
  Bibliography: p.
  Includes index.
  1. Problem solving.   2. Mathematics—Problems,
exercises, etc.   I. Goldin, Gerald A., 1943–
II. McClintock, C. Edwin.
  QA63.T37 1984   510   84-8074
  ISBN 0-89168-056-X

Perspectives on the Study of Task Variables:
A Preface to the 1984 Edition

For the past four years, *Task Variables in Mathematical Problem Solving* has been available to the research community as a Mathematics Education Report of the ERIC Clearinghouse for Science, Mathematics and Environmental Education.* The decision by The Franklin Institute Press to publish the book this year reflects a certain level of sustained interest that has developed in this work. Here I would like to offer a brief perspective on the meaning of task variables research, and its relationship to the broader study of problem solving.

In the experimental investigation of problem solving, a task (or sequence of tasks) is typically presented to a subject (or group of subjects), resulting in certain outcomes which are, in principle, observable. Among the considerations which inevitably enter into the design of a study, the following must be included.

First, what are the characteristics of the task or set of tasks? Which characteristics have been held constant across tasks, and which have been varied? What are the anticipated effects of changes in the task characteristics? This class of questions is particularly important because seemingly small changes in a problem's syntax, content, context, or structure can have large effects on problem difficulty or on subjects' problem-solving processes.[1]

Secondly what are the problem-solving outcomes that one intends to measure? What data are to be recorded, and what scoring system or coding system will be used? Is the method of scoring task-specific, task-independent, or does it apply to a category of tasks which have certain features in common? Many of the scoring systems that have been used in research can be grouped under six broad headings: *1.* problem difficulty measures, *2.* error patterns, *3.* strategy scoring systems, *4.* structured interview responses, *5.* paths through external representations, and *6.* verbal, written and enactive protocols. From

---

*The Ohio State University, Columbus, Ohio 43212. Publication was originally prepared with funding from the National Institute of Education, U.S. Department of Health, Education, and Welfare, under contract no. 400-78-0004. The opinions expressed do not necessarily reflect the positions or policies of NIE or HEW.

an operational point of view, the very definition of problem solving should include a description of how it is to be measured.[2]

In the present book, the reader will find extensive (but still incomplete) discussions of several categories of task characteristics, and their effects—problem syntax (Chapter 2), problem content and context (Chapter 3), problem representation structure (Chapter 4), and problem heuristic characteristics (Chapter 5). In addition, empirical studies exemplify not only the manipulation and control of task variables, but also many of the ways of recording and measuring problem-solving outcomes—measures of difficulty (Chapters 6, 7A, 7B, 7C), strategy scoring systems (Chapters 7A, 7B, 8A), structured questions (Chapter 7A), paths through external state-spaces (Chapter 7C), and process-sequence coding of protocols (Chapter 8B).

From the ways in which the measurements of problem-solving outcomes are observed to depend on task characteristics, one hopes to be able to model the structure of *competencies* in problem solvers. It is my present view that a realistic model of problem-solving competency should entail at least four higher-level language systems: *1.* a system for verbal and syntactic processing of "natural" language, which can account for observed effects of the manipulation of task syntax variables; *2.* a system for imagistic (non-verbal) processing, which can account for observed effects of task content and context variables; *3.* a system of formal notational language (toward which most mathematics teaching is directed), accounting for effects of task structure variables; and *4.* a system for planning and executive control, which can account for effects of task heuristic behavior variables. Output from any one of these systems can serve as input for any other. Furthermore, planning language can stand as a meta-language with respect to the others, taking their rules of procedure as input and modifying them. Planning language also has a self-referential capability, so that heuristic processes can be employed which act on the domain of heuristic processes, as well as on domains from other language systems. The theoretical analysis of task variables, together with empirical research, suggests these as the minimum number of language systems needed to simulate "intelligent" problem solving.[3,4]

Finally, supposing that one has constructed a sufficiently detailed model of problem-solving competency, there is the fundamental question of how *learning* takes place—i.e., how and under what conditions competencies are acquired during problem solving. Through what means does the individual construct new internal representational systems, and how do these facilitate the solution of classes of related problems? In the experimental investigation of these questions, control of task variables will again be crucial. The present book suggests some applications to instruction involving manipulation of problem syntax, content and context variables (Chapter 9), structure (Chapter 10A) and heuristic behavior (Chapter 10B) characteristics.

Thanks are due to Julia Hough of The Franklin Institute Press for her interest in ensuring the continued availability of *Task Variables in Mathematical Problem Solving.* The many people and institutions who contributed to its creation are acknowledged in the Editors' Preface of November 1979, which is included here.

Gerald A. Goldin
De Kalb, Illinois
April 1984

References

1. Goldin, G.A. Characteristics of Problem Tasks in the Study of Mathematical Problem Solving. In Zweng, M., Green, T., Kilpatrick, J., Pollak, H., and Suydam, M., *Proceedings of the Fourth International Congress on Mathematical Education.* Boston: Birkhäuser (1983), 452–454.
2. Goldin, G.A. The Measure of Problem-Solving Outcomes. In Lester, F.K. and Garofalo, J., *Mathematical Problem Solving: Issues in Research.* Philadelphia: The Franklin Institute Press (1982), 87–101.
3. Goldin, G.A. Mathematical Language and Problem Solving. *Visible Language* **16** (1982), 221–238.
4. Goldin, G.A. Levels of Language in Mathematical Problem Solving. In Bergeron, J.C. and Herscovics, N., *Proceedings of the Fifth Annual Meeting of PME-NA (N. Amer. Chapter of the Int'l. Gp. for the Psych. of Math. Educ.).* Montreal: Concordia Univ. Dept. of Mathematics (1983), Vol. 2, 112–120.

The following contributors to *Task Variables in Mathematical Problem Solving* have reported changes in their institutional affiliations:

Janet H. Caldwell
Glassboro State College
Glassboro, New Jersey

Harold C. Days
AT&T Technologies
Greensboro, North Carolina

Fadia Harik
Mount Holyoke College
South Hadley, Massachusetts

Max E. Jerman
BertaMax Inc.
Seattle, Washington

Howard Kellogg
Mercy College
Dobbs Ferry, New York

Gerald Kulm
University of Kentucky
Lexington, Kentucky

George F. Luger
University of New Mexico
Albuquerque, New Mexico

Alan H. Schoenfeld
University of Rochester
Rochester, New York

William Waters
Morris Hills Regional School District
Denville, New Jersey

Norman Webb
Dept. of Public Instruction
Madison, Wisconsin

iii

Table of Contents

APPLICATIONS TO RESEARCH

APPLICATIONS TO TEACHING

Editors' Preface

This book is intended for mathematics educators, psychologists, and others interested in mathematical problem solving as researchers, practitioners, or students. It could serve as a text for a graduate course, or as a source of supplementary readings and references.

Chapter I is introductory, and should be read by all who are interested in the subject of task variables. Chapters II-V describe in more detail the categories of task variables, and the various theoretical perspectives taken by the authors. Chapters VI-VIII consist of research studies, while Chapters IX-X contain teaching applications; these two groups of chapters may be read independently of each other. Finally, two invited reaction papers provide comment and criticism.

The ideas in the book are the products of several different lines of research, which eventually came to be unified within the task variables framework. The work on factors affecting problem difficulty, including the "linear regression" model, was begun in the 1960's by P. Suppes, M. Jerman, and others at Stanford University. It was carried further in the early 1970's at Pennsylvania State University by Jerman, and by J.C. Barnett as a graduate student working with R. Heimer. At the University of Pennsylvania the state-space and algorithmic analysis of problem structure, as well as efforts to control various task variables for experimental purposes, were advanced by J. Caldwell, J. Gramick, G.F. Luger, and W.M. Waters (with acknowledgments to R. McGee and C. Serotta); who, between 1971 and 1977, were graduate students working with G.A. Goldin. Another independent development was the description and analysis of heuristic behavior, enormously influenced by J. Kilpatrick while at Columbia University, and carried forward by his students, N. Branca, D. Goldberg, H. Kellogg, J.P. Smith, and others, during the 1970's. At the same time interest in heuristic processes evolved at the University of Georgia, with research by L.L. Hatfield and by J.W. Wilson, carried further by E.L. Kantowski and others.

In May 1975, many of these researchers came together with others in Athens, Georgia, for a conference sponsored by the Problem Solving Project of the Georgia Center for the Study of Learning and Teaching Mathematics. At this conference several working groups were organized, of which two remained particularly active--the Task Variables Group, chaired by G. Kulm, and the Heuristics Group, chaired by Smith. Under Hatfield's dedicated leadership as director, the Problem Solving Project continued to provide a framework for worthwhile collaboration. Out of the Task Variables Group emerged two projects--the National Collection of Research Instruments for Mathematical Problem Solving (a "Problem Bank" edited by Kulm at Purdue University), and the present book. From the Heuristics Group emerged the process-sequence coding system which we are fortunate to be able to include in this volume.

Conceptually the book is somewhere between a monograph and a collection

of invited papers. The categories of task variables, and the model in
Figure 1.1, were the product of considerable discussion and revision
by the authors of the first five chapters. Of course there remained
many differences of opinion among the contributors, so that the authors
of the chapters take ultimate responsibility for the viewpoints expressed.
As editors, we endeavored to impose a reasonably consistent use of
terminology throughout the book, and to encourage at least a modest
degree of fidelity to the framework described in Chapter I. We bear full
responsibility for the many editorial shortcomings which the reader will
find--particularly in view of the difficulties faced by all of the authors
who, in writing their chapters concurrently, had access only to preliminary drafts of other chapters.

Acknowledgments are due to the many individuals and institutions who
made publication possible. The Georgia Center, in addition to its support
for the Problem Solving Project, arranged for the independent critique of
preliminary versions of all of the chapters. We would like to thank the
following outside readers for their helpful suggestions: S.I. Brown (State
University of New York at Buffalo), P.G. O'Daffer (Illinois State University), J. Payne (University of Michigan), J. Sherrill (University of British Columbia), and P. Trafton (National College of Education, Chicago).
Special thanks are due to I. Isaacs (University of the West Indies, Jamaica)
who, while at the University of Georgia, read the entire manuscript. Valuable assistance with the index and bibliography was contributed by C.J.
Feltz, C.S. Goldin, and F. McClintock. In addition we appreciate the support and assistance provided by our own University departments.

Finally, we gratefully acknowledge the support of the ERIC center,
which provided the means for publication, and especially the patient and
tireless work of M.N. Suydam, who supervised the difficult technical
aspects of preparing the manuscript for printing.

Gerald A. Goldin
De Kalb, Illinois

C. Edwin McClintock
Miami, Florida

November 1979

Foreword

The Study of Problem-Solving Processes in Mathematical Education

by

Larry L. Hatfield
University of Georgia
Athens, Georgia

Goals of mathematical education usually assert the paramount value of learning to solve problems. It is a complex challenge to guide students to become competent problem solvers in mathematics. Indeed, there are numerous varied factors which may influence the learner's progress and the teacher's efforts (Hatfield, 1978).

In an effort to further our understanding of such factors, this volume on task variables has been prepared. The focus upon the qualities and influences of mathematical problem-solving tasks has been adopted intentionally. The authors have apparently used the heuristical precept: simplify the problem (of developing a theory of mathematical problem solving) by momentarily ignoring some of the conditions, variables, or questions. As overviewed by Kulm in Chapter I, this book seeks to provide information about the study of problem solving by clarifying the "instrument" (i.e., the task) used to stimulate and measure the phenomenon of problem solving.

This concentration upon the task at least temporarily ignores much of the other sources of variation due to the solvers or the solving situation. Critics may issue challenges to the viability of this tactic. But it is with considerable patience and detail that the authors of Chapters I-V have pursued their efforts to specify and clarify their scheme of task variables in mathematical problem solving. The potential uses of these conceptualizations are discussed as suggested applications of task variables to research (Chapters VI-VIII) and to teaching (Chapters IX-X). Finally, reaction papers by Jerman and Kilpatrick are included to commend and critique the ideas from the perspectives of two mathematics educators whose own earlier efforts influenced the authors, but who were not directly involved in the formulation of this book.

The treatment of task variables developed herein does not exhaust the possible sources of variation which might be attributed to problematic tasks in mathematics. The goal has been to identify potentially significant sources of task variation and to explicate their definitions, meanings, and effects as thoroughly as current understandings of human problem solving might allow. Any such effort must constitute a "means to an end": the long-range goal is to utilize these task variables in studies of problem-solving processes in mathematical education. Thus, the material herein is based upon an assumption that more precise, elaborate understandings of the influences of problematic task variations will further the search for better understandings of how students learn to solve mathematics problems.

It will be clear to the reader that the authors have produced a notable contribution toward these research and instructional goals. Yet, to the members of the Task Variables working group of the Georgia Center for the Study of Learning and Teaching Mathematics who initiated this book, it represents a challenge for continued work. The task variables developed to date need to be studied and possibly refined in terms of their meanings, measurements, and uses in teaching and learning how to solve mathematical problems. Comparable formulations of <u>subject</u> and <u>situational</u> variables need to be explicated. Eventually, the complex interactions of these variables must be studied.

Mathematics teachers need to understand how students might construct solutions to problematic tasks. But, perhaps more important, we need to understand how students construct their own increasing competence to solve problems across mathematical learning experiences. These constructions range from learning details of a specific solution to assimilating heuristical schemata used in several solutions to generalizing comprehensive meta-heuristical strategies across entire classes of problems and solutions. That is, the variety of constructions for, and about, solving mathematics problems which students will construct to become competent is extensive and complex. Yet it must be a central focus in studying processes to examine these constructions -- to the extent possible, as they are being constructed. Detailed case studies which identify and document a solver's existing competence structures for solving tasks are needed. But teachers are necessarily concerned with change, and they need knowledge of how such competencies might be built and reconstructed across time and tasks.

This constructive approach views mathematics as a human construction, learners as active builders of their own conceptions and competencies, and mathematics instruction as the context for stimulating and guiding these builders in their own constructive processes. Of course, mathematics can be viewed as a body of information and mathematical learning as information-processing. We should all be deeply aware of the growing influences of the information-processing framework in the study of human cognition. But Newell and Simon (1972) urge that we recognize the necessity to view the human processor as an adaptive system, possessing a capacity to develop and change the system while the performing system remains in reasonably good working order. Indeed, the crucial aspects of learning include changes in the processors. Thus, a learner is not a rigid, pre-wired machine with memory capacities, but rather a dynamic adaptable system where programs or routines are self-constructed and subsequently modified or reconstructed. Furthermore, the informational content of most learning experiences includes not only the surface, factual material but the meta-information relating to the means (processes) for dealing with the material. Among these conceptions of "how I learn" is an awareness of one's own processes of learning; in the problem-solving domain these make up heuristical emphases.

Problem solving as an endeavor requires the coordination of reflection and activity. The investigation of solutions as they are being constructed would involve attention to the solver's actions (both external and internal) and the interactive thoughts about these actions. An important antecedent to such actions and reflections is the structure of goals, both general and task/situation specific, held by the solver. To understand the genesis and control of a solver's actions and reflections, the teacher/researcher would know much about these goals. To date, little appears to be known, though much is often assumed about the solver, regarding the idiosyncratic goal structure. In devising ways of knowing a solver's goals, it will be important to recognize that goals, too, are constructed and often transitory. Indeed, an important purpose and outcome of instruction can be to bring about changes in the goals held by the student.

Today, the psychology of learning and teaching mathematics seems to be influenced by at least two rather differing viewpoints. A rationalist, scientific approach considers the educative situation as a cybernetic system involving adaptable but predictable beings, whose actions are describable from the point of view of general control theory. Instruction becomes an application of rules or algorithms for stimulating the information-processing capabilities of the student. Understanding problem-solving processes becomes a search for the production systems, invariant across solvers, responsible for controlling solving behavior (e.g., Landa, 1976b).

A constructivist approach views the educative situation as a complexity of perceptions, goals, dispositions, and interactions, all constructed by individual participants. These constructions are fluid and dynamic, being often in flux. The changes are often predictable only within broad terms. But to understand problem-solving processes is to search for the varied bases for, and qualities of, the constructions and reconstructions that constitute thinking. Any "theory" of problem solving would include attention to the rather uncontrollable variations in the possible constructions due to idiosyncratic goals and competencies.

It should be obvious that mathematical education cannot be fairly dichotomized this way. Yet perhaps elements of these two extremes do guide our thinking as teachers and researchers. The study of problem-solving processes in mathematical education can easily tolerate either framework, since we sorely need information to be generated for the teaching and learning of problem solving.

The analysis of task variables in the present book is a small but important step towards a theory of how students learn mathematical problem solving.

I.

The Classification of Problem-Solving Research Variables

by

Gerald Kulm
Purdue University
West Lafayette, Indiana

The development of problem-solving ability is a cumulative process which depends on the history of problem-solving experiences of the student. Crucial to any problem-solving experience is the task itself. In order to advance knowledge about problem solving, it is thus important that close attention be given to the characteristics of problem tasks.

The task or collection of tasks is the measuring instrument which is used to study the phenomena of problem solving. An understanding of how the variables describing the task itself interact with the total situation is a basic requirement for such a study. The ability to classify and define task variables would make it possible to control them systematically, in order to determine their effects on problem-solving behavior. Furthermore, the precise specification of problem tasks is necessary for the replication and extension of experimental studies. One purpose of this book is to provide researchers with categories and definitions of variables describing problem tasks, providing a framework for their control in problem-solving studies.

Throughout this book, the term "task variable" will mean any characteristic of problem tasks which assumes a particular value from a set of possible values. A task variable may thus be numerical (e.g., the number of words in a problem) or classificatory (e.g., problem content area).

In the past, standardized tests have been widely used to measure problem-solving ability. However, the emphasis in problem-solving research is shifting to the study of the *processes* used to arrive at an answer. The complexity of the written, verbal, or enactive sequences of behavior that characterize these processes makes it particularly necessary to examine the measuring instrument (i.e., the problem task) which elicits them. A *language* is needed to describe task variables, based on a model for the range of possible characteristics of mathematical problems. Such a development can assist the standardization of vocabulary, helping to distinguish between problem-solving variables which are intrinsic to the problem itself and those which describe other aspects of the problem-solving event.

The conclusions of problem-solving studies are sometimes stated in terms of processes which certain experimental groups are (or are not) capable of employing. On the other hand, *small* changes in the problem content, its setting, or the wording of the problem may result in *major* changes in the problem-solving procedures exhibited by subjects. Often these problem characteristics are not sufficiently described or analyzed, making it difficult to interpret or reproduce the findings. The payoff from a thorough description of task variables, and an investigation of their relationship to experimental observations, should be increased replicability and generalizability of research results.

The study of task variables also has important implications for classroom instruction. For example, the systematic teaching of a particular problem-solving strategy may require sets of problems of varying complexity to which the strategy is applicable. Problem complexity variables which are not relevant for a particular instructional segment must be controlled, while the relevant variables are emphasized. As teachers observe the capabilities of individual students and their difficulties with different types of problems, it can be helpful to recognize *which* characteristics of the problems pose particular difficulties, and to tailor discussion towards the explicit emphasis of these problem characteristics. Although these may seem to be simple ideas, the variables affecting problem difficulty are *not* simply described or easily characterized.

In this chapter, we shall develop the necessary background and introduce the model for the classification of task variables which underlies the structure of this book. Definitions for each of the major categories of task variables will be presented and discussed.

1.   Background for the Study of Task Variables

Kilpatrick's Categories of Problem-Solving Research Variables

In a position paper outlining categories of variables and methodologies in problem-solving studies, Kilpatrick (1975) attempted to clarify the role of task variables and to suggest possible methods of systematic problem description. This paper served as a forerunner to the development of the model described here. An outline of Kilpatrick's categories is presented in Table 1.1.

Independent Variables

Kilpatrick specified three main categories of independent variables in problem-solving research—*subject* variables, *task* variables, and *situation* variables. These three categories are derived from the necessary components of a problem-solving event, which are a problem solver (subject) solving a problem (task) under a set of conditions

Table 1.1 *Kilpatrick's Categories of Problem-Solving Research Variables (Kilpatrick, 1975)*

Independent Variables

Subject Variables

    Organismic Variables
    Trait Variables
    Instructional History Variables

Task Variables

    Context Variables
    Structure Variables
    Format Variables

Situation Variables

    Physical Setting
    Psychological Setting

Dependent Variables

Product Variables

Process Variables

Evaluation Variables

Concomitant Variables

(situation). Any problem-solving event involves a complex interaction among the variables describing these three components. In order to place the category of *task* variables in perspective, we shall outline briefly the nature of all three categories according to Kilpatrick.

Subject Variables

Subject variables are those quantities which describe or measure specific attributes of the subject—in this case the problem solver. They are of great importance in experiments of a clinical nature, including "teaching experiments" such as are frequently reported in the Soviet Union. The small number of subjects in such studies makes a sensitivity to subject variables particularly important in conducting them and in reporting the results.

Kilpatrick further classified subject variables according to the ease with which they can be modified. Those subject variables not open to change or experimental manipulation were called *organismic* variables. Examples of organismic variables are age, sex, socioeconomic status, and geographic residence. Kilpatrick noted that, except for age and sex, few problem-solving studies have considered organismic variables other than to describe the sample.

Of more interest are *trait* variables—those which can be modified by processes such as teaching. Traits such as cognitive style, attitude, persistence, mathematical memory, or the ability to estimate offer promise of being closely associated with problem-solving performance. Kilpatrick suggested that it might be fruitful to concentrate investigation on specific rather than general traits —for example, a study of the ability to estimate the magnitude of numerical solutions to equations might yield clearer information than studying the general ability to estimate. Many of the abilities listed in Krutetskii's (1976) outline of the structure of mathematical abilities (see Table 1.3) are traits in Kilpatrick's sense.

Finally, *instructional history* variables describe the schools attended, mathematical topics studied, or problem-solving instruction received by the subject. Some of these are more open to manipulation than others. Kilpatrick points out that the failure to consider them in selecting experimental groups may be partly responsible for the lack of differences often found between instructional methods.

Task Variables

The category of task variables as first introduced by Kilpatrick included three classifications—*context* variables, *structure* variables, and *format* variables. Although this classification scheme has been extensively redefined and elaborated in this book, it is of interest to summarize its initial conceptualization.

Context variables include those which characterize the physical situation of the problem, as well as the language in which the problem is expressed. They are intended to describe the differences between problems having the same mathematical structure. Kilpatrick noted that the term "content variable" may be appropriate, but suggested that there may be different interpretations of what is meant by "mathematical content." Whichever term is used, Kilpatrick intended "context variables" to include variables describing the semantic content or mathematical meaning of the problem.

Structure variables are intended to describe the intrinsic mathematical structure of a problem. One way to do so is to employ a mathematical formula or relation. Kilpatrick suggested that two problems with the same formula could be said to have the same "syntactic structure," evidently using this term to refer to the syntax of the formula or relation; i.e., the variables, the operations, etc. Another approach to the characterization of problem structure which Kilpatrick mentions is the "state-space" approach, described in Chapter IV of this book. The concept of problem structure is believed to be extremely important because of its implications for studying the effects of problem similarities and differences on problem-solving performance.

Format variables describe the different manners or settings in which a problem may be presented. For example, it may be presented along with other problems, with hints, or with the aid of some apparatus. Usually, format variables have been ignored by researchers with the assumption that problem-solving processes are not affected by them. Particularly relevant to this assumption are such format variables as the encouragement of scratch work, or whether or not the subject is asked to think aloud during problem solving. In Kilpatrick's opinion, format variables are important because they represent dimensions across which problem-solving results need to be generalized.

Situation Variables

In very general terms, situation variables describe the physical, psychological, or social environment in which the problem-solving event takes place. The category of situation variables is difficult to characterize since it includes a variety of components. In particular, some situation variables appear to overlap or merge with certain task variables, particularly those which Kilpatrick calls format variables, and it is important to resolve this difficulty.

The *physical setting* includes such variables as the type of space (classroom, laboratory, outdoors, etc.), the nature of the space (comfortable, stimulating, familiar, etc.), and the available resources (calculators, measuring instruments, manipulative materials, or amount of time). The *psychological setting* includes variables describing the purpose of the event (testing, instruction, practice, etc.), the type of procedure (evaluative, prescriptive, diagnostic, etc.), and the nature of the learning environment (type or amount of feedback, quantity or quality of interaction). These variables are most directly related to the motivation of the subject in solving the problem, and the resulting affective outcomes. The *social setting*, although not explicitly discussed by Kilpatrick, seems to fit as well into this category, including variables describing the group (size, purpose, type, etc.) or the relationship between subject and experimenter (personality, familiarity, etc.).

Situation variables are intended not to describe the task or the subject, but to be external to both. In this book, some of the above-mentioned variables, particularly the availability of resources such as calculators, are considered to be task variables and are discussed as such. As Kilpatrick pointed out, situation variables are often nuisance variables—of little direct interest, but possibly having unexpected effects on problem-solving performance.

Dependent Variables

The second major category of problem-solving research variables is derived from subjects' responses to the problem task. Kilpatrick identified four classifications of dependent variables: *product* variables, *process* variables, *evaluation* variables, and *concomitant* variables.

Product Variables

Product variables have to do with achievement of the solution to a problem. This classification includes the time to solution, the correctness or incorrectness of a solution, and the completeness of a solution. Perhaps the most important comment made about these variables is the recommendation that researchers consider product variables beyond those of speed and accuracy—including, for example, the elegance of the solution or the multiplicity of different solutions found.

Process Variables

Process variables are derived from a subject's verbal report during problem solving, from his or her written work, or from steps taken with a physical apparatus. Examples include variables describing the heuristic processes used, the algorithms employed, or the blind alleys encountered along the subject's path towards a solution. Kilpatrick was adamant about the importance of process variables, stating that "any respectable study of problem solving in mathematics should include measures of process variables."

While this is certainly a worthwhile goal, some caution is necessary, especially if subject self-reports are the sole process measure. Nisbett and Wilson (1977), for example, have argued convincingly that self-reports during problem solving may be inaccurate or incomplete, and that exclusive reliance on "thinking aloud" reports for obtaining process variables may result in distortion of the problem-solving process.

Evaluation Variables

Evaluation variables describe the views, thoughts, and opinions expressed by the subject after the problem has been solved. These variables include what the subject was trying to do, how the problem was perceived in relation to other problems, the subject's level of confidence in the solution, etc. While it may be difficult to obtain accurate measures of variables in this classification, Kilpatrick emphasized that they describe information which can be obtained only from the subject, and should not be neglected.

Concomitant Variables

Concomitant variables are those variables not included in the previous three categories, which may nevertheless change during the course of problem solving. Many of the trait variables mentioned above could be considered concomitant variables—for example, a subject's ability to estimate numerical solutions might improve after solving a set of problems. Similarly, more general abilities, or attitudes, might change. As Kilpatrick noted, concomitant variables cannot be expected to change greatly unless they are very specific or the number of problems solved is large.

Having placed the category of task variables in the context of Kilpatrick's framework of problem-solving research variables, let us digress to survey a few authors of importance to mathematics education who have placed special emphasis on the characteristics of problem tasks.

Problem-Solving Methods and Mathematical Abilities

Many of us have been fascinated and challenged, at one time or another, with the books by problemists such as Sam Loyd and Martin Gardner (1959a, b; 1966). These authors were concerned with creating, collecting, discussing, and solving a wide variety of problems, not with the experimental study of problem solving or with its teaching. Nevertheless, their work has great importance for these areas. They (and others) recognized and developed the concepts of the structure of a problem and the relationships between mathematically similar problems, which importantly affect problem-solving processes. Ideas such as problem *symmetry*, problem *isomorphisms*, and classification of problems in accordance with their *solution strategies* have been used extensively by Gardner. These ideas contribute importantly to the discussion of structure and heuristic behavior variables in the present book.

George Polya (1945, 1954, 1962, 1965) has been a major continuing influence on the teaching of problem-solving skills. His work has focused principally on the use of well-selected problem tasks to foster effective problem solving and on the application of general heuristic processes to problem solving. Table 1.2 presents Polya's summary of the stages involved in effective problem solving: (1) understanding the problem, (2) devising a plan, (3) carrying out the plan, and (4) looking back. In the present book, each category of task variable is envisioned as influencing some of these stages more strongly than others.

The *heuristic processes* suggested by Polya have motivated many experimental investigations. Perhaps the most intriguing of these processes, in relation to the study of *task* variables, is the advice to find a "related problem." It seems clear that the term "related" refers to some sort of underlying structural relatedness; but it is difficult in many cases to describe the precise nature of the relatedness in terms of problem structure. Polya mentions three ways in which problems may be related—by *analogy*, by *specialization*, and by *generalization*. Related problems can also be obtained by decomposing and recombining problems. In general, one wishes to identify the task variables that contribute to the relatedness. For example, Polya uses the following to illustrate *analogous* problems:

1.1 *Given the length of an edge of a regular tetrahedron, find the radius of the sphere circumscribed about the tetrahedron.*

1.2 *Given the length of the side of an equilateral triangle, find the radius of the circle circumscribed about the triangle.*

Polya was not explicitly concerned with syntax, but it is striking that two problems have the same number of words and the same sentence structure. They are also drawn from the same mathematical content area. In these senses they are "related" on a surface level. It becomes more difficult to describe their structural relationships. Problem *1.2* is the planar analogue of Problem *1.1*, so that analogous formulas which characterize structure exist. Problem *1.1* can be solved by use of a solid geometry analogue to the concurrency of the angle bisectors of a triangle, so that it possesses a solution strategy related to that of Problem *1.2*.

According to Polya, the difficulty with using related problems is not that of finding problems which seem relevant to the problem at hand, but that of finding problems related in such a way so as to help lead to a solution. The precise nature of such relatedness is a question which recurs in this book and which, in this author's opinion, can be answered through task variable analysis.

Like Polya, Wickelgren (1974) suggests methods for helping to improve problem-solving abilities. In an attempt to place problem-solving methods on a theoretical basis, Wickelgren borrowed many concepts from artificial intelligence. He considered the structure of the problem task to be extremely important. According to Wickelgren, a problem consists of information concerning (1) givens, (2) operations, and (3) goals. Problem types can be characterized by the amount and kind of information available in each of the three categories. For example, in a problem to find x (the goal), given the expression $7x + 3 = 24$ (the given), the goal is *incompletely* specified. The problem, therefore, can be classified as one in which the goal to be reached is not given. Other types of problems have *completely* specified goals. A "problem to prove" would be one in which the goal is given; e.g., given the expression $7x + 3 = 24$, prove that x = 3. Other problem classifications arise by varying the specification of the givens and the operations.

Wickelgren also discussed in his theory the ideas of problem *states*, operations on states, and solutions. The representation of possible sequences of actions and possible sequences of states is called a *state-action tree*. The state-action tree provides the framework for much of Wickelgren's discussion of problem-solving methods. Problems are characterized according to the properties of their state-action trees; and although not all problems are represented by such trees, concepts derived from them, such as the size of the search space and the identification of subgoal states, are used extensively in discussing solution methods.

Wickelgren also discussed the idea of related problems, focusing more directly on the relationships between solution methods than did Polya. Five types of related problems were identified: unrelated problems, equivalent problems, similar problems, special cases, and generalizations. The last three are very similar to the categories discussed by Polya. Wickelgren's analysis of related problems was based on the difficulty of solution of each. Both Wickelgren and Polya used the idea of problem structure to characterize the appropriate heuristic processes and solution strategies.

Unlike the aforementioned authors, Krutetskii (1976) was mainly interested in the experimental study of problem-solving ability. The development of problem tasks was an important component of his work. In an attempt to span the complete range of components of problem-solving abilities, 26 problem series containing a total of 79 problems were used. Rather than relying on answer-oriented instruments, Krutetskii emphasized the importance of relatively short tests which were designed to measure specific abilities. The problems were classified according to mathematical content area, as

Table 1.2 *Polya's Model for Effective Problem Solving (Polya, 1945)*

HOW TO SOLVE IT

UNDERSTANDING THE PROBLEM

First. *What is the unknown? What are the data? What is the condition?*

You have to *understand* the problem. Is it possible to satisfy the condition? Is the condition sufficient to determine the unknown? Or is it insufficient? Or redundant? Or contradictory?

Draw a figure. Introduce suitable notation.

Separate the various parts of the condition. Can you write them down?

DEVISING A PLAN

Second. Have you seen it before? Or have you seen the same problem in a slightly different form?

Find the connection between the data and the unknown. You may be obliged to consider auxiliary problems if an immediate connection cannot be found. You should obtain eventually a *plan* of the solution.

Do you know a related problem? Do you know a theorem that could be useful?

Look at the unknown! And try to think of a familiar problem having the same or a similar unknown.

Here is a problem related to yours and solved before. Could you use it? Could you use its result? Could you use its method? Should you introduce some auxiliary element in order to make its use possible?

Could you restate the problem? Could you restate it still differently? Go back to definitions.

If you cannot solve the proposed problem try to solve first some related problem. Could you imagine a more accessible related problem? A more general problem? A more special problem? An analogous problem? Could you solve a part of the problem? Keep only a part of the condition, drop the other part; how far is the unknown then determined, how can it vary? Could you derive something useful from the data? Could you

(continued)

Table 1.2 *(continued)*

think of other data appropriate to determine the unknown? Could you change the unknown or the data, or both if necessary, so that the new unknown and the new data are nearer to each other?

Did you use all the data? Did you use the whole condition? Have you taken into account all essential notions involved in the problem?

CARRYING OUT THE PLAN

Third.

Carry out your plan.

Carrying out your plan of the solution, *check each step*. Can you see clearly that the step is correct? Can you prove that it is correct?

LOOKING BACK

Fourth.

Examine the solution obtained.

Can you *check the result?* Can you check the argument?

Can you derive the result differently? Can you see it at a glance?

Can you use the result, or the method, for some other problem?

well as according to the ability characteristic they were designed to
elicit. Each series of problems was designed to reveal certain
aspects of a particular component of ability, so that it was necessary to compare results on several problem series. Krutetskii did
not specifically analyze the task variables in describing his problems or the processes they measured. Nevertheless, it is quite
clear that control and manipulation of task variables were central
to the development of the series. The description of students'
strategies and successes with the various tests were made with
reference primarily to the ability characteristic represented by
the test. Table 1.3 summarizes Krutetskii's outline of the structure of mathematical abilities, as it evolved from student performance on his problem series.

A great deal of information about the effects of task variables
on problem-solving behavior can be obtained directly from Krutetskii's
discussions. In one set of problems with identical context, a slight
change in the syntax of a problem produced a great change in structure. The following two problems illustrate this type of change:

> 1.3   *A horse moved at a speed of 12 km per hour for*
>   *half the time spent on a journey, and at 4 km*
>   *per hour for the rest of the time. Find the*
>   *horse's average speed.*

> 1.4   *A horse traveled half a journey at a speed of 12*
>   *km per hour, and at 4 km per hour for the rest*
>   *of the journey. Find the horse's average speed.*

The seemingly unimportant changes produce drastic changes in the
problem and the operations used to solve it. Many students had
difficulty in coping with the change, even when they knew that the
second problem was very different because of the seemingly small
change.

The problems constructed by Krutetskii, and the far-reaching
results that he obtained, provide an example of the value of well-
conceived and carefully-sequenced problem instruments.

Krutetskii's investigations are not rigorous empirical
studies, but are semi-clinical in nature. Some of the most
valuable data on task variables are provided by the work of
Suppes et al. (1966) and Jerman (1971). These and other studies
were aimed at investigating the problem characteristics affecting
difficulty through the use of linear regression models. Both syntax and structure variables are included in these studies. A
thorough summary of the linear regression analyses is provided
in Chapter II, while additional discussion of the work of
Krutetskii, Polya, and Wickelgren occurs in Chapters III through
V of this book.

Table 1.3 *Krutetskii's General Outline of the Structure of Mathematical Abilities (Krutetskii, 1976)*

1. Obtaining mathematical information

    A. The ability for formalized perception of mathematical material, for grasping the structure of a problem.

2. Processing mathematical information

    A. The ability for logical thought in the sphere of quantitative and spatial relationships, number and letter symbols; the ability to think in mathematical symbols.

    B. The ability for rapid and broad generalization of mathematical objects, relations, and operations.

    C. The ability to curtail the process of mathematical reasoning and the system of corresponding operations; the ability to think in curtailed structures.

    D. Flexibility of mental processes in mathematical activity.

    E. Striving for clarity, simplicity, economy, and rationality of solutions.

    F. The ability for rapid and free reconstruction of the direction of a mental process, switching from a direct to a reverse train of thought (reversibility of the mental process in mathematical reasoning).

3. Retaining mathematical information

    A. Mathematical memory (generalized memory for mathematical relationships, type characteristics, schemes of arguments and proofs, methods of problem-solving, and principles of approach).

4. General synthetic component

    A. Mathematical cast of mind.

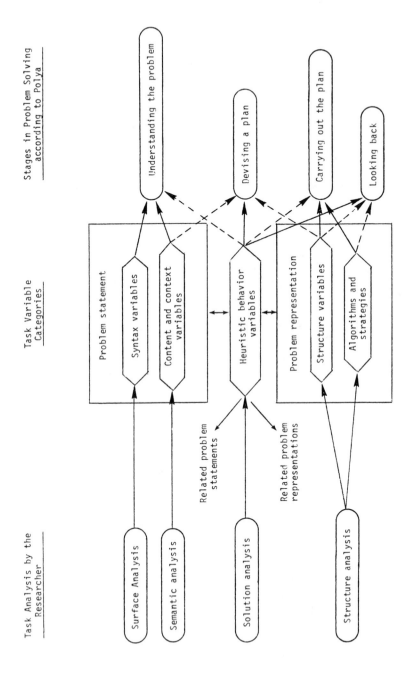

Figure 1.1. *A Hierarchy of Task Variables, Methods of Task Analysis, and Problem-Solving Stages*

2. Categories of Task Variables

The following discussion outlines four major categories of task
variables around which the present book is organized. Each
category will be more completely described in the four chapters which
follow, providing additional detail for the general model described
here. The categories are: (a) variables which describe the problem
syntax, (b) variables which characterize the problem's mathematical
content and non-mathematical *context*, (c) variables which describe
the *structure* of the problem, and (d) variables which characterize
the *heuristic processes* evoked by the problem.

These categories of task variables are hypothesized to stand in
a hierarchical relationship to each other, corresponding to increasingly complex levels of processing by the problem solver. The
hierarchy is represented in Figure 1.1.

The right column in the figure represents the stages in effective problem solving according to Polya. These stages are envisioned
to have a general sequential nature although, as with all such models,
the problem solver may frequently return to earlier stages in the
sequence. As indicated in the diagram by solid arrows, each category
of task variables is hypothesized to have primary importance for one
or two of these stages, and secondary importance for others indicated
by broken arrows. For example, syntax variables would primarily
influence the subject's initial understanding of the problem, and
have little influence over the later carrying out of a plan of a
solution.

The left column in the figure represents ways in which a teacher
or researcher might analyze the complexity of a problem task. A
surface analysis may yield information about the problem syntax—
the variables being for the most part explicit and susceptible to
direct observation or counting with a minimum of processing. A
semantic analysis also obtains information directly from the problem statement or embodiment; however, the analysis requires knowledge
of mathematical content and involves interpretation of the meanings
of the terms in the problem statement. *Solution* analysis requires
the generation of steps in the problem solution, and a description
of the heuristic processes or behaviors used in generating these
steps. Finally, the analysis of problem *structure* requires not only
the generation of solution paths, but examination of non-solution
paths, blind alleys, and other deeper attributes of the problem.
Except perhaps for certain standard problem types, it is not possible to obtain structure variables simply by inspection of the problem statement.

Thus, each method of task analysis in Figure 1.1 is primarily
related to obtaining a particular category of task variables. Next
we shall briefly survey the categories themselves.

Syntax Variables

Syntax variables are defined in this book to be those variables describing the arrangement of and relationships among words and
symbols in a problem. Note that the arrangement of words and symbols
may include the use of special mathematical vocabulary or symbols, as
well as ordinary English usage. In many arithmetic and algebra problems, the arrangement of words and symbols is closely associated with
or reflective of the more fundamental mathematical structure of the
problem.

A great deal of research has been done using syntax variables
as independent variables in regression equations for predicting the
difficulty of "word problems." Although these studies have not
examined syntax variables separately from variables in other categories, it has been found that, for algebra or arithmetic word
problems, syntax variables account for significant amounts of the
variance in the number of subjects achieving the correct numerical
answer (Jerman, 1971). It is less clear whether syntax variables
offer predictive power in geometry problems, or problems which do not
have a standard arithmetic or algebraic underlying structure.

The most useful syntax variables will be discussed in detail in
Chapter II. The categories of syntax variables include, for example,
problem length, grammatical complexity, and data sequence. New syntax variables can be generated by using combinations of two or more
previously defined variables. Further variables can also be generated by assigning indices to variables, producing measures such as
"number of sentences with more than ten words" or "number of words
unfamiliar to more than 50 percent of the subject population."
Although these somewhat complex derived variables may add predictive
power in regression studies, they may not be especially useful for
descriptive purposes or for instruction.

Research with syntax variables has provided clear indications
that linguistic variables must be considered in constructing problems, in order that syntactic difficulties do not interfere with
the variables or treatments of interest. On the other hand, little
research has been done on the effects of variations in syntax on
problem-solving behavior *processes*. Studies of reading comprehension in ordinary language do indicate that syntactic complexity
is an important determinant of the time and difficulty involved
in language processing. It is also well-known that subjects have
less difficulty with problems in which the syntax makes it possible
to translate directly from a verbal to an arithmetic or algebraic
expression. It would be useful to know much more precisely the
role of syntax variables in the decoding process of problem solving.
Because of their easy objective definition, it is in the category
of syntax variables that there is the most immediate opportunity
to obtain significant knowledge about problem-solving processing
that can be applied to the kinds of problems encountered in school
classrooms.

It is expected that syntax variables should most closely influence Polya's first stage, "understanding the problem."

Content and Context Variables

After a problem has been read, the problem solver responds to it in terms of its *meaning*. The term "content" is used here in its usual sense to refer to the main substance of a message, as opposed to its form. Thus by content we refer to *mathematical* meanings and by context to *non-mathematical* or incidental meanings in the problem statement.

Often, a problem is stated with respect to some particular mathematical or mathematically related *content area* such as number theory, measurement, probability, and so on. Such classifications of problems by mathematical content define one kind of content variable. Subcategories of content areas, as well as specific descriptors of mathematical characteristics, also define content variables. Among the latter are variables such as the type of mathematical expression (e.g., monomial, quadratic, linear) or type of mathematical operation appearing in a problem (e.g., binary, inverse, unary). The use of content variables to construct problems which vary according to mathematical complexity has always been a major focus in mathematics textbooks. Unfortunately, very little research has been done, beyond work with elementary arithmetic algorithms, to determine the best sequencing of mathematical content in problem solving.

Since many problems are presented in a verbal form, either written or oral, it is important to consider linguistic content variables; i.e., the use of mathematical words or phrases which have an impact on the meaning of the problem. For example, subtraction may be suggested by the *key words* "less," "decrease," "minus," "below," and so forth. Such key words have an enormous potential effect on students' comprehension of a problem.

It is somewhat difficult to distinguish *content* from *context* variables. The term *context* is used here to describe the *non-*mathematical meanings present in the problem statement. These may, however, help to give meaning to the mathematical content. Often the verbal context or setting of a problem provides a connection between mathematical content and its application or absence of application to the "real world." One important reason to study context variables is to examine the development of students' ability to extract essential mathematical information from the nonessential non-mathematical information in a problem.

Contexts may vary along dimensions such as concrete-abstract, applied-theoretical, or factual-hypothetical. Other context categories include those which make the statement of the problem more or less relevant to the problem solver's interests, age, or

experience. Also included as context variables are those which
relate to the mode of presentation: manipulative, pictorial,
verbal, etc.

Content and context variables should likewise influence Polya's
"understanding the problem" stage, as well as the stage "devising a
plan."

Structure Variables

To define syntax, content, and context variables requires little
or no processing of the problem statement. The term "structure," on
the other hand, is used to refer to the arrangement of and mathematical
relationships among all elements of a problem, and structure variables require some method of analysis in order to define them. The
attempt to represent the essence of problem structure often results
in an oversimplification or an incomplete representation of a problem.
On the other hand, the precise description and the potential for control of structure variables may be the most promising area in task
variable research.

In some research, the concept of problem structure has been
limited to a description of the algorithmic procedures or algebraic
equations which underlie many routine verbal problems. In these
cases, it is relatively easy to determine whether problems have
identical or different structures. On the other hand, even with
such problems, it is not clear *how closely* problems might be structurally related when they are *not* identical. Once the structure of
a problem has been clearly described, it is possible to investigate
problem-solving strategies which may be, in a sense, intrinsic to
the problem. This understanding of structure and applicable strategies is a necessary and valuable goal in developing the teaching of
problem-solving skills.

One of the promising approaches to studying problem structure
variables is state-space analysis, a generalization of Wickelgren's
state-action tree. Chapter IV will develop the necessary background
and provide details; however, a few of the potential outcomes of
state-space analysis should be mentioned here. Virtually any problem can be analyzed, providing a common ground for research. State-
space analysis makes it possible to study separately and simultaneously
the problem and problem solver, by utilizing the state-space to record
problem-solving behavior. This capability helps provide a way to
study how the problem solver builds internal representations of the
problem and processes information during the solution process. State-
space structures provide a framework within which to study chunking,
curtailment, problem symmetry, algorithms, working backward, decomposition, and other powerful problem-solving processes.

Problem structure variables principally affect Polya's stage "carrying out the plan," since they are descriptive of a *representation* of the problem which has been created.

Heuristic Behavior Variables

The usual interpretation of heuristic behaviors centers on the idea that they are general procedures or hints which help one discover or develop a plan for solving a problem. This characterization makes it appear that heuristic processes are independent of the particular problem being solved. There is no question that a given heuristic procedure may be widely applicable to many types of problems; it is this characteristic of heuristic processes that makes them valuable for problem solving. On the other hand, certain problems appear to be solved most efficiently, most quickly, most easily, or most often through the application of a *particular* heuristic process or set of processes. The structure of some problems may give rise to specific heuristic behaviors rather than others. An understanding of the heuristic processes that are *problem-specific* adds significantly to our ability to describe a problem task completely, and to use it in teaching or research.

It should be noted that heuristic behaviors, when regarded as task variables, are very different from the task variables discussed earlier. For example, rather than describing the difficulty level of problems, heuristic variables are simply informative. Thus, one can indicate that "working backward" is particularly useful for a given problem, but the difficulty level is not implied or suggested by such a statement. It is conceivable, however, that problems solvable by certain heuristic processes are less difficult than those not solvable by them.

As can be seen in Figure 1.1, heuristic behavior variables are hypothesized to affect all of Polya's stages, particularly those of "devising a plan" and "looking back." Heuristic processes form the bridge between the problem statement and a problem representation, as well as affecting the transition to related problem statements and representations. Of all the categories of task variables, they are certainly the most difficult to define and describe precisely.

3. Applications of Task Variables

The preceding section has introduced four main categories of task variables, which are further explored in Chapters II through V. Next let us survey some of the important areas of application of these ideas, described in the latter part of the book.

Applications of Task Variables to Research

Most of the research described in this book utilizes the concept of task variables to construct *sets* of problems, designed to measure the effects of a particular variable or set of variables on problem-solving outcomes. The key idea is to vary a single variable at a time, while holding constant other task variables. The degree of success in holding constant the variables which are not of experimental interest corresponds to one's degree of confidence that the observed effects are indeed due to the variable under study.

The study by Goldin and Caldwell, for example, is based on an instrument which holds constant a substantial list of syntax variables, content variables, and algorithmic structure variables, while studying the effects on problem difficulty of the classifications "abstract-concrete" and "factual-hypothetical." Likewise the studies by Waters and by Luger hold constant problem state-space variables while varying the problem embodiment, in order to observe the effects on strategy scores and transfer effects. The study by Days varies quantities describing the problem's algebraic representation to ascertain the effects on problem difficulty, and the study by Harik examines the consistency of the use of specific heuristic processes while problem structure variables are held constant and other task variables are modified. Taken together, these studies may be regarded as just the beginning of a program of research to explore various aspects of the model in Figure 1.1.

The chapter by Lucas et al. is of a very different sort. Addressing themselves to the difficult issue of measuring the use of particular heuristic processes (an obvious prerequisite to the reliable study of the problem-specificity of heuristic behaviors), a group of researchers has developed an elaborate *process-sequence coding scheme* for classifying subjects' heuristic behaviors. The scheme itself is intended to be *non*-problem-specific, but broad enough to permit the comparison of heuristic processes employed by subjects solving very different problems, as well as allowing the comparison of processes used by different subjects solving the same problem. Some preliminary results on the inter-coder reliability of the system are included.

Applications of Task Variables to Teaching

The main concept stressed in this book is the value of *explicit* treatment of task variables in the teaching of problem solving. Through the creation of sample unit plans, Caldwell demonstrates the value for teachers of systematically varying syntax, content and context variables, while holding structure variables constant. These are the variables which are characteristic of the problem statement, and thus are encountered first by students attempting to solve verbal problems. She also emphasizes the importance of

proper sequencing of problem content, in order to maximize the learning which takes place as a series of problems are solved.

Similarly, through the creation of sample teaching plans, Luger
argues for the use of structure variables to encourage learning
transfer through the systematic inclusion in instruction of problems
which stand in isomorphic and homomorphic relationships to each other.
This is an idea which has also received support from Usiskin (1968),
who urged the use of problems having identical algebraic structures
but widely varying content and context.

Finally, Schoenfeld discusses the explicit use of heuristic
behavior variables in teaching problem solving. Of particular
interest is his discussion of *cued* heuristic processes—that is,
the idea that identifiable cues within the problem statement itself
can serve to suggest the appropriate process to the student. By
calling attention to these cues in numerous examples, a convincing
case is developed that the *when* as well as the *how* of heuristic
processes can be taught by the sophisticated instructor.

It is likely that the ideas in these chapters, extensive as
they are, represent only a few of the many implications which the
study of problem task variables can have over the years for the
classroom teacher of mathematics.

II.

The Study of Syntax Variables*

by

Jeffrey Barnett
Fort Hays State University
Hays, Kansas

The role of language in the problem-solving process has received research attention for many years, and a significant amount of general information has been accumulated. For example, the relatively high correlation between mathematical problem-solving ability and the ability to read and comprehend written material has been confirmed by numerous studies since the beginning of the nineteenth century. If one subscribes to the view that the first stage of the verbal problem-solving process involves reading, decoding, and interpreting the problem statement, it is evident that linguistic variables should have a definite relationship to verbal problem difficulty.

One objective of Part I of this book is to establish subcategories of task variables more suitable for close examination. It is convenient to classify linguistic variables into two subtypes. Those that deal with the *meanings* of words and phrases—i.e., *semantic* variables—can be considered as *content* variables and will be discussed in Chapter III. Variables that describe the *form* of the problem statement—its grammatical and syntactic construction—are the subject of the present chapter.

The term "syntax" denotes those variables which account for the arrangement of and the relationships among words, phrases, and symbols in problem statements. The two examples below illustrate forms of a problem that are parallel with respect to content, context, and structure, but which differ in syntactic complexity.

2.1   *How much will Mary's puppy Spot weigh at the end of*
      1 year, if Spot weighs 2 pounds at birth and gains
      3 pounds every 2 weeks?

*The material in this chapter is based in part upon work supported by the National Science Foundation under Grant No. SED77-19157. Any opinions, findings, and conclusions or recommendations expressed in this chapter are those of the author and do not necessarily reflect the views of the National Science Foundation.

2.2 *Mary's dog had a puppy which she named Spot. She*
     weighed 2 pounds at birth. Mary observed that she
     gained 3 pounds every 2 weeks. At that rate, how
     many pounds will Spot weigh at the end of her
     first year?

The syntactic structure of Problem *2.1* is different from that
of the second problem. Problem *2.2* has more words and sentences.
It contains several pronouns, which take longer to process than
the nouns used in the first problem. The question appears at the
beginning of Problem *2.1* and at the end of Problem *2.2*. The data
in the two problems are presented in different orders, with the
order of data in Problem *2.2* farther removed from that required for
solution. The two problems also differ in the form used to represent numbers.

From this example, it is apparent that some types of syntax
variables, such as those describing grammatical structure and symbol
formats, may affect problem difficulty at the decoding stage, while
other types of syntax variables, particularly those involving the
sequencing of information and the positions of sentences and phrases,
interact with a problem's underlying structure and therefore directly
affect the ease or difficulty of processing the information contained
in the problem statement.

A wide variety of syntax variables have been identified and
studied in numerous investigations, particularly since 1969 when a
linear regression model was first applied to describe the difficulty
of mathematical word problems. Unlike many task variables which
depend on an interpretation of the processes to be used (such as
the number of steps needed to arrive at a solution), the definition
and quantification of syntax variables can be derived almost directly
from the problem statement, independently of the method of solution used by individuals. This not only permits a high degree of
reliability in the determination of these parameters, but also implies
that it may be possible for textbook writers and teachers to manipulate syntax easily, producing word problem statements with specific
characteristics.

The results of research related to syntax variables are discussed in the next section of this chapter. Although we would
consider it to be technically a content or context variable, "scope
of vocabulary" is included in this discussion, since it is related
to readability and has been used in the study of other syntax variables. The relationship of syntax variables to reading difficulty
in problem solving is examined from a historical perspective. A
discussion of research on syntax variables in arithmetic word problems is followed by an examination of research on syntax variables
in other content areas of mathematical problem solving, such as
algebra and logic. Although little has been reported on the effects
of training in syntax, or on the effects of variations of syntax on

problem-solving behavior, the section concludes with a discussion
of the few studies that have been done in these areas.

In the second half of this chapter, a verbal processing model
is suggested in an effort to clarify the role of syntax variables
in the problem-solving process. Five categories of syntax variables
are considered, with attention to *how* they are defined and made quantitative, and *why* they may be of importance in verbal problem solving.
These categories, presented in Table 2.1, include variables dealing
with (a) length, (b) formats for numerals and symbols, (c) grammatical structure, (d) characteristics of the question sentence, and (e)
sequencing of sentences and data.

In most of the discussion in this chapter, the *dependent* variables are *product* variables in the sense of Kilpatrick, such as the
correctness of the answers or the time in which the answers are
derived (Kilpatrick, 1975). Rarely have *process* variables been used
as dependent variables, although this might offer interesting possibilities for furthering knowledge about syntax variables in problem
solving. The second half of the chapter will include a discussion
of the potential role of process variables as dependent variables in
problem syntax research. Finally, an attempt will be made to summarize what has been learned about syntax variables in mathematical
problem solving, and some implications for future research will be
drawn.

1. A Review of Syntax Variables Research

Syntax Variables and Reading Difficulty

One of the strongest relationships that has emerged from research
is that between reading ability and mathematical achievement. Several
reviews of research in this area have shown correlations between reading ability and mathematics achievement (including mathematical problem solving) to range from .40 to .86 (Monroe and Englehart, 1931;
Aiken, 1972). Sizable correlations between problem-solving ability
and reading ability have also been demonstrated. For example, Martin
(1964) found that the partial correlation between reading comprehension and problem-solving ability, with computational ability partialed
out, was higher for fourth- and eighth-grade students than the partial
correlation between computational ability and problem-solving ability,
with reading comprehension partialed out. Other studies have shown
similar results.

Following the suggestions of earlier investigators (Monroe and
Englehart, 1931), efforts have been made to determine more precise
relationships between specific aspects of reading ability, and mathematics achievement and problem solving. Aiken (1972) reported that
the data included in the 1963 Technical Report on the California
Achievement Tests are representative of a number of findings which

Table 2.1 *Categories of Syntax Variables at the Surface Level of Analysis*

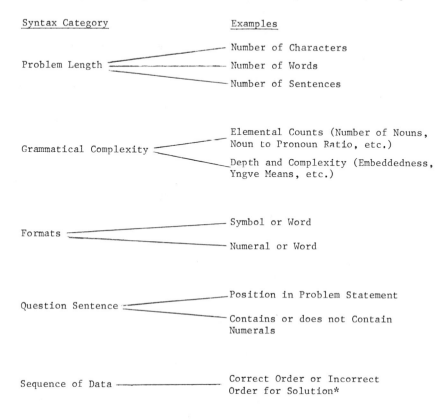

Syntax Category   Examples

Problem Length
— Number of Characters
— Number of Words
— Number of Sentences

Grammatical Complexity
Elemental Counts (Number of Nouns, Noun to Pronoun Ratio, etc.)
Depth and Complexity (Embeddedness, Yngve Means, etc.)

Formats
— Symbol or Word
— Numeral or Word

Question Sentence
Position in Problem Statement
Contains or does not Contain Numerals

Sequence of Data —————— Correct Order or Incorrect Order for Solution*

*The ORDER variable describes both syntax (sequencing of data in the problem statement) and mathematical structure (comparison with correct solution order), thus extending somewhat beyond the surface level of analysis.

show that "Reading Vocabulary" and "Reading Comprehension" (both involving semantic variables), "Mechanics of English" (involving syntax variables), and "Spelling" have sizable correlations with "Arithmetic Fundamentals" and even higher correlations with "Arithmetic Reasoning." A number of older studies, as well as several more recent investigations, have shown that knowledge of vocabulary (a component of reading ability) is an important factor in the ability to solve mathematical problems. For example, a study by Johnson (1949) revealed correlations of .45, .50, and .51 between three tests of arithmetic reasoning and the Primary Mental Abilities Vocabulary Test. A more recent survey of primary arithmetic texts by Willmon (1971) has shown that children are introduced to approximately 500 new *technical* words and phrases by the time they enter fourth grade. These results provide a clear indication of the importance of vocabulary as a variable influencing the ability to comprehend written mathematical problems.

A particularly interesting study designed to explore the relationship of difficult vocabulary and syntax to problem-solving ability was conducted by Linville (1970). Four arithmetic word problem tests were constructed. The problems in each were similar structurally, but varied according to difficulty of syntax and vocabulary. Fourth-grade students (n = 408) were randomly assigned to one of four treatments: Easy Syntax, Easy Vocabulary; Easy Syntax, Difficult Vocabulary; Difficult Syntax, Easy Vocabulary; and Difficult Syntax, Difficult Vocabulary. Significant main effects favoring the easy syntax and easy vocabulary tests were found. Not surprisingly, the investigator also found that in all four treatments, students of higher general ability and/or higher reading ability performed significantly better than students of lower ability.

During the past three decades, several attempts have been made to use the relationship of semantic and syntactic variables to reading difficulty as an index to classify mathematics materials. Several types of readability formulas have been used for English prose, and a few of them, particularly the Dale-Chall formula (Dale and Chall, 1948), the Spache formula (Spache, 1953), and the Cloze technique (Taylor, 1956) have been applied to mathematics texts and problems. A number of investigations which have employed one or more of these formulas have demonstrated a wide range of readability levels in selected mathematics textbooks (Shaw, 1967) and have provided evidence that the readability level of mathematics problems can have a significant effect on the problem-solving performance of children (Thompson, 1968).

The application of readability formulas to mathematics materials, however, has not, as yet, been widely accepted as a defensible approach. Kane (1968, 1970) maintains that readability formulas for ordinary English prose are usually not appropriate for use with mathematical materials, in that: (1) letter, word, and syntactical redundancies are different for English prose and mathematical material; (2) unlike ordinary English, the names of mathematical objects usually have a single denotation; (3) the role of adjectives becomes more important in mathematical English than in ordinary prose; and (4) the syntactic structure of mathematical English is less flexible than that of ordinary English. Despite these claims, in a more recent study Hater and Kane (1970) found the Cloze technique to be a highly reliable and valid predictor of comprehensibility of mathematical materials designed for secondary students.

Very little information is available on the readability level of mathematics problems as compared to the average reading ability of students at each grade level. The few studies that have been done offer conflicting conclusions. For example, after reviewing the literature on reading in mathematics, Earp (1969) concluded that the vocabulary of arithmetic texts is often at a higher readability level than the performance level of students in classes where the texts are used. He also noted that there is little overlap between the vocabulary of reading texts and that of arithmetic texts.

However, different results were reported by Smith (1971). After surveying the readability of sixth-grade arithmetic texts (as measured by the Dale-Chall formula), Smith found: (1) the average readability of problems fell within the normal bounds usually considered appropriate for that grade level, (2) the readability levels varied widely from problem to problem within the same text, and (3) the readability levels of the overall texts were generally comparable to those of related mathematics achievements tests. Based on these findings, Smith concluded that readability may not be the most important factor in arithmetic problem difficulty for this population of students. This conclusion, however, is based on the assumption that the Dale-Chall formula is an appropriate instrument to use with word problems in mathematics, an assumption that needs verification before these results can be meaningfully interpreted.

In another recent study, Knifong and Holtan (1976) analyzed the written solutions of 35 sixth-graders to the word problem portion of the Metropolitan Achievement Test. They concluded that poor reading ability could not have been a factor in 52 percent of the problems, since errors on these problems were strictly computational or clerical. The role of reading difficulty for the remaining 48 percent of the mistakes was not determined.

Although the evidence is not conclusive, it is still reasonable to assume that if the problem solver has difficulty reading a problem statement, he or she is less likely to be able to understand and solve it correctly than if the problem can be read with relative ease. The application of existing methods of determining readability to mathematics materials and problems is a plausible approach, but perhaps what is really needed are formulas or other techniques that are based on syntactic parameters specific to mathematical problems. To understand the importance of reading difficulty to problem-solving ability, researchers must address themselves to the question of determining what specific *components* of reading ability (understanding vocabulary, processing grammatical structures, etc.) affect problem-solving behavior, and how the roles of these components change over different age groups and problem sets. The linear regression studies discussed below offer a potentially fruitful method for investigating these questions.

Syntax Variables in Arithmetic Word Problems

The most common mathematical problems that students encounter are arithmetic word problems. These are the problems typically presented in textbooks from grades one through twelve. The number of steps needed to reach a solution may vary from problem to problem, but the student should be able to proceed by arithmetic methods. Often called *routine* problems, they differ from *exercises* only in that the student must sift through the problem statement to extract information and *select* the appropriate algorithm or algorithms to solve the problems. In an *exercise* the student knows which algorithms need to be used.

In recent years, a group of researchers has attempted to discover the relationship of various parameters of the problem statement to latency of response and problem difficulty through the use of a step-wise, linear regression model. Using the "counts" of these variables as the independent variables, it was hoped that linear regression would yield coefficients which could be used to predict the difficulty of a variety of verbal problems. Since a number of these studies will be examined, a brief description of the linear regression model seems warranted. The reader is referred to the original sources for a more detailed discussion of this model (Suppes, Hyman, and Jerman, 1966; Suppes, Jerman, and Brian, 1968).

Using the notation adopted in the original investigation, let v_{ij} denote the jth variable of problem i. The weight assigned to the jth variable is denoted by α_j. In a given group of subjects, let p_i be the observed proportion of correct responses on problem i. The purpose of the model is to predict the dependent variable, p_i.

To insure that the predicted values of p_i will always lie between 0 and 1, the following transformation is made:

$$z_i = \log \frac{1 - p_i}{p_i}$$

The regression model now becomes $z_i = \Sigma_j \alpha_j v_{ij} + \alpha_0$. For the special case when p_i is either 0 or 1, the following transformation is made:

$$z = \begin{cases} -\log (2n_i - 1) & \text{for } p_i = 0 \\ -\log \dfrac{1}{2n_i - 1} & \text{for } p_i = 1 \end{cases}$$

where n_i is the total number of students responding to problem i. It should be noted that in the first equation for z_i above, $1 - p_i$ appears in the numerator to make z_i increase monotonically in difficulty, as the magnitudes of the variables v_{ij} increase.

Using the above model in a step-wise linear regression analysis, the variables v_{ij} are introduced into the regression equation one at a time, and their contribution to the correlation coefficient R, and the estimate of the amount of error variance accounted for by the regression model, R^2, is calculated at each step. The majority of the studies that have employed this model have used R^2 as the major criterion for the relative importance of each variable in predicting the proportion of correct responses and success latency.

The first studies applying this multiple linear regression analysis to mathematical problems were conducted at Stanford University with elementary school children, operating in a computer-assisted instructional mode (Suppes, Hyman, and Jerman, 1966; Suppes, Jerman, and Brian, 1968). The problems studied were computational arithmetic problems, involving one or more of the four basic arithmetic operations. Since these studies did not deal directly with verbal problems, the reader is referred to other sources for a discussion of the procedures used in these investigations (Loftus, 1970; Segalla, 1973; Barnett, 1974).

Before discussing the outcomes of linear regression studies in the area of verbal problem solving, let us consider how syntax variables have been quantified in these studies. A major problem in the indentification of sets of well-defined parameters that relate to or influence mathematical problem-solving behavior continues to be that of achieving a high degree of reliability among experimenters. This problem is compounded by the fact that the quantification of many interesting variables may be dependent on the problem solver's method of solution, as well as the problem task. Most syntax variables, however, can be quantified with a high degree of reliability directly from the problem statement, once a few conventions are established. (An exception to this statement is the variable of "vocabulary difficulty," which depends upon the background of problem solvers.) In most cases, syntax variables are quantified by assigning a unique numerical value to the variable for each problem statement. These numbers become the v_{ij} in the regression equation.

In general, syntax variables can be quantified in one of three ways. The first method allows the variable to assume a positive integer value. For example, the *sentence* variable is given a value equal to the number of sentences in the statement of the problem. A *word* variable is given a value equal to the number of *unfamiliar* words in the problem statement. The majority of syntax variables are quantified by this method and are often referred to as "continuous" variables, in the sense that they can assume any integer value n = 0, 1, 2, ... (The term "continuous" is not used in the correct mathematical sense.)

A second method of quantifying syntax variables is to assign the variable a value of either "0" or "1". Such dichotomous variables are used to indicate the presence (1) or absence (0) of a particular characteristic. For example, an "order" variable can be assigned a value of "1" if the data contained in the problem statement are presented in the same order in which they can be used to solve the problem, and a value of "0" otherwise. Since this "order" variable involves a comparison between the sequencing of data in the problem statement (syntax) with the processing of data in the problem solution (structure), it might be considered to describe both syntax and mathematical structure, not syntax alone. For convenience it is included in this chapter on syntax variables. Many variables dealing with problem structure are of the dichotomous type but, in general, relatively few syntax variables are defined in this manner. Researchers have apparently assumed that measures on the *amount* of syntactic complexity rather than measures of the presence or absence of certain syntactic characteristics would yield better predictors of problem difficulty.

Combination of two or more variables to form a single "composite" variable constitutes a third method of quantification. This procedure allows each "sub-variable" to be differentially weighted, according to its assumed or proven importance. The result is a composite variable which assumes a value equal to a specified function of the values of its component variables. Although relatively few studies have employed this method with syntax variables, the procedure has the potential to generate sensitive variables with good predictive power that are relatively easy to manipulate.

A first attempt to extend the linear regression model to mathematics word problems was made in 1969 (Suppes, Loftus, and Jerman, 1969). In this study, 68 word problems were presented and solved in a computer-assisted instructional mode, using 27 above-average fifth-grade students. The LENGTH variable (a measure of the number of words in the problem statement) was used for the first time, along with five other variables related to operations, sequence, and verbal cues. The precise definition of the LENGTH variable, and a number of variables of length that have been used in linear regression studies, are presented in Table 2.2.

The results of the study were disappointing. The LENGTH variable and two others were found not to be significant. The three variables that were significant only accounted for approximately 45 percent of the variance in the proportion of problems done correctly. However, the organization and procedures used in the study provided a model for further investigations.

A 1970 study by Loftus used the six variables from the previous study, plus two new ones, the syntax variables of ORDER (indicating the sequence of data presented in the problem) and DEPTH (a measure of grammatical complexity). The definition of the DEPTH variable and several other definitions of grammatical complexity variables are presented in Table 2.3. A set of 100 problems was administered to 16 sixth-grade students, characterized as "low ability." The students solved the 100 problems after four weeks of practice on a computer teletype. The results showed an R^2 value of .70, a

Table 2.2 *Definitions of Variables of Length*

Variable	Definition
1. WORDS:	The number of written words in the problem statement, excluding numerals. A count of one is assigned to a single word, hyphenated word, or group of words that would appear as a single entry in a dictionary.
2. NUMWRD:	Numerals converted to words is defined as the number of words obtained by converting numerals to word form and counting the number of words.
3. LENGTH:	The number of words in the problem statement, that is, the sum of variables 1 and 2 (LENGTH = WORDS + NUMWRD).
4. NUMERL:	A count of one is given to each numeral in the problem.
5. WRDNUM:	The number of words and the number of numerals are defined as the sum of variables 1 and 4 (WRDNUM = WORDS + NUMERL).
6. DIGITS:	A count of one is given to each digit in each numeral.
7. WRDGTS:	The number of words and digits, that is, the sum of variables 1 and 6 (WRDGTS = WORDS + DIGITS).
8. SYMDGT:	The number of symbols and digits in each numeral.
9. WRDSYM:	The number of words and symbols, that is, the sum of variables 1 and 8 (WRDSYM = WORDS + SYMDGT).
10. LETTRS:	Each letter (and each apostrophe and hyphen) are given a count of one.
11. PUNCT:	A count of one is given for each punctuation mark.
12. CHRCTR:	A count of one is given for each character in the problem, that is, the sum of variables 8, 10, and 11 (CHRCTR = SYMDGT + LETTERS + PUNCT).
13. SYLBLS:	A count of one for each syllable of every word (in WORDS).
14. AVGWDL:	The average word length as defined by the ratio of variables 10 and 1, that is, AVGWDL = LETTRS/WORDS.
15. SENT:	The number of sentences in the problem.
16. SENTLN:	The average number of words per sentence, that is, SENTLN = LENGTH/SENT.
17. LGNUWD:	A count of one for each word occurring after the first number and before the last number in the problem.
18. LGMXST:	A count of one for each word in the longest sentence.

Table 2.3 *Definitions of Variables Describing Grammatical Structure*

Variable	Definition
1. VERBS:	The number of verbs in the problem.
2. ADJECTIVES:	The number of adjectives in the problem.
3. NOUNS:	The number of nouns in the problem.
4. ADVERBS:	The number of adverbs and adverbial clauses.
5. PRONOUNS:	The number of pronouns.
6. NOUN TO VERB RATIO:	The number of nouns divided by the number of verbs (NOUNS / VERBS).
7. NOUN TO ADJECTIVE RATIO:	The number of nouns divided by the number of adjectives (NOUNS / ADJECTIVES).
8. PRONOUN TO NOUN RATIO:	The number of pronouns divided by the number of nouns (PRONOUNS / NOUNS).
9. VERB TO ADVERB RATIO:	The number of verbs divided by the number of adverbs (VERBS / ADVERBS).
10. SUBCL:	The number of subordinate clauses in the problem.
11. PREPHR:	The number of prepositional phrases in the problem.
12. MAINCL:	The number of main clauses in the problem.
13. CLAUSE:	The total number of clauses (CLAUSE = MAINCL + SUBCL).
14. WDMAIN:	The number of words in the main clauses of the problem.
15. SUBLEN:	The number of words in the subordinate clauses.
16. MCLTH:	The average number of words in each main clause (MCLTH = WDMAIN / MAINCL).
17. SCLTH:	The average number of words in the subordinate clauses (SCLTH = SUBLEN / SUBCL).
18. AVGCLS:	The average clause length (the number of words in the problem divided by the total number of clauses) (AVGCLS = LENGTH / CLAUSE).
19. DEPTH:	The highest value of the means of the Yngve numbers computed for each sentence of the problem statement (Yngve numbers measure the degree of "embeddedness" of each word in the sentence. See Figure 2.2 in Section 2 of this chapter).

respectable amount of variance accounted for. Both the DEPTH and
LENGTH variables made significant contributions to the amount of
variance in proportion correct accounted for, and entered the
regression equation in the third and fourth steps respectively.
It should be noted, however, that the number of subjects was *very*
small, and it was assumed that using the partial correlation
coefficients was a valid measure of importance.

In the following year, a number of studies included some of
the previously defined variables, defined new ones, and extended
the mode of presentation of problems to paper and pencil. Jerman
(1971) reported the results of two studies. In the first, Searle
reanalyzed the data from the 1969 Suppes, Loftus, Jerman study,
using 14 new variables, including an ORDER variable. Both the
ORDER and LENGTH variables were found to be significant. Jerman
followed up this study with an investigation using 30 word problems administered to 20 fifth graders. This was the first study
that was conducted in paper-and-pencil mode. Five variables,
including the syntax variable LENGTH, were found to account for
87 percent of the variance in problem difficulty. Further support
for the LENGTH variable was found in a study by Jerman and Rees
(1972) and in a follow-up study by Jerman (1972).

At this point it should be noted that direct comparisons of
the importance of variables from one study to another became
impossible. Investigators modified the definitions of the variables in each study, and used different problem sets and various
grade levels. More recent studies, however, have attempted to
show similarities between the variables, and have tried to
generalize results to several grades and problem types.

After six years of experimentation with variable definitions
and the linear regression equations, the time seemed right to
apply these previous results predictively. Using the data from
Jerman's 1971 study with students in grades 4 to 9, Jerman and
Mirman (1972) took the top six variables found in that study and
coded them on a new problem set. Using the resulting regression
model, they then attempted to predict, before administering the
problem set, the proportion of students in a new population that
would correctly solve each of the problems. The results indicated
that the regression model based on pooled data from grades 4 to 9
was unsatisfactory. The data were then reanalyzed, using the same
six variables for each grade level separately. The resulting
regression equations for each grade level gave much better predictions, with residuals of percentage correct ranging from 4 to
15 percent. Although these results were not as good as the
researchers would have liked, the study did establish a model
for further investigations. It still remains for the predictive
equations to be refined so as to yield results in an acceptable
range.

The application of the regression model to arithmetic word problems was extended to the junior college population in a comprehensive study by Segalla (1973). Convinced of the importance of syntax variables, Segalla defined 30 variables that included many syntax variables not previously defined. A set of 172 word problems was administered to 44 low-ability junior college mathematics students. Based on the size of the drop in R^2 when the variable was removed from the regression equation, the set of the six most significant variables included the syntax variables of ORDER, NOUNS, DEPTH, LENGTH, and ADVERBS.

As interest in the regression model began to grow, it became apparent that syntax variables played an important role in determining problem difficulty for subjects of all ages. In 1973, Krushinski investigated the relative importance of 14 syntax variables, including eight describing aspects of length, four describing grammatical structure, and two describing numerals and the question sentence. Three sections of preservice elementary school teachers enrolled in a course in the teaching of arithmetic were administered a problem-solving test. The amount of time permitted on the problem-solving test varied from 20 minutes for section one, to 60 minutes for section two, to one day for section three. Krushinski found that six variables, NUMBER OF SENTENCES, NUMBER OF CLAUSES, CLAUSE LENGTH, NUMBER OF PREPOSITIONAL PHRASES, NUMBER OF WORDS IN THE QUESTION SENTENCE, and NUMERALS IN THE QUESTION SENTENCE, entered the regression analysis within the first six steps in at least two of the three sections. After the sixth step, the multiple R's for the three sections, in order of decreasing time limits, were .856, .738, and .626. These interesting results suggest that as time becomes a crucial factor, some syntax variables may decrease in importance with respect to other (non-syntax) factors.

Following the Krushinski study, Beardslee and Jerman (1973a) attempted to apply Krushinski's 14 syntax variables to a problem set appropriate for students in grades 4 to 8. Three test forms of 30 problems each were prepared using a problem set from a previous study. The number of words was systematically varied, so that Form 1 was the original problem set (Form 2) with one-third fewer words, and Form 3 was the original problem set (Form 2) with one-third more words. Eighteen separate analyses were conducted on the data. Only two of the six variables which Krushinski found to be significant, CLAUSE LENGTH and PREPOSITIONAL PHRASES, entered consistently among the first six variables in the linear regression analyses. In addition to these two variables, two other variables, SENTENCE LENGTH and WORDS IN SUBCLAUSES, entered the regression consistently within the first six steps on two or more test forms. These results suggest that it may be possible to identify syntax variables that are important for both college and pre-college students. This study is one of the few attempts to observe the effects on problem-solving performance resulting from systematic variations of syntax.

Using the same set of data, Beardslee and Jerman (1973b) extended the previous study to include syntax variables not used in the 1973 Krushinski study. In addition, they investigated a wide variety of measures of length, to determine which definition accounted for the most variance in proportion correct. This second purpose was of particular importance since the many definitions of length employed in several different studies made interpretation of results extremely difficult. Seventeen variables were defined in the investigation. The first four, LENGTH, SUBCL, PREPHR, and NUMINQ, were used in the Krushinski study and the first Beardslee and Jerman study. The remaining 13 variables included WORDS, NUMWRD, NUMERL, WRDNUM, DIGITS, SYMDGT, WRDGTS, WRDSYM, LETTRS, PUNCT, CHRCTR, SYLBLS, and AVGWDL. Nine of these, including LENGTH, WORDS, WRDNUM, WRDGTS, WRDSYM, LETTRS, CHRCTR, SYLBLS, and AVGWRL, were considered to be variables of length. The definition of each of these variables appears in Tables 2.2 and 2.3. Although none of the variables was found to account for a significant amount of the variance for all grades, five of them, NUMERL, PUNCT, AVGWDL, SUBCL, and PREPHR, were significant for several grades for one or more test forms. None of the nine length variables was shown to be superior to any of the other length variables. It would appear that, although the many different definitions of length use different size units to obtain elemental counts, they are all about equally correlated with problem difficulty.

Although most of the linear regression studies included a number of kinds of task variables, the dominance of any particular category of variable (structural, computational, syntactic, etc.) in determining problem difficulty was not established. This question was investigated by Beardslee and Jerman (1974) in a study involving five "structural" variables, four "syntax" variables, and twelve "topic" variables. A 50-item achievement test was administered to fourth- and fifth-grade students. Based on a regression analysis involving only the twelve topic variables, four were selected to be combined with the five structural and four syntax variables. The results showed that three variables made significant contributions to the amount of variance accounted for; the topic variable GEOMETRY and the two structural variables NOMC2 (a variable dealing with the number of "carries" in multiplication) and COG LEVEL (a variable reflecting the cognitive level of a problem, based on a classification by Avital and Shettleworth). Although none of the syntax variables were found to be significant, the total amount of variance accounted for was only .47. Despite this disappointing result, this study established the need for a more inclusive model. The experimenters stated, "None-the-less some encouraging signs seem evident. One, that a combination of different classes of variables produces a higher R than using only one class" (Beardslee and Jerman, 1974, p. 10).

Another study which investigated classes of structural variables was conducted by Barnett (1974). After analyzing the results of the previous regression studies, it was noted that the variables investigated reflected either the *linguistic, computational, operational*, or *procedural* complexity of arithmetic word problems. Defining for each of the above categories a *composite* variable, the resulting set of four independent variables accounted for approximately 64 percent of the variance in difficulty. The LINGUISTICS variable consisted of the *sum* of two *syntax* variables of length and the semantic (*content*) variable of "mathematics words." Using the four independent composite variables as a basis, four instructional units were constructed to help students overcome the difficulty attributable to each variable. Five parallel forms of a 20-item verbal problem-solving test were constructed, in which the composite variables were systematically varied. The four instructional units were separated by the five parallel forms of the test, and administered to 150 college juniors, randomly assigned to either an experimental group or to one of two control groups (the control groups received instructional units unrelated to problem solving). The results showed that the instruction based on each of the variables was significantly effective in improving problem-solving performance. Interestingly, the amount of variance accounted for by the set of variables, and the position of each variable in the regression equation, remained relatively stable across the five tests. These results present a further case for the use of composite variables and suggest that these can be rather stable measures in predicting problem difficulty.

To summarize, the results of several of the studies that have used the regression model are shown in Table 2.4 (based on data suggested by Segalla, 1973, p. 60, and Barnett, 1974, p. 37). The reader is cautioned in interpreting the table, since the data are based on a variety of subjects, populations, problem sets, and different definitions. Subject to these limitations, the table reveals that syntax variables, particularly measures of length, consistently enter the regression equation in the first six steps. It would appear from these studies that the syntactic complexity of arithmetic word problems is a definite contributor to problem difficulty. As we shall see in the next section, the linear regression model has also been used with success to predict the difficulty of problems other than arithmetic word problems.

Syntax Variables in Algebra and Logic Problems

One expects to find relationships between syntax variables and problem difficulty, using problem sets involving algebraic solutions as well as arithmetic solutions. Problem statements which lend themselves to translation into algebraic form may include well-defined variables that can be used to predict difficulty with high reliability, due to *consistencies* in the "language" of equations.

Cook (1973a) attempted to apply the results of previous regression studies to a set of algebraic word problems solved

Table 2.4 *Variables Entering in the First Six Steps for Major Studies Since 1969*

	1	2	3	4	5	6
Suppes (1969)	SEQ	CONV	OPER	V. CUE	STEPS	LENGTH
Loftus (1970)	SEQ	OPER	DEPTH	LENGTH	CONV	V. CUE
Jerman (16 var.)	OPER	V. CUE	DIV	LENGTH	FORMULA	S_1
Jerman (21 var.)	OPER	CONV	LENGTH	ORDER2	DIV	S_2
Jerman (CAI, 19 var.)	OPER2	LENGTH	ORDER	RECALL	S_2	
Jerman (Pen., 19 var.)	LENGTH	NOMC2	QUOT	DIST	COLC2	S_1
Jerman & Rees (1972)	LENGTH	NOMC	QUOT	DIST	COLC2	S_1
Jerman (1972)	NOMC	QUOT	LENGTH	RECALL	CONV	DIST
Beardslee & Jerman (1973)	CL. LEN	PREP	SEN.LE.	SUBCL		
Krushinski (1973)	SENT.	CLAUSE	CL. LEN.	PREP	NWOQUE	NUMERL
Merman (1973)	LENGTH	QUOT	NOMC2	RECALL	OPER3	CONV
Segalla (1973)	MEMORY2	ORDER1	V. CUE	OPER	PRO. N	DIST
Beardslee & Jerman (1974)	GEOMTY	COGLEV	NOMC2			
Barnett (1974)	OPER	PROCED	LING			

Note: Variables describing length and syntactic complexity are underlined. The variables that have not been previously defined in this section include: Variables describing the sequence of problems and operations (SEQ, S1, ORDER2), conversions of units (CONV), needed recall of facts and formulas (RECALL, FORMULA), required operations and steps (OPER, STEPS), and computations with numbers and specific operations (DIV, NOMC, QUOT, COLC2).

by college students. Twenty-six variables, including five arithmetic variables from the 1972 Jerman study; thirteen algebraic variables (dealing with translations and equations); the syntax variables WRDNUM (a measure of problem length), SENT (the number of sentences), NUMQS (a variable relating the presence of numbers in the question sentence), and PREP (the number of prepositions) from the 1973 Krushinski study; and four additional syntax variables (NUMERL, QUENL, LGREL, and LGMXST) were computed for 28 word problems. LGREL was defined as a measure of the numerical relationships in the problem, and LGMXST was defined to be the number of words in the longest sentence of the problem statement. The problem set consisted of one consecutive-integer problem, two distance problems, three age problems, four angles-of-triangles problems, four direct variation problems, and seven miscellaneous problems.

Two *translation* variables, three *syntax* variables, three *arithmetic* variables, and four *equation* variables entered the regression equation on the first 12 steps, accounting for over 96 percent of the variance in proportion correct. The variable LGMXST had the highest correlation with the observed proportion correct, with an R^2 value of .2962. The variables LGREL and NUMQS entered the regression equation in the eighth and twelfth steps respectively. The study indicates additional support for the effect of syntax variables of length, although the definition of length in this study is different from that used in previous studies. Perhaps the most encouraging aspect of this investigation, however, is the relatively high value for R^2 at the sixth step (.8040). This result suggests real potential for the use of the linear regression model with problems of this type.

In a second study conducted the same year, Cook (1973b) investigated the relationships of 41 variables to problem difficulty using 19 algebraic word problems selected from the National Longitudinal Study of Mathematical Abilities Y and Z Test Batteries. All problems selected required the set-up and solution of linear or quadratic equations in one variable. The syntax variables investigated included those from the previous study except PREP, QUENL, and NUMQS. A new variable, LGNUWD (a count of 1 for each word that occurred after the first number and before the last number in the problem statement) was also added.

The results showed one arithmetic, one translation, three equation, and one syntax variable, SENT, entering on the first six steps of the regression equation. Three other syntax variables (LGREL, LGNUWD, and WRDNUM) entered the regression equation on the ninth, tenth, and twelfth steps respectively. Although the variable LGMXST, which entered the regression equation first in the last study, was one of the last to enter in this study, the continued presence of variables of length in all but a few studies is a strong indication that this variable plays an important role in problem difficulty, and deserves continued systematic investigation.

Jansson (1974) applied the linear regression model in an exploratory investigation designed to identify which variables strongly influence the relative difficulty of judging *simple deductive arguments* in verbal form. A simple deductive argument was defined to be a chain of reasoning involving two premises and a conclusion. Combining results and suggestions from previous studies with research on logic development, Jansson defined 12 variables which included the syntax variable WORD and the new ones listed in Table 2.5.

Three tests of class and conditional reasoning were used. (Class reasoning is of the form "All P's are Q's." Conditional reasoning is of the form "If P then Q.") On each item, the student was required to decide if the conclusion was valid or invalid, or if there was not enough information to decide. The number of items ranged from 22 to 40.

On two of the three tests, the variable NEGP1 entered the regression equation on the second step, with an average R^2 value of .73. The variables WORD and NEGP2 also entered consistently in the first six steps. Although the positions of each variable changed on each test, a relatively high amount of variance in the proportion correct was accounted for. Further evidence for the effects of length variables (the variable WORD) was obtained, as well as new evidence for variables reflecting the frequencies of negations.

The results of the Jansson and Cook studies are encouraging. R^2 values in all three studies are respectable, and the repeated occurrence of many of the same variables lends support to the effects of syntax variables in many types of verbal problems.

Our discussion throughout has focused on verbal problems of a routine nature. The question remains as to how syntax variables affect the difficulty of non-routine verbal problems. Unfortunately, there is almost no research on the role of syntax variables in non-routine problems. It seems reasonable to conjecture that a complex syntax will make any type of verbal problem more difficult to solve. However, non-routine problems tend to require higher cognitive processes for solution, and therefore other categories of task variables, such as structure variables, may play a more important role.

Critique of the Linear Regression Model

The linear regression model previously discussed has shown promise as a research tool to identify which task variables affect problem difficulty. The technique is based on the assumption that the relationship between selected task variables and problem difficulty is linear. While the results of some

Table 2.5 *Definitions of Variables Describing Simple Deductive Arguments*

1. WRDP1: A count of 1 for each word in the first premise.

2. WP1/P2: The ratio of the number of words in premise 1 to the number of words in premise 2.

3. WRDL: The average word length in number of letters in the total argument.

4. NEGP1: The number of negations in the first premise.

5. NEGP2: The number of negations in the second premise.

6. NEGC: The total number of negations in the conclusion of the argument.

7. TOTNGS: The total number of negations in the entire argument.

studies suggest that a linear model fits the data reasonably well, it is not clear that a different model would not fit the data better.

Since the linear regression model was first applied to verbal problems in mathematics, it has fallen short of being an acceptably precise technique for predicting problem-solving behavior. This may be due to the inappropriateness of the linear model in explaining the relationship of task variables to problem difficulty, or to the lack of methodological paradigms and inconsistencies in the use of the model. Furthermore, research in problem solving has shown that a large variety of task variables (content, context, syntax, structure, etc.), as well as subject and situation variables, have an influence on problem solving. It is unreasonable to expect that a model which does not take all of these variables into account will be able to predict accurately problem-solving success *across subject populations* and *across problem types*. In a study dealing with only one category of task variable, say variables of syntax, the total amount of variance accounted for in the proportion correct may reasonably be much less than 100 percent. If it does approach 100 percent, this may be due to inadvertent correlations in the problems themselves between syntax variables and other task variables (see below). The real value of the linear regression model, then, may be in its use to determine the *relative* importance of major categories of variables, or the relative importance of specific variables within a particular category. Thus, the development of a *complete* linear regression model may not be a valuable undertaking.

Another concern with the linear regression model is the lack of independence of the variables that have been investigated. Although some variables are independent of each other in terms of the method used to quantify them, they are often not independent conceptually. For example, the *length* variable is clearly related to a number of variables which also are quantified by elemental counts. It is also very probably correlated with such *non*-syntax variables as the number of givens and the number of steps to solution. The significance in the regression equation of the length variable alone does not convey a great deal of information in helping to understand the problem-solving process or contributing to the development of a model of problem-solving behavior. The important question here is, "What particular aspects of problem length *make* it important in the problem-solving process?" Questions of this nature have not, as yet, been addressed in linear regression studies. It is important to create problem sets in which particular syntax variables are intentionally held constant and others intentionally varied, in order to approach such questions. It is also important to note that the linear regression model makes no provision for *interactions* among the variables. These can be incorporated only by defining new task variables as (non-linear) functions of previously defined variables, and then carrying out a new linear regression.

The use of the regression model as an indicator of the relative importance of specific variables could also be improved. Investigations using *comparable populations* would be helpful in refining the regression coefficients to form a model that is acceptable for a particular population. More comprehensive studies across grade levels could help to establish which variables are the most important for each level of student development. This information would be most useful in designing instructional material. The use of similar problem sets by different researchers would permit greater replicability of findings.

Additional applications of the linear regression model itself might include the use of different *dependent* variables (such as latency of response) and the proportion of the use of a correct *method*, in addition to the proportion of correct answers. Different criteria for establishing the importance of each variable should also be examined, such as the size of the regression coefficient, the size of the partial correlation coefficient, the order of entry into the regression equation, the contribution to the total variance in the proportion correct, and size of the drop in R^2 caused by removing the variable from the regression equation.

To summarize, the linear regression model is valuable for identifying task variables *associated with* problem difficulty, but yields little information on how the variable in question affects the difficulty of the problem.

Syntax Variables and Instruction

It seems reasonable to expect that instruction designed to help children with syntax and semantics could reduce the difficulty of many problems. Research on this hypothesis has been conducted for many years. A number of studies showed that instruction in the interpretation of specific mathematical terms produced significant gains in problem-solving ability (Dresher, 1934; Johnson, 1944). Fewer studies have been directly concerned with instruction in syntax. In one study, Sax and Ottina (1958) demonstrated that specific instruction in syntax resulted in improvement in mathematics achievement for seventh graders who had no previous training in mathematics in their earlier schooling.

At this point, it should be emphasized that any discussion of training in syntax must include a discussion of reading instruction, for it is clear that the ability to understand the meanings of words and the syntax of written statements is essential in learning to read all types of material (Aiken, 1972). However, as Henney (1971) notes, students often find reading mathematics to be different and, in general, more difficult than reading other materials. Spencer and Russell (1960) have pointed out that students experience difficulty in reading arithmetic material because: (1) the names of certain materials are confusing; (2) number languages which are patterned differently from the decimal system are used; (3) the language of expressed fractions and ratios is complicated; (4) charts and other diagrams are frequently confusing; and (5) the reading of computational procedures requires specialized skills.

The question of whether reading instruction, particularly reading instruction in mathematics, can have a positive effect on the ability to understand mathematics and mathematics problems has only recently been investigated. Perhaps due to emphasis in the modern mathematics programs of the early 1960s on increased use of symbolism and verbal explanations, a number of studies were conducted to determine the effectiveness of reading instruction on mathematical achievement and problem solving. Gilmary (1967) found that elementary school children in an experimental group who received instruction in both reading and arithmetic gained one-third of a grade more on the Metropolitan Achievement Test— Arithmetic than did a control group which received instruction in arithmetic only. The results were even more pronounced, favoring the experimental group, when differences in I.Q. were controlled statistically.

However, in a later study, Henney (1969) tested the effects of 18 lessons on reading verbal problems with 179 fourth-grade students. Approximately half of this group received the lessons over a nine-week period. During the same time period on alternate days, the other half of the students studied and solved verbal problems in any way that they chose, under the supervision of the same teacher. The results showed significant gains for both groups over the nine-week period, but *no* significant differences were found between the groups on the posttest.

A few recent studies have examined specific instructional techniques. Earp (1969) noted that verbal problems which have a high conceptual density factor include three types of symbolic meanings--verbal, numerical, and literal--within a single problem task. He maintains that three kinds of reading *adjustments* are required (that is, adjustments from the reading pattern used in ordinary English prose): (1) adjustment to a slower rate than with narrative materials; (2) varied eye movements, including some regressions; and (3) reading with an attitude of aggressiveness and thoroughness.

A number of suggestions for helping students read word problems have emerged from the literature. Earp (1970), for example, has suggested five steps in reading verbal problems:

(1) Read first to *visualize* the overall situation.

(2) Read again to get the *specific facts*.

(3) Note *difficult vocabulary* and concepts.

(4) Reread to help *plan the solution.*

(5) Reread the problem to *check* the procedure and solution.

The effectiveness of the use of the above five steps was tested in the study by Barnett (1974) described in the previous section.

Several other attempts have been made to design instructional procedures to help children read mathematics materials. Taschow (1969) suggests a remedial-preventive program in reading mathematics. Students are first given a Group Informal Reading Inventory to determine which students have difficulty with mathematical reading. In the second phase, a five-step program called the Directed Reading Activity in Algebra is given to each child. The five-step DRA consists of: (1) readiness, (2) guided silent reading, (3) questions, (4) oral reading when needed, and (5) application. While this program does not provide instruction in specific syntax variables, the exposure and practice with reading mathematics materials can help students learn to cope with the more difficult syntax structure found in verbal problems.

Another program offers more specific instruction in processing syntactic structure. Dahmus (1970) suggests a "direct-pure-piecemeal-complete" (DPPC) approach to solving verbal problems. In this method, the student is encouraged to translate the data presented in the problem into mathematical sentences, by concentrating on a few words at a time. He or she gradually learns to put together the "piecemeal" mathematical statements into equations, and, finally, into systems of equations. It is clear that the ability to *translate* data in problem statements into mathematical symbols is one of the most important aspects of general problem-solving ability. It seems that it is also one of the most difficult abilities to cultivate. Several procedures similar to the one above have been suggested, but it is not yet clear that any of these procedures are effective across a variety of student populations and problem types.

In conclusion, two points should be noted. First, the ability to process English syntax is crucial to reading ability. The studies discussed above suggest that instruction in syntax results in improved reading comprehension. Secondly, the ability to read and the ability to engage successfully in mathematical problem solving are directly related. As Aiken notes,

> .... instruction in reading in general or the reading of mathematics in particular improves performance in the latter subject. It seems reasonable that attempting to cultivate the skill of reading carefully and analytically in order to note details and understand meanings, thinking about what one is reading, and

translating what is read into special symbols would improve
performance on many types of mathematical problems. (Aiken,
1972, p. 18)

What is not clear at this point is the relative importance of the
various syntax variables to the design of instructional material.
It is hoped that future research will address this question through
coordinated investigations to vary systematically individual syntax
variables in a variety of verbal problem settings.

2. The Classification and Definition of Syntax Variables: A Verbal Information Processing Model

In the previous section, a number of investigations of the role
of syntax variables in verbal problem solving have been considered.
It may now be productive to examine in more detail how syntax parameters are incorporated into the hierarchy of task variables introduced in Chapter I (Figure 1.1). The purpose of that hierarchy is
to suggest the relationship between Polya's stages of problem solving and the types of task variables, and between the types of task
variables and the levels of task analysis. Here we shall consider
syntax variables with respect to the detailed sequence of processes
used by the problem solver.

Figure 2.1 proposes a verbal information processing model on
which the present section is based. The model magnifies a portion
of Figure 1.1, expanding the "understanding the problem" stage described by Polya. We shall then redefine the more significant syntax
variables discussed in the literature and examine them in relation
to the proposed model.

When the problem solver is confronted with a problem statement,
he or she enters a *translation* or *verbal processing* stage, which can
be thought of as divided into two parts. During the *decoding* substage, the problem solver interprets the problem statement. This
is followed by an *encoding* substage, where the data contained in
the problem statement are transformed into a usable form (for
example, mathematical sentences) that assists with the problem
solution. This process of decoding and encoding enables the problem solver to translate the original words, phrases, numerals, and
symbols into meaningful expressions, before proceeding to the computational stage of problem solving.

It is in the decoding substage that the problem solver must
process syntactic and semantic information; thus, syntax variables
are expected to affect the verbal problem-solving process at the
surface level, during the decoding substage. We suggest that this
substage may be usefully thought of as composed of three separate
processes which interact with each other as the problem solver

Figure 2.1 *Problem Syntax and Information Processing*

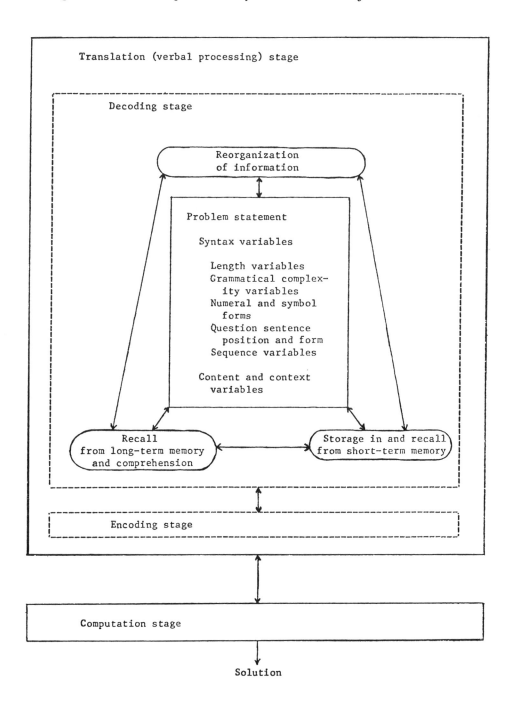

reads through the problem statement: recall from *long-term memory*, storage in and recall from *short-term memory*, and *reorganization* of information.

As each word or phrase in the problem statement is encountered, the problem solver must recall and comprehend its meaning in its grammatical context, drawing on long-term memory. Complicated or unfamiliar grammatical structures may make this recall and comprehension more difficult. Lengthy problems contain more words, more grammatical structures, and often quantitatively more information, necessitating greater use of recall and comprehension from long-term memory. The formats of symbols or numerals which are unusual or unfamiliar may cause momentary pauses in language processing, pending recognition (access to long-term memory) or conversion to more familiar formats.

Concomitantly with recall and comprehension, the problem solver may store selected items of information in short-term memory for future use. It should be noted here that for the purpose of examining *task* variables, the term "short-term memory" refers to storage of information contained in the problem statement at hand, while "long-term memory" refers to knowledge possessed prior to encountering the given problem. The usage of these terms is therefore slightly different from that found in the psychological literature.

As the problem solver reads the problem statement, information may be stored in a variety of ways, as illustrated in the following example:

> *2.3 Ms. Fuller drives due north for 100 kilometers, and then due east for 358 kilometers to International Airport. She then takes a plane which flies in a straight line back to her home where she started her trip. How many miles did the plane fly (with respect to the ground) between International Airport and Ms. Fuller's home?*

Reading this problem will elicit information from long-term memory, and produce a number of mental images which are stored in short-term memory. These images may be augmented as more information is processed. For some problem solvers, "due north ... and then due east" may produce an image of a right triangle. The numbers "100" and "358" may be stored as numerals, or even added to the triangle image as labels. Mathematical terms such as "kilometers" may also be stored in short-term memory, along with the relationships between items of data and quantifiers. For other problem solvers, the words "due north ... and then due east" may suggest a perpendicular relationship of two vectors, without generating the clear mental image of a triangle. This relationship may or may not trigger the recall of the Pythagorean Theorem from long-term memory. It is also possible that the *presence* of the numbers

100" and "358" could be noted in short-term memory, but not the actual numbers themselves—in this situation, the problem solver might scan the problem statement again to pick out the numbers when they are later needed in a mathematical equation.

Consider a second example:

> 2.4 *Five oak trees dropped 37, 56, 108, 87, and 25 acorns respectively on Monday, and 45, 53, 68, 40, and 38 acorns respectively on Tuesday. Based on this group of five oak trees, what is the average number of acorns dropped by an oak tree during this two-day period?*

In this problem it is likely that many problem solvers would not actually form and store mental images of the action specified in the problem statement—i.e., acorns being dropped by oak trees. Some items of information might be stored directly, such as the key word "average." The presence of numbers such as "37, 56, ..." might be noted, without their actual values being stored. The term "five" might be stored as a word, or more likely as the translated numeral "5." In short, it is clear that the kinds of information which are stored in short-term memory, and the form of the information stored, will vary widely from individual to individual.

Again, some generalizations about the effects of syntax variables can be made. Lengthy problems which contain many items of information may place considerable demand on short-term memory. The problem solver may have difficulty keeping track of all the data or deciding which items will be needed and should be stored. Grammatical structure variables, such as the number of pronouns, may place additional demands on short-term memory, since the problem solver must remember to which noun each pronoun refers.

Finally, in many problems the data may be presented in a sequence which requires reorganization as the information is stored, into more usable or recognizable forms. The position of the question sentence may influence how the given information is initially stored in short-term memory, and whether or not subsequent reorganization takes place. Thus the model in Figure 2.1 includes "reorganization" processes as a third and crucial component in the decoding substage. The reorganization process may take place before the data are stored in short-term memory or, as more information is accumulated, whenever it becomes useful to rearrange the information in short-term memory. Reorganization, as well as recall-comprehension and storage, is not necessarily a conscious, willful action on the part of the problem solver; it may take place in a rapid, nearly automatic fashion.

After interpreting and decoding the problem statement, the problem solver may begin a structural analysis of the task, attempting to encode the relevant data into a representation suitable for solution by algorithmic procedures. During or after this encoding substage, the problem solver may discover a contradiction, error, or difficulty; or insufficient information may prevent the completion of the encoding process. Any of these happenstances may necessitate a return to the decoding substage, where the problem solver will reread and reprocess the problem statement to correct any discrepancies, reorganize away any difficulties, and store additional needed information.

Thus the verbal processing stage is characterized by dynamic mental activity, involving a great deal of movement between the decoding and encoding substages. Within the decoding substage, there is similarly considerable movement among recall-comprehension, reorganization, and short-term memory. These three processes occur *during* the act of reading the problem statement, not necessarily in any particular order after the entire statement has been read.

During the decoding substage, syntax variables influence the amount and complexity of the processing that is required. It is clear that content and context variables, discussed in Chapter III, will influence this substage as well. For example, familiarity with the meanings of mathematical terms facilitates recall-comprehension from long-term memory, as well as storage in and access to short-term memory.

The following problems illustrate certain qualitative aspects of the verbal information processing model.

> 2.5 *If the hypotenuse of an isosceles right triangle is 16 cm, what is the sum of the lengths of the two legs?*

In Problem *2.5*, interpretations of the mathematical terms "hypotenuse," "isosceles," "right," "triangle," "cm," and "legs" may be recalled from long-term memory, and reorganized to form a mental image of the overall situation. Alternatively, some of these terms may trigger the recall from long-term memory of the Pythagorean Theorem. Many of these terms, and others such as "16" and "sum," may be stored in short-term memory and used later in the encoding stage. Since the problem cannot be solved directly from the Pythagorean formula by treating the hypotenuse as the unknown variable, some reorganization of the data will eventually be necessary. In this problem, mathematical *content* variables (mathematical topic, key words, and mathematical vocabulary) directly and importantly affect the decoding substage. With respect to *syntax* variables, the problem length is comparatively short, and the major complexity of grammatical structure is the nesting of the prepositional phrases in the question sentence.

*2.6 Beth lives on the corner of a square city block, and
her friend Nancy lives on an adjacent corner of the
same block. Nancy's friend Sue lives on the other
corner adjacent to Nancy. The length of the diagonal
from Beth's house to Sue's house is 280 meters. How
far does Beth have to walk to Sue's house if she must
stop to pick up Nancy on her way?*

Although Problem *2.6* requires the same mathematical procedures
as Problem *2.5*, its syntax is more complex. The very first independent clause contains nested prepositional phrases. Many of the
words which must be recalled from long-term memory are relational
terms (such as "adjacent"), which must be interpreted in their
proper syntactic context. This problem also contains several action
verbs which must be processed and stored for use during the encoding
stage. The pronouns "she" and "her" may cause momentary pauses
while the problem solver looks back or recalls from short-term
memory the nouns which they modify. Some of the technical mathematical vocabulary is absent, which might for this problem delay
the needed access to the Pythagorean Theorem in long-term memory.

Problem *2.7* represents one version of a well-known non-routine
problem. Its structure will be examined in more detail in Chapter
IV.

*2.7 Three missionaries and three cannibals are on one
bank of a river, with a rowboat that will hold at
most two people. How can they cross to the other
side of the river, in such a manner that missionaries are never outnumbered by cannibals on either
riverbank?*

Again in this problem, interpretations of terms such as "missionaries," "cannibals," "rowboat," "outnumbered," etc., may be
recalled from long-term memory. Although the problem can be
solved without actually understanding the meanings of the words
"missionaries" or "cannibals," knowledge of these terms may permit more effective storage of the rule that cannibals must never
outnumber missionaries. This rule must be held in short-term
memory, and probably accessed several times during the course of
problem solving.

Figure 2.1 proposes a rather naive, idealized version of the
process of decoding the problem statement, which we have examined
partially and qualitatively for a few problems. In the remainder
of this section we shall discuss in detail five categories of
syntax variables which have been studied in the literature in
the previous section, and attempt to understand using the model
how they are most likely to affect problem difficulty. In some

cases, this will guide us towards preferred definitions or suggested redefinitions of the variables for purposes of research.

Length Variables

Table 2.2 contains a list of 18 variables of length which have been investigated in the literature. Let us discuss these variables with respect to the decoding processes in Figure 2.1.

Lengthy problems usually contain more items of information and more information not directly related to the problem solution. As the problem length increases, greater stress may be placed on short-term memory. If the problem solver is not able to hold all of the information in an accessible form in short-term memory, *repeated* processing of the problem statement may be necessary, or additional *reorganization* may be required simply for the purpose of retaining the information. The effort to try to "hold" all of the present information may result in a loss of direction, or foster a feeling of confusion or frustration.

Problem length has been studied by means of the number of words, phrases, or sentences in the problem statement, as well as by means of the number of characters or letters and the number of syllables. It seems apparent that the number of character, letters, or syllables ought not to affect directly the stress on short-term memory, since words and phrases are usually remembered without the separate and distinct processing of each individual character or syllable. Thus the variables LETTRS, CHRCTR, and SYLBLS probably do not directly describe stress on short-term memory. Similarly, it is extremely rare for units as small as individual characters or symbols to be reorganized during the course of problem solving, or individually to evoke recall from long-term memory and comprehension. Thus, the verbal processing model suggests that these variables are inappropriate for the prediction of problem difficulty, being associated with it only by virtue of their correlation with other length variables.

The variables WORDS, LENGTH, WRDNUM, WRDGTS, and WRDSYM are all versions of word counts, with various combinations of symbols, digits, and numerals added for completeness. Length variables of this type are appropriate for the prediction of problem difficulty under the assumption that each word represents a syntactic and semantic processing unit which can be stored in short-term memory or evoke recall from long-term memory. It is evident that this assumption is a kind of approximation, for in many cases it is a *phrase* which functions as a unit in this sense (the variable WORDS takes this into account to the extent of assigning a count of "1" to a group of words which would appear in the dictionary as a single entry). From the standpoint of syntactic and semantic units of processing, it seems most appropriate to count each numeral

as equivalent to a single word (rather than to count each digit or
to count the number of words in the word form of the numeral). Similarly it would seem most appropriate to count each symbol (such as $)
as a single word.

Often, but not always, a problem with many sentences is more
difficult than a problem with only one or two sentences. This
variable (SENT) is not simply another way of counting words, but
is based on the assumption that each sentence contains at least
one complete idea, action sequence, or organizational relationship. Indeed, the problem solver may treat the ends of whole
sentences as natural places to pause (even momentarily) to reflect
on what has been read. The new idea may then be reorganized and
integrated with other ideas or action sequences from other sentences, before more material is read. Thus, SENT would be expected
to affect problem difficulty principally through the increased load
on the reorganization of information.

However, inversely related to the "number of sentences"
variable SENT is the "average sentence length" variable SENTLN.
If, indeed, sentences are considered to be the appropriate units
for reorganization of information, it is reasonable to expect that
the longer the unit, the more items of information it may contain,
the greater the load on short-term memory prior to reorganization,
and the more complex the reorganization that is necessary. Carrying this idea one step farther, the LGMXST variable is defined on
the assumption that a problem may be as difficult as its *longest*
sentence.

The variable LGNUWD is the length variable that reflects
the "distance" between the first and last numeral in the problem
statement. The rationale for this definition rests on the assumption that it may be more difficult to solve a problem when the
data are spread far apart, since in this situation it is more
likely that the problem solver will lose track of how the data
fit together. This definition is appealing in terms of the
verbal processing model, because it refers directly to the
reorganization process in its rationale.

Finally, the average word length variable AVGWDL is intended
to be indicative of overall word comprehension. The ability to
recycle and process words with many letters develops gradually
as the child matures; thus, this variable may affect problem
difficulty, particularly for young children, by placing greater
strain on the recall/comprehension process. For older children
and adults the effect is likely to be much less pronounced, or
in some cases negligible.

To summarize, the verbal processing model (Figure 2.1) suggests
the following hypotheses with respect to length variables: (a)
variables describing the number of words and/or symbols affect
problem difficulty due to the increased load on short-term memory;

(b) variables describing average word length or vocabulary difficulty affect problem difficulty due to the increased load on long-term memory and comprehension; (c) variables describing the number of sentences and the degree of separation of data within the problem affect problem difficulty due to the increased load on the reorganization of information; while (d) variables describing the number of letters or characters are inappropriate, being associated with problem difficulty only by virtue of their correlation with the length variables.

Grammatical Structure Variables

Although problem length has been shown to be an important parameter in the study of problem difficulty, length variables are the most superficial of the syntax variables. We now turn our attention to syntax variables which reflect the grammatical complexity of problem statements.

Variables describing the numbers and types of clauses and phrases are included in Table 2.3. In terms of the verbal processing model, variables such as the number of main clauses (MAINCL), the number of subordinate clauses (SUBCL), and the number of prepositional phrases (PREPHR) would principally affect the process of reorganization of information. Main clauses, containing subject and verb, represent the main idea or main action sequences in the problem statement. Subordinate clauses represent ideas which are secondary in a grammatical sense, although not necessarily in a mathematical sense. The problem solver is hypothesized to process smaller "units" such as words into short-term memory and reconstruct larger "units" through reorganization. With this interpretation, the fact that variables such as MAINCL and SUBCL do not enter nearly as importantly as LENGTH (see Table 2.4) into the regression equation seems to imply that the increased difficulty of longer problem statements results from greater load on short-term memory, rather than from greater need for the reorganization of information. It should also be noted that an increase in the number of clauses may be associated with increased mathematical complexity, which is not a syntax variable but will obviously affect problem difficulty.

The following two problems, at two different levels of difficulty, illustrate this last point.

2.8 (*The Easter Bunny hid 10 dozen eggs*) but (*the children could only find 20 of them.*) (*How many eggs were left?*)

2.9 (*Larry Bonecrusher weighed 420 pounds.*) (*He ate 15 pounds of chocolates.*) *If* ((*he gained 8 pounds,*)) (*by what percent did he increase his body weight?*)

In the above examples, single parentheses indicate main clauses, double parentheses indicate subordinate clauses, and prepositional phrases are underlined. The counts for these two problems are shown below.

Variable		Problem *2.8*	Problem *2.9*
MAINCL		3	3
SUBCL		0	1
WDMAIN	(number of words in the main clauses)	20	22
SUBLEN	(number of words in sub. clauses)	0	4
CLAUSE	(total number of clauses)	3	4
PREPHR		1	1

The variable counts above can also be used to generate other variables, particularly those involving ratios. For example, AVGCLS (average main clause length) can be computed by taking the ratio of WDMAIN to MAINCL; i.e., AVGCLS = 20/3 = 7 for Problem *2.8* and 22/3 = 7 for Problem *2.9*.

While the values of the variables for Problem *2.9* are higher than for Problem *2.8*, the greater difficulty of Problem *2.9* can be accounted for without reference to these variables. For example, Problem *2.9* contains irrelevant numerical information and utilizes the concept of percent, while Problem *2.8* does not.

Parts of speech variables are also defined in Table 2.3. As the problem solver reads through the problem statement, the meanings of nouns and verbs must be recalled from long-term memory, and those that appear important in reaching a solution must be retained in short-term memory. Adjectives and adverbs may provide the context to help the problem solver decide which nouns and verbs are important; however, it is often the case that they are distractors which do not supply useful information, but merely increase the length of the problem and increase its complexity. Consider the following two problems:

2.10 The brown horse can run 5 miles per hour faster than the black horse, which can run 10 miles per hour faster than the old grey mare. If the old grey mare can run at 10 miles per hour, how fast can the brown horse run?

2.11 The large, green spotted dragon ran quickly up to the castle and demanded that the fair damsel be given to him to eat. Sir Dull, the boring Knight,

killed five of his last eleven dragons, while Sir
Oscar killed seven of his last 15 dragons. Based
on his record, which knight has the greater prob-
ability of killing the large green dragon?

In Problem 2.10, the adjectives "brown," "black," and "grey" are
necessary to distinguish the horses from each other. While the adjective "old" is not necessary it does help to reinforce the fact that
the grey mare is the slowest. The adverb "faster" helps describe the
action of the problem and provides an item of information essential
to the problem's structure. Again it is apparent that there is considerable interaction among the task variable categories of syntax,
context, and structure. In Problem 2.11, the adjectives and adverbs
"large," "green," "spotted," "fair," "boring," and "quickly" provide
no useful information and place greater strain on short-term memory
unnecessarily. These adjectives and adverbs do not interact with
the problem structure. They may, however, serve a useful purpose
in stimulating the problem solver's interest in the problem (see
Chapter III).

In view of the two situations illustrated in the above problems,
it is difficult even to decide in which direction the correlation
between the variables ADVERBS and ADJECTIVES and problem difficulty
will be. Here again, we find the major limitations of the linear
regression model.

Segalla (1973) attempted to quantify a number of somewhat sub-
jective aspects of problem statements. To measure the "richness"
of a problem statement, he hypothesized that a high NOUN TO ADJECTIVE
RATIO would be a characteristic of more difficult problems, since
the problem statement would tend to be barren of information. However, it is just as possible that a problem with a low NOUN TO
ADJECTIVE RATIO would contain many unnecessary descriptors which
would function as distractors, making the problem more difficult.
This variable therefore seems inappropriate to a verbal processing
model.

A particularly interesting variable studied by Segalla is the
PRONOUN TO NOUN RATIO. This variable is a measure of the indirectness of a problem. In statements which contain many pronouns but
few nouns, it is difficult to remember which nouns are referred to
by which pronouns. This places strain on short-term memory, slowing
down verbal processing and necessitating rereading. More movement
among the three processes in Figure 2.1 may be necessary. Problem
2.2, for example, has a high "indirectness" index.

Thus far, we have considered syntax variables that describe
only the surface structure of sentences. However, Ruddell (1964)
noted that variables which employ element counts, such as the
LENGTH variable or any of the "parts of speech" variables, have
been successful in accounting for only 26 to 51 percent of the
variance in reading comprehension scores. It is apparent that
a syntax variable which reflects more of the organizational

complexity of language structure might account for a significant portion of the variance in problem difficulty. In 1970, Loftus defined such a variable, based on a measure of "depth" proposed by Yngve (1960). In the Yngve model, each sentence is broken down into its constituent parts by a binary rewrite rule. In the resulting "phrase structure tree diagram," a number is assigned to each word, reflecting the level of "embeddedness" of the word in the sentence. These "Yngve numbers" are determined by the number of left branches leading to each word in the sentence. Figure 2.2 illustrates the "phrase structure tree diagram" for the sentence "The best students are always very punctual."

Yngve hypothesizes that this concept of depth is a measure of the number of constituents of the sentence that the reader must keep in short-term memory when considering each word. In this particular example, the reader must recall that "best" preceded the noun "students" and the verb phrase "are always very punctual", and therefore it receives a depth of "2". However, after reading the word "best" the reader will usually anticipate a noun and a predicate to follow, since this is a familiar pattern in English language structure. The depths of the words "students" and "are" are therefore not as great as the depth for "best."

The validity of the use of Yngve's measure has been supported in several studies, and Yngve himself was successful in applying his model to algebraic sentences. However, his results were not nearly as valid when applied to ordinary sentences in English. Rohrman (1968) and Perfetti (1969) noted difficulties associated with coding the depth of a sentence, and the results of their investigations do not support the Yngve hypothesis. One problem is that, for some sentences, more than one structure tree may be possible, resulting in a different mean depth for each. Since there does not exist an explicit set of rules for determining the numbers assigned to the words of a sentence, the question of reliability becomes significant.

Although the difficulties cited above imply that the Yngve measure of depth may be of questionable value in recall tasks, Loftus (1970) and Segalla (1973) attempted to show that the Yngve hypothesis may have some value in determining the relationship of syntax structure to word problem difficulty. In each of these studies, the investigators overcame the problems of ambiguous sentences and inter-experimenter reliability by choosing sentences carefully and comparing their "sentence trees" with those obtained by experts in psycholinguistics. In each case, the results for each problem correlated well with those obtained by the original researchers.

The syntax variable DEPTH can be defined as it was in the Loftus study by the following procedure: (1) compute the mean of the Yngve numbers for each sentence in the problem; and (2) the highest value of this set of Yngve "means" is taken as a measure of syntactic complexity, DEPTH, of the problem. The procedure for computing this variable is illustrated with the following example. The reader is invited to quantify the DEPTH variable for this problem and compare the results with those obtained by Loftus.

Figure 2.2 *Computation of Yngve Numbers*

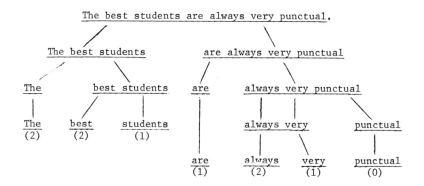

2.12 *Jim has 40 bottles. Ken has 30 bottles. They*
      have how many bottles together?

In the first sentence, the Yngve numbers are 1, 1, 1, 0, yielding a
mean of .75. The third sentence is characterized by the Yngve numbers
1, 1, 3, 2, 1, 0, with a mean of 1.33. The number 1.33 is therefore
taken as the measure of DEPTH for this problem.

It is clear from this procedure that the definition of the DEPTH
variable is based on the assumption that a problem is as complex as
its most complex sentence. This notion of "embeddedness" is essentially based on short-term memory. It would seem, however, that DEPTH
represents only one dimension of grammatical complexity, since it does
not reflect the types of words present in the problem statement.

Another technique for representing syntactic complexity has been
suggested by Botel, Dawkins, and Granowski (1973). Their formula for
computing syntactic complexity is based on a theory of transformational grammar in which complex sentences are considered to be
derived from changing and combining underlying structures such as
simple sentences. Like the Yngve measure, the Botel, Dawkins, and
Granowski formula yields a numerical coefficient for each sentence,
but the latter formula is more reliable and inclusive. Methods for
computing the syntactic complexity coefficient and implications for
researchers are discussed in detail by Goldin and Caldwell in Chapter
VI.

To summarize, the verbal processing model suggests the following
hypotheses with respect to grammatical structure variables: (a)
variables describing the number of clauses and prepositional phrases
affect problem difficulty due to the increased load on the reorganization of information; (b) the effects of different parts of speech
depend on whether the information is essential or inessential to the
problem solution and thus no clear effect is anticipated; and (c)
variables describing syntactic complexity (e.g., DEPTH) affect problem difficulty due to the increased load in short-term memory.

Variables Related to Numerals and Mathematical Symbols

It is obvious that in mathematical problem solving the numbers
and symbols contained in the problem statement are of great importance, since these are the data that learners must manipulate to
reach a solution. What is not so obvious is the relationship, if
any, of the syntax of the numbers and symbols to problem difficulty.
A step-wise linear regression analysis of the effects of the form
of numbers and symbols has not been done in any of the major studies
that have employed this technique.

Syntax variables describing the number of digits, numerals and
symbols have already been considered as components of various length
variables. The question remains as to which form of these variables

is likely to most affect problem difficulty based on Figure 2.1.
Most problem solvers are exposed to numbers in numeral form much
more often than in English form. In the encoding stage of verbal
processing, numerals (and not English words) are placed together
in mathematical sentences. It would seem therefore that word problems which contain numbers in numeral form may require less processing, and are more readily recognizable. Numbers in word form must
be recalled and translated into numerals before they can be used in
the later stages of the problem-solving process.

The relationship of symbol form to problem difficulty may likewise depend on the extent to which the problem solver is familiar
with the symbols used. If a particular symbol is new to the problem
solver, recall of its meaning may take longer and storage in short-
term memory may be slower than if the symbol had appeared in the
problem in written form. In actual practice, however, the symbols
used in linear regression studies (such as $ and %) have been
familiar to the problem solvers.

Several number and symbol form variables can be defined by taking
combinations of the variables in Table 2.6 (Tripp, 1972). For example,
consider the following problem:

> 2.13 At a sale, three children received a 10% discount
> on the purchase of a gift for their teacher. If
> the gift cost the children 5 dollars, how much
> was its original price?

The word "three" is a number that appears in word form, so the count
for NURD is 1. "10" and "5" are numbers that appear in the problem
statement in numeral form, so the count for WORAL is 2. The symbol
"%" was used in the problem statement to replace the word "percent,"
yielding a WOSBL count of 1. Conversely, "dollars" is a word in the
problem statement that replaces the symbol "$", so SYMRD receives a
count of 1.

The definitions of these four variables indicate that NURD and
WORAL, as do WOSBL and SYMRD, measure the same factors but in
opposite directions.

To summarize, the verbal processing model suggests that variables
describing the form of numerals and symbols will affect problem difficulty based on the familiarity of the form to the problem solver, and
the similarity of the form to the form required for a mathematical
equation.

Table 2.6 *Variables Describing Number and Symbol Forms*

1. NURD: A count of 1 for each number in word form which must be used to solve the problem or serving as a distractor.

2. WORAL: A count of 1 for each number in numeral form.

3. WOSBL: A count of 1 for each word in symbolic form

4. SYMRD: A count of 1 for each symbol in word form.

Variables Describing the Question Sentence

An important part of any problem statement is the sentence or phrase that contains the question to be answered. If the problem solver does not understand the question, the problem will be meaningless. Teachers have noted that students often find the correct answer to the wrong problem; that is, their calculations are correct but their answer is not what was asked for in the problem statement. Syntax variables describing the form, length, and position of the question sentence or phrase have been defined in order to observe the effects on problem difficulty of variations in question sentence. One kind of variable is the *length* of the question sentence. From the standpoint of the verbal processing model, there is no obvious reason to treat the length of the question sentence differently from any other sentence length.

A few researchers have suggested that certain types of problems may be more difficult if the question sentence contains one or more numerals than if no numerals are present in that sentence. It is possible that the presence of numerals would distract the problem solver from identifying the goal in the question sentence, encouraging instead the immediate processing of this information.

A third type of variable in this category relating to the organization of information is that of sequence. In problems which contain several sentences, difficulty may be influenced by whether the question sentence appears first or last in the problem statement. Similarly, for one-sentence problems the question may be asked before or after the data are presented. It is not clear whether the question functions as an advanced organizer when presented in the beginning of a problem. If it does, it may help the problem solver determine the relevance of data and assist in storage in short-term memory and in reorganization. It is also possible, however, that the "distance" of the question from the end of the problem may cause the problem solver to lose sight of the exact nature of the task.

The previous discussion suggests the definitions in Table 2.7.

The reader is invited to consider the following examples with respect to QUENL and QUESQ. For determining QUNLC, we shall consider the entire problem as the question sentence. The counts for the above variables will change if the variables are defined with respect to the "question phrase" rather than the "question sentence."

2.14 *How many more dollars will John need if a bike costs $50 and he has already saved $35?*

2.15 *John has $35. He wants to buy a bike that costs $50. How many more dollars does he need?*

Table 2.7 *Variables Describing the Question Sentence*

1. NUMQS: A count of 1 for each word in the question sentence (a similar variable can be defined for the number of words in the "question phrase" for single sentence problems.

2. QUENL: A count of 1 if the question sentence (or phrase) contains a numeral. A count of 0 otherwise.

   QUNLC: Another variable, QUNLC, can also be defined, with a count of 1 for <u>each</u> numeral in the question sentence.

3. QUESQ: A count of 1 if the question sentence (or phrase) appears before the presentation of the data. A count of 0 if the question sentence (or phrase) appears at the end of the problem statement (or follows the pre-sententation of the data).

2.16 If a block of wood is 9 inches long by 7 inches wide
by 5 inches thick, what is its surface area in square
inches?

2.17 In how many years will Mrs. Brown be 3 times as old
as her daughter? Mrs. Brown was 20 on her daughter's
second birthday.

Problem	QUENL	QUNLC	QUESQ
2.14	1	2	1
2.15	0	0	0
2.16	1	3	0
2.17	1	1	1

To summarize, from the standpoint of verbal processing it would
be expected that NUMQS should have no particular effect that has not
been already incorporated under length variables, and the QUENL and
QUESQ may affect the problem difficulty by making easier or more
difficult the process of reorganization of information.

Sequence Variables

The sequencing of information in problem statements has long
been known to contribute to problem difficulty. Problems with data
presented in the same order as they will be used to reach a solution
tend to be easier than those in which the data are out of order.
Data in the proper order facilitate understanding of the relationships in the problem statement and allow the problem solver to construct relational mathematical expressions with minimum reorganization.

In recent years, a number of researchers have used some form
of ORDER variable in linear regression studies (Loftus, 1970;
Segalla, 1973; Barnett, 1974). This variable has been defined both
as a dichotomous variable and as a whole-number-valued variable,
as in Table 2.8.

Brennan (1972) has suggested a different version of an ORDER
variable. The ORDER3 variable in Table 2.8 reflects the position
of the question statement with respect to the data interval. This
variable is similar to question sentence variables discussed previously.

The following examples illustrate the three ORDER variables.

2.18 A businesswoman was getting 23 miles per gallon of
gasoline. Changing her spark plugs reduced this by

Table 2.8 *Sequence Variables*

ORDER1: A count of 0 is given if the numbers in the statement of the problem appear in exactly the same order as they are needed for solving the problem, and a count of 1 otherwise.

ORDER2: The minimum number of permutations required to change the sequence of the numbers in the statement of the problem to the sequence customarily required to solve the problem.

ORDER3: A count of 1 is given if the data interval is interrupted by the statement of the question. A count of 0 is given if the data interval is not interrupted by the question statement. (The data interval has its end points on the first and last numerals.)

10 percent. However, a carburetor tune-up increased that by 5 percent. What was her new mileage?

2.19 *A grocer bought 17 dozen pears for $4.65. If 5 dozen spoiled, at what price per dozen must he sell the remaining pears to make a profit equal to 3/5 of the total cost?*

Problem	ORDER1	ORDER2	ORDER3
2.18	0	0	0
2.19	1	2	1

Note that in Problem 2.19 the numeral $4.65 must be moved from the second position of the four items of information (17, $4.65, 5, 3/5) to the fourth position, since it is used last in the problem. Therefore, the count for the ORDER2 variable is 2.

Order variables are not exclusively syntax variables, since they involve *comparison* of the sequencing of information in the problem statement with the ideal sequence from the standpoint of mathematical structure. They may affect the reorganization process in the decoding stage, but their effects may also be due to effects of problem structure on problem solving, thus extending beyond the scope of the translation stage.

3. The Effects of Syntax on Problem-Solving Processes: Recommendations for Research

The effects of variation of problem syntax on the *processes* used by problem solvers have been studied very little (an exception is the study by Hayes and Simon, 1975, describing effects of syntax and semantics on the representations created by subjects). Given two problems with the same mathematical structure, let us hypothesize about how variations within each of the categories of syntax variables might affect problem-solving processes. In a previous section, the role of variables of length was discussed with respect to the verbal processing model. The point was made that lengthy problems can place stress on short-term memory in the decoding stage. We might therefore expect problem solvers to depend less on short-term memory in lengthy problems than in short problems. It seems reasonable to hypothesize that the changes in processes used might include: the increased use of paper-and-pencil techniques to record information; the greater use of diagrams, tables, and/or graphs to help organize the data; and, perhaps, the increased use of algebraic labels for unknown quantities. Reading patterns might vary following an initial reading of the problem statement (such as a greater tendency to reread part or all of the problem, or increased skimming of the problem statement to pick up individual items of information). It might be particularly interesting to investigate the effects of the *appearance* of a lengthy problem on the processes used to solve it. That is, do the processes used to solve a lengthier problem change due to the actually greater amount of language processing necessary, or does the mere appearance of a long problem influence how the problem solver approaches it?

Varying the number of sentences (the SENT variable) while keeping the content, context, and mathematical structure constant might also produce differences in the processes used to solve word problems, since the information in the problem statement would be contained in different size organizational units. For example, a problem with one sentence might lead the problem solver to construct a single equation incorporating all the relevant data. A structurally similar problem with several sentences (each containing an action sequence or information item) might lead the problem solver to construct several small equations or mathematical relationships before combining them into a single, all-encompassing equation.

Many of the above comments on the possible relationship of variations in length to solution processes apply to grammatical structure variables as well. Faced with a problem having complex grammatical structure, the problem solver is likely to show increased use of the same aids to short-term memory as in the case of lengthy problems. However, a more interesting question to ask is whether there is a relationship of the number or form of the equations developed by the problem solver to the amount of action (as measured by, say, the VERBS variable), or to any of the other grammatical structure variables defined in Table 2.3.

The point was made earlier that the position of the question in a problem task may influence the storage of data in short-term memory. If the appearance of the question sentence at the beginning of a problem statement acts as an advanced organizer, this may be reflected in the *form* of mathematical sentences used by the problem solver. Recent developments in instruments of protocol analysis could be of great value in determining the relationship of the position of the question to the form of equation and method of solution employed.

Speculating on possible changes in process as a result of changes in number and symbol formats is somewhat difficult. If the formats of these two aspects of a problem statement are unfamiliar to the problem solver, it is possible that he or she will write information expressed in one form in a more familiar form. For example, if the numbers are presented in a problem task in English form, the problem solver may write them in numeral form while reading through the problem statement, as an aid to short-term memory.

Changes in the sequence of data are likely to influence the sequence type or length of the equations developed by the problem solver. Information obtained by investigations of this relationship may lead to a better understanding of the nature of the reorganization substage of the verbal processing phase.

In order to investigate the effects of syntax on problem-solving processes as suggested in this section, a reliable method of recording and classifying such processes is evidently needed. Chapter VIII.B of this book may be an important step in developing such a method.

4. Conclusions

In the previous discussion, an attempt has been made to (1) establish the importance of syntax variables as a special class of task variables related to verbal problem solving in mathematics; (2) examine the current state of knowledge based on linear regression in syntax variable research; (3) suggest a verbal processing model compatible with the general problem-solving model shown in Chapter I, which may help explain the role of syntax in the verbal processing phase; (4) suggest some categories and subcategories of syntax variables for future research; and (5) propose some possible extensions of syntax variables research to look at problem-solving *processes* as the dependent variables.

The identification of the five major categories of syntax variables (Length, Grammatical Structure, Numerals and Symbols, Question Sentence, and Sequence) is based on the research to date, particularly those studies that have employed the linear regression model. While this technique has made a valuable contribution to the identification of specific syntax variables that may contribute to verbal problem difficulty, it may be time to progress beyond it.

A purpose of this book is to demonstrate that describing task variables by means of various categories is a useful procedure that should help researchers gain information about the interrelationships of different attributes of problem tasks. The relationship of specific syntax variables to the other characteristics of verbal problem tasks discussed in the following chapters needs intensive study across age and ability groups. Of particular importance are studies that attempt to determine directly the role of syntax variables in the decoding process at the first stages of problem solving.

A commitment to the development of new research and methodological paradigms on the part of researchers is of paramount importance. In the opinion of this author, significant advancement in the field of problem-solving research will only be possible if results can be replicated and extended by coordinated series of investigations. Such efforts imply a commitment to common definitions, notation, shared problem sets, and similar subject populations. The various components of the verbal processing model suggested in Figure 2.1 may provide an organizational framework for a portion of these efforts.

III.

Content and Context Variables in Problem Tasks

by

Norman Webb
University of Wisconsin
Madison, Wisconsin

One purpose of this chapter is to identify different dimensions across which the content and context of a task can vary. The categorization scheme is designed to be used by teachers and curriculum specialists to analyze the range of problem-solving experiences children are receiving, or should be receiving, in school.

A second purpose is to clarify the role which content and context variables play in problem-solving research. It is essential that content and context variables be well defined to increase the validity and the generalizability of research findings. Small variations in the content or context of a task can result in large variations in the solution process, and consequently in the findings of a study. The categorization scheme for content and context variables should help researchers in designing research, selecting problems, and interpreting their findings. Brownell and Stretch (1931) caution,

> ...the act of solving verbal problems in arithmetic is exceedingly complicated and ... investigations which oversimplify the process and attempt to measure a single aspect of it without regard for other aspects are certain to secure only partially valid results and to misrepresent the true situation (p. 74).

The content of a problem is the mathematical substance of the task. The four main subdivisions of content variables to be discussed in this chapter are: (1) variables describing the *mathematical topic*, (2) variables describing the *field of application*, (3) variables describing the *semantic* content, and (4) variables describing the *problem elements*. Here "semantic content" refers to the meanings of critical words or phrases in the problem statement, such as keywords or technical mathematical vocabulary. "Problem elements" are phrases in the problem statement which contain essential items of information such as givens, allowed operations, and goals.

Where content refers to "substance of a problem," the context refers to the *form* of the problem statement. "Form" is interpreted very generally to include: (1) variables describing the problem embodiment or representation, (2) variables describing the verbal context or setting, and (3) variables describing the information format.

Certain boundaries have been set in this chapter between content/ context variables and other categories of task variables. Both syntax variables and content/context variables describe the problem statement. Content and context variables tend to be classificatory in nature, and describe the types of words, elements, operations, and applications of the task. Syntax variables tend to be quantitative measures describing the problem statement. Content and context variables describe surface characteristics that can be observed directly from the problem statement or its immediate surroundings. Structure variables describe the underlying mathematical characteristics of the tasks, in contrast to its surface characteristics.

In developing the categorization of task variables, we must take account of certain difficulties. Often a very fine distinction determines the placing of a variable in one or another category. Some variables which we consider to be *context* variables, and thus *intrinsic* to the task, are very similar to some *situation* variables which are *external* to the task. Even among the categories of task variables, ambiguity can arise. For example, we shall consider "problem type" as a content variable. However, this is distinguished from certain structure variables by a thin line. If the "type" of the problem can be identified from the *problem statement*, without mathematical processing, then the problem type is a content variable. However, if the problem "type" is identifiable only after beginning to solve the problem mathematically, then it is a structure variable. The point is that any categorization scheme for task variables is somewhat arbitrary: its value comes from the extent to which it helps identify possible confounding factors and provides a means of communication.

The next section reviews some research that is related to content and context variables. Sections 2 and 3 delineate the proposed classification scheme for these variables.

1. Review of Research Related to Content and Context Variables

In this section, research will be reviewed which illustrates the major questions that have been asked concerning context and content task variables.

Content variables have been investigated both directly and indirectly, depending upon the purpose of the study. "Mathematical topic" has not often been regarded as a variable to be manipulated. For example, Lucas (1972) investigated the teaching of problem solving using calculus as the content and Kantowski (1974) has worked with high school students using geometry. In these studies the mathematical topic was fixed *a priori* and problem-solving behavior studied *within* the topic area.

Studies that have considered the generalization of heuristic processes *across* tasks have sometimes used "mathematical topic" as an independent variable to study the effects of instruction. Wilson

(1967) gave high school students instruction in heuristic processes on two different kinds of tasks, algebra and logic; he then tested their ability to solve problems on these topics, their use of different levels of strategy on each task, and their ability to solve a transfer task in geometry. He concluded that the different levels of heuristic processes may complement each other, since superior problem-solving performance resulted when different levels of heuristic processes were demonstrated in the two training tasks. Heuristic processes demonstrated on one task tended to be used on successive tasks. A similar type of study was done by Smith (1973) to investigate the effect of giving advice on task-specific heuristic processes as opposed to general heuristic processes. He gave college students three programmed booklets to study, each on a different mathematical topic: finite geometry, Boolean algebra, and symbolic logic. The task-specific group did better on the logic and Boolean algebra tasks. The general heuristic process group did *not* solve more transfer problems, and did not solve them faster.

Both of these studies investigated a fundamental pedagogical issue: teaching specific means of solving problems in each content area vs. teaching general means of solving problems that can be applied to problems from different content areas.

Krutetskii (1976) developed problem sets that varied *problem type* in order to study the ability of children to generalize. He found that capable pupils tended to generalize the problems before solving them, on the basis of a grasp of the general features of the structure of the problems. Most capable pupils were able to recall the type and the general character of the operations of a problem they had solved, but not the problem's specific data or numbers. Less capable pupils usually recalled only specific data or numbers.

In most of Krutetskii's series, problems from more than one mathematical topic were used. The topics included arithmetic, algebraic, geometric, logical, and general mathematics problems. The names of the problem series that varied content or context variables are as follows (see Table 5.3, Chapter V for more detail):

- Problems with an unstated question
- Problems with incomplete information
- Problems with surplus information
- Problems with interpenetrating elements
- Systems of problems of a single type
- Systems of problems of different types
- Problems with terms that are hard to remember

The first three series were used to study the characteristics of information-gathering by mathematically capable pupils. Each of these series had a high loading on a single factor labeled "formalized perception of mathematical material."

Using some of the same problems as Krutetskii, Silver (1978) examined student perceptions of "relatedness" among mathematical word problems. He administered a card-sorting task to one group of eighth-grade students and later to a second group. The card-sorting task consisted of 24 verbal problems varied systematically along two dimensions, *mathematical structure* and *contextual details*. Students were instructed to form groups of problems that they judged to be "mathematically related" and to explain their basis for categorization. The students appeared to use four general problem similarity dimensions--(a) mathematical structure, (b) contextual details, (c) question form, and (d) pseudostructure. The latter dimension referred to associations among problems based on the presence of a common measurable quantity, such as age, weight, or time. Silver's four dimensions are similar to those identified by Chartoff (1976) in administering a card-sorting task of algebra verbal problems to 500 students ranging from seventh graders to college freshmen. Chartoff also identified four dimensions--(a) how the problems are solved, (b) the contextual setting, (c) comparison with a generic problem of the same type, and (d) the question posed by the problem. Chartoff's third dimension corresponds to Silver's "pseudostructure."

The population used by Silver was composed of students in regular eighth-grade classes, in contrast to the very capable students predominantly described by Krutetskii. However, the results are very similar in that the *structure* dimension tended to dominate students' perceptions of problem relatedness. On the other hand, it was not uncommon for students in the Silver study to associate problems using the pseudostructure dimensions. Further, a negative relationship was found between mathematical ability and the tendency to associate problems according to their contextual details.

The distinction between "typing" problems by their mathematical structure and by their pseudostructure needs to be developed further. In general, Krutetskii used the term "problem type" to group problems having similar mathematical structures. In our scheme of analyzing task variables, such a classification would represent a "structure" variable rather than a "content" variable. The pseudostructure, as defined by Silver, refers to the concept of "problem type" as a content task variable, since the classification of the problem can be done strictly from the problem statement. Some of the classifications of problem type by pseudostructure include "age" problems, "work" problems and "coin" problems. Much of the problem-solving experience students receive in school involves working problems grouped by problem type.

During a part of the Mathematical Problem Solving Project at Indiana University, elementary-age students were asked to select problems they would like to solve. The criteria used to select the problems were observed to be very superficial, such as the name of the person mentioned in the problem or the length of the problem statement. Rarely did students select problems on the basis of

problem complexity or difficulty level. When given a choice between
problems stated with a few words and a picture or those stated only
with words, students selected the former more often than the latter.
For example, a problem like *3.1* was chosen more often than *3.2*. There
are other factors involved, but one suspects that the differences in
semantic content are among the reasons the students found *3.1* to be
more interesting and require less outside help.

> *3.1 Use each number from 1 to 8 once to fill in the small
> squares so that no two numbers that follow in order
> (such as 4 and 5) are in squares that touch.*

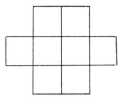

> *3.2 A bowl has 24 pieces of fruit. Some are oranges and
> some are grapefruit. It has twice as many oranges as
> grapefruit. How many oranges are in the bowl?*

Studies of the "semantic content" of mathematical problems have
examined mathematical vocabulary and the use of "key words." Kane
(1968, 1970) argues strongly that mathematical English and ordinary
English differ on at least four factors--the level of redundancy of
words, *the unique denotation of names of mathematical objects*, the
importance of adjectives, and the flexibility of grammar and syntax.
He questions the validity of the use of standard readability formulas
to assess the readability of mathematics textbooks and problems.

Nesher and Teubal (1975) identify three ways that research studies
have dealt with verbal cues and their relationship to attaining solutions of arithmetic problems. One group of studies emphasizes the need
for *training* in specialized mathematics vocabulary (Dahmus, 1970; Lyda
and Duncan, 1967; Vanderlinde, 1964; Willmon, 1971). Other studies
(Jerman and Rees, 1972; Loftus, 1970) view verbal cues as a factor in
determining the relative difficulty of verbal arithmetic problem
solving. Following this line of investigation, a distinction is made
between verbal cues, words that cue for specific mathematical operations, and distractors or potential verbal cues which are not in fact
cues for operations. In a third approach, Paige and Simon (1966)
raise the question of exactly how verbal cues affect the transition
from the verbal formulation to a mathematical expression.

Each of the three types of studies is concerned with how the task variable of "key words" may affect problem-solving performance. However, research findings do not always substantiate the importance of key words, particularly in relation to problem difficulty. Nesher and Teubal found that, for first graders, key words actually deterred finding the correct operation rather than facilitating the process. Of the three groups of studies, they felt the third group held the most promise, where verbal cues are studied as they affect the transition from a verbal formulation to a mathematical expression. Loftus kept track of verbal cues in the word problems such as "and" for addition, "left" or a comparative for subtraction, and "each" for multiplication. She found that such cues did not enter as a significant regression effect once other variables with larger multiple correlates were entered into the equation. These other variables, in order of importance, were: operations, sequence, length, depth, and conversion.

More studies have investigated context variables than content variables. The majority of these studies have considered the effects of different settings on problem difficulty or problem-solving performance. In general the findings are inconclusive: the setting of a problem makes a difference in some studies, while in others the variation of setting has no effect. Most of the studies have been restricted to standard word problems similar to those found in textbooks. Little is known about the variation of context on the difficulty of nonroutine problems.

A classic study on the effects of unfamiliar settings on problem solving was done by Brownell and Stretch (1931). More important than the findings of this study is the approach taken by the researchers. They sought not only to determine what the effects were, but also to understand why and how they occurred. The undertaking was to study whether the success of children in solving arithmetic problems is conditioned by the familiarity or lack of familiarity in the settings described in the problems. In particular, it was asked whether unfamiliarity of setting causes a loss of efficiency in the understanding of the arithmetic involved in the problem, in computation, or in both.

"Familiar" was defined as included in immediate personal experience, as opposed to experiences secured through pictures and reading. Brownell and Stretch took the position that there may be degrees of unfamiliarity and used four varieties of the same problem with successive versions designed to make the setting more "unfamiliar." The first version was designed to be a situation from the students' immediate experience. The setting of the fourth version was a situation that was probably unknown to the students, and included some nonsense terms.

An arithmetic problem was assumed to have five separate features: (1) certain numbers, (2) one or more operations, (3) one or more verbal clues to the operations(s) ("How many . . . together"), (4) a setting or situation, and (5) the language (words, sentence structure) necessary to bind together the preceding four parts. The first three features are content variables, "setting" is a context variable, and sentence structure falls under the heading of "syntax variables" (see Chapter II). In studying the setting of problems, Brownell and Stretch kept the other four variables constant. An example of a problem and its variations is the following:

> 3.3 *There are 34 Boy Scouts in Dick's troop. Each scout is to bring 3 of his old toys to school to give to poor children in the town. The Scout Master says that altogether 91 toys have been brought. How many are there yet to be brought? (47 words)*
>
> *Soldiers grooming cavalry horses.*
> *(3 x 34) - 91*   *(47 words)*
>
> *Refining plant; tank cars of oil in the yards.*
> *(3 x 34) - 91*   *(47 words)*
>
> *Hindu village, with bimlecks and toros.*
> *(3 x 34) - 91*   *(47 words)*

(Brownell and Stretch, 1931, p. 19)

The tests were administered to fifth-grade students with each child solving all four versions of each problem. A Latin square design was used to ensure that the tests were taken in different orders. The number of children used in the analyses was 256.

Just by considering the number of problems scored correctly, a significant increase in difficulty was found as the familiarity of the problems decreased. Brownell and Stretch examined the data further to try to explain these results, and found them to be deceiving. There was little change in the accuracy of computation as problems became more unfamiliar. The children's choices of operations varied considerably across problems having the same number relationships, even when there were no changes in the familiarity of the setting. Unfamiliarity of setting is not universal in its effect on problem solvers. From 65 percent to 80 percent of the children were *unaffected* by changes in the familiarity of settings. The unfamiliarity of the setting had the *most* effect on the *least* skilled children, in their choice of operations and their computation. The final conclusion by Brownell and Stretch was that problems are not made unduly difficult for children by unfamiliar settings, except under a limited set of conditions.

Travers (1967) contrasted "social-economic," "mechanical-scientific," and "abstract" problem settings, and found only a slight relationship between students' preferences and the types of problems they were successful in solving. Scott and Lighthall (1967) examined the possible relationship between "higher needs" (e.g., love and belongingness) and "low needs" (e.g., food and shelter) in the settings of arithmetic problems, and the background of students; they found no statistically significant relationship. Cohen (1976) investigated "outdoor," computational, and "scientific" settings with regard to problem difficulty, by testing over 200 eighth graders. Results indicated that "area of student interest" alone was *not* sufficient to predict the type of problem on which they would be most successful.

Another dimension of context variables is the presentation of the tasks, the forms of which can be varied considerably in problem-solving research. Some examples include: (a) oral; (b) pictorial; (c) with physical equipment and apparatuses (particularly with younger children); (d) in game forms or as "twenty questions"; and (e) in a written verbal form, sometimes even on overhead projectors with strict time limitations.

In spite of the variety of options, research that has been done on different forms of task presentations has been predominantly restricted to verbal problems, and conflicting results have been reported. Multiple-choice word problems from the Y and Z population of NLSMA which were presented with an accurate picture were less difficult than the same set of problems presented with prose only or with a distorted picture (Sherrill, 1970; Webb and Sherrill, 1974). These results were not supported in a study by Kulm et al. (1972), who presented 50 tasks on overhead transparencies and used five different stimulus situations: "textbook," "student-generated," "pictorial," "textbook and pictorial," and "student-generated and pictorial." In this study, students were limited to one minute to read the problem, followed by three minutes to solve the problem. Students were most effective on the textbook version of the problems and least effective on the "textbook and pictorial" version.

Kennedy, Eliot and Krulee (1970) included both number problems and word problems in their investigation of error patterns in the problem-solving formulations used by 28 high school juniors. Examples of a number problem and a word problem as given by these authors are:

3.4 $\quad \dfrac{3y-4}{8} \ = \ \dfrac{4y+8}{4}$

3.5 *A man is three times as old as his son. Eleven years from now he will be only twice as old as his son. How old is the son at present?*

In general the number problems offered little difficulty for the subjects of this study. The word problems, however, were considerably more difficult for the less-able students. Rosenthal and Resnick (1971) also found word problems to be more difficult than number problems in research involving 63 elementary students.

Another study that looked at varying the form of presentation used four problem-solving test forms to compare advantaged and disadvantaged second and fourth graders (Houtz, 1973). The four forms varied from "abstract" to three increasingly "concrete" forms. The *abstract form* contained written statements of the problems. The *picture book* form had drawings representing the problem placed in the test booklets above the response alternatives. A third form had *slides* made of the drawings and used these in depicting the problems. Finally, the *model* form included three-dimensional full-color models of the drawings. The three concrete forms resulted in a higher level of performance than the abstract form for both the advantaged and the disadvantaged children. The model form did not result in the highest level of performance, and appeared to result in a decrease in the level of performance of the non-white children in the study.

Loftus (1970) investigated "structural variables" that affect problem-solving difficulty, using word problems with a small group of disadvantaged sixth-grade students. One variable identified was how a problem was embedded in a set of "like" and "different" problems. A word problem was found to be more difficult to solve when it was of a different type from the problem preceding it. This variable that Loftus identified as "structural" fits the definition of a *context* variable since it relates to *how* the problem is presented.

This sampling of studies that have investigated content and context variables provides illustrations of the kinds of questions that can be asked, rather than a definitive description of the effects of content and context variable manipulation. These studies are representative in that no strong results emerge. More studies like that of Brownell and Stretch are needed, making an effort to understand not only *if* there is an effect, but also *why* there is an effect.

2. The Classification and Definition of Content Variables

The two categories of task variables which refer to the main essence of mathematical problems are content and structure variables. Content variables describe the substance of the task, while structure variables describe the models that represent the solution process of the task. The analysis of content variables, then, is important because of their direct link to the mathematical aspects of the tasks.

Table 3.1 provides an overview of the classification of content variables proposed in this chapter.

Problem Classification by Mathematical Topic

Our discussion of mathematical topic is divided into two parts: classification by *subject area* and classification by *problem type*. The subject area of a task is typically a field of mathematics.

Table 3.1 *A Summary of Content Task Variables*

1. Mathematical topic of the task

   A. Subject area classifications

   <u>broad</u> arithmetic   <u>narrow</u> ratio and proportion
           algebra   binomial theorem
           geometry   quadratic formula
           analysis   etc.
           etc.

   B. Traditional "problem types"

           rate problems
           age problems
           money problems
           mixture problems
           etc.

   These classifications usually imply reference to mathematical
   information which may not be explicitly stated in the problem,
   such as the quadratic formula, the equation "distance = rate x
   time" or the monetary value of coins.

2. Field of application of the task (if relevant)

           biology
           chemistry
           physics
           etc,

   A problem may require the use of specific mathematical relationships understood to hold within the field of application. For
   example, a physics problem may require application of the law of
   conservation of momentum in order to obtain a relevant equation.

3. Semantic content of the problem statement

   A. Key words

           greater than
           reduced by
           altogether
           etc.

   Particular verbal clues often (but not always) suggest specific mathematical operations. Verbal clues may sometimes be
   misleading.

   B. Mathematical vocabulary

           average
           root of an equation
           polynomial
           etc.

   Technical mathematical terms may appear in the problem whose
   interpretation is important for solution.

Table 3.1 *(continued)*

4. Variables describing the problem elements

   A. Given information

   > given conditions or numerical information
   > conditions implied but not explicitly stated
   > hints
   > etc.

   B. Goal information

   > number of required items of goal information
   > goals implied but not explicitly stated
   > problems "to find" vs. problems "to prove"
   > etc.

5. Mathematical equipment available for the task (if applicable)

   > calculator
   > compass
   > protractor
   > etc.

Krutetskii chose to use problems representing the five broad subject
areas of arithmetic, algebra, geometry, logic, and general mathematics. Within each of his problem series, he included items
representing different subject areas. For example, two problems
from Krutetskii's series III (problems with surplus information),
representing different subject areas, are given below (the superfluous information is underlined):

Arithmetic Test

3.6 *In a store, 24 sacks of potatoes weigh 3 kg and 5
kg each, with more in the former than in the latter.
The weight of all the 5-kg sacks was equal to the
weight of all the 3-kg sacks. How much did each
weigh?*

Geometry Test

3.7 *Given an isoceles triangle, with one side 2 cm,
another 10 cm, and the third equal to one of the two
given ones. Find the third scale.* (Krutetskii, 1976, pp. 110-111)

The identification of a broad subject area classification for
many problems is straightforward. The following five tasks are from
a book of problems for junior and senior high school students; each
has an obvious classification (Hill, 1974).

3.8 *Find all real numbers x such that*

$$\sqrt{5 - \sqrt{5 - x}} = x \ .$$

3.9 *Given a regular tetrahedron, find the ratio of the
volume of the inscribed sphere to that of the circumscribed sphere.*

3.10 *Find the number of terminal zeros in the standard
numeral for 100! (100 factorial)*

3.11 *Fifty tickets numbered consecutively from 1 to 50 are
placed in a jar, and two of them are drawn at random
(without replacement). What is the probability that
the difference of the two numbers drawn is 10 or less?*

3.12 *Given the equation $\sin x = \frac{x}{100}$, determine the number
of solutions.*

Hill classified these problems respectively in the domains of
algebra, geometry, number theory, probability, and trigonometry.

The classification of these problems can be obtained by considering
the givens, the possible operations, and the goals that are explicit
in the statement of the problem or assumed. It is not necessary to
solve each problem in order to classify it.

Krutetskii and Hill both used traditional subject areas which
can be found in most standard textbooks to classify the content of
problems. However, these classifications are not the only way to
partition the domain of mathematics. For example, in the Unified
Mathematics Program, the table of contents lists the following
topics: Finite Number Systems, Operational Systems, Mathematical
Mappings, The Integers, Multiplication of Integers, Lattice Points
in a Plane, Sets and Relations, Theory of Numbers, Rational Numbers,
Probability and Statistics, Transformations in a Plane, and Using
Rational Numbers (Fehr, Fey, and Hill, 1972).

A problem task does not always fall clearly into a single subject area. The statement of the task may be in general terms, so
that the solution can be derived by using methods from different
mathematical subject areas. Thus a task may be labeled as "arithmetic" or "algebra" depending upon how the problem is expected to
be solved. In this situation the problem task is categorized as
belonging to a particular subject area based upon the mathematical
structure of the task and what *processes* are to be used to find the
solution. This distinction is important in considering subject area
classification as a content variable rather than a structure variable.
Subject area as a content variable is based upon the problem statement
--the givens, the stated operations, and the goals of the task. For
example, consider Problem *3.13*. The subject area classification of
this task is geometry, since the givens are all elements of a figure,
the goal is to find a geometric element in terms of three others, and
the implicit operations and needed properties are mostly within the
domain of geometry. The solution, however, has the appearance of an
algebraic relation.

3.13

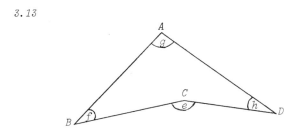

Find angle e in terms of angles f, g, and h.

(Webb, 1976)

Next consider Problem *3.14:*

> *3.14 A barrel of honey weighs 50 pounds. The same barrel
> with kerosene in it weighs 35 pounds. If honey is
> twice as heavy as kerosene, how much does the empty
> barrel weigh?*
>
> (Webb, 1976)

For those who have studied algebra, the most obvious way to
solve Problem *3.14* is to set up simultaneous linear equations and to
solve them using algebraic rules of procedure. Pre-algebra students
are more likely to solve the problem using trial-and-error and computations. One possible solution is to double the weight of the
barrel full of kerosene and then subtract the weight of the barrel
full of honey. Whether this task is classified as an arithmetic
task or an algebraic task depends upon some knowledge of the mathematical experience of the students and their approaches to solving
the task. In this case, to say that the subject area of Problem *3.14*
is "algebra" refers more to the *structure* of the task and one efficient way of solving it than to the content of the task.

The degree of specificity of the mathematical topic of a task
will depend upon the purpose of the task. If a goal of a researcher
is to seek a contrast or variation in approaches resulting from solving algebra problems as opposed to geometry problems, then the tasks
can be chosen to accomplish that goal. This implies varying the
global, traditional subject areas. However, if a teacher is structuring experiences for the students in order to cover a variety of
algebra tasks, then more refined subject area stratifications need
to be used, such as "quadratic equations," "exponents," etc.

Another means of adding specificity to the mathematical topic
of a task is by identifying the *problem type.* "Problems of a similar
type" commonly refers to a set of problems that can be solved by
using the same algorithm. Students are taught how to recognize a
certain type of problem and then how to apply an appropriate algorithm. "Rate problems" and "work problems" are two such problem
types that most students encounter sometime during their first year
of algebra. As a content task variable, the term *problem type* will
be used more generally and will refer *to a class of problems with
similar attributes of the problem statement* but not necessarily
solvable by the same algorithm. This definition corresponds to what
Silver labeled "pseudostructure." Problems of the same "type" often
draw on specific mathematical formulas or relationships which are
not explicit in the problem statement (such as, distance = rate x
time); these may be essential to the translation of the problem
statement into a mathematical representation.

Formally, the *elements* of a problem are: the givens, the stated
or implied operations that transform one or more expressions into one
or more new expressions, and the goal or goals. The problem statement

generally includes a full or partial specification of the givens, the operations, and the goal(s). For two problems to be of the same problem type, the givens and the goal *as described in the problem statement* must be "similar" and from the same mathematical content area. As an illustration, examine these two problems:

> 3.15 *A spherical balloon is inflated with gas at the rate of 100 ft³/min. Assuming that the gas pressure remains constant, how fast is the radius of the balloon increasing at the instant when the radius is 3 ft.?*

> 3.16 *Water is withdrawn from a conical reservoir 8 ft. in diameter and 10 ft. deep (vertex down) at the constant rate of 5 ft³/min. How fast is the water level falling when the depth of water in the reservoir is 6 ft.?*

(Thomas, 1969, p. 112)

Each problem statement specifies the shape of the container, the dimensions of the container, and the rate at which an amount of fluid is changing. The goal in each problem is to find the instantaneous rate at which a specified dimension is changing. "Calculus" is the mathematical topic of these problems, with "related rates" being the problem type in the traditional sense. The above problems are very easy to recognize as being similar and of the same problem type in the sense defined here. The important thing to note, however, is that these are examples for which two problems can be of the same type as we have defined it, but for which no common solution algorithm exists. Thus, as a content variable, "problem type" is not a *sufficient* condition for ascertaining the structure of a problem. To determine the type of a problem just by considering the surface characteristics of the problem can be misleading for the solution process. In conducting research or providing instruction on problem solving, both surface and structure characteristics are important. Hence, in contrasting problems, or varying problems according to type, two task variables are simultaneously involved: the type of the problem determined from the problem statement, which is a content variable, and the algorithmic method of solution, which is a structure variable.

Problem Classification by Field of Application

Many interesting mathematical problems are derived from real-life situations, or from disciplines other than mathematics. The "mathematical topic" of these problems does not adequately describe the content of the problem. Thus a second major dimension of content variables is the "applied field" of the task, which is the discipline or real-life situation from which the task arises. This dimension cannot be used to describe every task, since many problems are "purely" mathematical, and contain no reference to an applied field.

Genuine applied problems add a new dimension to problem-solving instruction and research. In its most general characterization, applied problem solving requires the building, development and testing of a mathematical model. Four steps in a model-building process given by Maki and Thompson (1973) are illustrated in Figure 3.1. The original task arises from a "real world" situation where observations are made and questions posed. Initially the task is general, global, and not necessarily well-defined. The next step is to make the task as precise as possible by making certain idealizations and approximations. In this step irrelevant information is identified, and significant points are considered. The terminology that is used still reflects real things, "but the situation may no longer be completely realistic." The third step is to convert the real model into a mathematical model in which the real quantities are represented by symbols and mathematical operations. Now the task is in such a state that appropriate mathematical ideas and techniques can be used to reach the conclusions and predictions (step 4). To complete the cycle, results are compared to the original situation to verify that the conclusion (solution) is in agreement with the "real world" task. If not, the cycle begins again.

A distinction needs to be made between genuine applied problems and those problems that are merely embedded in a story or which merely borrow words from a discipline other than mathematics or from real-life situations. For the latter type of task, the discipline or real-life situation provides a *context* for the task, but cannot be considered as a *bona fide* applied field.

An illustration of this distinction is given by Pollak (1978). He discusses five different forms, three of which have an applied field.

1) Problems with immediate use of mathematics in everyday life:

> *3.17 A boy has 24 ft. of wire fence to make a rectangular pen for his pet rabbit. He plans to use all the fence in making the pen. Could he make a pen 12 ft. long and 12 ft. wide?*
>
> *Why or why not? Could he make a pen 8 ft. long and 3 ft. wide? How about 8 ft. long and 4 ft. wide? Give five examples of lengths and widths he could use for his pen.* (Applied Field: real-life situation.)

Figure 3.1 *Four Steps of the Model-Building Process (Maki & Thompson, 1973, p. 10)*

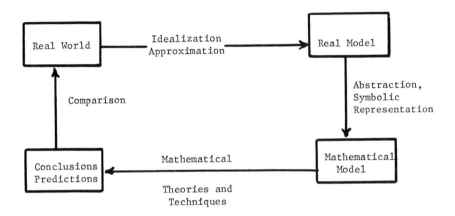

2) Problems that use words from everyday life and pretend to be applications:

    3.18 An electric fan is advertised as moving 3375 cubic feet of air per minute. How long will it take the fan to change the air in a room 27 ft. by 25 ft. by 10 ft.? (Assume all old air must be removed first.) (This problem does have an applied field.)

3) Problems of Whimsy — use of words from daily existence or from another discipline, when it is quite clear no real application is intended:

    3.19 A bee and a lump of sugar are located at different points inside a triangle. The bee wishes to reach the lump of sugar, while traveling a minimum distance. under the requirement that it must touch all three sides of the triangle before coming to the sugar. What is the shortest path? (No applied field.)

4) Genuine applications in real life:

    3.20 What is the best way to get from here to the airport? (Applied field: real-life situation.)

5) Genuine applications to other disciplines:

    3.21 A body moves without friction over a horizontal table. If its initial velocity is 4 ft. per second, how far will it travel in 12 seconds? What if there is friction? (Applied field: physics.)

                                             (Pollak, 1978, pp. 233-238)

The problems having an applied field are those that have (a) immediate use in everyday life; (b) genuine application in real life; or (c) genuine application to another discipline such as physics, computer science, anthropology, social science, business, or economics. The "applied field" of the task is then the discipline (other than mathematics) or the real-life application.

Applied problems have both an applied field and a mathematical topic classification. For example:

    3.22 What is the likelihood of a couple having a hemophiliac son when it is known that the wife's two brothers are both afflicted with the disease?

(This situation is depicted below.)

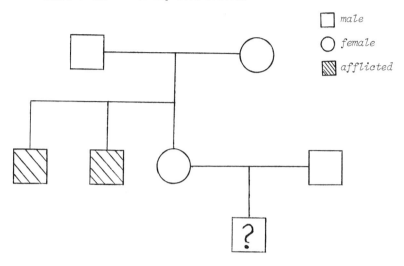

The applied field of this task is genetics, while the subject area of the task is probability.

The mathematical topic of an applied problem is not always apparent from the problem statement alone. Problem *3.20* is stated very generally, and could be answered without any mathematical considerations at all: the best way to get to the airport may be by private automobile, since all public means of transportation are not in operation due to a strike, and the distance to the airport precludes walking or taking a bicycle. If a quantitative criterion is set to determine the best way, then this will establish the mathematical topic of the task. Some applied problems, due to their breadth, may fall in more than one mathematical subject area.

Recently, more emphasis is being given to applied problems in instruction, as evidenced by the algebra series, <u>Algebra Through Applications with Probability and Statistics</u> (Usiskin, 1976). Even in this series, however, several problems are merely embedded in a context from a real-life situation or other discipline and do not have a genuine applied field content. However, there are many problems which do come from real-life situations, as illustrated by the following:

> *3.23 Monthly electric rates for a residence in Illinois*
> *(as of April, 1974) were as follows (quoted from*
> *Commonwealth Edison pamphlet):*

Monthly charge   *$0.95*
1st 100 kw hrs. of use   *.0385 per kw hr.*
Next 225 kw hrs. of use   *.0282 per kw hr.*
Over 325 kw hrs. of use   *.0279 per kw hr.*

Tax is added to this and adjustments are made if the price of energy to Commonwealth Edison changes. What would be the monthly charge for each amount of energy?

5.   *100 kw hours*   6.   *200 kw hours*
7.   *400 kw hours*   8.   *700 kw hours*

(Usiskin, 1976, p. 191)

Applied problems as used in problem-solving research may evoke different behaviors and solution processes from those evoked by problems in pure mathematics. Knowledge of specific mathematical relationships which pertain to an applied field, such as equations of motion in physics, may be necessary. There may be an increased complexity in the translation process, and several alternative solutions may exist. Because of their special nature, applied problems deserve special attention in research and in the teaching and learning of mathematics. A greater understanding of this content variable would facilitate the increased use of applied problems in instruction.

Semantic Content Variables

The third major category of content variables in Table 3.1 describes the meanings of the mathematical words and phrases that form the statement of the problem. This dimension we shall call "semantic content," and divide it into two parts for discussion--*key words* and *mathematical vocabulary*. This dimension is used to describe the semantics of natural and technical language that may affect problem-solving performance.

Natural language is related to problem-solving performance through the large number of written problems students face during their mathematics experiences in school. Such problems require comprehension of the written statement and translation of the problems into mathematical expressions that model the mathematical structure of the problem. Of course, very complex and difficult problems can be stated using a few easily understood words; for example:

3.24   *Show that it is impossible, using a compass and straightedge, to trisect an angle.*

On the other hand, trivial mathematical problems can be embedded in lengthy or semantically complex statements. The words used to state a problem do not necessarily reflect the structural complexity of the problem, but do affect the comprehension and translation of the problem statement. Performance on word problems thus is influenced by a combination of linguistic and mathematical abilities.

Key words have been given a great deal of attention over the years in solving computational word problems.* Students are taught to use certain words such as "less," "more," "each," "gained," and "altogether" as verbal cues for specific operations. Loftus (1970), however, found that the verbal cue variable did not have a significant regression effect on problem difficulty for a group of sixteen disadvantaged sixth-grade students solving arithmetic problems. The verbal cues that were used were "and" for addition, "left" for subtraction, and "each" for multiplication.

The benefit of using "key words" as an approach to instruction is open to question. Nesher and Teubal (1975) point to the fact that the same words appear at times as valid cues, and at other times as distractors with a meaning contrary to the most common usage. For a group of approximately 120 students toward the end of first grade, they found that a greater percentage of students answered the problem correctly when a key word was given that corresponded to its usual operation, than when a key word was given that did not correspond to its usual operation. Eighty-seven percent of the children who attempted an addition problem which used "more" as a verbal cue answered the problem correctly. Only 62 percent of the children answered correctly a similar addition problem which used "less" as a verbal cue. The two addition problems were:

"More" as a verbal cue

    3.25 The milkman brought on Sunday 4 bottles of milk more than on Monday. On Monday he brought 7 bottles. How many bottles did he bring on Sunday?

"Less" as a distractor

    3.26 The milkman brought on Monday 7 bottles of milk. That was 4 bottles less than he brought on Sunday. How many bottles did he bring on Sunday?

(Nesher and Teubal, 1975, p. 51)

Placing too large an emphasis during instruction on the identification of key words in word problems can thus mislead students.

---

*These are words from natural language which commonly have a specific mathematical interpretation.

Figure 3.2 *Misinterpretation of Problem 3.28*

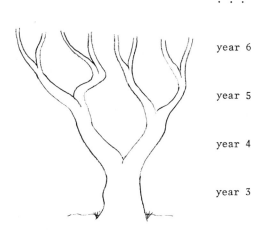

Figure 3.3 *Correct interpretation of Problem 3.28*

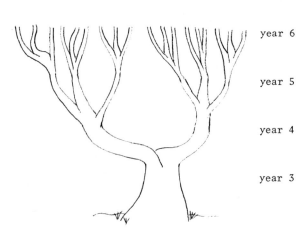

Here is another example:

> 3.27 *Two piles of coal are in a yard; pile A has 15 tons*
> *and pile B has 12 tons. A truck takes away all but*
> *5 tons of the coal from pile A. A second truck takes*
> *away all but 4 tons from pile B. How much coal is*
> *left in the yard?*

(Weaver)

The key words in this problem, "take away" and "left," all naively
suggest a subtraction problem, but the correct operation is addition.
This type of problem is useful in investigating whether students are
focusing on the superficial characteristics of the problem (rote
translation of key words) or are able to comprehend the meaning of
the problem statement and select the correct mathematical representation.

Up to now we have been discussing key words as either verbal
cues or possible distractors. Another important type of word is
one which is essential to the meaning of the problem, but which
does not suggest an operation. This type of word will be called a
critical word. The critical words of the following problem are
underlined.

> 3.28 *During the first three years of growth, a tree grows*
> *only its trunk. During the fourth year the trunk*
> *divides and grows into two main branches. During*
> *the fifth year and every year thereafter, it grows*
> *two new branches on each old branch. How many new*
> *branches are grown during the eighth year of growth?*
> *How many new and old branches does the tree have after*
> *eight years of growth?*

(Gimmestad, 1977)

As the task is worded, it is very easy for someone to misinterpret
the problem and assume that as the trunk divides into two branches,
so will the branches. The word "divides" can create a "mind-set"
for the remainder of the problem. The word "on" is crucial to the
meaning of the problem.

A misinterpretation of the problem is a "tree diagram" with
each branch dividing in two (see Figure 3.2). The correct interpretation has the two new branches growing on the existing branches,
so that where there was only one branch before, there are three (see
Figure 3.3).

A critical word, such as "on" in problem *3.28*, is essential to
understanding the mathematical relationships described in the problem. One means of investigating critical words and the comprehension
of word problems is the Cloze procedure. When using this procedure,

a number of words of the problem are replaced by blanks, anywhere from only one word to every fifth word being omitted. The student is asked to fill in the correct words. A good indication of how students comprehend Problem *3.28* can be obtained by replacing the word "on" with a blank, and asking the student to fill it in.

The second part of our discussion of semantic content concerns mathematical vocabulary. Natural language words used in the problem statement have their standard meaning as they are used in everyday life, while mathematical language refers to words that take on *special* meaning as they are being used in a mathematical context. The word "function," for example, in mathematics means mapping from one set to another; the common meaning of "function" is the specific action or use of a thing, such as the "function" of the brain.

Even when the words in the statement of a problem assume their ordinary meaning, Kane (1968) argues that reading mathematics texts or problems requires a special ability, different from that required to read ordinary prose. However, mathematical vocabulary is particularly important in problem-solving research studies that use a control group which has not been exposed to a particular form of instruction. When presenting unfamiliar problems to control groups, differences in performance may be due to a lack of familiarity with the mathematical vocabulary in the problems, rather than to differences in the ability to carry out mathematical operations. Thus it may be relatively easy to produce an "effect" on measured problem-solving ability in an experimental group, merely by the introduction of technical mathematical vocabulary.

Variables Describing the Problem Elements

A fourth category of content variables concerns the problem elements. The "elements" of a problem correspond to the three types of information of which formal problems are normally composed: givens, operations, and goals. The attributes of each set of elements provide another means of describing the content of the problem. Are all of the givens stated explicitly, or are some conditions implied but not explicitly stated? What are the given conditions or items of numerical information? Are the givens related conjunctively (and) or disjunctively (or)? What operations are stated or implied by the problem statement? The goals of a mathematical problem can likewise be classified. One important classification of goals is into the categories "to find" or "to prove." "To find" goals can be classified further by describing that which is to be found. The list below gives some examples of how the goals of problems "to find" can vary.

A number as the goal:

> 3.29 *Find a four-digit number which is an exact square, and such that its first two digits are the same and also its last two digits are the same.*
>
> (Shklarsky et al., 1962, p. 27)

A set of numbers as the goal:

> 3.30 *Find five positive whole numbers a, b, c, d, and e such that there is no subset with a sum divisible by 5.*
>
> (Posamentier and Salkind, 1970)

A process as the goal:

> 3.31 *Three cannibals and three missionaries are on the bank of a river. All of them want to cross the river, but they have only one boat that holds two people. How can they all get across the river without ever having the cannibals outnumbering the missionaries on either side of the river?*

An expression as the goal:

> 3.32 *In quadrilateral ABCD, $\overline{BA}$ and $\overline{BC}$ are each equal to t, and $\sphericalangle ABC = \sphericalangle A + \sphericalangle C$. Express $\overline{BD}$ in terms of t.*

A construction as the goal:

> 3.33 *Given a line AB, construct, when possible, a point P in AB such that the sum of the squares on AP and PB is equal to the area of a given square. When is it impossible?*
>
> (Durell, 1960, p. 28)

A geometric figure as the goal:

> 3.34 *Draw a rectangle with a perimeter of 81 cm and with the maximum possible area.*

A logical conclusion as a goal:

> 3.35 *Twelve persons were traveling and brought a dozen loaves of bread. Each man brought 2 loaves, each woman brought half a loaf, and each child a quarter of a loaf. How many men, women and children were traveling?*
>
> (Krutetskii, 1976, p. 150)

Problems "to find" can also be partitioned in other ways by considering the nature of the goal. In the following problem, the goal is to find the configuration of coins that satisfies the conditions:

> 3.36 *Judy has 32 coins with the total value of $2.00. She does not have any nickels. What coins does she have?*

This differs from the following problem, where the goal is to exhaust all of the possibilities that meet the conditions:

> 3.37 *Find the number of ways in which 20 U.S. coins consisting of quarters, dimes and nickels can have a value of $3.10.*

(Webb, 1976)

Even though both problems "to find" can be classified as money problems, the nature of the goal varies. Such a distinction is particularly important when selecting problems which are more likely to be solved using one approach than another. Problem *3.36* is well suited for a "guess and test" approach, since the conditions are explicitly specified and it is easy to generate possible sets of coins. The solution can be verified by ensuring that the set contains 32 coins, does not have any nickels, and totals $2.00. Guessing and testing is one approach for Problem *3.37* as well, but will generally not lead to a solution without additional refinement. The problem solver needs to develop some means of analysis to ensure that all of the possibilities have been exhausted.

Problems "to prove" vary in a similar fashion. Such problems can have as their goals proofs of theorems, lemmas, statements, or expressions. This categorization of goals is to be distinguished from the classification of problems by possible type of proof--direct, indirect, inductive, reductio ad absurdum--which would represent a structure classification.

Mathematical Equipment

Other categories of content variables exist, such as the type of equipment required for the task. In this category, problems could be classified in accordance with the requirement for use of mathematical materials, such as a calculator or straightedge and compass. The content variables given here, and summarized in Table 3.1, are not exhaustive. The more important areas, those that appear most often in instruction and research, have been identified.

3. The Classification and Definition of Context Variables

The context of a task refers to circumstances, surroundings, formats and instructions that are included as part of the task and which influence the understanding of the task. The distinction we make between context variables and situation variables (which are not task variables) is that context variables are intrinsic to the task, and not descriptive of the external environmental circumstances in which the problem is solved. On the other hand, the content-context dichotomy is analogous to the substance-form dichotomy. Whenever a problem is given, choices are made about the form of the problem. It may be presented orally, in written form, or pictorially. The essential information of the problem can be embedded in a story. Hints may be included or made available. Extraneous non-mathematical information may be included. All of these choices determine the context of the problem.

This section describes a set of context variables, which are summarized in Table 3.2. Awareness of the possible variations of problem context can improve the teaching of problem solving and guide the development of sets of problems to be used in the study of problem solving.

Problem Embodiments or Representations

The essential elements of a problem are the givens, the operations, and the goals. The most succinct statement of these will be called the *kernel* of the problem. Often the kernel is embedded in a verbal statement or story that has no mathematical relevance to the problem, although it may affect motivation as well as overall problem difficulty. The verbal embodiment of the problem then is the statement that is used to present the essential information of the problem. Variations in the verbal embodiment of a problem are illustrated below. The simplest version of the problem is given first. The next two versions increase in both syntactic complexity and the complexity of the story context that is described.

Sum Problem

> 3.38 *Find the smallest set of whole numbers such that every integer from 1 to 7 is either an element of the set or a sum of the elements in a subset.*

Modified Golden Chain Problem

> 3.39 *A woman has a chain with seven gold links. She would like to take a seven-day trip by carriage. The driver has agreed to take her for one link of the golden chain for each day, payable at the end of the day. If it costs the woman five dollars to have a jeweler open one link, what is the least amount of money she would have to spend to open links so the driver can have one link the first day, two links the second day, and so on?*

Table 3.2 *A Summary of Context Task Variables*

1. Problem embodiments or representations

> manipulative
> pictorial
> symbolic
> verbal
> etc.

2. Verbal context or setting

> familiar vs. unfamiliar
> applied vs. theoretical
> concrete vs. abstract
> factual vs. hypothetical
> conventional vs. imaginative
> etc.

The verbal context or setting refers to such extraneous non-mathematical information as may be contained in the problem statement.

3. Information format

> presence or absence of hints
> multiple-choice vs. free-answer
> etc.

Golden Chain Problem

> 3.40 *A Chinese prince who was forced to flee his kingdom*
> *by his traitorous brother sought refuge in the hut of*
> *a poor man. The prince had no money, but he did have*
> *a very valuable golden chain with seven links. The poor*
> *man agreed to hide the prince, but because he was poor*
> *and because he risked considerable danger should the*
> *prince be found, he asked that the prince pay him one*
> *link of the golden chain for each day of hiding. Since*
> *the prince might have to flee at any time, he did not*
> *want to give the poor man the entire chain; and since*
> *it was so valuable, he did not want to open more links*
> *than absolutely necessary. What is the smallest number*
> *of links that the prince must open in order to be cer-*
> *tain that the poor man has one link on the first day,*
> *two links on the second day, etc.?*

The most common form of embodiment of a problem is a story. The general opinion is that presenting a problem as part of a story will increase the level of interest of the student in finding the solution to the problem. In some cases, this backfires and the embodiment actually retards interest in the problem; this may occur if the difficulty in extracting the relevant information is excessive.

In addition to purely *verbal* embodiments, problems may be presented in *manipulative, pictorial,* or *symbolic* form. For example, a problem presented in a manipulative embodiment might include a physical model of a river, a dock on either side, one ferryboat, and a number of cars. The problem is to transport the cars on the ferry to the other side of the river. The conditions of the problem can be varied by changing the size of the ferry and the number of cars. The goal of the problem can be varied by restricting the number of trips or the number of cars allowed on the ferry boat at one time, stipulating that the smallest possible number of trips is desired.

The problem is a partitioning problem for younger children. The solution may be found by manipulating the objects in the model. The conditions of the problem do not have to be interpreted exclusively from the verbal problem statement, because the child can determine these from the physical objects themselves, being limited in the number of cars that will fit on the ferry boat at one time, or by the total number of cars. Another benefit of using the manipulative form, besides the ease with which students can understand the problem, is that an observer can more easily describe the processes that students use in finding the solution. It is very easy to record the trials that are made and the sequence of steps that is followed.

A second manipulative problem involves a cube that is painted red on the outside and is divided into 27 equal cubes as shown.

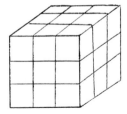

The subject is asked to determine how many small cubes are painted on
4 sides, 3 sides, 2 sides, 1 side, and 0 sides. If a real cube is
placed in front of the subject, even though the cube cannot be
handled, the problem can be considered to have a manipulative component in its embodiment. As the solution of the problem progresses,
the subject may be allowed to look at one of the smaller cubes as a
hint. Which small cube the student selects, and what information is
derived from the small cube, will help the observer determine what
the student is considering in solving the problem.

Manipulative problems are not restricted in their appeal to
children only. The problem of "instant insanity" is a good example
of a concretely presented problem suitable for adults. The puzzle
has four cubes with each face painted with one of four colors. The
object is to stack the cubes so that exactly one of the four colors
is showing on each side of the stack. Even though the problem is
presented in a manipulative embodiment, adults will often create a
symbolic embodiment to solve this problem.

A third type of problem embodiment is the pictorial. As an
example, problems can be presented pictorially with no words or very
few words accompanying the picture, such as the following:

3.41

The pictorial embodiment is generally considered to be a more abstract
form of presenting a problem than the manipulative embodiment. Conceivably, a person could create a physical model of the problem and
solve the problem manipulatively. However, it is more likely that
translation will be in the direction of a *more* abstract (i.e.,
symbolic) representation. Pictorial presentations do not have all
of the advantages of manipulative presentations, but they do reduce
the interaction between problem-solving performance and verbal ability.
At the same time other variables may be introduced in addition to
simply that of presentation. For example, pictorial presentations may

introduce variables of spatial relationships as well. The reader is referred to studies by Moses (1977), Schonberger (1976), and Frandsen and Holden (1969) for examples of this phenomenon.

Finally we have the *symbolic* embodiment, which is the most commonly used. This category includes problems presented exclusively in written form, or by using symbols such as those in an equation. This is the most abstract of the forms of problem embodiment.

The three forms of problem presentation: manipulative, pictorial, and verbal-symbolic, parallel the three forms of representation used by children to store and retrieve information as identified by Bruner (1966). These are: *enactive*, things we know through *action; iconic*, things that depend upon visual or other sensory organization; and *symbolic*, representations in words or language. Bruner suggests that intellectual development proceeds with the development of each of these systems until all have been mastered. Thus we expect the ease of working within a particular type of problem embodiment to be directly related to a subject's level of cognitive development, as well as to variables such as verbal and spatial ability.

Verbal Context or Setting

The verbal embodiment of a problem can have different characteristics with respect to the problem solver. One dichotomous set of characteristics is the abstract versus concrete embodiment, discussed by Goldin and Caldwell in Chapter VI. An "abstract" word problem involves a situation which describes only abstract or symbolic objects, while a "concrete" word problem describes a real situation dealing with real objects.

Abstract

  3.42 *There is a certain given number. Three more than twice this given number is equal to fifteen. What is the value of the given number?*

Concrete

  3.43 *Susan has some dolls. If she had four more than twice as many, she would have fourteen dolls. How many dolls does Susan really have?*

A slightly different version of the abstract-concrete dichotomy was used by Krutetskii in one of his series of problems. The problem set consisted of problems that made a gradual transformation from "concrete" to "abstract," where the most abstract problem used only

variables and the concrete problem used only numbers. The problems
in between included both variables and numbers. The two extreme
variants of a problem in one set are given below:

> 3.44 *The length of a room is 6 m, its width is 3 m, and
> its height is 3 m. What is the volume of 4 such
> rooms? (Concrete)*

> 3.45 *The length of a room is b̲ m, and its width and
> height are a̲ m each. What is the volume of n̲
> such rooms? (Abstract)*

(Krutetskii, 1976, p. 124)

A second characteristic of the embodiment of a verbal problem,
discussed in Chapter VI, is the factual-hypothetical dimension.
Problem 3.42 illustrates a factual problem and Problem 3.43 a
hypothetical one. The distinction between the two is that a
factual problem merely describes a situation, while a hypothetical
problem suggests a possible change in the situation.

Many other characteristics of verbal problem contexts have
already been mentioned in the review of the literature--familiar
vs. unfamiliar contexts (Brownell and Stretch, 1931), social-economic
vs. mechanical and scientific vs. abstract (Travers, 1967), low needs
vs. higher needs (Scott and Lighthall, 1967), and outdoor vs. computational vs. scientific (Cohen, 1976). The preponderance of evidence is
that most of these variables do not greatly affect problem difficulty
when other variables are controlled.

Information Format

Another dimension of problem context is the way in which the
problem is partitioned when it is presented. Is all the information
given at once, or is only part of the information given initially,
with time allowed for processing before new information is given?
Is there some information which is given only when requested by the
problem solver? Is information given in the form of "hints"?
Different parts of the problem may even be presented in different
embodiments--manipulative, pictorial, or verbal-symbolically.

The most common information format is to present the problem as
a whole, including sufficient information for a unique solution. The
use of other formats may depend upon the purpose of the problem. For
example, if the purpose is to study how a child uses different conditions of the problem, one condition can be given at a time. For
example,

> 3.46 *How many chickens and pigs are there, if there is
> a total of 50 legs?*

A fourth grader working this problem will in most cases discover that
there are many solutions. The problem becomes one of organizing the

information and defining some system so that all possibilities can be exhausted. If a second condition such as: "There are twenty heads" is given, the child can use the information already derived, together with the new condition, to obtain a unique answer. The researcher or a teacher may acquire more information in this way about the problem-solving procedure used by the child than if both conditions had been given together.

"Hints" are another way of varying the formats of problems. Some studies have allowed the problem solver to work on the problem as far as possible alone, and then have given hints to see what the problem solver does with the new information. Some researchers include hints that will eventually lead to the solution, to ensure that the subjects reach a solution and to reduce the likelihood of frustration.

Roman and Laudata (1974) constructed a CAI program to instruct elementary school children in grades 4 and 5 on word problems. They used a series of three hints to help identify the general steps taken in solving word problems. For example:

3.47 *The problem: In April Harvey held some toys. Yesterday, he divided the toys into 45 boxes. How many toys did he hold in April, if there were 3 toys in each box?*

First hint: Restate the question: Find the number of toys Harvey started with. Now reread the problem. (Identifies the unknown.)

Second hint: Restate the question: It is similar to Harvey's toys divided into 45 boxes given 3 toys in each box. ? = toys Harvey started with. Now reread the original problem. (Restatement of problem in single syntactic form, omitting superfluous information.)

Third hint: Translate the problem to a number sentence: ? toys/45 boxes = 3 toys in a box, or ?/45 = 3. Now solve the number sentence. (A mathematical statement that relates the variables in the problem to an appropriate number sentence.)

(Roman and Laudata, 1974)

Hints can provide useful information not only for the problem solver but also for the researcher and the teacher. *How* the hints are being used, *how many* are needed, and *which* hints provide the key to solution all yield useful information about the thought processes students are using.

In this section, we have reviewed three categories of context variables: problem embodiments, characteristics of the verbal

contexts or settings, and information format. In Chapter IX, this
classification is applied to derive some suggestions for the more
effective teaching of problem solving.

4. Summary

In this chapter, schemes have been proposed for the classification of content and context variables. Content is taken to refer to
the substance or meaning of the problem statement, while context
refers to the form or inessential characteristics of the problem.
The main categories proposed for content variables are: Mathematical
Topic, Field of Application, Semantic Content, Problem Elements, and
Mathematical Equipment. The main categories proposed for context
variables are: Problem Embodiment, Verbal Context, and Information
Format.

The proposed categories are not exhaustive. As more research
on problem solving is performed, and as research interests change,
new categories and subcategories may have to be added. For example,
current interest in sex-related differences in mathematics education
suggests that attention will be paid to gender in describing the
verbal context of problems. To list all possible content and
context categories would be an insuperable task. The classification
schemes described here provide a useful framework for studying the
effects of varying content and context in mathematical problems.

IV.

Structure Variables in Problem Solving

by

Gerald A. Goldin
Northern Illinois University
De Kalb, Illinois

While syntax, content, and context variables principally describe
the *statement* or *embodiment* of the problem, structure variables describe
the mathematical properties of a problem *representation* (see Chapter I,
Fig. 1.1). In order to derive syntax variables, it may be necessary to
carry out a linguistic analysis of the problem statement; in order to
derive content and context variables, one may classify terms in the
problem statement in accordance with their mathematical meanings or
one may classify the given problem embodiment in accordance with its
characteristics. These variables do not require a mathematical analysis of the problem for their definition. By contrast, structure
variables are those which are obtained only by means of some such
analysis.

Structure variables may depend for their definition on the particular representation of the problem within which the analysis takes place.
For example, a structure variable which has been studied fairly extensively is the "number of steps" required in solving a problem. However,
this number will obviously depend upon the method of problem solution
which is selected as the standard. In addition, it will depend on *what*
one chooses to call a "step"--to pass from the equation $2x + 3x = 10$
to the equation $5x = 10$ might be thought to require only one step; or
it might be thought to require two steps $[2x + 3x = 10, (2 + 3)x = 10,
5x = 10]$; or even more steps $[2x + 3x = 10, 2x + 3x = (2 +3)x, (2 + 3)x
= 10, 2 + 3 = 5, 5x = 10]$. Is there, then, such a thing as "intrinsic"
problem structure, apart from the particular problem solver?

Certainly different problem solvers may formulate different representations from the same problem statement. There may be a wide
variety of different and creative approaches to gaining insight into
a problem, including reference to related but distinct problems. Rules
of procedure may be open to interpretation. Nevertheless, it is the
viewpoint of this chapter that, given a set of well-defined rules or
operational procedures, a well-defined structure will be generated that
is subject to formal analysis. Furthermore, a mathematical problem
translates into just such a system of rules of procedure, sometimes
stated explicitly in the problem and sometimes to be understood from
the mathematical framework within which the problem is presented. This
is the sense in which we interpret problem structure variables as *task*
variables.

When rules of procedure are subject to more than one interpretation, it is necessary to make explicit the *possible* interpretations, and these become part of the description of intrinsic problem structure. Likewise, when different representations of the problem may be obtained through translation of the problem statement, it will be necessary to select one or more of them for analysis in order to obtain problem structure variables. For example, if asked to find the minimum value of the expression $y = x^2 - 2x + 3$, a first-year algebra student might construct a table of values, proceeding by systematic trial-and-error to arrive at a minimum value. Another possibility is to draw a graph of the function $y = x^2 - 2x + 3$ and, from a visual inspection, determine the minimum. A calculus student, having available additional rules of procedure, might set the derivative equal to zero, solve for x, and substitute. Thus, the problem might be represented by means of a sequence of values of x and corresponding values of y; or by means of a graph, or by means of a sequence of equations beginning with $\frac{dy}{dx} = 0$. But the existence of such different representations does not mean that intrinsic problem structure variables are impossible to define. Rather it means that we must be explicit about our choice of representation in performing the analysis. It will usually be desirable to consider those representations most commonly employed by the population of subjects for whom the problem is intended.

In this chapter we shall develop and apply methods of *state-space analysis* to define and examine problem structure variables. Some of the development is familiar to students of "artificial intelligence" but not in general to mathematics educators; this includes much of the material at the beginning of Section 2, which is included for completeness. After introducing the basic definitions, we shall return to the question of characterizing "relatedness" among problem representations. We shall also discuss the sense in which *algorithms* and *strategies* may be regarded as part of the "intrinsic" problem structure.

In the study of problem-solving processes and the teaching of problem-solving skills, task variables are usually taken to be the independent variables--they are subject to the control of the researcher or the teacher through the selection or creation of appropriate problems. Dependent variables of interest include variables describing the amount of success in problem solving (problem difficulty), variables describing the employment of specific processes (patterns of behavior, strategy scores), and variables which measure the learning which has taken place during problem solving (transfer to related problems). Thus, we shall most frequently be interested in defining problem structure variables which are likely to influence these outcomes. The term "complexity variables" can be used to highlight those variables expected to affect directly the problem difficulty.

Before proceeding with the development, we shall briefly survey some of the research related to problem structure variables.

1. Review of Related Research

A dramatically increasing body of research employs "artificial intelligence" models, or mechanical models, to describe human problem solving. Some of this research is oriented toward finding the most efficient algorithms or strategies for solving problems with a computer, which necessitates the formal analysis of the structure of problem representations (Arbib, 1969; Banerji, 1969; Hunt, 1975, Nilsson, 1971). Such formal analysis is reproduced and extended in the present chapter, from the standpoint of examining task structure variables which can affect the outcomes of problem solving.

The "state-space representation" of a problem provides the basis for much of our formal analysis (Hunt, 1975; Nilsson, 1971). One goal of artificial intelligence research has been to program high-speed computers to solve problems in logic, to play games such as chess and checkers, or to make decisions in specified situations to obtain the most favorable possible outcome. Thus, an entire branch of the field is devoted to obtaining efficient *search algorithms*, by means of which the mechanical problem solver can "look ahead" in the state-space or game tree, or "foresee" the outcomes which are possible following a particular choice. Nilsson discusses "breadth-first" and "depth-first" search algorithms—roughly speaking, in the former all possible continuations are examined, a single step at a time; in the latter, a single continuation is followed to its end before another one is tested. In addition there are search algorithms which combine features of both these approaches. Complications arise because there must be an efficient means for the mechanical problem solver to "remember" which states have already been entered, and which have not.

Since for most problems or games the number of possible branches rapidly becomes more than astronomical, the field of choice must somehow be narrowed. In order to avoid searching to the very end of every path, a value may be assigned to each state based on information available in that state. This *evaluation function* represents a measure of expectation for future success. An example of this technique is the use of "positional judgment" in chess, whereby such features as "control of the center" and "safety of the king" affect the desirability of a position. Once criteria for such an evaluation have been established, the search algorithm may be constructed to look only n moves ahead, to calculate the evaluation function for the terminal states reached, and to make the choice which maximizes the terminal value. Procedures based on such evaluation functions are called "hill-climbing" by Wickelgren (1974), and form an important component in his survey of problem-solving methods. In a competitive game, the choice is made which maximizes the *minimum* value (across opponent's moves) of the terminal states resulting from the choice. A modification of this "minimax" procedure which further reduces the number of states in the search is to select only a narrowed class of moves whose continuations are to be investigated, based on pre-specified criteria.

The "General Problem-Solver" of Newell, Shaw, and Simon has greatly influenced the field of artificial intelligence, as well as providing a take-off point for the modelling of human problem solving (Ernst and Newell, 1969; Newell, Shaw, and Simon, 1960). It embodies a kind of depth-first search algorithm in which the first object of the program is to identify a *subgoal* state which might eventually lead to solution of the main problem. The subgoal state is chosen to be "less distant" in some suitable sense from the goal state than is the initial state. When such a subgoal has been identified, control switches to the task of attaining the subgoal, prior to returning to the task of obtaining the original goal. This technique is to be applied *recursively*, until a string of attainable subgoals has been generated that extends from the problem's initial state to its goal state. Thus Newell, Shaw, and Simon take the position that utilization of the subgoal and subproblem structure of a problem is fundamental to efficient problem solving. In this chapter, we shall utilize these concepts in defining some of our task structure variables.

The geometry theorem-proving machine of Gelernter (1959, 1960) utilizes the "syntactic symmetries" of a problem to facilitate the state-space search. When the program has succeeded in reaching a particular state, it proceeds to generate those states which are *syntactically equivalent* to the state that was reached—that is, equivalent by permutation of syntactically equivalent elements in the problem statement. This procedure eliminates the necessity of reproducing all of the equivalent paths, and is more efficient in situations where symmetry exists. Nilsson also discusses states in the problem state-space which are equivalent by symmetry. In this chapter, we make extensive use of problem symmetry in defining certain task structure variables which may be expected to affect problem-solving outcomes.

The methods that have been mentioned are directed towards more efficient machine programming of problem-solving capabilities. While the techniques are often motivated by introspectively or empirically obtained information about actual human problem solving, their main purpose has been effective programming. Another branch of research motivated by artificial intelligence is directly concerned with describing or modelling human problem solving.

One approach taken by researchers has been to try to *simulate* human problem-solving with mechanical procedures. Here the goal is to generate some human-like behaviors during the course of problem solving. For example, Newell and Simon compare the *trace* of the General Problem Solver solving a logic problem (that is, the actual sequence of routines and subroutines employed) with the *protocol* of a human subject solving the same problem, finding many parallels. Minsky and Papert (1972) discuss Piaget's conservation experiments from the standpoint of the acquisition of specific descriptive and deductive procedures. Paige and Simon have compared Bobrow's STUDENT program for solving verbal problems with subjects' protocols (Bobrow, 1968; Paige and Simon, 1966) —STUDENT is discussed at greater length in Chapter VI of this book.

A detailed information processing model has been developed simulating
the observed behaviors of subjects solving "concept attainment" problems (Bruner, Goodnow, and Austin, 1956; Johnson, 1964). Efforts
along these lines, however, are sometimes subject to the limitation
that the programming methods employed do not lend themselves to generalization beyond a specific problem domain.

Beyond trying to simulate human problem solving with specific
programs, Newell and Simon have proposed a comprehensive model for
the human problem solver as an information-processing system. They
introduce the concept of a "problem space" to represent the task
environment *within* the information-processing system; they then hypothesize that human problem solving takes place by means of a search in
such a space. The problem space of Newell and Simon (1972) is described
in Table 4.1. The first four components of the problem space correspond
almost exactly to the definition of a problem state-space representation
--with the important difference that instead of states of the problem
itself, the reference is to states of *knowledge* about the problem.
Newell and Simon obtain what they call the "problem behavior graph" of
a subject in the "external problem space." It is the structure of this
"external problem space" which is the principal concern of the present
chapter.

The missionary-cannibal problem and its variants, described in
detail in Section 2 of this chapter, has been used extensively with
subjects whose moves have been recorded in such an "external problem
space" or state-space. Thomas used a variant of the problem called
"Hobbits and Orcs" with young adult subjects (Thomas, 1974). Hobbits
correspond to missionaries, and orcs to cannibals (see Problem *4.2*
below). In Thomas' study, a control group solved the problem once;
an experimental group solved the problem first by beginning with a
state in the middle of the problem, and a second time beginning with
the initial state. Thus the experimental group solved a subproblem
prior to attempting the main problem. The total number of moves, legal
and illegal, required to solve the first part of the problem (through
the first five moves in the state-space as depicted in Figure 4.2)
decreased significantly for the experimental group as compared to the
control group. Thus practice on a later part of the problem improved
performance on the earlier part. However, this practice did *not*
improve the subsequent performance of the experimental subjects on
the later subproblem segment as compared with their own earlier performance on this segment. Furthermore, there was *negative* transfer
for the control group from the first part of the problem to the later
segment--that is, their performance on the subproblem was significantly poorer than that of the experimental subjects in their *first*
attempt. These and other results lead Thomas to conclude that there
may well have been *little* correspondence between the external moves
of subjects in the state-space, and the sequence of *knowledge* states
entered.

Two other aspects of this paper are interesting in relation to
the study of task structure variables. One is the description of the

Table 4.1   *The Problem Space of Newell and Simon*

A problem space consists of:

1. A *set of elements*, U, which are symbol structures, each representing a state of knowledge about the task.

2. A *set of operators*, Q, which are information processes, each producing new states of knowledge from existing states of knowledge.

3. An *initial state of knowledge*, u_o, which is the knowledge about the task that the problem solver has at the start of problem solving.

4. A *problem*, which is posed by specifying a set of final, desired states G, to be reached by applying operators from Q.

5. The *total knowledge available* to a problem solver when he is in a given knowledge state, which includes (ordered from the most transient to the most stable):

   (a) *Temporary dynamic information* created and used exclusively within a single knowledge state.

   (b) The *knowledge state* itself--the dynamic information about the task.

   (c) *Access information* to the additional symbol structures held in LTM or EM (the *extended knowledge state*).

   (d) *Path information* about how a given knowledge state was arrived at and what other actions were taken in this state if it has already been visited on prior occasions.

   (e) *Access information to other knowledge states* that have been reached previously and are now held in LTM or EM.

   (f) *Reference information* that is constant over the course of problem solving, available in LTM or EM.

Abbreviations: LTM   long-term memory
EM   external memory

relative "difficulty" of *each state*, as measured by the proportion of
incorrect responses and the mean response time associated with that
state. A second is the discussion of *stages* which occurred during the
problem solving--an estimate of three or four main stages is reached.
In an accompanying paper by Greeno, further evidence in support of
such stages is presented (Greeno, 1974). Subjects seem to organize
their sequences of moves into small subsequences or clusters, rather
than making equally-paced, discrete moves. From the patterns of
pauses within the solution sequences, and differences between groups
receiving feedback information during problem solving, it is concluded
that the solution process is "organized forward" in the state-space,
in contrast to the "retroactive organization" of the General Problem
Solver.

Reed, Ernst, and Banerji (1974) designed a transfer study based
on the missionary-cannibal problem and a variant called the Jealous
Husbands problem (see Problem *4.9* in this chapter). These problems
differ not only in context but in structure--the states of the Jealous
Husbands problem stand in a many-to-one relationship with the states
of the missionary-cannibal problem. In one experiment, a group of
(adult) subjects solved the missionary-cannibal problem first, followed
by the Jealous Husbands problem (MC1-JH2); another group took the problems in the opposite order (JH1-MC2). Subjects were required to solve
each problem once, in the given order, and to solve both problems
within a 30-minute time limit. The result was that *no* significant
reduction in time, total number of moves, or number of illegal moves,
took place between the JH1 and JH2 groups, or between the MC1 and MC2
groups. In a second experiment, one group solved the missionary-
cannibal problem twice (MC1-MC2), and a second group solved the Jealous
Husbands problem twice (JH1-JH2). Significant improvement was found in
the time to solution for JH2 over JH1, and in the number of illegal
moves made by both groups. A third experiment was like the first one,
except that subjects were *told* the relationship between the two problems. Here there was significant improvement for MC2 compared to MC1,
both in the time to solution and in the total number of illegal moves;
however, there was no corresponding improvement for JH2 compared to
JH1. Thus, there was significant transfer from the Jealous Husbands
problem to the missionary-cannibal only when the problem relationship
was pointed out, and no significant transfer when the problems were
presented in the other order.

The difficulty of the missionary-cannibal problem and its
variants does not originate from the complexity of the state-space
itself, but from that of transforming one state into another; that
is, finding which moves are legal. In Section 3 of this chapter,
we shall see that this difficulty can be regarded as originating
from blind alleys in a more detailed, expanded state-space. This
leaves open the question of whether there would be effects similar
to those described above in problems where the moves from state to
state were more elementary, and where the difficulty rested in the
selection of one move from among several available at each step.

Many problems of this sort are described later in the chapter; one which has been studied extensively using the state-space to graph behavior is the Tower of Hanoi (see Problem 4.11).

Goldin and Luger have proposed a set of hypotheses describing possible patterns in the paths generated by subjects through the state-space of a problem such as the Tower of Hanoi, and Luger investigated these hypotheses for adult subjects in detail (Goldin and Luger, 1975; Luger, 1973, 1976). Included in the investigation is an analysis of the non-randomness and goal-directedness of paths, the subgoal-directedness of paths, the special role of certain "subgoal" states in establishing the direction of the paths, *stages* in problem solving corresponding to the solution of particular subproblems, and symmetry patterns in the paths. The hypotheses are extended and discussed in the present chapter (Section 3). In Chapter VII.C, Luger reports additional results in which similar techniques are used to examine transfer between the Tower of Hanoi problem and a variant, the Tea Ceremony problem.

Other variants of the Tower of Hanoi problem have been used by Hayes and Simon (1975) to study the consequences of changing the problem *statement* upon the representations adopted by subjects. The tasks used were eight different "monster-globe" problems, presented verbally, all of which have state-spaces which correspond to the 3-ring Tower of Hanoi problem. The problems differ from each other in two ways. In "Transfer" problems, a monster or globe is *moved* from one place to another, while in "Change" problems, a monster or globe is changed in size. Secondly, in "Agent" problems, the monsters move or change the globes, while in "Patient" problems, the monsters move or change themselves. In one of the experiments, half of the subjects solved a Transfer problem followed by a corresponding Change problem, while the other half solved the problems in reverse order. In a second experiment, one group of subjects solved an Agent problem followed by a corresponding Patient problem, while the other group solved the problems in reverse order. The results of these studies showed that both the Agent-Patient and the Transfer-Change variation affected the notation used by subjects to solve the problem (i.e., the problem representation). Problems of the Transfer type were solved much more quickly than problems of the Change type. In the first experiment, transfer of learning from Transfer to Change problems was greater than that for Change to Transfer problems; that is, there was greater learning transfer when the *less* difficult problem was solved first. This result is in contrast to the results of Reed, Ernst, and Banerji mentioned previously, those of Dienes and Jeeves discussed below, and those of Waters (Chapter VII.A) and Luger (Chapter VII.C). Agent problems were found to be slightly less difficult than Patient problems. In the second experiment, transfer effects were greater than in the first experiment--and there was greater learning transfer when the *more* difficult problem was solved first. A limitation of these experiments is that while the state-spaces for all of the experimental problems are mutually isomorphic, the solution paths are not--that is, the initial state for the second problem solved by a subject does not always correspond to the initial state for the first problem solved by that subject,

Next let us mention some studies in which the use of problem state-spaces has not entered into the characterization of problem structure. Dienes and Jeeves (1965, 1970) have studied the processes used by children and adults in learning sets of rules for predicting the appearances of cards in a window, where a set of rules corresponds to the structure of a mathematical group. The apparatus in the first report consisted of a board with a window in which a number of different symbols or cards could be placed. The subject was given the same cards as those which could appear in the window. On each turn, the card which appeared in the window depended on the card which was there previously, and the card that was played by the subject. Each subject played cards in succession and made predictions, in an attempt to learn the "rules of the game." The underlying structures corresponded to: (a) the two-element group, (b) a symmetrical two-element structure (not a group), (c) the cyclic group with four elements, and (d) the Klein group. In the second report, the study of transfer, more complicated groups were introduced, and an electrical machine replaced the manual apparatus.

One feature of these studies which is of interest to us is the definition of *strategy scores*, based on actual patterns of choices made by subjects. For example, an *operator score* is obtained by taking the total number of cards played when the same card is being played three or more times in succession, divided by the total number of freely selected instances. This score is intended to reflect use of an *operator strategy*, in which the card played is "operating" on the card in the window. For the four-element groups, a *pattern score* is obtained by partitioning the table of card-pairs into three sections correspond-ing to frequently-mentioned patterns. Runs of three or more card combinations from the same section count toward the pattern score (for technical reasons, runs are counted here even if they are interrupted by single correctly-predicted instances from other sections). There are some logical difficulties with these strategy score definitions--for example, a subject may find in the case of the Klein group that a particular card cannot be played three times in succession without one of the plays being a repeat of a previous play (and thus, presumably, unnecessary). Such difficulties are reminiscent of similar problems which have arisen with Bruner, Goodnow, and Austin's strategy scoring system for concept attainment tasks, discussed in Chapter VII.A (Bruner, Goodnow, and Austin, 1956). It also seems to be the case that the same sequence of card choices can count toward more than one strategy score--for example, repeated plays of the card corresponding to the identity element in the group. Despite these difficulties, it is striking that the main strategies seem to emerge naturally from the underlying group structures, and in some sense are "intrinsic" to the problems themselves.

Dienes and Jeeves compare the strategies used by subjects (as measured by strategy scores) with the *retrospective evaluations* of the subjects. Three categories of evaluations were established: *operator, pattern* and *memory*. A subject was considered to give an operator evaluation if he or she described the card played as somehow "acting on" the card in the window. A subject was considered to give a pattern evaluation if he or she attempted to split up the combinations of cards played into subsets or regions. The memory evaluation consisted of the assertion that the subject had simply memorized all of the possible combinations. Based on these retrospective evaluations, subjects could be classified as "pure operator," "combined operator-memory," and so forth.

Among the main results are the following: (a) a positive relationship between the subjects' evaluations and their measured strategy scores; (b) an association of particular evaluations with success in the tasks in the following order (from most successful to least successful): (1) operator, (2) pattern, (3) memory; (c) a greater ability among adults than children to give explicit evaluations; (d) a consistency in the types of evaluations given by the same subject solving a two-element game and a four-element game; (e) more explicit evaluations tending to occur when the more complex task is given first than when the simpler task is given first.

In the study of transfer effects, Dienes and Jeeves define three kinds of structural relationships which may exist between tasks: *embeddedness, overlap,* and *recursion* (including both generalization and particularization). These relationships are intrinsic to the group structures which underlie the tasks--"embeddedness" refers to the situation where one group is isomorphic to a subgroup of the other; "overlap" to the situation where the two groups contain isomorphic subgroups; and "recursion" to the situation where the two groups are generated by similar procedures (for example, cyclic groups of different orders). The relationships are not mutually exclusive--often two groups are related to each other in more than one way.

A motivating theme of the transfer study is the *deep-end hypothesis.* This is the conjecture that, under appropriate conditions, learning can be accelerated on a sequence of tasks by presenting the more difficult task first: this is analogous to learning to swim by entering the deep end of the pool. We have already seen some confirmation of this conjecture in the study by Reed, Ernst and Banerji, and conflicting results in the study by Hayes and Simon. In the present book, the reports by Waters and by Luger tend to support the conjecture. Among the main results of Dienes and Jeeves with respect to transfer are the following: (a) children particularize with less difficulty than adults, and generalize with greater difficulty; (b) children and adults both find overlap more difficult than generalization, and embeddedness much more difficult than generalization; (c) children are more successful when the more difficult task is presented first than when the less difficult task is presented first, at least when the relationship is that of recursion.

In a follow-up to the work by Dienes and Jeeves, Branca and Kilpatrick (1972) employed three tasks. The first task replicates the card game employed by Dienes and Jeeves, having the structure of the four-element Klein group. The second task consists of a wired board with four light-bulbs and four switches, labelled with the names of

planets. One bulb is lit at the beginning of the task; the next bulb
to light up depends upon the bulb previously lit and the switch which
is thrown. The second task also embodies the structure of the Klein
group. In the third task, both the embodiment and the structure are
changed. The task consists of a map of the United States on which
several cities and highways are marked. Highways can be closed, open
in one direction, or open in both directions. The subject starts in
one city at the beginning of the game, and must learn the condition
of each highway. This is done by choosing another city, and being
informed which city the subject must pass through first if the most
direct route to that city is taken.

Branca and Kilpatrick found that successful subjects' retrospective evaluations show more consistency than change in passing between
the first two tasks. Thus the effect of the change of embodiment was
not significant for successful subjects' retrospective evaluations.
However, in contrast to Dienes and Jeeves' findings, subjects' retrospective evaluations frequently did not correspond to their actual
behaviors as measured by strategy scores. In addition, contrary to
expectations, higher operator strategy scores were associated with
more trials to solution. These discrepancies are traced by the authors
to the fact that Dienes and Jeeves' tasks are not truly "free selection"
tasks. The subjects are constrained in the choice of which two elements
they can combine on any turn, by the fact that one card is already showing in the window of the apparatus. The strategy scoring rules depend
heavily on this feature. Branca and Kilpatrick suggest that because of
this constraint, subjects are not free to implement any desired strategy;
and that in future experiments, either new scoring rules should be
established or the game should be modified to permit free choice of
both elements. This study illustrates further how strategy scores
depend for their validity on intrinsic task structure.

We conclude this section with mention of some studies which have
examined structure variables in relation to problem difficulty. In
the domain of routine arithmetic problems, multiple linear regression
analyses of problem difficulty and latency of response have been
carried out (Suppes, Hyman, and Jerman, 1966; Suppes, Jerman, and
Brian, 1968). Data for these studies were obtained from computer-
assisted exercises in addition, subtraction, and multiplication
presented to elementary school children. The analysis for both the
addition and subtraction problems showed the variable NSTEPS to be
the most significant for predicting the percent of errors and the
latency of response. This variable corresponds to the number of steps
needed to solve the problem by means of a standard algorithmic procedure: it thus makes reference not only to the task, but to the method
of solution. NSTEPS is broken down into three components: TRANSFOR-
MATIONS, OPERATIONS, and MEMORY; and these were examined for order of
importance in the case of addition problems. It was found that MEMORY
ranked first, followed by TRANSFORMATIONS, and lastly OPERATIONS. Other
variables included in the analysis were for addition problems MAGSUM
(the magnitude of the sum) and MAGSMALL (the magnitude of the smallest
addend; for subtraction problems MAGDIF (the magnitude of the difference) and MAGSUB (the magnitude of the subtrahend).

In the domain of verbal problems, it has been reported that a problem is less difficult when the data are presented in the order in which they are used to solve the problem than when they are presented in reverse order (Burns and Yonally, 1964; Rosenthal and Resnick, 1971).

Multiple linear regression studies have found the following task structure variables to affect significantly the difficulty of verbal problems: OPERATIONS (the minimum number of different operations required to solve the problem correctly) and variations in which weights are assigned to the occurrences of particular arithmetic operations; NOMC2 (the total number of multiplication carries); and QUOT (the number of digits in the quotient). Also included but less importantly were STEPS (the minimum number of steps required to solve the problem correctly); COLC2 (a count of 1 for each column and each regrouping in addition and subtraction); S_1 (a count of 1 for each displacement of the order of operations in successive problems); and S_2 (a count of 1 for each displacement between the order of operations required to solve the problem and that given in the problem statement)(Jerman, 1971; Loftus, 1970; Suppes, Loftus, and Jerman, 1969). An extensive discussion of the linear regression model has already been provided in Chapter II.

A number of researchers have attempted exhaustive classifications of arithmetic problems into narrow classes, which would be *homogeneous* in the sense that if a subject could solve one problem in a class, he or she could solve any problem in that class (Durnin, 1971; Ferguson, 1969; Gramick, 1975; Hively, Patterson and Page, 1968). Of interest in these classifications is the use of *equivalence classes* of problems, defined with reference to the *path* or directed graph through an algorithm that each problem requires. Gramick, for example, formed such equivalence classes for eight different subtraction algorithms, five based on the "decomposition" (or "borrowing") method, and three based on the "equal additions" method. She then formed the mutual intersections of these equivalence classes with each other and with a set of "item forms" derived from those of Hively, Patterson, and Page, to obtain 39 "problem types" for subtraction. Thus, two problems of the same "type" required the same path through all eight algorithms, as well as falling into the same "item form" categories. Gramick used a diagnostic instrument based on these "types" to determine that children in need of remedial instruction whose initial behaviors more closely resembled the structure of a particular algorithm, benefited more from instruction in that algorithm than did children whose initial behaviors were at variance with its structure.

In this highly abbreviated survey, many studies of importance have been omitted. We have tried to touch on the main ideas which are central to the present chapter. The main point of this chapter is to develop the use of problem state-space representations as a unifying framework, in which task structure variables such as those mentioned above can be defined with precision, and their consequences for problem-solving outcomes investigated systematically.

2. The Definition of Task Structure Variables

State-Space Analysis of Problem Structure

As defined by Nilsson, a *state-space* for a problem is a set of distinguishable problem configurations, called *states*, together with the permitted steps from one state to another, called *moves*. A particular state is designated as the *initial state*, and a set containing one or more states which can be reached from the initial state by successive moves is singled out as the set of *goal states*.

Let us illustrate this concept with several elementary examples of well-known problems, and at the same time introduce certain task structure variables.

> 4.1 *You are standing at the bank of a river with two pails. The first holds exactly three gallons of water, the second exactly five gallons, and the pails are not marked for measurement in any other way. By filling and emptying pails, or by transferring water from pail to pail, find a way to carry exactly four gallons of water away from the river.*

A state of this problem can be represented by a pair of numbers, standing for the number of gallons in the respective pails. The initial state is then the state $(0,0)$; a goal state is any state of the form $(x,4)$; and the entire state-space is depicted in Figure 4.1. Note that there are two distinct *solution paths*: a path of six moves (seven states) leading to the goal state $(3,4)$, and a path of eight moves (nine states) leading to the goal state $(0,4)$. Note also that not every move is reversible--for example, it is permissible to move from $(1,5)$ to $(0,5)$ directly, by emptying the first pail; but it is not permissible to move from $(0,5)$ to $(1,5)$.

The missionary-cannibal problem was introduced in Chapter II (Problem 2.7). Its use to study transfer of learning was discussed in Section 1 above.

> 4.2 *Three missionaries and three cannibals are on one bank of a river, with a rowboat that will hold at most two people. How can they cross to the other side of the river, in such a manner that the missionaries are never outnumbered by cannibals on either riverbank?*

A state of this problem corresponds to a configuration of missionaires, cannibals, rowboat and river. Letting M stand for missionary, C for cannibal, * for the rowboat and : for the river, we can conveniently

Figure 4.1 *State-Space for the Problem of the Two Pails*

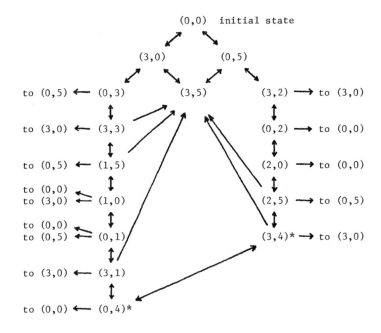

(0,0)   initial state

* denotes a goal state

represent the initial state by the configuration (MMMCCC*:) and the goal state by the configuration (:MMMCCC*). From the initial state, it is permissible to move to (MMCC:MC*), (MMMC:CC*), or (MMMCC:C*); but a move to (MCCC:MM*) is *not* permitted, since the cannibals would then outnumber the missionaries three to one on the left bank of the river.

Figure 4.2 depicts the complete state-space for this problem, which is actually quite small. Every move is reversible, and the state-space is completely symmetrical when reversed. Figure 4.2 also includes forbidden states, which violate the problem condition that the cannibals are not to outnumber the missionaries on either riverbank. These forbidden states may importantly affect the problem-solving process and the overall difficulty of the problem.

The following is another variation of the problem.

> 4.3 *Three missionaries and three cannibals are on one bank of a river, with a rowboat that will hold at most two people. Only one of the cannibals knows how to row. How can they cross to the other side of the river, in such a manner that missionaries are never outnumbered by cannibals on either riverbank?*

This version of the missionary-cannibal problem is more complicated than the preceding version, because of the additional condition that only one of the cannibals knows how to row. Let us develop the state-space for this problem so that the similarities and differences between the two versions are highlighted. In Figure 4.3, the cannibal who knows how to row is represented by C̄, and the other cannibals by C. Figure 4.3 should be contrasted with Figure 4.2.

It is, of course, possible to characterize the fact that the second version of the missionary-cannibal problem is more complex by means of the problem *statements* only (i.e., by *surface* analysis)—the latter problem statement contains more words, more sentences, and one additional problem condition. However, the state-space analysis permits a much more detailed characterization of the increased complexity by means of the following task *structure* variables:

(a) *Total number of states* in the state-space: Problem *4.2* has 16 states, Problem *4.3* has 24.

(b) *Length of the shortest solution path*: Problem *4.2* requires 11 steps to reach the goal state from the initial state, while Problem *4.3* requires 13 steps.

(c) *Number of blind alleys*: A blind alley is defined to be a state from which there is no legal move except (possibly) the reversal of the immediately preceding move. Then Problem *4.2* has only one blind alley, namely the state (MMMCC:C*)

Figure 4.2 *State-Space for the Problem of the Missionaries and the Cannibals*

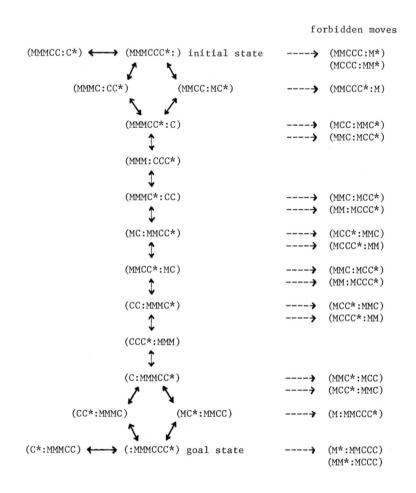

forbidden moves

(MMCC:C*) ⟷ (MMMCCC*:) initial state   ----→ (MMCCC:M*)
                                                (MCCC:MM*)

(MMMC:CC*)   (MMCC:MC*)   ----→ (MMCCC*:M)

(MMMCC*:C)   ----→ (MCC:MMC*)
              ----→ (MMC:MCC*)

(MMM:CCC*)

(MMMC*:CC)   ----→ (MMC:MCC*)
              ----→ (MM:MCCC*)

(MC:MMCC*)   ----→ (MCC*:MMC)
              ----→ (MCCC*:MM)

(MMCC*:MC)   ----→ (MMC:MCC*)
              ----→ (MM:MCCC*)

(CC:MMMC*)   ----→ (MCC*:MMC)
              ----→ (MCCC*:MM)

(CCC*:MMM)

(C:MMMCC*)   ----→ (MMC*:MCC)
              ----→ (MCC*:MMC)

(CC*:MMMC)   (MC*:MMCC)   ----→ (M:MMCCC*)

(C*:MMMCC) ⟷ (:MMMCCC*) goal state   ----→ (M*:MMCCC)
                                              (MM*:MCCC)

Figure 4.3 *State-Space for a More Complex Variation of the Missionary-*
Cannibal Problem

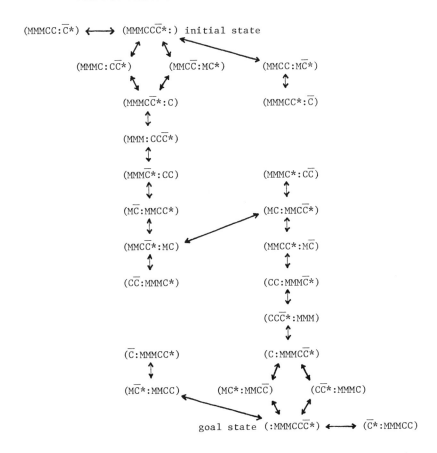

reached directly from the initial state. Note that we do not count the state (C*:MMMCC) as a blind alley, since there is no way to arrive there without first entering the goal state (:MMMCCC*). Problem *4.3* has four blind alleys: the states (M̲M̲MCC:C̄*), (MMMCC*:C̄), and most importantly (MMMC*:CC̄) and (CC:MMM*C).

(d) *Number of possible first moves*: three for the first version of the problem, four for the second.

Problem complexity variables such as these may reasonably be expected to be predictors of problem difficulty. In investigating such a question, it may also be of interest to define additional complexity variables based on those mentioned above; for example:

(e) The *number of goal states* is equal to one for both problems.

(f) The *ratio of the number of goal states to the total number of states* is 1/16 for the first problem, and 1/24 for the second.

The next set of problems further illustrates the use of structure variables, and highlights their *necessity* in the description of intrinsic problem complexity.

4.4a Two nickels and two dimes are placed in a row, the nickels on the left and the dimes on the right, with a single space between them, as shown:

$$N \; N \qquad D \; D$$

Nickels move only to the right, and dimes only to the left. A coin may move into the adjacent empty space, or may jump over one coin of the opposite kind into the empty space. Show how to exchange the positions of the nickels and the dimes.

4.4b Three nickels and three dimes are placed in a row, ...

4.4c Four nickels and four dimes are placed in a row, ...

For these three problems, by any reasonable definitions, the values of syntax, content and context variables will be identical. Consequently, the obvious differences in complexity *require* the use of structure variables for their quantitative characterization. Figure 4.4 depicts the state-spaces for (a) the trivial problem of one nickel and one dime, (b) the problem of two nickels and two dimes, and (c) the problem of three nickels and three dimes. Each state-space is symmetrical when the move of a nickel to the right is replaced by the corresponding move of a dime to the left, and Figure 4.4(c) represents only a little more than half of the state-space. Each problem thus possesses two solution

Figure 4.4 *State-Spaces for the Problems of Exchanging Nickels and Dimes*

(a) One nickel and one dime:

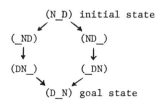

(b) Two nickels and two dimes:

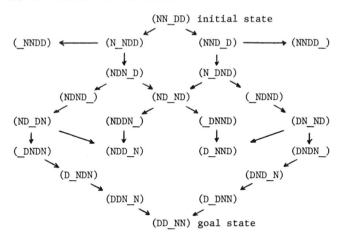

Figure 4.4 *(continued)*

(c) Three nickels and three dimes:

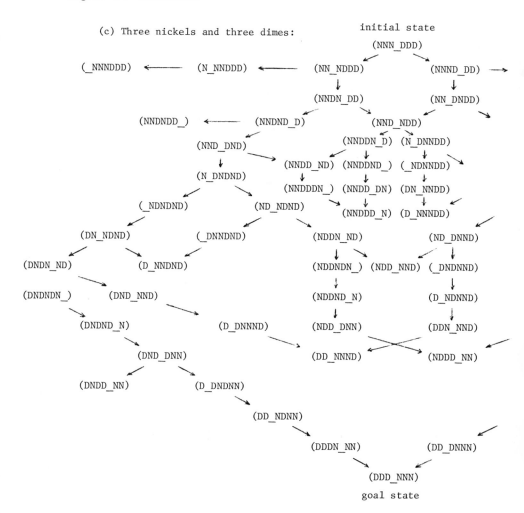

Figure 4.4 *(continued)*

(d) Solution paths for the problem of four nickels and four dimes:

```
                    (NNNN_DDDD)
                  ↙          ↘
      (NNN_NDDDD)            (NNNND_DDD)
          ↓                      ↓
      (NNNDN_DDD)            (NNN_DNDDD)
          ↓                      ↓
      (NNNDND_DD)            (NN_NDNDDD)
          ↓                      ↓
      (NNND_DNDD)            (NNDN_NDDD)
          ↓                      ↓
      (NN_DNDNDD)            (NNNDDN_DD)                . . .              . . .
          ↓                      ↓                       ↓                  ↓
      (N_NDNDNDD)            (NNNDND_D)           (D_NDNDNDN)         (DNDNDND_N)
          ↓                      ↓                       ↓                  ↓
      (NDN_NDNDD)            (NNNDND_DND)          (DDN_NDNDN)         (DNDNDND_DNN)
          ↓                      ↓                       ↓                  ↓
      (NDNDN_NDD)            (NND_DNDND)           (DDNDN_NDN)         (DND_DNDNN)
          ↓                      ↓                       ↓                  ↓
      (NDNDNDN_D)            (N_DNDNDND)           (DDNDNDN_N)         (D_DNDNDNN)
          ↓                      ↓                       ↓                  ↓
      (NDNDNDND_)            (_NDNDNDND)           (DDNDNDD_NN)        (DD_NDNDNN)
          ↓                      ↓                       ↓                  ↓
      (NDNDND_DN)            (DN_NDNDND)           (DDND_DNNN)         (DDDN_NDNN)
          ↓                      ↓                       ↓                  ↓
      (NDND_DNDN)            (DNDN_NDND)           (DD_DNDNNN)         (DDDNDN_NN)
          ↓                      ↓                       ↓                  ↓
      (ND_DNDNDN)            (DNDNDN_ND)           (DDD_NDNNN)         (DDDND_NNN)
          ↓                      ↓                       ↓                  ↓
      (_DNDNDNDN)            (DNDNDNDN_)           (DDDDN_NNN)         (DDD_DNNNN)
          ↓                      ↓                        ↘            ↙
        . . .                  . . .                     (DDDD_NNNN)
```

paths which are equivalent by virtue of this symmetry. The state-space for Problem *4.4c* is too large to diagram conveniently, but the solution paths are indicated in Figure 4.4(d).

There are many interesting patterns which can be found in the solution paths for these problems (Charosh, 1965; Rising, 1956). Structure variables which emphasize the differences in complexity include the following:

(a) Total number of states in the state-space:

    1 nickel and 1 dime   6
    2 nickels and 2 dimes   23
    3 nickels and 3 dimes   72

(b) Length of the shortest solution path:

    1 nickel and 1 dime   3 steps
    2 nickels and 2 dimes   8 steps
    3 nickels and 3 dimes   15 steps
    ....
    n nickels and n dimes $(n+1)^2 - 1$ step

(c) Number of blind alleys:

    1 nickel and 1 dime   0
    2 nickels and 2 dimes   4
    3 nickels and 3 dimes   13

Variables which are the same for all versions of these problems include the number of possible first moves (2), the number of goal states (1), and the number of solution paths through the state-space (2).

A comment is in order here. The discussion in this chapter focuses on the states of a representation ("nodes") and the permitted moves or transitions between them ("arcs"). In many problems, the moves can be characterized by means of a finite set of *operators* from the set of states into itself. More precisely, each operator possesses a *domain* of states to which it is applicable, and a *range* of *successor* states; thus it is a partial function. Finding a solution path corresponds to finding a sequence of operators which, when applied successively to the initial state, produces a goal state.

In Problem *4.4*, we might define the four operators "moving right with a nickel," "moving left with a dime," "jumping right with a nickel," and "jumping left with a dime." Each of these operators applies only to certain states, and is inapplicable to others. When an operator does apply to a state, it generates a unique successor state.

Given a set of states and a set of operators, we can define a move to be permitted from state s_1 to state s_2 if and only if there exists an operator which maps s_1 into s_2; thus we can always recover the state-space as a collection of configurations and permitted moves (a directed lattice). However, *different* families of operators may correspond to the *same* permitted moves among the states (for example, the states may be grouped into domains in different ways for different families of operators). Problems *4.4* are equivalently characterized by two operators, "moving or jumping right with a nickel" and "moving or jumping left with a dime."

Often the set of states in a problem representation is extremely large. Nevertheless, one can fully characterize the state-space by specifying a list of operators together with an initial state. Operators are also essential to the characterization of *algorithms* which may be used to solve families of problems. But, except where otherwise specified, the structure variables discussed in this chapter are defined without reference to any particular choice of a set of operators from among the possible choices.

For an N-player game, the structure analogous to the state-space is the *game tree* or *game graph*. Here the opposing players typically have disjoint sets of goal states, and the information as to which player has the move must, if applicable, be included in the description of a state. A problem may then be regarded as a 1-player game. A very simple version of the well-known game of "Nim" provides an example.

4.5 *In 2-pile Nim, three matchsticks are placed in one pile, and two in another. The object of the game is to be the player to remove the last match. Each player, in turn, may take away as many matchsticks as desired, but only from one pile.*

The game graph for 2-pile Nim is represented in Figure 4.5. Each state is designated by a pair of numbers representing the matches remaining in the respective piles, and by a letter, A or B, denoting the player whose turn it is to move. Again, it is possible to define variables describing the complexity of the game, such as the total number of states in the state-space, the maximum number of moves possible in a play of the game, the number of goal states for each player, and so forth.

We saw earlier that a concern of artificial intelligence research has been to develop efficient search algorithms within the state-spaces of problems or games. However, the emphasis of this chapter is not the development of techniques for more sophisticated computer problem solving, but the study of problem-solving outcomes as they are affected by intrinsic problem structure. For this purpose, it seems worthwhile to select problems whose intrinsic structure is sufficiently complex to be interesting, but sufficiently simple so that the task structure variables can be completely determined. That is, problems used for the study of problem solving should be thoroughly analyzed prior to

Figure 4.5 *Game Graph (State-Space) for 2-pile Nim*

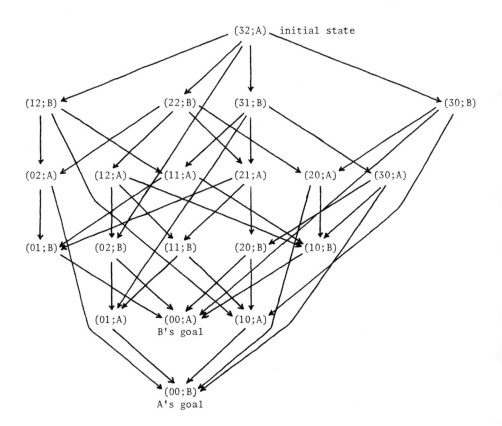

the study, so that in the course of research we can gain insight into the problem *solvers*, and not merely additional insight into the structure of the tasks. Likewise, if the teacher is aware of problem structure, instruction in problem solving can be guided more effectively.

State-Space Homomorphisms and Isomorphisms

Define two state-spaces (or game graphs) to be *isomorphic* if there is a mapping from the states of the first onto the states of the second, having the following properties: (a) the mapping is bijective (a one-to-one correspondence); (b) a move from one state to another is permitted in the first state-space if and only if the corresponding move is permitted in the second; (c) the initial state of the first state-space is mapped onto the initial state of the second; and (d) a state is a goal state in the first state-space if and only if the corresponding state is a goal state in the second. Occasionally we shall speak loosely about two state-spaces being isomorphic when only conditions (a) and (b) are intended; for example, when a variety of initial states or goal states are being considered.

Representations of problems and games which have isomorphic state-spaces will have identical values of the structure variables which were defined above. Any algorithm which works to solve such a problem or win such a game within one representation will have a corresponding algorithm within the isomorphic representation.

We mentioned earlier that different problem solvers may formulate different representations from the same problem statement. However, if two such representations are isomorphic, they can be said to have the "same" structure. One individual may represent the missionary-cannibal problem with nickels and dimes, while another uses M's and C's as we did; the state-spaces for these representations are obviously isomorphic. The equation $2x + 3x = 10$ may be obtained by one individual from an algebra word problem, while another individual writes $2A + 3A = 10$. Again the state-spaces are isomorphic--for any equation which can be validly obtained from $2x + 3x = 10$, there is a corresponding equation which can be validly obtained from $2A + 3A = 10$. On the other hand, a "table of values" representation for finding x has no natural correspondence of states with an algebraic representation.

Thus the valid representations of a given problem fall into equivalence classes or *isomorphism classes*. When we speak of problem "structure variables," we are actually discussing a particular isomorphism class of representations of the problem. The usefulness of structure variables depends on the fact that, for most unambiguously stated problems, relatively few classes of representations will find actual use by a given population of problem solvers.

A more interesting aspect of state-space isomorphisms is the fact that quite distinct problems may turn out to have isomorphic representations. Consider for example the following games.

4.6 In the game of Number Scrabble, the integers 1, 2, ...,
9 are written on slips of paper. The opposing players
take turns, each selecting one number for himself or
herself. Neither player may select a number already
taken. The goal is to obtain exactly three numbers which
add up to 15.

(Simon, 1969)

4.7 In the game of Jam, each player has a different color
pencil. The players in turn color a straight line in
the diagram below along its entire length. The object
is to obtain three lines in one's own color intersecting
at any single point.

Diagram for the game of Jam:

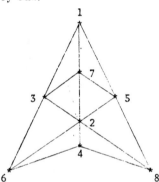

4.8 In the Horse Race game pictured below, there are eight horses
on the starting line, and nine cards to be picked one at a
time by the two players. Each card has the numbers of
several horses. When a player picks a card, the following
things happen: if a horse is unowned, that player takes
possession of it and advances it one. If a horse is already
owned by that player, it advances one. If a horse is owned
by the player's opponent, it is disqualified. The first
player to bring home a horse wins.

Cards for the Horse Race game: a. 1 3 6   d. 3 7   g. 2 3 8

b. 4 6   e. 1 2 4 7   h. 4 8

c. 2 5 6   f. 5 7   i. 1 5 8

Diagram: Horse #

	1	2	3	4	5	6	7	8
START								
		X						
FINISH								

*In the diagram, for purposes of illustration, card "e"
has been played by the first player, and card "g" by
the second.*

The three preceding games, which differ from each other radically
in syntax, content, and context, are all isomorphic in the sense of
state-space structure to the familiar game of tick-tack-toe. The
isomorphism of Number Scrabble with tick-tack-toe is illustrated by
the well-known magic square in Figure 4.6(a). The game of Jam is
based on the projective dual of tick-tack-toe, in which points correspond to lines and lines to points; the correspondence with tick-tack-
toe is noted in Figure 4.6(b). Finally, each card in the Horse Race
game corresponds to a tick-tack-toe square, and each horse to a straight
line. The cards have been constructed so that each horse appears on
exactly three cards; the correspondence with tick-tack-toe is tabulated
in Figure 4.6(c).

In Chapter I, Figure 1.1, it is noted that problem solving may
involve the use of *related* problem statements or problem representations. Isomorphism of problem representations is the closest possible
relationship from the standpoint of structure. Solving a problem isomorphic to a given problem may be easier due to differences in syntax,
content, or context, but it will be no easier in structure (and no more
difficult). Next we consider less stringent structural relationships
between problems.

A generalization of the idea of state-space isomorphism is that
of state-space *homomorphism*. The concept of homomorphic problems has
been approached in different ways; the development here is the author's
own.

Suppose that we have two state-spaces S and T. A *homomorphism* is
a mapping f from S into T, not necessarily one-to-one and not necessarily onto, which satisfies the following: if s_1 and s_2 are states in S
such that there is a legal move from s_1 to s_2, then either there is a
legal move in T from $f(s_1)$ to $f(s_2)$, or else $f(s_1) = f(s_2)$. A homomorphism is *goal-preserving* if it maps goal states of S into goal
states of T. We shall now define some special kinds of homomorphisms
and look at some examples.

(a) For an *injective homomorphism*, the mapping f from the first
state-space to the second is required to be one-to-one. For example,
consider the game of 2-pile Nim in which the initial state has two
matchsticks in each pile (Figure 4.7). The states of this game may
obviously be placed into one-to-one correspondence with a *subset* of
the states in the more complex game which is generated by an initial
state having more matchsticks, more piles, or both. (Compare Figure
4.7 with Figure 4.5.) Such a correspondence defines an injective
homomorphism.

Figure 4.6 *Games Isomorphic to Tick-tack-toe*

(a) Magic square illustrating the isomorphism with Number Scrabble:

4	3	8
9	5	1
2	7	6

(b) Correspondence between points of Jam and lines of tick-tack-toe:

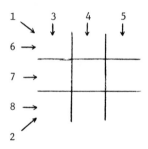

(c) "Horse Race" cards correspond to tick-tack-toe squares; horses to tick-tack-toe lines.

a	b	c
d	e	f
g	h	i

Figure 4.7 *A Symmetrical Subspace of the 2-pile Nim State-Space*

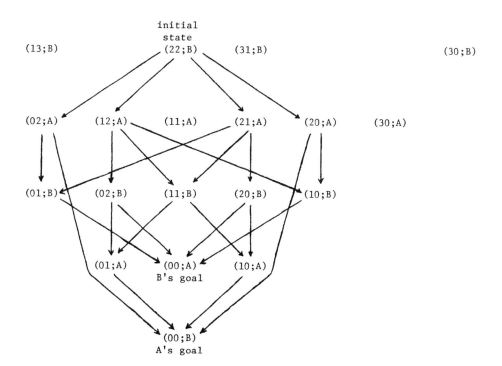

As a second example, consider the nickel-dime problems illustrated in Figure 4.4. The states for the problem of one nickel and one dime may be mapped into the states for the problem of two nickels and two dimes by adding a nickel to the left and a dime to the right of any given configuration. Likewise the states for the problem of two nickels and two dimes may be mapped into the states for the problem of three nickels and three dimes, and so forth. Each of these mappings defines an injective homomorphism. Note that in this example, the goal state for the less complex problem is *not* mapped into the goal state for the more complex problem, as it was for the case of the Nim games. Furthermore, the goal state for the less complex problem is not even mapped into a state which is on a solution path for the more complex problem; it is mapped into a "blind alley" state. Thus these are not goal-preserving homomorphisms.

(b) We define a *surjective homomorphism* to be one for which the mapping f from the first state-space to the second is an onto or surjective mapping. That is, for every state t in the second state-space T, there exists at least one state s in the first state-space S, such that f(s) = t. For example, consider the two versions of the missionary-cannibal problem illustrated in Figures 4.2 and 4.3. Define a mapping f from a state in Figure 4.3 to a state in Figure 4.2 which associates to every state in the more complex state-space the state obtained by removing the bar above the C. For instance, the two states (M$\bar{\text{C}}$:MMCC*) and (MC:MMC$\bar{\text{C}}$*) are both mapped into (MC:MMCC*) by f. The mapping f is thus in general many-to-one; but it clearly preserves the structure of legal moves in the sense that if a move is legal between two states in Figure 4.3, then it is legal between the corresponding states in Figure 4.2. This is a surjective homomorphism because every state in Figure 4.2 has at least one state in Figure 4.3 associated with it by the mapping f.

Given initially the more complex statement of the problem, Problem *4.3*, one might decide to solve first the "related" problem obtained by neglecting the condition that only one cannibal knows how to row, Problem *4.2*. The problem *statements* are related in that one condition has been removed. The goal-preserving surjective homomorphism described above characterizes the "relatedness" of the problem *structures* which results.

Next consider the "Jealous Husbands" problem discussed in Section 1 (Reed, Ernst, and Banerji, 1974).

4.9 *Three husbands and three wives are on one bank of a river, with a rowboat that will hold at most two people. How can they cross to the other side of the river, in such a manner that no wife is ever in the presence of a man other than her husband on either riverbank, unless her husband is also present?*

We have reworded the problem in order to highlight the parallels and differences with Problem *4.2*. The three husbands correspond to the three missionaries and the three wives to the three cannibals. However, interpretation of the condition that no wife be left with a man other than her husband, unless her husband is also present, seems to require the problem solver to keep track of the individual identities of the husbands and the wives. Such a representation of the problem leads to a fairly complex state-space, a small portion of which is depicted in Figure 4.8. In this figure the husbands have been labelled H_1, H_2, H_3, and their respective wives W_1, W_2, W_3.

Define a mapping f from a state in Figure 4.8 to a state in Figure 4.2 which associates to every state in the more complex state-space the state obtained by removing all the subscripts, and relabelling H by M and W by C. It is evident that f defines a many-to-one correspondence of the states in the two representations, and that every state in Figure 4.2 has at least one state in Figure 4.8 to which it is associated by f. To deduce that f is a homomorphism (i.e., that it preserves the structure of legal moves), it is necessary to reason that if no wife is left with a man other than her husband unless her husband is also present, then the wives can never outnumber the husbands on either riverbank. Thus if a move is legal in Problem *4.9*, the corresponding move will be legal in Problem *4.2*. Note that the converse of this statement is false--it is quite possible for a proposed move to be *illegal* in the Jealous Husbands problem, with the corresponding move in the missionary-cannibal problem perfectly legal. Again, we have a goal-preserving surjective homomorphism which characterizes the "relatedness" between the two problems.

Thus far we have observed that an injective homomorphism allows us to view one problem or game as a *subproblem* or *subgame* of another; while a surjective homomorphism allows us to describe the relationship of a problem with a related problem obtained by *disregarding some attribute* of the states of the original problem.

Finally we shall define a less stringent notion of "relatedness" of problem structure than that of a homomorphism. Suppose that we have two state-spaces S and T. A *weak homomorphism* will be a mapping f from S into T, not necessarily one-to-one or onto, which satisfies the following: if s_1 and s_2 are states in S such that there is a legal move from s_1 to s_2, then either $f(s_1) = f(s_2)$, or there exists a *sequence* of legal moves in T from $f(s_1)$ to $f(s_2)$ such that the intermediate states are not in the image of f. That is, there is a legal *path* in T given by $(f(s_1), t_1, \ldots, t_n, f(s_2))$, and there are no states in S mapped into $t_1, \ldots, t_n$. It is clear that every homomorphism is a weak homomorphism, since $(f(s_1), f(s_2))$ qualifies as a path in T having no intermediate states. Furthermore, a weak homomorphism that is surjective is also a homomorphism. A weak homomorphism from S into T which is injective will be called an *embedding* of S into T.

Figure 4.8 *A Portion of the State-Space for the "Jealous Husbands" Problem*

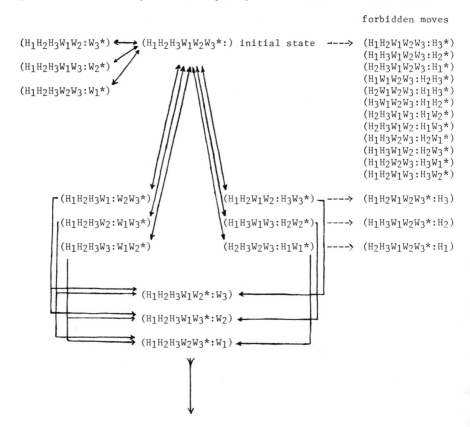

forbidden moves

The concept of an embedding of one problem representation into another allows us to classify further the alternative representations which may be constructed for a given problem statement. For example, it is commonly asserted that the state-space in Figure 4.2 "is" the state-space for the missionary-cannibal problem; we have already noted that such an assertion must be interpreted as referring to a class of isomorphic state-spaces. However, there is still greater flexibility in specifying the state-space, even without the device of including the "illegal states" in Figure 4.2. For example, we may choose to record separately the intermediate configurations in which one or two missionaries or cannibals is in the rowboat, part-way across the river. In this more complex representation of the missionary-cannibal problem, there are not only many more states, but there are many more blind alleys than in Figure 4.2. For example, the path from the initial state (MMMCCC*:) to (MMCC:MC*) may now be represented by the three states (MMMCCC*//), (MMCC/MC*/), (MMCC//MC*), where the two slashes stand for the two banks of the river. From the state (MMCC:MC*) there were formerly no legal "blind alley" moves; now, however, the move from (MMCC//MC*) to (MMCC/C*/M) is still legal and represents a blind alley, since if the cannibal lands on the left bank, the conditions of the problem are violated. Some, but not all, of the "forbidden moves" in Figure 4.2 now have legal intermediate "blind alley" states heading towards them.

In short, there is an embedding of the state-space in Figure 4.2 in the more complex state-space, and the latter is certainly an equally valid representation of the problem structure.

This example is not merely a trick; it illustrates a fundamental issue in the definition of structure variables such as the number of steps or the number of blind alleys. Indeed, one could carry forward the expansion of the missionary-cannibal state-space still further. Suppose that we define a state of the missionary-cannibal problem to be a configuration of missionaries and cannibals, rowboat and river, together with the label t for "tested" or u for "untested." Untested states have not been examined with respect to the condition that cannibals are not to outnumber missionaries, and are therefore legal--however, the only move permitted from an untested state is to test it. From a tested state, one is only permitted to move to an untested state. In this expanded state-space, the "forbidden moves" in Figure 4.2 have become legal, "untested" states. There is an embedding of the state-space in Figure 4.2 in the expanded state-space which assigns to each original state the corresponding "tested" configuration.

We see that given a problem statement, it will often be possible to construct alternate state-spaces which are accurate representations of the problem, and which are not isomorphic. Typically they will be related to each other by means of an embedding, and will have different values of important structure variables. This is a more precise characterization of the difficulty which we noted at the beginning of this chapter in specifying the number of steps needed to pass from the equation $2x + 3x = 10$ to the equation $5x = 10$.

It is not meaningful, then, to specify structure variables in an absolute sense; that is, we cannot say "the number of steps needed to solve this problem *is* n." However, we can specify the values of structure variables *in a specified representation* of a problem. This permits us to *compare* problems having different values of structure variables, as long as we are consistent in our choice of representation for the problems.

Symmetries and Subspace Decompositions

Utilization of intrinsic problem symmetry can often contribute to insightful problem solving (Goldin and McClintock, in press). Likewise, the decomposition of a problem into subproblems through the selection of subgoals can be an effective procedure. Here we shall define task structure variables associated with problem symmetries and subproblem decompositions. These characteristics of task structure may be thought of as representing the *potential* for use of appropriate heuristic processes.

An *automorphism* of a problem is an isomorphism of the problem state-space onto itself. Such an automorphism is also called a *symmetry transformation* of the problem representation. For example, automorphisms of the tick-tack-toe game tree may be obtained by rotating the tick-tack-toe grid by 1/4, 1/2, or 3/4 of a complete turn, or by reflecting the grid vertically, horizontally, or diagonally (see Figure 4.9). Corresponding automorphisms may therefore be obtained for the representations of all of the games isomorphic to tick-tack-toe.

The set of symmetry transformations of a system always forms a mathematical *group*. Any ordered pair of symmetry transformations may be performed in succession to obtain a third symmetry transformation, thus defining an associative binary operation. The identity transformation is always included as a symmetry transformation by convention, and for every symmetry transformation, there exists the inverse transformation which returns the system to its initial configuration. The symmetry transformations of a state-space thus form a group which we shall call the *symmetry group* of the problem or game representation.

For any problem or game, we may now consider as a new task variable the *number of symmetry transformations* of a representation; i.e., the order of the symmetry group.

Many of the problems and games already discussed display some sort of state-space symmetry; for example, the nickel-dime problems (Problems *4.4a-c*) possess bilateral symmetry (symmetry group of order 2), as does the Nim subgame depicted in Figure 4.7. In tick-tack-toe, the symmetry group of the state-space is of order eight, and corresponds to the geometric symmetry of the tick-tack-toe grid; while in

Figure 4.9 *Tick-tack-toe States Equivalent by Rotation and Reflection Symmetry*

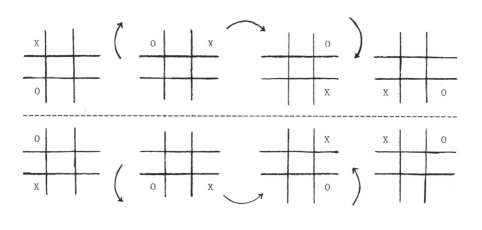

Figure 4.10 *3-Pile Nim States Equivalent by Permutation Symmetry*

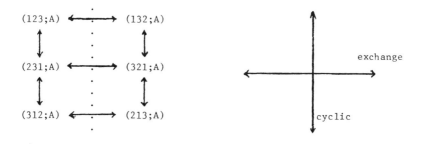

Number Scrabble, the embodiment of the game is such as to conceal the symmetry which is in fact present. Thus problem symmetry may be more or less overt, depending upon the problem embodiment.

Whenever a state-space possesses symmetry, it is possible to construct a smaller, *reduced* state-space in which states equivalent by virtue of symmetry transformations have been identified with each other. To develop this concept precisely, let s be a state in a given state-space S, and let G be the symmetry group of S. Consider the set of all states which can be obtained by applying elements of G to the fixed state s; this set, denoted Gs, will be called the *orbit* of s under the action of G. Two states in S will be called *equivalent modulo G* if they are in the same orbit under the action of G. The orbits in the state-space form mutually disjoint equivalence classes of states.

For example, the eight tick-tack-toe states in Figure 4.9 all belong to the same orbit. Of course some orbits in the tick-tack-toe state-space contain fewer than eight states. The state with X in the center square, for example, the other squares being empty, stands alone in its equivalence class.

Given a state-space S having a symmetry group G, a new and smaller state-space S' may be constructed as follows. Let each equivalence class in S (*modulo* G) be a state in S'; let the initial state in S' be the equivalence class containing the initial state in S; and let the goal state(s) in S' be the equivalence class(es) containing the goal state(s) in S. Define a move to be permitted from one state of S' to another state of S' if and only if there exists a state s_1 in the first equivalence class and a state s_2 in the second equivalence class, such that (s_1, s_2) is a permitted move in S.

The state-space S' thus obtained will be said to have been *reduced modulo the symmetry group* G. It may sometimes be convenient to represent S' by selecting one representative state from each orbit in S.

By way of illustration consider the following generalization of the game of Nim.

> 4.10 *In the game of n-pile Nim, a_1 matchsticks are placed in the first pile, a_2 in the second pile, and so forth, with a_n matchsticks in the nth pile. The object of the game is to be the player to remove the last match. Each player, in turn, may take away as many matchsticks as desired, but only from one pile.*

The state-space for n-pile Nim may be mapped by means of an injective homomorphism into a state-space possessing n-fold permutation symmetry.

Let m be the maximum of all of the a_i for i = 1, 2, ..., n; let the
state-space consist of all configurations which can be reached by
applying legal moves to the state (mm..,m;A). Any permutation of
the n piles now defines an automorphism of this state-space. Figure
4.10, for example, illustrates six 3-pile Nim states which are equivalent by permutation symmetry. In depicting the reduced state-space,
only one of these states--for instance, the state (123;A)--might be
used to stand for the equivalence class of the six states.

In Figure 4.11 the symmetrical subspace of the 2-pile Nim state-
space, which was pictured in Figure 4.7, is reduced *modulo* the exchange
symmetry. Now the state (21;A) stands for the *equivalence class* containing (21;A) and (12;A). Note the legal move in Figure 4.11 from
(21;A) to (10;B), which is present because the move from (21;A) to
(01;B) is legal in Figure 4.7.

Given a state-space S having a symmetry group G, and letting S'
be the reduced state-space, define the mapping f from S to S' which
assigns to each state in S its corresponding equivalence class in S'.
f defines a surjective homomorphism from S onto S'. Thus there is a
surjective homomorphism from Figure 4.7 onto Figure 4.11.

Returning to the question of alternative representations for a
given problem statement, we remark that when symmetry is present, a
choice must be made--to incorporate the symmetry from the start by
utilizing a reduced state-space, or to neglect the symmetry by treating states equivalent by symmetry as distinct states. From the
standpoint of efficient problem-solving, it may be desirable to
incorporate as much of the symmetry as possible. However, many
problem solvers will not recognize all of the symmetry which is in
fact present, at least at the outset of problem solving. Thus from
the standpoint of defining and investigating task structure variables,
it is desirable to characterize the expanded state-space, the symmetry
group, and the state-space reduced *modulo* the symmetry group.

The symmetry group G of a state-space may have various *subgroups*,
each of which contains only certain specified symmetry transformations. Then, for any subgroup H of G, it will be possible to define
S", the state-space reduction of S *modulo* H. S" will be a state-space
intermediate in size between S and S', into which some but not all of
the available symmetry has been incorporated.

Finally let us remark that certain problem representations
possess *forward-backward* symmetry. Given a problem with a single
goal state, one may construct the *inverted* problem as follows: (a)
the goal of the original problem becomes the initial configuration
of the inverted problem; (b) the initial configuration of the original problem becomes the goal of the inverted problem; and (c) given
the two problem configurations s_1 and s_2, a move is permitted from s_1
to s_2 in the inverted problem if and only if the rules of the original
problem permit a move from s_2 to s_1. We note, however, that for a

Figure 4.11 *Reduced Symmetrical Subspace of the 2-Pile Nim State-Space (compare with Fig. 4.7)*

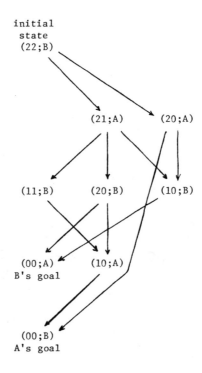

configuration to be a state in the state-space of the inverted problem, it is neither necessary nor sufficient that it be a state in the
state-space of the original problem. The configuration might not be
reachable from the initial state of the original problem, although
reachable by "working backward" from the goal state of the original
problem. A problem is said to possess forward-backward symmetry when
the state-space of the inverted problem is isomorphic to that of the
original problem.

Many of the examples that we have mentioned thus far have forward-
backward symmetry. In the various versions of the missionary-cannibal
problem (Figures 4.2 and 4.3) and the Jealous Husbands problem (Figure
4.8), the problem statements are such that any legal move is reversible. The state-space for the inverted problem is the same set of
states as the state-space for the original problem. The forward-
backward symmetry is apparent in the state-space diagram, and
corresponds simply to exchanging the two banks of the river in the
problem statement. In the nickel-dime problems (Figure 4.4), the
permitted moves are not reversible. With the exception of Figure
4.4(a)--the problem of one nickel and one dime--the state-space
diagrams do *not* display forward-backward symmetry. Nevertheless, when
one constructs the state-space for the inverted problem, it is isomorphic to the state-space for the original problem; it includes configurations which are not present in Figure 4.4 because they cannot be
reached from the initial state in Figure 4.4, and it excludes other
configurations which are present in Figure 4.4. The forward-backward
symmetry corresponds to exchanging "dimes" and "nickels" in the original
problem statements.

The problem of the two pails (Figure 4.1) is an example of a problem which does not possess forward-backward symmetry.

We have seen that one way of reducing the state-space for a problem or game, and establishing equivalence classes of states, is with
respect to a group of symmetry transformations. A second way of
reducing the state-space is with respect to its infrastructure of subproblem or subgame state-spaces. A *subspace* of a state-space S is a
subset T of S, together with the moves which are permitted from one
state in T to another state in T. From time to time we may designate
a state in T as the "initial" state for the subspace, and a particular
set of states in T as "subgoal" states.

Figure 4.7 illustrates a subspace of the 2-pile Nim state-space.
In fact, given a homomorphism f from a state-space R into a state-space
S, define the *image* of the homomorphism to be the set of all states s
in S for which there is at least one state r in R such that $f(r) = s$.
Then the image of the homomorphism is a subspace T of S. The initial
state in T may be characterized as the image of the initial state in R,
and the set of subgoal states in T as the image of the set of goal
states in R.

An interesting situation arises when the state-space of a problem can be partitioned into mutually disjoint subspaces, in such a manner that for any pair of subspaces, there is at most one permitted move between a state in one subspace and a state in the other. An example is provided by the well-known Tower of Hanoi problem.

> 4.11 *Four concentric rings (labeled 1,2,3,4 respectively) are placed in order of size, the smallest at the top, on the first of three pegs (labeled A,B,C), as in the diagram below.*

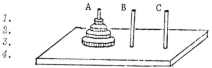

> 1.
> 2.
> 3.
> 4.

> *The object of the problem is to transfer all of the rings from peg A to peg C in a minimum number of moves. Only one ring may be moved at a time, and no larger ring may be placed above a smaller one on any peg.*

Figure 4.12(a) depicts a state-space for the Tower of Hanoi problem. In Figure 4.12(b)-(c), the state-space has been partitioned into mutually disjoint subspaces in various ways.

Given a state-space S which has been thus partitioned, a new and simpler state-space S' may be defined by considering each subspace of S to be a state in its own right in S'. The initial state in S' will be the subspace containing the initial state of S, and a goal state in S' is any subspace containing a goal state of S. A move is permitted from one state of S' to another state of S' if and only if there exists a state s_1 of S in the first subspace, and a state s_2 of S in the second subspace such that the move (s_1,s_2) is permitted in S.

The state-space S' obtained in this fashion is said to have been *reduced modulo the subspace decomposition* of S. S' may sometimes be conveniently represented by selecting a representative state from each subspace of S.

In the Tower of Hanoi problem, a "1-ring subspace" is isomorphic to the task of transferring a single ring from one post to another; a "2-ring subspace" is isomorphic to the task of transferring two rings from one post to another; and so forth. In Figure 4.12(b), we see that when the state-space for the 4-ring problem is partitioned into 2-ring subspaces, the *reduced* state-space is isomorphic to a 2-ring Tower of Hanoi state-space. Likewise, when the 4-ring state-space is partitioned into 3-ring subspaces, the reduced state-space is isomorphic to a 1-ring Tower of Hanoi state-space; and when the 4-ring

Figure 4.12 *State-Space Representation for the 4-Ring Tower of Hanoi*
Problem, and its Partitioning into Subspaces

(a) The Tower of Hanoi state-space. The four letters labelling
a state refer to the respective pegs on which the four rings
are located.

```
                         . AAAA (start)
                 CAAA . . BAAA
                     .   . BCAA
             BBAA . . . . CCAA
                  .        . CCBA
                 . .      . .
               .   .    .   .
       CCCA . . . . . . . . BBBA
           .                . BBBC
          . .              . .
         .   .            .   .
  AACB . . . . BBCB     . . . . AABC
       .        .   .     .    .
      . .      . .   . .   . .
     .   .    .   . .   . .   .
 BBBB . . . . . . . . . . . . . . . CCCC (goal)
```

(b) Decomposition of the 4-ring state-space into 2-ring subspaces.

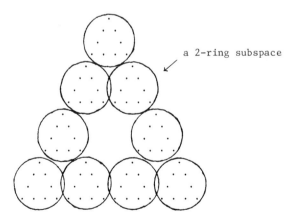

a 2-ring subspace

Figure 4.12 *(continued)*

(c) Decomposition of the 4-ring state-space into 1-ring and 3-ring subspaces.

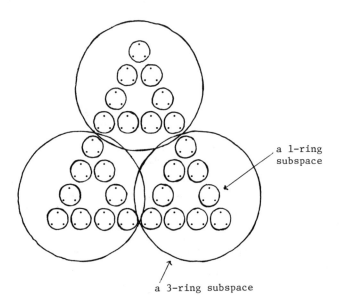

a 1-ring subspace

a 3-ring subspace

state-space is partitioned into 1-ring subspaces, the reduced state-space is isomorphic to a 3-ring state-space (Figure 4.12(c)).

The Tower of Hanoi problem has the additional interesting feature that in the subspace decompositions illustrated, all of the subspaces are themselves mutually isomorphic in each decomposition.

The reduction of a state-space with respect to a symmetry group G, and the reduction with respect to a "subspace" decomposition, are similar to each other in that both reductions involve the establishment of equivalence classes of states. For the case of a symmetry group, two states are equivalent if they are conjugate by virtue of a symmetry automorphism of the state-space; for the case of a subspace decomposition, two states are equivalent if they are contained within the same subspace. We have shown for each type of reduction how to obtain a smaller state-space S' from the original state-space S. For reduction *modulo* a subspace decomposition, as for reduction *modulo* a symmetry group, there always exists a surjective homomorphism from S onto S' which is obtained by mapping each state in S to the equivalence class in S' which contains it.

We have spent a considerable portion of this chapter developing the concepts of state-space homomorphisms and isomorphisms, and symmetries and subspace decompositions, purely from the point of view of the formal analysis of intrinsic task structure. Let us digress at this point, and discuss the psychological meaning that these features may potentially have for the problem solver.

Consider first the case of a particular subproblem of a given problem. Associated with the subproblem is a subspace of the problem state-space. We may imagine that during the course of problem solving, a problem solver might succeed in solving the subproblem, so that every time it is encountered, it is solved directly and nearly automatically. Perhaps a special name is even conferred on the subproblem, which suggests the use of a particular solution algorithm. In some sense the subproblem is abstracted from the main problem by the problem solver, and "chunked" as a single entity. This is suggestive of the process which Krutetskii (1969, 1976) calls "curtailment."

Selection of a *subgoal* (or specification of a set of subgoals) by the problem solver establishes a subproblem of the main problem. Thus we might envision an ideal sequence of events, in which the problem solver (1) establishes a subgoal, (2) solves the corresponding subproblem, and (3) "chunks" the solution algorithm to the subproblem. Conceptually, the latter step corresponds to replacing the subspace of the state-space by a single state, without altering the overall network structure of the state-space (except, of course, for the elimination of the moves that are internal to the subspace).

If the state-space can be partitioned into subspaces, with each subspace corresponding to a particular subproblem (as with the Tower of Hanoi), we may anticipate the possibility of *stages* during problem solving, corresponding to the solution of particular subproblems and the curtailment of thinking with respect to those subproblems. When the state-space is partitioned into *isomorphic* subspaces, there may exist stages corresponding to the solution of particular isomorphism classes of subproblems.

Next consider the case of a problem for which the state-space possesses symmetry. We may suppose that at the outset, a problem solver might regard the various problem states or configurations as distinct from each other, even though they may be symmetrically conjugate (and thus equivalent as far as the problem structure is concerned). During the course of problem solving, such states may *come to be recognized* as equivalent, causing perhaps a profound change in the problem solver's "perception" of the problem.

Recognition of the symmetry which is present in a problem representation is often a key to *insightful* problem solving. Thus problem state-spaces which possess such symmetry offer the opportunity to study the process whereby this kind of insight occurs. Again we have the possibility of *stages* corresponding to the recognition of particular features of the problem symmetry (*subgroups* of the problem symmetry group), and curtailment of thinking whereby states are considered "the same" when they are equivalent by virtue of a symmetry transformation.

Problems with isomorphic or homomorphic representations present the opportunity to study *transfer* of learning from one problem-solving experience to another. The process whereby problem solvers come to recognize analogy of problem structure corresponds to the component of mathematical ability Krutetskii calls "generalization."

Comparison of a problem representation with a representation of the inverse problem provides the structural framework necessary for the study of "reversibility of thinking," a third component of mathematical ability in Krutetskii's model. For problems having forward-backward symmetry, any algorithm or strategy which solves the inverse problem has a corresponding algorithm or strategy which solves the original problem; thus the inverse problem is no easier than the original. Nevertheless, problem solvers who can carry out a certain strategy "working forward," and then carry out the corresponding strategy "working backward," may be able to "connect" these paths, thus arriving at a solution by different means than those who work exclusively in one direction. At the other extreme, problems with representations which in the "forward" direction have a multiplicity of branches, and in the "backward" direction have very few branches, possess the structural characteristics for "working backward" to be more successful than "working forward."

To sum up, as examples of the usefulness of state-space analysis, we have seen that it permits us to characterize with some rigor the problem characteristics which facilitate the study of three of

Table 4.2 *Structure Variables Defined with Reference to State-Spaces*

Numerical variables describing a problem state-space S

    Total number of states
    Length of the shortest solution path
    Number of blind alleys
    Number of possible first moves
    Number of goal states
    Ratio of the number of goal states to the total number of states
    Number of elements in the symmetry group G

Non-numerical structural characteristics of the state-space S

    Equivalence classes of states under the action of the symmetry group G
    Subgroups of the symmetry group G
    Subspace decompositions of the state-space (particularly, decomposition
      into mutually isomorphic subspaces)
    Forward-backward symmetry within the state-space S

Relationships to other problem state-spaces T

    Existence of an isomorphism between S and T
    Existence of a homomorphism between S and T; in particular:
      An injective homomorphism from T to S (subproblem of S)
      A surjective homomorphism from S to T (reduction of S)
    Characteristics of the inverse problem of S (particularly, isomorphism
      of S with its inverse problem)

Krutetskii's components of mathematical ability--curtailment, generalization, and reversibility of thinking (see Chapter I, Table 1.3). In
Chapter X.A, Luger explores the possibilities for using problems having
some of these characteristics in teaching, in order to foster the development of mathematical ability.

Table 4.2 summarizes the structure variables which have been
defined with reference to state-spaces.

Algorithms and Strategies

An algorithm is a well-defined procedure for solving a class of
problems in a given representation. Algorithmic analysis may be considered an alternative to state-space analysis for the definition of
task structure variables. However, the two approaches are quite
compatible, since an algorithm may be described with reference to the
set of operators on a state-space. Thus an algorithm will accept the
initial state as input, and, by successive application of operators,
will generate a sequence of successor states until a goal state is
reached. In this manner, given an initial state, an algorithm defines
a *unique* path through the state-space. We may imagine the path generated by an algorithm as an "overlay" on the collection of problem
states, with alternative algorithms generating possibly distinct
solution paths.

Choice of a particular algorithm permits the comparison of problems with respect to task structure variables that are defined with
respect to the algorithm. These include: (a) the number of steps in
the solution path generated by the algorithm; (b) the number of times
any particular loop in the algorithm is traversed; (c) the number of
times any particular branch point in the algorithm is crossed; and (d)
the number of times any particular operator is called for by the
algorithm. Structure variables defined with respect to algorithms seem
to make the most sense in highly routinized, computational tasks, where
standard algorithms are widely taught to students. Their definition
depends not only upon the choice of a mathematical representation for
a problem, but also upon the choice of a *method* of solution within the
representation.

Let us now approach the concept of a *strategy* as a generalization
of an algorithm. A strategy is any procedure which *narrows* the set of
possible moves, without necessarily singling out a unique move. Thus,
while an algorithm is defined with reference to operators which are
partial functions on the state-space, a strategy may be defined with
reference to *partial relations* on the state-space. A partial relation
maps each state in its domain into a *set* of possible successor states.
Thus a strategy does not necessarily lead to a unique path within the
state-space. Instead it generates a set of possible paths, which may
or may not include a solution path.

This definition of the term "strategy" is quite consistent with ordinary usage. In chess, for example, a strategy associated with a particular opening variation might be, "seek to obtain control of an open Queen's Bishop file." Such a strategy does not single out a unique move or sequence of moves, but it is considerably more precise (and more problem-specific) than a *heuristic process* as the term is used in this book by McClintock and by Schoenfeld. A strategy establishes a well-defined subset of moves for consideration on a particular turn. Sometimes a heuristic process will suggest a particular solution strategy (or algorithm) in a particular situation.

In our sense of the word, a strategy is no more vague than an algorithm, when it is well-defined. It merely allows for a set of possible continuations, rather than a single continuation, at each juncture. To be well-defined, the set of possible moves must be unambiguously described for any state to which the strategy is applicable. Our use of the term "strategy" is similar to the use by Landa (1976a) of the term "semi-algorithm" (p. 37).

Sometimes a problem is susceptible to an easily-described strategy, when an attempt to write a detailed algorithm leads to a cumbersome and artificially complicated procedure. For example, consider a routine problem involving two independent simultaneous linear equations in two unknowns, X and Y, with non-zero coefficients. The procedure, "solve for Y in the second equation and substitute in the first equation; then solve for X," represents the outline of an algorithm; but it may not generate the simplest solution. In contrast, the procedure "solve for *one* of the variables in *one* of the equations and substitute in the other equation; then solve for the other variable," outlines a strategy. The first procedure, when sufficiently elaborated, will define a unique sequence of steps; the second procedure will define four possible sequences. However, if we attempt to turn the second procedure into an algorithm by spelling out in precise detail *how* to select the variable to be solved for first, and the equation in which it is to be solved for, a cumbersome result emerges which is contrary to the spirit of the strategy.

Just as task structure variables may be defined with respect to a particular algorithm, they may be defined with respect to a particular strategy. For example one may compare problems with respect to (a) their susceptibility to solution by means of a particular strategy, (b) the minimum number of steps in a solution path generated by a particular strategy, and so forth.

If two state-spaces are isomorphic, any strategy which may be defined in one state-space has a corresponding strategy which may be defined in the other.

Structure Variables in Routine Problems

Up to now the problem examples we have taken--the problem of the two pails, the missionaries and cannibals, the Tower of Hanoi, etc.-- have been principally of the *non-routine* variety. Such problems have two features which make the state-space analysis particularly easy. First, the rules of procedure stated in the problems are few, making it possible to identify a small number of operators which characterize the state-space. Frequently the state-space itself is small enough so that it can be fully displayed. Secondly, the states themselves correspond to configurations of physical objects described in the problem statements--pails of water, rings and posts, and so forth. When we turn to routine problems in, say, elementary algebra, these features are no longer present. Nevertheless, a state-space analysis is possible which does not differ in principle from the kind we have already performed.

In routine problem solving, which includes most of the problem- solving instruction offered in schools, there usually exists a *standard* representation which is *taught* to the students, and which it is expected they will use in writing solutions. Such a representation, then, should be used as far as possible in defining the task structure variables. It may also be valuable to consider representations *expanded* from the standard representation; i.e., in which the standard represen- tation can be embedded, or from which the standard representation can be obtained by state-space reduction.

A routine word problem in elementary algebra can be translated into a representation by means of finitely many equations in finitely many unknowns. It is such a configuration of symbols which we shall treat as a *state* in a state-space, for the purpose of studying struc- ture variables. This is not to deny the importance of other (non- standard) representations which might also be worthy of examination.

For example, consider a problem such as the following.

> 4.12 *Seven children each have the same number of marbles.*
> *In addition there are eleven marbles in a bag. All*
> *together, there are 102 marbles. How many marbles*
> *does each child have?*

The problem might be translated into the equation "$7x + 11 = 102$." This configuration of symbols then becomes the initial state for the problem state-space. In other words, the state-space analysis begins *after* the translation has been completed, as suggested by Figure 1.1 in Chapter I. The goal state for this problem is any state of the form "X = [numeral]" which can be obtained from the initial state by "legal moves."

The context of the problem ("marbles") may suggest a solution which is a positive integer, encouraging the use of (non-standard) "guess-and-check" procedures. These procedures, too, can be recorded in a state-space (see Chapter VIII.A).

The left-hand side of Figure 4.13 shows a solution path for the above problem in an *expanded* state-space; on the right is a solution path in a *reduced* state-space. The right-hand side of the figure depicts a path likely to correspond to the written work of many students. *Curtailment* may result in some of these steps being skipped or abbreviated, as shown. On the other hand, the left-hand column is intended to represent some of the theoretical *possibilities*, steps which *might* be taken by *some* students at various times. The following are some of the features of state-space reduction which were discussed earlier that have application to the correspondence between the expanded state-space and the reduced state-space in this diagram.

(a) States related by virtue of the associative property for addition may be taken as *equivalent*, and the "unnecessary" parentheses removed. Likewise, states related by virtue of the associative property for multiplication may be taken as equivalent. Furthermore, states related by virtue of the inclusion of superfluous parentheses may be taken as equivalent. For example, the two states "$(7x + 11) + (-11) = (102) + (-11)$" and "$7x = (11 + (-11)) = (102) + (-11)$" may correspond to the same state, "$7x + 11 + (-11) = 102 + (-11)$." The removal of parentheses amounts to the disregard of certain "irrelevant" attributes which formerly distinguished the states from each other. In the language of this chapter, a surjective homomorphism (many-to-one) is defined from the expanded state-space onto a reduced state-space. The more experienced the problem solver is in algebra, the more rapidly and "automatically" the irrelevant parentheses are removed or ignored.

(b) States incorporating expressions for addition of a negated quantity may be taken as equivalent to corresponding states incorporating subtraction of the quantity. Thus, the state "$7x + 11 + (-11) = 102 + (-11)$" can be reduced still further, to the state "$7x + 11 - 11 = 102 - 11$."

(c) States related by virtue of the addition of zero, or multiplication by unity, may be taken as equivalent. Disregard of these "irrelevant" attributes of the states results in further reduction of the state-space.

(d) Computational algorithms may be considered a single "step" in a reduced state-space. When we focus on the *algebraic* structure of a problem, each arithmetic computation becomes a self-contained *subproblem*, with an associated subspace of the state-space that can be identified with a single state in the reduced state-space. Again, more experienced problem solvers in algebra "chunk" such computations, so that possibly complicated numerical computations do not result in lengthy detours from the main argument.

Figure 4.13 *A Solution Path for a Linear Equation in One Variable in an Expanded State-Space, with Possible Reductions*

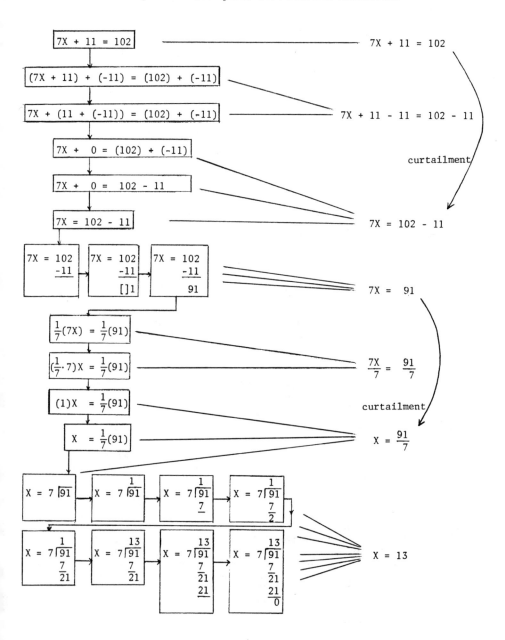

(e) Any letter might have been consistently substituted for X
without changing the structure of the solution path. The arbitrari-
ness of the choice of letter symbols is an overall *symmetry* of the
standard representation for problems in algebra.

The steps in the expanded state-space which are displayed in
Figure 4.13 may be thought of from two perspectives. On the one
hand, some of the steps resemble those presented in the rigorous
"justifications" of algebraic manipulations given in some texts,
in which each step is accompanied by the appropriate "reason":
"addition axiom for equality," "associative property of addition,"
"additive inverse property," "additive identity," and so forth. On
the other hand, other steps resemble those taken by a rather dull
"plodder," who cannot perform any steps mentally or see two steps
ahead in the problem and who finds it necessary to write "+0" in
place of "+11 - 11" before dropping the expression altogether. Of
course, these interpretations are merely metaphors. The steps in
Figure 4.13, along with many other possible valid expressions for
the "same" mathematical procedures, are simply "there"; they form
a part of the task environment for the solution of elementary algebra
problems as taught to a substantial population of students.

The state-spaces of Figure 4.13 may be expanded or reduced still
further. For example, the step from "$(\frac{1}{7}.7)x = \frac{1}{7}(91)$" to "$(1)x = \frac{1}{7}(91)$"
may be considered to pass through the intermediate step "$\frac{1}{7}.7 = 1$,"
which is then followed by a substitution. At the other extreme, the
steps from "$7x + 11 = 102$" to "$7x = 102 - 11$" may be taken as a single
move ("bring the constant term to the other side with a change of
sign"). In short, many levels can be defined in which state-spaces
of symbol-configurations for routine algebra problems are *embedded* in
more complicated state-spaces. We note again that very different
paths are obtained when "guess-and-check" moves for finding the value
of X are examined. It is not the purpose of this section to describe
exhaustively all of the possibilities, but to lay some groundwork for
the definition of structure variables in routine algebra problems.

Diagrams such as Figure 4.13 may be constructed for more complicated problems involving more equations and more unknowns. Each
"method" for solving such systems of equations yields particular
sequences of moves. For example, there are moves based on substitution for the value of one of the unknowns in terms of the others;
there are moves based on addition or subtraction of one equation from
another. All of the considerations mentioned above about the level
of expansion or reduction of the state-space apply as well.

In general, the skilled mathematics teacher is cognizant of the
alternative paths which may lead to solutions of routine algebra
problems, as well as the alternative levels of detail with which
steps can be represented. The well-instructed student should be
able to *describe* a step such as "bring the constant term to the
other side with a change of sign" as a shortcut for a sequence of

more detailed steps, while using the shortcut naturally and freely as a single step during problem solving.

With all of these considerations in mind, let us look at the prospects for definition of task structure variables in routine problems.

Controlling for Problem Structure

In problem-solving studies, it is often important to develop routine problems which have the "same" mathematical structure, in order to study the effects of other, experimental variables. Despite the different possible choices of state-spaces, the concept of a state-space isomorphism permits us to call problem structures "the same" when the algebraic equations into which the problems may be translated are the same, except for the choice of arbitrary letters to stand for unknowns. The state-spaces for such problems will be isomorphic regardless of which level of expansion or reduction is used.

A more difficult situation arises when it is desired to characterize problem structures as "the same" when the values of numerical constants differ. The characterization then depends upon the selection of a representation. In Figure 4.13 we may distinguish between the *algebraic* moves and the *computational* moves which occur, and require two conditions in order that problem structures be "the same"--(a) that the algebraic equations into which the problems may be translated be the same, except for the choice of arbitrary letters to stand for unknowns, and except for the choice of numerical constants; however, corresponding numerals should have the same number of digits, and the single-digit numbers "0" and "1" should not be taken as equivalent to other single-digit numbers; and (b) the computational moves for the problems should be in one-to-one correspondence, requiring corresponding paths through all standard computational algorithms. These conditions that problem structures be "the same" are employed in the study by Goldin and Caldwell described in Chapter VI.

Selection of a representation other than the standard algebraic representation of solution paths may drastically alter the assertion that two problems have "the same" structure. The study by Harik described in Chapter VIII.A utilizes a "search space" representation for algebra problems which is based on "guess-and-check" moves. Changes in the values of numerical constants have a major effect on the size of the search spaces. Again we have the situation that task structure variables describe the problem *representation*, not the problem statement.

Defining Task Variables in a Standard Representation

In order to assign numerical values to structure variables such as those listed in Table 4.2, it is necessary to fix once and for all an arbitrary level at which states will be considered to be distinct, and to specify once and for all the steps which will be considered to constitute individual moves from state to state. The following conventions for a standard representation of elementary algebra problems are proposed:

(a) Symbol-configurations related by virtue of the associative property of addition or multiplication represent equivalent states. Symbol-configurations related by virtue of superfluous parentheses represent equivalent states. Thus the states "$7x + (11 - 11) = 102 - 11$," "$(7x + 11) - 11 = (102) - 11$," etc. are equivalent, and may all be abbreviated "$7x + 11 - 11 = 102 - 11$."

(b) Symbol-configurations related by virtue of the commutative property of addition or multiplication represent equivalent states.

(c) Symbol-configurations related by virtue of the symmetric property of equality represent equivalent states. Thus "$7x = 91$" is equivalent to "$91 = 7x$."

(d) A single move is required for any of the following: (1) to change both sides of an equation by adding, subtracting, multiplying by, or dividing by identical expressions (exclusive of division by zero); (2) to change both sides of an equation by adding, subtracting, multiplying by, or dividing by previously obtained equations; (3) to change both sides of an equation by performing a single operation on each side, such as negating each side, taking the reciprocal of each side, squaring each side, etc.; (4) to perform a single arithmetic computation (regardless of complexity); (5) to substitute an expression for a variable consistently throughout an equation; (6) to distribute multiplication over a sum or difference of terms; (7) to distribute a negation over a sum or difference of terms; (8) to cancel terms of opposite sign, or to cancel like factors in the numerator and denominator of a rational expression.

With the above conventions, it is possible to characterize the length of the shortest solution path in a problem such as "$7x + 11 = 102$" in an unambiguous fashion. Six steps are required, as shown on the right of Figure 4.13. With these conventions, it is also possible to *compare* problems having *different* systems of equations with respect to the lengths of their minimal solution paths, and to keep track of steps taken by the problem solver which deviate from the most direct paths. As the domain of problems under consideration is widened, additional conventions may be assumed.

Once standard conventions for describing the states and moves in elementary algebra problems have been established, we can examine any particular category of moves as they are required for solution of a problem. For example, the computational moves may be classified with reference to the paths through standard arithmetic algorithms which they require; the substitution moves may be classified with reference to the complexity of the substituted expression; the distributive moves may be classified with reference to the number of terms over which the distribution takes place; and so forth.

Comparing the Characteristics of Problem States

Another way to approach the study of structure variables in routine problems is to examine the characteristics of the corresponding systems of equations (the initial problem states), without becoming involved in tracing solution paths through a standard state-space. For example, problem states may be compared with respect to the number of equations, the number of unknowns, the operation symbols in the equations, etc. Of course, it is assumed that these characteristics have consequences for the solution paths in the state-space.

The study by Days described in Chapter VII.B classifies verbal problems by means of the characteristics of the corresponding systems of equations, as well as by the number of steps in the solution paths (using conventions for defining "steps" which are somewhat different from those proposed above).

Comparing Problems with Respect to a Solution Algorithm or Strategy

A final method which may be used to define task structure variables in routine problems is to select a particular algorithmic procedure or strategy which may be applied to a class of such problems (see above). A well-defined solution algorithm will accept the initial state as input and generate a unique solution path through a standard state-space. Correspondingly, a well-defined strategy will generate a set of possible-solution paths, which may or may not contain an actual solution path. One may then consider task variables defined from characteristics of the paths, or from characteristics of the application of the algorithm or strategy.

In this approach, task structure variables are defined not only with respect to a particular mathematical representation of the task, but also with respect to a particular method of solution within the representation.

3. Structure Variables and Problem-Solving Behavior

Symmetries and Conservation Operations

We saw earlier that the set of symmetry transformations of a state-space always forms a group. The concept of a group is the paradigm in mathematics of the methodology which has been termed "structuralist"

(Lane, 1970; Piaget, 1970). According to Piaget, a structure in the most general sense is a system or set within which certain relations or operations have been defined, embodying the properties of wholeness, transformation, and self-regulation. Structuralist methodology has been applied to fields as diverse as anthropology and linguistics as well as psychology and mathematics (Bourbaki, var.; Harris, 1951; Levi-Strauss, 1963, 1969; Piaget and Inhelder, 1969).

In Piagetian developmental psychology, the acquisition of conservation operations by children--conservation of number, volume, etc.--defines sequential stages in their cognitive development. In view of the parallel fundamental roles played by group structures in mathematics and cognitive structures in the structuralist view of developmental psychology, it is natural to try to look at the acquisition of conservation operations as equivalent to the acquisition of a group of symmetry transformations.

In a problem representation, the states may be distinguished from each other by virtue of having different discrete values for a set of variables we shall call *observables*. The observables may or may not be numerical--they may include color, position, and so forth. Let us say that a symmetry group G in the state-space *conserves* a set B of observables when, for every state s, all states which are in Gs (the orbit containing s) have exactly the same values for the observables in B. That is, the observables conserved by G are those whose values are left unchanged by the symmetry transformations of the problem. Of course, for the states to be regarded as different at all, there must be other observables which do change in value under the symmetry transformations.

Let us look at the state-space for a conservation of number task from this viewpoint. Consider the rearrangement of $\underline{n}$ objects on a table or two-dimensional surface, such as might occur during a number conservation experiment. This is not a problem-solving task *per se*, since it does not have an established set of goal states. Nevertheless, it is a highly structured task environment, for which a state-space description may be useful. A configuration of objects may be described by vector coordinates $(x_1, x_2, \ldots, x_n)$. A new configuration of objects, described by vector coordinates $(x_1', x_2', \ldots, x_n')$, may be obtained from the initial configuration by means of a rearrangement mapping or deformation which appropriately transforms the points in the two-dimensional plane. Such a rearrangement must be one-to-one, so that two objects do not wind up at the same point. It must also be surjective, so that it is invertible. Noting that any two mappings of this kind may be applied successively to yield a third, we have the fact that the set of all such mappings forms a group, G.

Now take the collection of states to be the set of all possible configurations of $\underline{n}$ objects on a two-dimensional table surface, for $\underline{n} = 0, 1, 2, \ldots$. (For the purpose of this discussion, we shall not worry about the boundary of the table.) A move consists of changing the position of a single object, or of removing an object, or of

Figure 4.14 *Rearrangements of n Objects in 2-Dimensional Space*

(a) A general rearrangement by means of a spatial deformation.

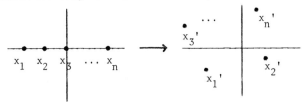

(b) Rearrangement of n objects by means of a translation mapping.

(c) Rearrangement of n objects by means of a rotation mapping.

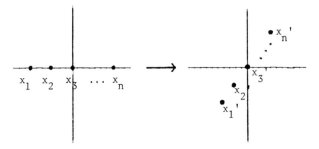

(d) Rearrangement of n objects by means of a dilation mapping.

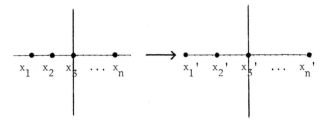

adding an object, The group defined above maps the set of states onto itself and satisfies the definition of a symmetry group for this state-space.

To say that number is conserved means that when a given state is transformed into an altered state by moving the objects around, not by adding any or taking any away, then the value of the observable "number" remains unchanged at n. Thus, the acquisition of number conservation by the child (that is, the ability to respond directly that the number of objects remains unchanged when only the positions of the objects have been altered) corresponds to the acquisition of the structure of the symmetry group G (that is, the ability to undo or invert any rearrangement transformation, and to perform two such transformations successively to obtain a third).

Mathematically, the group G has a rich structure of subgroups-- translations, rotations, reflections, dilations, etc. Some of these are illustrated in Figure 4.14. Each subgroup defines a corresponding system of equivalence classes of states. This suggests that *stages* in the acquisition of a symmetry group structure might actually correspond to the acquisition of particular subgroups. For example, a child might at some stage recognize that the number of objects remains unchanged when a configuration is merely translated a certain distance in space, without its being spread out or otherwise rearranged. If this were to occur, it would be possible to say that the subgroup of G composed of all rigid translations had been acquired as a symmetry structure. Effectively, the state-space will have been reduced *modulo* the subgroup.

Just as the group G conserves the observable "number," its subgroups conserve not only "number" but other observables as well. Thus the rigid motions conserve the distances between objects. In addition, translations conserve their orientation to the horizontal. Dilations preserve the orientations of the objects, but only the ratios of the distances between them.

In general, specification of a symmetry group in a state-space is *logically equivalent* to specification of the observables conserved by the action of the group.

The point of the above analysis is to assert that the various groups described are intrinsic to the conservation task environment, and thus may be regarded as task structure variables. For a Piagetian conservation task, we have *syntax* variables characterizing the manner in which the task is verbally described and in which questions are posed; we have *context* variables characterizing the attributes of the objects which are transformed (e.g., familiar *vs.* unfamiliar objects, or objects which have a "natural" one-to-one correspondence, such as eggs and egg-cups); and we have *structure* variables relating to the hierarchy of symmetry groups of the state-space. In much of the research on conservation tasks, the syntax and context variables are

modified in various ways, in order to verify that the observed stages
are not sensitive to these changes in the task. A less-explored
question has been the relationship, if any, of the observed stages
to the intrinsic task structure variables.

State-Space Representation of Problem-Solving Behavior

The value of state-space analysis in characterizing problem
structure suggests the utility of mapping actual problem-solving
behavior as paths through the state-space. A *path* is a sequence of
states s_1, ..., s_n such that for $\underline{i} = 1$, ..., $\underline{n}$-1, the pair (s_i, s_{i+1})
is a permitted move. A *solution path* for a problem (or subproblem)
is a path in which s_1 is the initial state and s_n is a goal (or subgoal)
state, with s_2, ..., s_{n-1} neither initial states nor goal (or subgoal)
states. Two paths within respective isomorphic problems are said to
be *congruent (modulo* the isomorphism) if one path is the image of the
other under the isomorphism.

In problem solving it is frequently the case that the solver acts
sequentially upon problem situations (states) in an external representation to generate successor states. Ideally the process can be
described by means of paths through a state-space which has been
constructed and analyzed by the (omniscient) researcher. In practice
it may not be easy or even possible to record behavior in this fashion.
The best experimental situation is a problem whose states correspond to
different discrete configurations of an actual physical device, such as
the Tower of Hanoi board utilized by Luger (see Chapter VII.C). The
study by Harik (Chapter VIII.A) is indicative of the possibilities in
an experimental situation involving paper-and-pencil computations.

The decision to represent problem-solving behavior as paths through
an external state-space is motivated by the desire to establish precisely, ahead of time, a set of *possible* behaviors which is of manage-
able size. The problem solver's *actual* behaviors then constitute a
portion of the data which need to be explained by a theory of problem
solving. Problem solvers' protocols do offer considerable information
beyond the mere description of states entered in sequence; protocol
classification schemes are discussed further in Chapters V and VIII.B.
Thus it is important to stress that, in looking at state-space paths,
we are singling out a *subset* of the available data for particular
attention.

It is worthwhile to mention a distinction between this approach
and that taken by Newell and Simon, in which the problem space for a
single problem is permitted to vary from subject to subject (see Table
4.1). Instead of "states of the problem" as a structured external
environment, they place their focus on "states of knowledge" about
the problem. Their approach thus permits, in principle, a very
detailed interpretation of an individual's problem-solving protocol
as steps in information processing. However, it also lends to their

model a somewhat *post hoc* character--no definite commitment concerning the structure of the problem space needs to be made until after a problem-solving attempt has been observed. Here we wish to regard the problem solver and the task environment as two separate, inter-acting systems. By characterizing the states of a problem representation ahead of time, we describe for a population of subjects a structured set of possible behaviors together with their environmental consequences. Then it is possible to formulate hypotheses regarding the effects of problem structure variables on these behaviors, and correspondences between the individual's "knowledge states" and the problem's state-space can be explored.

The state-space description of behavior is limited in its appli-cability to localized problem-solving episodes during which the solver understands the rules of procedure, and is able to discriminate among the different values of the perceptual variables which characterize the states. The acquisition of these rules and discriminative abili-ties prior to the commencement of problem solving is not addressed. Nevertheless, some notion of how one intends to proceed from the study of local problem-solving episodes to an understanding of the global process of cognitive change needs to be made explicit. The acquisition of symmetry group structures during problem solving may be an important means of making this transition. The fact of which symmetries are incorporated by the problem solver, and which are neglected, determines which states are treated as equivalent and which as distinct. Thus, as described in the preceding section, such manifestly global changes as the acquisition of conservation operations might be described in principle using symmetry group structures.

An approach to the study of patterns in the state-space paths generated by problem solvers is to formulate general hypotheses, repre-senting anticipated *possible* effects of problem structure variables (Goldin and Luger, 1975; Luger, 1973, 1976). Whether or not these effects *actually* occur may depend not only on problem structure, but also on syntax, content, and context variables. Even more importantly, their occurrence will depend on characteristics of the problem *solvers* (i.e., subject variables). Thus, what is proposed in the following list is not a set of hypotheses expected to hold universally, but a set of patterns which can be *tested for* in particular situations.

Hypothesis 1. In solving a problem, the subject generates non-random, *forward-directed* paths in a state-space. By a forward-directed path, we mean one which does not "double back" within the state-space; that is, the distance (as measured by the number of steps) from the initial state is non-decreasing. A special case of a forward-directed path is a *goal-directed* path, for which the distance from the "nearest" goal state is non-increasing; the hypothesis may be modified to test for goal-directed paths.

Given a decomposition of the state-space into subspaces, *Hypothe-sis 1* may be tested separately for the paths through each subspace, taking the state of entry to the subspace as the initial state for the subproblem, and using a set of pre-established subgoal states to define subgoal-directed paths. Furthermore, it may be hypothesized that, when a subgoal state is entered, the subject leaves the state in such a manner as to exit also from the subspace.

Hypothesis 2. Identifiable stages occur during problem solving corresponding to the solution of subproblems within the main problem. That is, path segments occur in the state-space which do not constitute solutions or at least are not the most direct solutions) to the main problem, but which do constitute direct solution paths for pre-specified subspaces of the state-space. Where appropriate, this hypothesis may be investigated for various alternative decompositions of the state-space into subspaces.

Hypothesis 3. When two subproblems of a problem have isomorphic state-spaces (that is, are of identical structure), the subject's paths through the respective subspaces tend to be congruent. This hypothesis would be particularly interesting to test insofar as it might depend on the problem embodiment--perceptual similarities and differences among the isomorphic subspaces.

Hypothesis 4. Given a symmetry group G of automorphisms of the state-space, and a sequence of paths corresponding to trials by a single subject, there tend to occur *pairs* of paths (for adjacent trials) which are congruent *modulo* G. Such occurrences often culminate in the immediate and direct solution of the problem. This hypothesis, intended to describe an aspect of "symmetry acquisition," is motivated by the "insight" phenomenon that changes the "Gestalt" of the problem solver.

In the event that the set of goal states is not invariant under the symmetry group (that is, taking G to include non-goal-preserving automorphisms), then there will be a class of congruent paths for which only certain ones terminate in goal states. It may then be hypothesized that the occurrence of pairs of paths congruent *modulo* G in a subject's trials is correlated with an initial move by that subject along a *non*-solution path. An illustration of *Hypothesis 4* is provided for the case of a subject solving the Tower of Hanoi problem in Figure 4.15.

Hypothesis 5. Identifiable stages occur during problem solving corresponding to the acquisition of *subgroups* of the problem symmetry group G. This hypothesis might be testable by seeking discontinuities in state-space paths, where in effect the subject has moved from a state to another state which is conjugate to the first by virtue of an automorphism. The set of automorphisms for which moves of this sort take place, if not the whole group G, could characterize a subgroup of G.

Figure 4. **15** *Paths through the Tower of Hanoi State-Space which are Congruent*
Modulo the Symmetry Automorphism (Hypothesis 4)

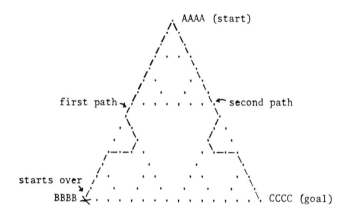

Hypothesis 6. Given two problems having isomorphic state-spaces, significant *transfer of learning* will occur from solution of one problem to solution of the other, even when the isomorphism is not perceptually apparent. Measures of success on the tasks may include the number of trials prior to successful solution, the total number of moves prior to successful solution, or the time to solution. A question of particular interest is that of how the task embodiments affect the validity of this hypothesis.

Alternatively, *Hypothesis 6* may be reformulated for problems having *homomorphic* state-spaces, and tested for each of the types of homomorphisms described earlier in this chapter.

Hypothesis 7. Given two problems having homomorphic state-spaces, it is more advantageous to present the more complex task first than to present the simpler task first, from the standpoint of measures of success on both tasks. This is one way to restate the "deep end" hypothesis of Dienes and Jeeves. Alternatively, given two problems having isomorphic state-spaces, it may be more advantageous to present first the task having the greater complexity of syntax.

While some of the above hypotheses, particularly the first few, may seem to be intuitively obvious or necessary, it is not difficult to construct mechanical problem-solving algorithms which violate any or all of them. The hypotheses are intended not as a definitive list, but as suggestions of the kinds of analysis of paths through state-spaces that are possible.

4. A Summary of Independent and Dependent Variables

In accordance with Kilpatrick's classification of problem-solving research variables described in Chapter I, the task structure variables which we have discussed are taken as the *independent* variables in the study of problem solving. We interpret the problem task, or collection of tasks, as a *measuring instrument,* designed to yield information about problem solvers either individually or collectively. A thorough analysis of task structure tells us the characteristics of the measuring instrument, permitting us to separate more effectively information which is about the task itself from information about the problem solvers.

In Table 4.3, we have attempted to outline some of the anticipated effects on problem solving of structure variables. This table summarizes many of the points already made in the chapter, and goes somewhat beyond them to anticipate directions of experimental inquiry which are included in the second portion of this book.

Some words of caution are in order. The table is *not* intended to be a complete or exhaustive listing of task structure variables, but rather to be indicative of the possibilities which are available for defining them. The anticipated effects listed are *not* being claimed

Table 4.3 *Summary of Anticipated Effects of Task Structure Variables on Problem-Solving Outcomes*

Task Variable	Anticipated Effect
Problem Complexity Variables	
(a) Total number of states	(a) With increasing total number of states, any state-space search is likely to be lengthier, increasing problem difficulty.
(b) Length of shortest solution path	(b) As the length of the shortest solution path increases, search procedures which limit the depth of search become less likely to approach goal states, and problem difficulty should increase.
(c) Number of blind alleys	(c) With an increase in the number of blind alleys, depth-first search becomes more likely to generate "dead-end" paths, and problem difficulty should increase.
(d) Number of possible first moves	(d) This variable may be indicative of the number of paths which "go wrong;" if so, problem difficulty should increase as the number of possible first moves increases. In addition, a large set of possible first moves may have a bewildering effect upon the problem-solver, discouraging trial-and-error.
(e) Number of possible first moves which lie on solution paths	(e) This variable may tend to offset the effect of (d), if random choices of first moves are more likely to be "correct."
(f) Number of possible state-space paths of length less than or equal to n, for any n	(f) This variable might describe the lengthiness of a state-space search of depth approximately equal to n.
(g) Number of goal states	(g) More goal states may be associated with a greater likelihood of a goal being encountered during a state-space search.
(h) Ratio of the number of goal states to the total number of states	(h) As this ratio increases, problems should become less difficult, since searches should be more likely to encounter goal states.
(i) Ratio of the number of possible first moves which lie on solution paths to the total number of possible first moves	(i) This ratio may describe the off-setting effects of variables (d) and (e).

continued

Table 4.3 *(continued)*

(j) Total number of solution paths

(j) As the total number of solution paths increases, depth-first search procedures should become more likely to succeed, and problems should become less difficult.

(k) Ratio of the total number of solution paths to the total number of state-space paths of length less than or equal to n, for any n (counting solution paths as distinct only if they separate in fewer than n steps)

(k) As a measure of the "density" of solution paths among all paths, this ratio may describe the likelihood of success of a state-space search having depth approximately equal to n.

Variables Defined with Respect to Algorithms or Strategies

(1) Length of a solution path generated by a particular algorithm

(1) To the extent that the algorithm resembles the problem solver's actual attempt, this variable may be predictive of problem difficulty.

(m) Number of times any particular loop in the algorithm is traversed $(0,1,2,...)$

(m) Assuming a fixed probability of error in each traversal for each subject, this variable may quantitatively predict the likelihood of specific error patterns.

(n) The number of times any particular branch point in the algorithm is crossed $(0,1,2,...)$

(n) Similar to (m).

(o) The number of times any particular operator is called for by the algorithm

(o) Similar to (m).

(p) The susceptibility to solution of the problem with respect to a particular strategy

(p) This variable may predict the effect (or lack of it) of prior instruction in the strategy in question.

(q) The minimum number of steps in a solution path generated by the strategy.

(q) A whole set of variables such as this one should be predictive of the ease or difficulty with which various problems are solved using the strategy.

continued

Table 4.3 *(continued)*

Variables Describing the Initial State
in a Standard Representation

(r) Number of equations and unknowns

(r) Variables such as these are indicative of more or less complex paths generated by standard algorithms, and thus may be predictive of problem difficulty without the need for detailed algorithmic or state-space analysis.

(s) Number of occurrences of any particular operation $(0,1,2,...)$

(s) Operations occurring explicitly within the initial state are likely to be called for by standard algorithms. Thus this variable may be associated with (o).

(t) Number of parentheses

(t) Each pair of parentheses may be associated with the use of particular operations by standard algorithms (the distributive property, for example).

Symmetry and Subproblem Characteristics

(u) Number of elements in the symmetry group G

(u) As this variable increases, problems possess more and more symmetry, and the likelihood of utilization of the symmetry by the problem solver should grow.

(v) Equivalence classes of states under the action of G

(v) These states may come to be treated as equivalent by problem solvers during the course of problem solving.

(w) Subgroups of G

(w) The infrastructure of subgroups may be predictive of stages during problem solving, corresponding to partial recognition of the problem symmetry by the solver.

(x) Forward-backward symmetry

(x) Problems without forward-backward symmetry may yield to "working backward"; while problems with this symmetry may evoke the technique of working forward a certain number of steps, working backward along the corresponding path, and connecting in the middle.

(y) Subspace decompositions of the state-space

(y) Subspace decompositions may be predictive of stages during problem-solving corresponding to the solution of particular subproblems.

continued

Table 4.3 *(continued)*

(z) Subspace decompositions into mutually isomorphic subproblems

(z) Stages during problem-solving may correspond to the solution of isomorphism classes of subproblems.

Variables Describing Relationships Between Problems

(a') Existence of an isomorphism between problem state-spaces

(a') Such an isomorphism may predict transfer of learning from one problem-solving experience to another. Consistency of strategy usage may be examined.

(b') Existence of a homomorphism between problem state-spaces

(b') Homomorphic relationships may also be predictive of learning transfer. The type of homomorphism (injective, surjective, embedding, etc.) may affect transfer in specific ways (e.g. the "deep end" hypothesis).

to occur under all or even most circumstances, but are proposed as effects which *might* be observed under some conditions when other task variables, unrelated to the specific variable under discussion, are held constant.

Table 4.3 contains references to two categories of *dependent* variables. Product variables include measures of task *difficulty*, such as the number of correct solutions by a given population of subjects, the mean time to solution, or the mean number of trials to solution. Process variables include measures of the *methods* used in problem solving.

Many of the dependent variables are examined in the studies which are described in the second portion of this book. One branch of research examines the effects of task structure variables on task difficulty (Days, Chapter VII.B). A second branch of research studies transfer of learning. Here the independent variables are the task variables of a *pair* of tasks, together with the order of presentation; the dependent variables are measures of success on the two tasks (Waters, Chapter VII.A; Luger, Chapter VII.C). Some process variables can be studied by examining paths through the state-space corresponding to subjects' behaviors (Luger, Chapter VII.C; Harik, Chapter VIII.A). Other process variables include strategy scores and heuristic behavior scores (Waters, Chapter VII.A; Harik, Chapter VIII.A; Lucas et al., Chapter VIII.B).

These studies taken collectively represent a tiny beginning in the effort to investigate systematically the effects of task structure variables, in conjunction with other factors, on problem-solving outcomes.

V.

Heuristic Processes as Task Variables

by

C. Edwin McClintock
Florida International University
Miami, Florida

Heuristic reasoning and the behaviors that reflect it are generally considered to be characteristics of the problem solver. However, it is suggested in this chapter that heuristic processes may be viewed from another standpoint as inherent in mathematical problems. The nature and degree of this inherency varies from problem to problem. For some problems the inherency may be fairly easily characterized, based on a logical analysis of the problem structure. For example, the three-ring Tower of Hanoi problem must be "accomplished" several times in the process of solving the four-ring Tower of Hanoi problem, within the representation discussed in Chapter IV. In this sense, the four-ring problem "contains" the heuristic process called "subproblem decomposition." This does not imply that a problem solver necessarily employs that process consciously in solving the problem, only that it is a reasonable and plausible one based on the logical analysis of the puzzle.

For other problems, heuristic processes appear to be less task specific and more related to the problem solver. Even then, however, the task environment provides the stimulus that sets the course of reasoning. It is the interaction between the mental operations of the problem solver and the task itself that evokes the heuristic processes that occur during the problem-solving episode.

Section 1 of this chapter reviews the related research, which is described under three headings. *Theoretical* perspectives refer to the characterization of heuristics from the standpoint of effective or efficient problem solving. *Experimental* perspectives refer to the investigations in controlled studies of the use and efficacy of heuristic processes. *Exploratory* investigations include the clinical study of the learning and teaching of heuristics. In the author's view, all three types of research are equally important and necessary to progress in our understanding of problem solving. This section includes a description of various techniques for coding and recording problem-solving processes, techniques carried considerably further in Chapter VIII.B of the present book.

Section 2 of this chapter offers a broad classification of heuristic processes in accordance with the distinction between problem statements and problem representations described in Chapter I (Figure 1.1).

Table 5.1 *Definitions and Descriptions of "Heuristic"*

AUTHOR

We can therefore say that insistent analysis of the situation, *especially the endeavor to vary the appropriate elements sub specie of the goal* must belong to the essential nature of a solution through thinking. We shall call such relatively general procedures *heuristic methods of thinking* (1945, p. 20). Duncker

Heuristic reasoning is reasoning, not regarded as final and strict, but as provisional and plausible only, whose purpose it is to discover the solution of the present problem (1957, p. 113). Polya

Heuristic, or heuretic, or *ars inveniendi* was the name of a certain branch of study, not very clearly circumscribed, belonging to logic, or to philosophy, or to psychology.... The aim of heuristic is to study the methods and rules of discovery and invention (1957, p. 112). Polya

Modern heuristic endeavors to understand the process of solving problems, especially the *mental operations typically useful in* this process (1957, pp. 129-130). Polya

I wish to call *heuristics* the study . . . of means and methods of problem solving.... I am trying . . . to entice the reader to do problems and to think about the means and methods he uses in doing them (1962, p. vi). Polya

We shall consider that a heuristic method (or a heuristic, to use the noun form) is a procedure that may lead us to a shortcut to the goal we seek or it may lead us down a blind alley. It is impossible to predict the end result until the heuristic has been applied and the results checked by formal processes of reasoning. If a method does not have this characteristic that it may lead us astray, we would not call it heuristic, but rather an algorithm. The reason for using heuristics rather than algorithms is that they may lead us more quickly to our goal and they allow us to venture by machine into areas where there are no algorithms (1958, p. 337). Gelernter and Rochester

continued

Table 5.1 *continued*

We use the term heuristics to denote any principle or
device that contributes to the reduction in the average   Newell, Shaw,
search to solution (1959a).   and Simon

All that can be said for a useful heuristic is that it
offers solutions which are good enough most of the   Feigenbaum
time (1963, p. 6).   and Feldman

An heuristic is a decision mechanism, a way of behaving,
which usually leads to desired outcomes, but with no
guarantee of success. It is plausible in nature, giving
guidance in the discovery of a solution (1967, p. 3).   Wilson

An heuristic is any device, technique, rule of thumb,
etc. that improves problem solving performance (1967,
p. 19).   Kilpatrick

Heuristics may be described as rules for selecting
search paths through a problem space; the theory of
problem solving is concerned with systems of heuristics
or methods of search which will exploit the information
in the task environment (1974, p. 7).   Kantowski

An heuristic is a path a problem solver chooses in his
search for a solution (1974, p. 103).   Kantowski

In Section 3, the inherency of heuristic processes in problem tasks is explored, and the interactions of syntax, content, context, and structure variables with heuristic behaviors are discussed.

1. Review of Research on Heuristic Processes

Theoretical Perspectives

The work of Polya toward resurrecting the ancient, ill-defined discipline called "heuristics" is the natural beginning point of a review of theoretical aspects of heuristic processes. The terms "heuristic" and "heuristic process" have been defined in a variety of ways, as Table 5.1 will reveal. Polya, a renowned research mathematician, teacher *par excellence*, and artist in solving problems and in teaching others to solve problems, has contributed several of these definitions.

At the very core of the subject "heuristics" is the disciplined attempt to understand the process of human reasoning. The third definition by Polya in Table 5.1 suggests this notion. Further, related to the "...mental operations typically useful in this process...," Polya identifies twelve principal articles in his "Short Dictionary of Heuristic" (1957, p. 37ff, pp. 129-130):

1. Analogy
2. Auxiliary Elements
3. Auxiliary Problems
4. Decomposing and Recombining
5. Definition
6. Generalization
7. Induction and Mathematical Induction
8. *Reductio ad absurdum* and indirect proof
9. Specialization
10. Symmetry
11. Variation of the Problem
12. Working Backwards

It is within the context of these twelve principal articles that different aspects of a problem are considered in turn, and that the mental operations characterizing *heuristic* produce a provisional and plausible guess as to the solution. However, these provisional and plausible guessing processes should, according to Polya, be seen as distinct from and complementary to rigorous proof; they should never be confused with nor sold as a replacement for strict and formally justified solutions (1957, pp. 113-130).

In addition to the construct of reasoning processes, another sense in which the term "heuristic" is used by Polya is that of a means to the end of developing the mental operations typically useful in the heuristic reasoning process. Wilson (1967, p. 6) indicates that "His (Polya's) list of questions may be regarded as a set of heuristics." Examples of such questions are: (a) What is the unknown? (b) Do you know a related problem? (c) Can you see clearly that the step is correct? (d) Can you derive the result differently? (See Ch. I, Table 1.2 for this list.) The list is structured around the four stages of problem solving:

1. Understanding the problem

2. Devising a plan

3. Carrying out the plan

4. Looking back

They represent Polya's classification of the major heuristic processes of problem solving. Two important points need to be emphasized about this model. First, there is no sequence of processes for solution implied by this model. Secondly, the questions contained in this model are heuristic processes only in the sense that they may initiate a mental operation or a sequence of mental operations typically useful in the problem-solving process. As Polya has stated it, the intent of these heuristic questions is that

> The student may absorb a few of the questions of our list so well that he is finally able to put to himself the right question in the right moment and perform the corresponding mental operation naturally and vigorously. (1957, p. 4)

The fourth of Polya's definitions in Table 5.1 suggests the importance Polya attaches to the relationship between heuristic processes and problem solving. It also suggests the hypothesis that studying processes of problem solving is essential for effective use and transfer of those processes. This is much like the view expressed by Henderson and Pingry (1953):

> Unless students study the process of solving problems as an end in itself there is scant likelihood that they will learn the generalization which will enable them to transfer their ability to solve problems to new problems as they arise. (p. 233)

Polya offers much to the conception of teaching as an art. He focuses upon the development of the mental operations that form the basis of invention and discovery in his illustrations and discussion of teaching. Further, he repeatedly develops the theme of "independent thinking" as the aim of instruction and suggests the importance of informal, intuitive thought along with formal, finished forms of mathematics. This theme is a characteristic corollary to heuristic teaching. Polya emphasizes its use in teaching in many of his works as exemplified in the following:

Trying to prove formally what is seen intuitively and to see
intuitively what is proved formally is an invigorating mental
exercise. (1957, p. 72)

Information Processing Systems

Drawing from the foundations of Polya, Newell and Simon (1971,
1972) have proposed a theory of problem solving for which heuristic
processes are fundamental elements. Their contribution to Artificial
Intelligence through, particularly, General Problem Solver (GPS), and
their subsequent empirical comparison (using protocols of human subjects "thinking aloud") with an alternate Information Processing System
(IPS) has led to their IPS theory of problem solving, as discussed in
Chapter IV. It has provided a substantial underpinning for mathematical problem solving. Based on symbol manipulation and "thinking in
symbols," this information processing theory bears some similarity to
the problem-solving theory of Gestalt psychologists (especially Wertheimer, 1959) in that past experience and its role in ongoing problem
solving are a central part of both theories (Newell and Simon, 1959,
p. 11; Wertheimer, 1959, p. 68). The nature of the past experience
and its organization represent the main difference in these two views
of problem solving. Whereas a sudden, ill-defined reorganization of
elements of experience is purported, in the Gestalt view to occur
and to provide bursts of insight, Newell and Simon suggest that basic
processes occur in an orderly, sequenced manner and represent the postulated organization of past experiences. The basic processes such as
reading and comparing symbols, transforming symbol structures, and
associating one symbol with another are postulated to exist and are
of interest in information processing; however, the crux is organization
of experience. This organization arises from ordering these basic processes into a hierarchy of operations in problem solving. These
operators of mathematical problem solving are the fundamental components
of an IPS *program*. A *program*, in IPS language, is a hierarchically
ordered set of methods related to goal types, and executive control mechanisms for executing the methods and evaluating the achievement of the
methods with respect to the goal (see Newell, Shaw, and Simon, 1959b,
p. 7 for an example and explanation of a *program*).

Similarly, heuristic processes are key elements of problem-solving
programs. Efficiency and organizational simplicity have depended upon
and paralleled the nature of the heuristic processes embedded in the
program.

The influence of Polya on the work of researchers involving the
simulation of human thought is expressed well in this comment by
Gelernter (1963):

A machine that functions under the full set of principles
indicated by Polya would be a formidable problem solver in
mathematics.... (p. 137)

Miller, Galanter, and Pribram (1960, p. 16) speak continually of the
impact of Polya and the influences of Newell, Shaw, and Simon as they
describe the role of heuristic processes on "the plan," a crucial
element in computer simulation of human problem solving. The planning heuristics and means-ends analysis are two very general systems
of heuristic processes developed by Newell, Shaw, and Simon; these
will be discussed later. As such, they are important elements of a
theory of problem solving. Newell, Shaw, and Simon (1959) define
heuristic processes as follows: "We use the term *heuristics* to denote
any principle or device that contributes to the reduction in the average search to solution" (p. 22). In so doing, they are implying that
problem-solving processes are viewed as search processes in which the
appropriate solution is being sought from the space of possible solutions. Heuristic processes are, then, those efficient search processes
that reduce the field of search to a plausible set of alternatives and
that order and sequence the search.

To clarify further the conception of heuristics in the sense of
use in IPS, we refer to the "problem space" of Newell and Simon (Table 4.1).
It bears a striking resemblance to "state space" for a problem, as
described in Chapter IV. Like the state-space for a problem, problem
space depends upon the task environment, which in turn is shaped into
the subject's internal representation of the problem.

The internal representation that is set up by a problem solver is
the problem space for that problem solver. As such (until another
internal representation replaces it), it becomes the space in which
the problem-solving activity takes place. Such a search space is, of
course, dependent upon the knowledge and experience of the problem solver. Problem solving, in this theoretical view, becomes a
search for solution(s) in the space of possible solutions. Heuristic
processes, then, are rule-governed processes that guide the selection
of the search path. In a program of artificial intelligence research
may be found the combination of plausible methods and an executive
structure that selects and sequences the plausible methods. Thus, a
program incorporates methods, algorithms, and the like; but, more
importantly it incorporates heuristic processes as a means of making
methods and algorithms more efficient and more effective.

The aspect of the decision mechanism as a plausible, yet fallible,
mechanism is expressed by Gelernter and Rochester (1958) in the following way:

> We shall consider that a *heuristic method* (or a heuristic, to
> use the noun form) is a procedure that may lead us to a short
> cut to the goal we seek or it may lead us down a blind alley.
> It is impossible to predict the end result until the heuris-
> tic has been applied and the results checked by formal
> processes of reasoning. If a method does not have this
> characteristic that it may lead us astray, we would not call
> it heuristic, but rather an algorithm. The reason for using
> heuristics rather than algorithms is that they may lead us
> more quickly to our goal and they allow us to venture by
> machine into areas where there are no algorithms. (p. 337)

In a sense, then, Newell, Shaw, and Simon define algorithms "into" heuristic processes, while Gelernter and Rochester exclude algorithms from the class of heuristic processes. There are advantages and disadvantages with both conceptions. Further, the question cannot be resolved on logical grounds nor on grounds of "profit," for the "gray area" makes the distinction difficult if not impossible. (For a discussion of this issue, see Kilpatrick, 1967, pp. 9-20; Landa, 1976a, pp. 29-39.)

Following the further development of the conception of heuristic processes, we return to a discussion of computer programs that initially appeared to model human problem-solving behavior in "line by line" comparison (see Kleinmuntz, 1966). An examination of the heuristic processes embedded in these machines and the extent to which heuristic programming allows for the development of efficiency and organizational simplicity will be made.

In contrast to the more specific types of programs and more task-specific heuristic processes embedded in programs such as "Artificial Geometer," "Student," and "Logic Theorist," the more sophisticated "General Problem Solver" (GPS) employs two very general systems of heuristic processes as well as more task-specific systems of heuristics. Developed by Newell, Shaw, and Simon, GPS uses *planning heuristics, means-ends analysis,* and *task-specific heuristics.*

The systems of *planning heuristics* embedded in GPS easily evolve from Polya's model. Two vital phases of that model for problem solving involve planning; one involves "developing a plan" and the other involves "carrying out the plan." From Polya's perspective, a plan involves "...knowing at least in outline, which calculations, computations, or constructions we have to perform in order to obtain the unknown" (Polya, 1957, pp. 8-9).

In Newell, Shaw, and Simon's theory of problem solving, planning heuristics play a significant role. As a system of heuristic processes, the planning processes allow for the construction of a potential solution in an abstract form prior to carrying out the concrete detailed solution. Newell, Shaw, and Simon (1959) speak of it as being farsighted (as opposed to means-ends analysis which "sees" one step ahead). The original conception of the planning heuristics is described by Newell, Shaw, and Simon as follows:

> (a) abstracting by omitting certain details of the original objects and operators, (b) forming the corresponding problem in the abstract task environment, (c) when the abstract problem has been solved, using its solution to provide a plan for solving the original problem, (d) translating the plan back into the original task environment and executing it. (pp. 18-22)

Specific features that make the planning heuristics (in the strict IPS sense) particularly powerful are (1) the provision of auxiliary problem capability in a different task environment, and (2) the fact that the plan, along with its ordered set of subproblems, is simpler in composite (as measured by the number of total steps to solution) than the original problem. This is assured through the embedded heuristic principle:

> The principle of subgoal reduction. Make progress by substituting for the achievement of a goal the achievement of a set of easier subgoals. (p. 8)

This brief review of the planning heuristics indicates its generality and importance. The generality is evident through the embedding within the planning heuristic of means-ends analysis, the use of auxiliary problems, and certain aspects of "learning."

From one perspective, the planning heuristics system may be the most powerful system that exists in the IPS problem-solving model and will probably remain so until the *learning heuristics* system moves beyond the stage of rote learning (Slagle, 1971).

Much of Polya's writing centers on *means-ends analysis*. For example, the idea of decomposing and recombining as a general strategy is based in this heuristic approach. Another related strategy involves analyzing the solution process of a simpler related problem so that the method or the result may be applied to the problem under investigation. A third major technique that Polya recommends is that of solving special cases of the problem so as to establish a pattern that becomes a means to the end of the solution to the original problem.

Duncker (1945) considers the heuristic method of reasoning to be fundamentally that of replacing a problem goal with a series of easier subgoals. This, he says, is the critical element of thinking. Further, he declares that "the solution of a new problem typically takes place in successive phases which . . . have in retrospect, the character of a solution, and in prospect, that of a problem" (p. 21). This breaking of a problem into subproblems and the process that shows the retrospective view of a solution and the new end of another problem characterize means-ends analysis for Duncker. It is in these combined senses of means-ends heuristics that Newell, Shaw, and Simon evolved means-ends heuristics in GPS.

As one of the two strategic heuristic principles in GPS, Newell, Shaw, and Simon (1959) discuss the general principle implicit in means-ends heuristics. This principle is that of replacing a goal by the achievement of a sequence of easier subgoals. They list three basic elements of means-ends analysis as outlined below:

1. If the goal is not obvious from the given, determine the essential differences between given situation and goal situation.

2. Choose appropriate operators based on the changes they make in situations and the features that remain unchanged,

in order to reduce the differences between given and
goal.

3. Order the differences on difficulty and apply operators
to the ordered situations in such a manner that the new
situation resulting from the application of an operation replaces the difficulty with a lesser difficulty.

The process implicit in means-ends analysis is obviously iterative.
One typical form of iteration is that of selecting a subgoal, applying
an appropriate operator, evaluating the resulting state, reordering the
situations on difficulty, selecting another subgoal, and so on. Thus,
the generality of the means-ends process has a sense of mathematical
structural reasoning inherent within it.

Wickelgren's Classification of Methods

The work of Wickelgren (1974) in the area of problem solving (mathematics, science, engineering, etc.) has obviously been greatly influenced
by the information processing theorists and by Polya. As Wickelgren
himself states it:

My greatest intellectual debts are to Allen Newell, Herbert
Simon, and George Polya. Newell and Simon's analyses of
problems and problem solving constituted my starting point
. . . many other good ideas were taken more or less directly
from Polya, . . . rich source(s) of methods and a stimulus
for thought. (pp. ix-x)

In his book, Wickelgren illustrates and systematizes seven basic methods
of solving mathematical problems. Each of these methods is either a
heuristic process in the IPS sense of the concept or in Polya's sense
of the concept. The methods that he analyzes are (1) inference, (2)
classification of action sequences, (3) state evaluation and hill climbing, (4) subgoals, (5) contradiction, (6) working backward, and (7)
relations between problems. These methods are defined in Tables 5.2 and 5.3.

Wickelgren says he ". . . aims to guide you to discover how to
apply general problem-solving methods to a rich variety of problems"
(p. xi). With the intent of improving one's ability to solve problems
through *teaching by example*, Wickelgren shares style, method, and purpose with Polya. On the other hand, the contribution of his work to
"Elements of a Theory of Problems" is more explicit than that of other
authors, including Polya, though admittedly far from precise. Wickelgren, then, in a rudimentary way focuses very clearly upon the problem,
the task itself, along with its interrelationship to heuristic processes, as a key element in ". . . A Theory of Problems and Problem
Solving."

The first method Wickelgren describes is the one he says is the
natural beginning point for attempts to solve a problem, the method of
inference. This method is definitely in the category of heuristic

advice. It suggests characteristics of the task that imply a way of selecting and ordering plausible alternatives in the search. In essence, Wickelgren suggests as heuristic advice prioritizing possible inferences that can be drawn. The ordering begins with the most productive inference in "like situations"; at the same time, the suggestion is made that certain types of "insight problems" are considered challenging simply because they are most easily solved by drawing a "low priority" inference.

In a discussion on "Classification of Action Sequences" Wickelgren distinguishes among (a) Random Trial and Error, (b) Systematic Trial and Error, and (c) Classificatory Trial and Error, as is indicated in Table 5.2. The three basic trial-and-error methods Wickelgren describes are hierarchically arranged with respect to the general IPS heuristic precept, ordered devices for reducing the average search to solution. The implications of this method for teaching are clear. For a theory of problems, the implications center upon the characteristics of the problem as a means of producing equivalent representations for seeing order or symmetry and for choosing the most appropriate "equivalent action sequence."

The method related to "State Evaluation and Hill Climbing" is a second method designed to reduce the amount of search necessary for achieving the solution. This method has, as its description suggests, two separate but related concepts as indicated in Table 5.2. Clearly this idea of "hill climbing" is related to the IPS heuristic principle: "Make progress by substituting for the achievement of a goal the achievement of a set of easier subgoals (the principle of subgoal reduction; Newell, Shaw, and Simon, 1959, p. 8). Wickelgren operationalized this principle to make it applicable outside of computer programs.

The fourth problem-solving method described by Wickelgren is that of subgoals. This method

is advantageous for attacking problems that require a
sequence of more than two or three actions to solve...
If the problem seems likely to be a multistep rather than
insight problem, it is usually advantageous to spend more
time trying to generate plausible subgoals, because of the
enormous power of the method. (pp. 92-93)

Wickelgren gives some very direct clues for the type of task variables that will induce the use of this heuristic process. Classes of examples implied by his advice are: (1) multi-step arithmetic problems, (2) problems of two (or more) loci in geometry, (3) alphanumeric problems, and (4) some logic problems.

The fifth problem-solving method described is the method of contradiction. This method, which essentially involves proving that some goal(s) cannot be obtained from the givens, is described as having four strategies (see Table 5.2).

Table 5.2 *Problem Solving Methods According to Wickelgren (1974)*

INFERENCE

> Draw inferences from explicitly or implicitly presented infor-
> mation that satisfy one or both of the following two criteria:
> (a) the inferences have frequently been made in the past from
> the same type of information; (b) the inferences are connected
> with the properties (variables, terms, expressions, and so on)
> that appear in the goal, the givens, or inferences from the
> goal and the givens (p. 23).

CLASSIFICATION OF ACTION SEQUENCES

> Random Trial and Error: Applying the allowable operations to
> the givens in the problem . . . analogous to random sampling
> with replacement . . .

> Systematic Trial and Error: A generation method that auto-
> matically produces a mutually exclusive and exhaustive listing
> of all sequences of actions up to some maximum length . . .
> analogous to random sampling without replacement . . .

> Classificatory Trial and Error: The organization of sequences
> of actions into classes that are equivalent (or probably equiv-
> alent) with respect to the solution of the problem (pp. 46-47).

STATE EVALUATION AND HILL CLIMBING

> Defining an "evaluation function" over all states, including
> the goal state.

> Choosing actions at any given state that achieves a next state
> with an evaluation closer to that of the goal (p. 67).

SUBGOALS

> Defining subgoals in order to facilitate solving the original
> problem . . . [or] "analyzing a problem into subproblems" or
> "breaking a problem into parts." In essence, the purpose is
> to replace a single difficult problem with two or more simpler
> problems (p. 91).

continued

Table 5.2 *continued*

CONTRADICTION

    Indirect Proof: To assume that the contrary is true and
show that the contrary statement in combination with the
given results in a contradiction (p. 111).

    Multiple Choice--Small Search Space: In the solution of
. . . problems [for which we] are guaranteed that exactly
one of a small set of alternative goals is consistent
with the given information, systematically examine each
and derive a contradiction for all but one of them (p. 115).

    Classificatory Contradiction--Large Search Space: Use some
efficient search strategy for contradicting large subgroups of alternative goals at a time (p. 126).

    Iterative Contradiction in Infinite Search Spaces

    [A method of contradiction] . . . used in problems that
have an infinite number of possible solutions . . . [in
which we] rule out large or infinite classes of alternatives . . . (p. 133).

WORKING BACKWARDS

    We start with the goal, but instead of drawing inferences
from it, we try to guess a preceding statement or statements that, taken together, would imply the goal statement.
Hence, the direction of inferences is the same as working
forward--namely, from the given information to the goal.
We start at the end point and try to determine preceding
statements, which need not necessarily be given statements
but which, when taken together, will produce the goal.
Then we try to determine statements that will determine
those statements, gradually working our way back. We hope
to arrive at given information that is sufficient to derive
everything in between the givens and the goal (pp. 137-138).

The sixth method described by Wickelgren is the method of working backwards. It is what Pappus has called "analysis" (see Polya, 1957, pp. 141-147) and is suggested as plausibly useful whenever a task satisfies two conditions. One of these "... is that the problem should have *a uniquely defined goal*," while the other is that the operations should be unitary and one-to-one. Task variables that suggest this heuristic process are rather explicit in these two stated characteristics and imply its applicability to such broad classes of problems as geometric proofs, inequalities, and algebraic and trigonometric identities. Problems of the "to find" classification are not as apt to yield to working backwards, although Wickelgren presents several such problems, such as the "Nim" family of games, in his exposition.

Wickelgren further suggests that there are five fundamental relationships between pairs of problems. These are shown in Table 5.3.

Suffice it to say that for similar problems the method(s) of solving one generally provide(s) a substantial amount of useful information about the method(s) of solving the other. As the description of similar problems (see Table 5.3) implies, the task variables involved change in content (quantities) rather than in structure. However, problems are also considered "similar" whenever minor structure characteristics are varied. In particular, variations of problems that preserve most essential elements and relations also preserve, generally, processes appropriate for solution.

Wickelgren does not completely characterize *similar problems*, although he gives a heuristic discussion of ways one problem may be simpler than another. It is frequently the case, for simpler problem creation, that the preservation of abstract relationships among givens and operations is more important than the preservation of more concrete similarities. An example of a way to create simpler problems is the heuristic process "create a special case."

The logical inverse of "simpler problems" is "more complex problems." One can, generally, "invert" the heuristic advice for working with simpler problems in order to obtain appropriate advice for "more complex problems." Thus, for example, a way to create a more complex problem is the heuristic process "generalize."

The significance of generalization to problem solving as it relates to problem relationships is threefold, in Wickelgren's view.

First, as a necessary part of problem solving, we usually abstract from a problem certain properties belonging to a more general class of problems and thus relevant for determining the previously established principles for solving our present problem. Second . . . it is often useful to consider whether we could generalize a solution from it [our problem] to a wider class of problems, in order to derive a more general conclusion . . . . Third, it may be useful to pose and attempt to solve a more general problem prior to working on the current problem . . . . (p. 180)

Table 5.3 *Relations Between Problems According to Wickelgren (1974,*
         pp. 153-168)

Equivalent problem: Problems that differ only with respect
to the names attached to different elements of the problem,
but all of whose relations and operations are identical . . .
they are completely analogous or *isomorphic*.

Unrelated Problems: Problems that are unrelated have no
elements in common.

Similar Problems: Problems are similar if they . . . differ
only in the quantities of certain elements of the problem
. . . [and have] all of the qualitative or structural characteristics . . . identical or when they are . . . partly
analogous problems in which the structure is somewhat different
in the two problems being compared but still highly similar.

Simpler Problems: Problem a is simpler than problem b (a and
b may well be similar) implies that many of the methods used
in solving a are also methods useful in solving b (the more
complex problem may require one or a few additional methods);
simplicity generally relates to the number of different elements
or complications, but it is by no means a simple quantitative
idea.

More Complex Problems: Posing a problem that is more complex
is the logical inverse of posing a problem that is simpler
than the given problem.

In his discussion of "Relations Between Problems," the combined influence of IPS and Polya is clear. From his discussion of isomorphic problems (cf. Chapter IV) to his discussion of generalization and specialization, the underlying idea of developing a theory of problems is dominant. The nature of Wickelgren's presentation is that of heuristic advice; thus, he is implying a close tie between a theory of problems (of task variables) and heuristic processes.

Research Perspectives (Experimental)

Several studies of the comparative effectiveness of heuristic methods and other methods, or comparisons of one heuristic approach to another heuristic approach, have been conducted. Three of these will be reviewed here. Ashton (1962) performed an experiment involving ten ninth-grade algebra classes. One of two classes of students of above average ability in each of five schools was taught to use heuristic methods of solving algebra problems while the other was taught the "textbook" method. In each school the same teacher taught both contrasting methods.

The heuristic method consisted of aiding students in the discovery of the solutions of algebra problems through suggesting questions from Polya's list. The "textbook" method provided model solutions or problem types for imitation and practice, with model solutions being presented by the teacher and by the textbook. The hypothesis that students taught to solve algebra problems by using Polya's heuristic processes would, after ten weeks of treatment, show significantly greater gains in solving problems than those using the "textbook" method was sustained by the results of the one-tailed t-test for independent samples. Five separate t-tests, one for each of the five schools, were reported; each showed significant differences in gain scores favoring the heuristic method (one was significant only at $p = .07$).

Ashton points out that the subjects of this experiment were all females. This limitation, as well as the fact that intact classes were used and individual subjects were considered as the experimental unit rather than classes, must be noted.

Each of two other studies proposed to determine the effects of instructing subjects in the use of general versus task-specific heuristic processes. These studies, by Wilson (1967) and Smith (1973), hypothesized that instruction in the use of general heuristic processes would facilitate transfer to tasks dissimilar to those of instruction, while instruction in task-specific heuristic processes (advice not readily generalizable) would be more useful in solving problems similar to those encountered in instruction. In each experiment, the main dependent variables were time to solution and the number of correct and relevant steps to solution.

Wilson developed two units of self-instructional materials "algebra-proofs" and "expressions" (logic proofs), with each unit

containing three sets: a set on means-ends analysis and one on planning
heuristic processes (with characteristics of the concepts paralleling
those of Newell, Shaw, and Simon), as well as one set on task-specific
heuristic processes. These variables, along with the order of presentations of instructional tasks, constituted the three independent variables of this experiment. Thus, a 3x3x2 factorial design with three
levels of training in the "expressions" task (specific, means-ends,
and planning), three levels of training in the algebra task (specific,
means-ends, and planning), and two levels of "order" (expressions-
algebra, algebra-expressions) were used. The problem-solving tasks
that served as posttests were the Expressions Task, Algebra Task, and
Functions Task; transfer tests used as posttests were the Geometry Tests,
Box 9 Test, Maps Test, and Pentominoes Test.

One-hundred forty-four high school students who had completed a
course of algebra and a course of geometry served as the subjects of
this experiment. Analysis on fourteen dependent measures (seven for
time; seven for correct steps) yielded the following results:

1. Main effects were found for:

   A. "order" on the Expressions Task on both the time and
      correct steps favored the algebra-expressions order.

   B. level of heuristic processes on the Algebra Task
      favored planning heuristic processes over both other
      forms on the time.

   C. level of heuristic processes on the Box 9 Test favored
      planning and means-ends processes over task-specific
      processes on the time variable.

2. Interaction occurred on some dependent measure for each
   combination of independent variables.

The general hypothesis was not supported.

The study done by Smith was similar in many ways to that of Wilson.
The general conception of the study was to "strengthen" the instructional
aspects of the Wilson study. This was done by using three rather than
two different task environments of problems representing the general and
task-specific heuristic processes. Further, the planning heuristic process became the only form of general heuristic processes so that greater
emphasis could be placed on the varied ways that this process could be
used.

The Smith study, which involved college subjects (but with only
one year of algebra and one year of geometry as mathematics background),
employed a 2x3x3 factorial design. Two levels of heuristic processes
(planning and task-specific); three levels of order of presentation
(geometry/logic/Boolean algebra, geometry/Boolean algebra/logic, and
Boolean algebra/geometry/logic), and three levels of order of tests

(same as order of presentation) constituted the treatment. In addition
to learning tests that contained problems related to the instructional
units, Smith administered two transfer tests. One of the transfer tests
was similar to Wilson's Functions Test, while the other involved transformation tasks on ordered triples of integers. Again "time" and
"number of correct, relevant steps toward solution" were the dependent
variables.

The results of the analysis of data showed that the task-specific
instructional group solved significantly more logic problems and completed the logic test and the Boolean algebra test significantly faster;
the general heuristic processes instructional group completed the
geometry test significantly faster. No other main or interaction
effects were significant. In addition to the data described above,
Smith obtained information through questionnaires and interviews.
From this evidence, Smith concluded that few subjects used the heuristic advice on transfer problems, but even those who did not use such
advice did use other heuristic processes in the solution of the test
problems.

Research Perspectives (Exploratory)

The review of the research literature will be limited to those
studies that have investigated heuristic behavior variables. It will
attempt to determine (1) what heuristic processes have been shown to
"exist" in the process sequences of subjects, and (2) what heuristic
behaviors have been developed as a result of heuristic instruction.
In the review, both experimental and empirical-behavioral research
will be included. In a later section, a discussion of the progress
that has been made toward developing process-sequence coding systems
and process-product scoring schemes will be pursued.

The use of "thinking aloud" techniques for acquiring data (to be
discussed later) has been employed by researchers to capture the nature
of the heuristic processes that subjects may have acquired, independen-
dently (supposedly) of formal and systematic study of heuristic
processes. Additionally, it has been used by some researchers who
attempted to monitor the development of subjects' use of heuristic
processes during instruction. Duncker (1945) used thinking-aloud
techniques to obtain data in an attempt to determine how and in what
ways solutions of problems are attained from a problem environment. His selection of problems was quite atypical of research in the
1930s and 1940s in that the problems would be classified as non-routine
mathematical and practical problems. They were also probably more
difficult than those used in the typical research of that day in that
they required the invention of solution processes while at the same
time assumed mathematical and practical knowledge. Examples of problems posed by Duncker include:

> 5.1 *For a clock to go accurately, the swing of the pendu-
> lum must be strictly regular. The duration of a*

*pendulum's swing depends, among other things, on
its length, and this of course in turn on the temperature. But the clock should go with absolute
regularity. How can this be brought about?*

*5.2 Why are all six-place numbers of the form abc,abc,
such as 254,254, divisible by 13?*

Through analysis of protocols of subjects, Duncker was able to
identify heuristic processes that ranged from general to task-specific.
Further, the observed solution processes paralleled those identified by
Polya. The identified heuristic processes that arose from Duncker's
analyses included what was called   (1) analysis of the situation and
(2) analysis of the goal. Analysis of the situation included: (a)
analysis of material, a more surface form of analysis involving direct
deductions from the problem elements without (necessarily) "foresighted-
ness" into the use to which the deductions might be put; and (b) analysis of conflict, which focused on varying certain elements in attempts
to gain "insight" into the relationships among the elements and the
goal. Analysis of the goal was seen by Duncker as of paramount importance and included a focus not only on what was demanded by the problem,
but on what might be the predecessor (as stated by Duncker, "what do I
really want" [p. 23]) and what might be nonessential to the goal.

Duncker's analyses of protocols led to his belief that powerful
heuristic processes are those that (1) are goal oriented and (2)
involve the selection and accomplishment of a sequence of easier
subgoals. Although the work from which these conclusions are drawn
predominantly involves the direct analysis of protocols derived from
independent attempts of subjects to solve problems, on occasion hints
and preparatory problems are provided in order to determine their
effects on the solution process. Thus, Duncker recognizes (1) the
difference between task-specific and general heuristic processes, (2)
subgoal reduction and goal-oriented heuristic processes, (3) processes
of variation of a problem, and (4) means-ends heuristic processes.

Like Duncker, Kilpatrick (1967) asked subjects to think aloud as
they solved mathematical problems. Other points of similarity between
the Duncker and the Kilpatrick studies include: (1) the complex
nature of the problems used, and (2) the assumption of content knowledge in addition to the requirement of invention of solution processes.

Much of Kilpatrick's work is developmental in the sense of creating mechanisms for analyzing protocol material. His aim is to develop
a way of classifying subjects according to the heuristic processes used
in solving word problems and to determine how the variables of classification relate to such variables as aptitude, achievement, and cognitive style. As a part of the process, he develops a protocol coding
system that includes both heuristic processes and non-heuristic
processes, with the heuristic processes being derived from the work
of Polya. A series of preliminary pilot studies was used to perfect

a workable coding system. Although Polya's checklist (see Chapter I) was the starting point for the heuristic processes of the coding system, considerable refinement (predominantly elimination and clarification) was necessary for the production of a reliable system that included the processes used by the eighth-grade subjects of the study. The major divisions of the processes are: (1) preparation, (2) production, and (3) evaluation. The heuristic processes included in these divisions, as well as the process coding systems, will be presented later in this chapter.

Although the coding system developed by Kilpatrick was a major part of the research effort and has served to spark the development and use of related coding systems and process research in mathematics education, we shall forego further discussion of it at this time and return to the heuristic processes that Kilpatrick observed in his subjects. The processes used by subjects and found to be reliably codable (high intercoder reliability) included: (1) drawing a figure, (2) using successive approximation, (3) questioning the existence/uniqueness of the solution, (4) using a deduction process, (5) using an equation, (6) using trial and error, and (7) checking the solution. These were taken from the final coding system that contained both a checklist and a process-sequence code. Of these processes, drawing a figure and questioning the existence/uniqueness of the solution were coded only on the checklist.

Kilpatrick found that the tape-recorded protocols of his 56 above-average eighth-grade subjects contained the use of only a few of Polya's heuristic processes. Those observed were: (1) the drawing of figures while solving problems (found to be unrelated to success in solving the problem or to the use of other processes); (2) the use of trial and error (frequently) and, to a much lesser extent, successive approximation trial and error (related to success in solving problems); and (3) checking work (seldom used except on two or three specific problems).

In an attempt to produce meaningful clusters of subjects by use of the coding system, Kilpatrick found that the most promising differences appeared to be in the use of trial-and-error forms in contrast with forms of deductive inference. His final classification of subjects was into four equal-sized groups as follows:

(a) subjects who, at least once, attempted to set up an equation in solving the problem.

(b) subjects who attempted trial and error before attempting deduction.

(c) subjects who, by comparison, used trial and error with moderate frequency, and

(d) subjects who did not use algebra and who used trial and error infrequently.

Kilpatrick found the subjects from the first group, when classified in this way, were, on the average, high in quantitative ability,
high in mathematical achievement, and of a reflective conceptual tempo.
Those of the second group were high on quantitative ability, moderately
high in mathematics achievement, and of a reflective conceptual tempo.
In contrast, the third group stood between the second and the fourth
group in aptitude and achievement and were moderately impulsive, while
the fourth group were, in general, lowest in mathematics achievement
and aptitude and were the most impulsive (pp. 100-101).

The coding system and the analysis of problem-solving processes
as suggested by Kilpatrick's work have been modified in several subsequent studies. For example, Webb (1975) conducted an exploratory study
involving 40 high school students in a second year of algebra. Three
aims of the study were:

(1) to determine relations among cognitive ability, problem-
    solving ability, and the use of problem-solving processes.

(2) to categorize selected heuristic processes as problem-
    specific or general (categorization to be accomplished
    with respect to use by the subjects of the research).

(3) to use "sets of processes" as a means of identifying
    clusters of students according to the problem-solving
    modes they employed.

In terms of the analysis, Webb employed regression analysis to
answer the first question, the Cochran Q test to answer the second,
and cluster analysis to answer the third. From these analyses, Webb
found that mathematics achievement was, by comparison, highly related
to the problem-solving scores; it accounted for 50 percent of the
variance of the total scores. Verbal reasoning accounted for an
additional 5 percent (a significant amount at the .05 level), and the
heuristic process, *pictorial representation*, accounted for 8 percent
of the variance beyond that for which the pretest components had
accounted.

Webb, like Kilpatrick, limited the detailed analysis of heuristic processes to those of relatively frequent occurrence and to those
with intercoder reliability in excess of .88 (with two exceptions for
particularly interesting processes). The Cochran Q test was used to
determine, based on the use of the heuristic processes by the subjects,
the ones that were problem-specific as opposed to general processes.
Problem-specific heuristic processes identified were: uses mnemonic
notation, draws a representative diagram, recalls a related problem,
uses inductive reasoning, uses specialization, uses successive approximation, checks the solution by substituting in an equation, and checks
that the solution satisfies the condition. Webb used the decision rule
that, "a process is a *general heuristic process* provided the percentage
of use of the process is no greater for some problems than for others."
Applying this rule, "deriving a solution by another method" and "having

a bright idea" were found to be general heuristic processes (p. 95).
A more complete description of research related to general versus
task-specific heuristic processes was included in the review of the
studies by Wilson and by Smith.

Finally, Webb described three problem-solving modes as characterized by heuristic processes. The three groups representing the
modes were as follows:

(1) subjects who used a wide range of strategies,

(2) subjects who did not use "checks the solution by sub-
     stituting in an equation," "checks by specialization,"
     or "derives the solution by another method," and

(3) subjects who did not use inductive reasoning, general-
     ization, specialization, or successive approximation.

In comparison with Kilpatrick's subjects, Webb's subjects performed as follows:

(1) those who used equations and trial and error moderately
     and who made few structural errors performed best on a
     problem-solving performance measure,

(2) those who used equations relatively more frequently but
     used trial and error relatively infrequently were more
     intermediate in their problem-solving performance, and

(3) those who used trial and error relatively more frequently
     and equations relatively less frequently were the least
     adept problem solvers (p. 96).

Thus, Webb found that subjects involved in a second year of
algebra, in contrast to high-ability eighth-grade subjects of Kilpatrick who had not been taught algebra, were more successful as
problem solvers when they made greater use of equations and supple-
mented this process with trial and error.

Blake (1975), like Webb, examined problem-solving processes of
eleventh-grade subjects who were engaged in a second course of algebra.
He obtained thinking-aloud protocols on each of five problems from 40
subjects randomly selected from 14 different schools. The subjects
had an I.Q. range of 115 to 125. Blake administered the Embedded
Figures Test to the subjects to classify them as field independent or
field dependent. He also administered two types of tasks which were
classified by context as either real-world setting or mathematical
setting.

Using a model of mathematical problem solving based on the work
of MacPherson, Blake sought answers to the following questions:

(1) What heuristic processes are used by students of algebra
     in the solution of mathematical problems?

(2) What patterns are exhibited in the use of heuristic
processes in solving word problems?

The MacPherson problem-solving model involves three major components:
(a) knowledge of mathematical content (called "core"), (b) heuristic processes, and (c) application (called "lore"). Blake devised a process
coding system (to be discussed in more detail later) that incorporated
the elements of the MacPherson model. In particular, it included the
heuristic processes: (a) smoothing, (b) analysis, (c) cases, (d) templation, (e) deduction, (f) inverse deduction, (g) invariation, (h)
analogy, (i) symmetry, (j) preservation, (k) variation, and (l) extension.
Except for smoothing, templation, and preservation, each of the processes
was defined similarly to processes from Polya's list. Templation is
essentially a category that includes recalling related problems and
recalling results and methods, much as Polya defines them. Preservation deals with extending the properties of a mathematical system consistently, while smoothing is defined as altering a problem so as to
produce an isomorphic problem in a mathematical system. Smoothing is,
in a sense, a heuristic process appropriate for the "mathematical model-
ing" in "applied" problem solving.

In mild contrast to the study of Webb, who found a relatively large
percentage of variance attributable to mathematical achievement (20 percent) and a smaller percentage attributable to heuristic processes (13
percent), Blake concluded that heuristic processes and "core" account
for approximately equal amounts of variance. His analysis indicated
that 41 percent of variance could be attributed to heuristic processes
and 40 percent attributed to "core," with a "common-shared" 20 percent
of variance (in comparison to 40 percent "shared" in the Webb study).
In addition, Blake found considerable evidence of the use of random
cases (three-fourths of the subjects used it at least once) and sequential cases (over half of the subjects used it more than once), as well
as some evidence of critical (special) cases. He further concluded that
these trial-and-error processes related closely to correct solutions.
In contrast, Webb concluded that trial-and-error processes were related
to success in problem solving only when used moderately in conjunction
with deduction.

Blake found that templation and "random cases" were the most frequently occurring processes in the protocols, with three-fourths of the
subjects using these processes (over half of the protocols contained
multiple occurrences). He also found analysis (subproblem decomposition), smoothing, and sequential cases (successive approximation) in
protocols of one-fourth of the subjects. Further, trial and error,
direct deduction, variation, and inverse deduction (working backwards)
were the only other heuristic processes observed, and they were observed
infrequently.

Further conclusions from this exploratory study that involved no
instruction are:

(1) Total number of heuristic processes used and the number of
different heuristic processes used are positively related

to success in problem solving and contributed significant amounts of variance to the number of correct solutions.

(2) Field independent subjects use "higher order" heuristic processes, use a greater variety of heuristic processes, change their problem solving mode more readily, and solve more problems correctly than do their field-dependent counterparts.

(3) Subjects rely heavily on "core" in their attempt at solution, and they use "templation" most frequently of any heuristic process. However, Blake concludes that they are "ineffective" in their use of templation.

In contrast to the research of Duncker, Kilpatrick, Webb, and Blake, who sought to find out what heuristic processes were used by subjects independently of instruction designed to prepare subjects in heuristic processes, researchers such as Lucas (1972) and Kantowski (1974) sought to find out what heuristic processes would be used by subjects who were specifically taught by and about Polya's maxims. The research of both Lucas and Kantowski was clinical-exploratory; both described the associated teaching as heuristic teaching. The following paragraphs will describe the studies of Lucas and Kantowski, respectively, and summarize their findings as they relate to the development of heuristic processes.

The Lucas study was a diagnostic-behavioral study in the sense that audio-taped problem-solving interviews of subjects were collected both before and after diagnostic instruction. The pre-instructional problem-solving interviews contributed to the design of instruction. The subjects of the study were classes of 27 and 25 students of Calculus I. The class of 27 received heuristic-oriented instruction, while the class of 25 was the control group. Eight of the 27 and six of the 25 students were interviewed prior to their respective instructional phase; the same eight and six students and an additional nine and seven students were involved in individual tape-recorded post-instruction problem-solving interviews (pp. 273-275).

Lucas modified and extended the process coding scheme of Kilpatrick for use with the first-year college students of his study. The major changes were the addition of several heuristic behavior categories and the omission of several non-heuristic behavior categories. These changes, which were based on a pilot study, will be discussed in more detail in a later section of this chapter.

A summary of the results of the study will answer the questions posed by Lucas:

(1) He found that Kilpatrick's system of behavioral analysis (a process-sequence code and a checklist) could be satisfactorily modified in terms of reliably codable processes for analysis of problem-solving in the content area of calculus.

(2) In answer to the main question, "What heuristic processes are subject to change under heuristic instruction," Lucas found the following:

(a) the kind of notation,

(b) applying the method of a related problem,

(c) applying the result of a related problem,

(d) reasoning by analysis, and

(e) organizing data.

He did not find effects on such heuristic processes as drawing or modifying a diagram, looking back, trial and error, reasoning by synthesis, or productivity (relationships, equations, or algorithmic processes) (Lucas, 1972, pp. 427-428).

Kantowski performed a "teaching experiment" (in the sense of Soviet research) on eight students of above-average ability. Using geometry as the mathematical content area, the longitudinal clinical study involved four phases. Students were asked to "think aloud" as they solved eight problems at the outset of this exploratory study of mathematical processes. Then came a "readiness for instruction" phase that accustomed the subjects to heuristic instruction. Following the administration of another pretest, students were taught three units of geometric content through heuristic instruction. Interspersed throughout this instructional period were mid-unit and end-of-unit tests. The final phase involved a prerequisite knowledge test and a geometry and verbal problems test on which the students were again asked to think aloud.

The written and the tape-recorded thinking-aloud protocols were subjected to a protocol analysis and each problem was given a process-product score. The process-sequence was again based on a modification of the coding scheme of Kilpatrick. Process-product scores were given for each of 44 problems solved by each of the eight subjects. Each individual's median score on the 44 problems was computed and was used as a basis for judging the relationship among problem-solving processes as problem-solving ability developed (over time).

Ten questions were posed to guide the analysis. Six of these questions are directly related to heuristic processes and will be discussed in the following paragraphs. In answer to the question "Is there a relationship between the tendency to use heuristics and success in problem solving?", Kantowski found that heuristic processes were evident in 59 to 95 percent of the solutions which had scores above the individual's median score, while 52 percent or fewer of the problem solutions with scores below the individual's median contained evidence of the use of heuristic processes (pp. 52-67).

Taking process-product scores above the individual's median as evidence of "success in problem solving," Kantowski concluded that "the tendency to use heuristics increases as problem-solving ability develops."

Support for this conclusion was that on the pretest, there was from 14 to 72 percent use of heuristic processes (with the median subject having a percentage of 36), while on the posttest there was from 14 to 100 percent use of heuristic processes (with a median percentage of 72). Additional support was obtained from the unit tests. On Test Block I there was from 17 to 50 percent use of heuristic processes (with a median percentage of 25), on Test Block II there was from 32 to 84 percent use (with a median percentage of 47), and on Test Block III there was from 31 to 100 percent use (with a median percentage of 77) (pp. 68-69).

Kantowski found strong evidence to indicate that successful problem solvers exhibit more regular patterns of analysis ("decompose" heuristic process) and synthesis ("recombine" heuristic process) in their process sequences. From 77 to 100 percent of the subjects' solutions (with a median percentage of 95) did exhibit such patterns, considering only solutions for which scores were above the subject's median process-product score. From 18 to 41 percent of the solutions with scores below the subject's median exhibited such patterns (with a median percentage of 23). Furthermore, the interrelationship between analytic-synthetic patterns and heuristic processes was quite evident in problem solutions. Kantowski concluded that goal-oriented processes, those processes specifically related to the conclusion of the problem, tended to occur in solutions that are more efficient, and they tended to precede immediately regular patterns of analysis and synthesis (p. 106). In fact, from 50 to 92 percent of solutions with scores above the subject's median contained the use of analytic-synthetic processes and other heuristic processes in combination. At most, 33 percent of the less-successful attempts at problem solution contained these processes in combination (p. 71).

With respect to "looking back" heuristic behaviors, protocols provided very little evidence of the use of these behaviors. Further, an increase in the use of these processes was not evidenced as problem-solving ability developed.

Finally, there was evidence of the use of related problems in problem solutions. The evidence relating previously solved problems and success in problem solving was gathered on problems that occurred in more than one of the test batteries. Subjects were observed to recall and use both the results of related problems and the methods of related problems.

In summary, Kantowski's teaching experiment suggests that subjects given heuristic instruction were observed to increase their use of heuristic processes as problem-solving ability developed and that success in solving problems was directly related to their use of these heuristic processes. Most pronounced in the protocols were regular patterns of analysis and synthesis and goal-oriented processes. "Insight" in the form of either a general or a task-specific heuristic process related to the goal tended to initiate the regular patterns of analysis and synthesis. Little use of such processes as "looking back" was observed.

The investigation of processes used in solving mathematical problems is a prominent area of research in the Soviet Union. One of the most thought-provoking and penetrating series of analyses centers around the work of Krutetskii and his colleagues (1976). This investigation, of more than twelve years duration, was based on some 26 series of problems, containing from one to eight tests per series and from one to sixteen problems per test. The layout of the problem-solving task instruments is given in Table 5.4.

The table demonstrates the breadth and depth of problem types, classified by Krutetskii's view of mathematical abilities. Any problem of a set, according to the design of the sets, was apt to evoke the "ability" from subjects with the ability to which the set related. For example, "flexibility of thinking" is a general label for an ability hypothesized by Krutetskii. Four sets of problems: Series XIII (Problems with Several Solutions), Series XIV (Problems with Changing Content), Series XV (Problems on Reconstructing an Operation), and Series XVI (Problems Suggesting Self-restriction) were used by Krutetskii to assess the existence and the quality of development of the ability "flexibility of thinking."

Examples of "problems with several solutions" are given below:

5.3 *In how many ways can 78 rubles be paid if the money is in 3-ruble and 5-ruble notes?*

5.4 *Four liters of water at room temperature (15°C) were added to 3 liters of water at a temperature of 36°C. What temperature was established in the vessel?* (p. 136).

Examples of "problems with changing content" are the following:

5.5 *A horse moved at a speed of 12 km per hour for half the time spent on a journey, and 4 km per hour for the rest of the time. Find the horse's average speed.*

5.6 *(2nd variant: "travelled half a journey at a speed of 12 km per hour, and at 4 km per hour for the rest of the journey")* (p. 138).

These problems represent *tasks* designed to evoke activity from which Krutetskii inferred the existence of flexibility of thought in subjects who were "successful" in solving them. Additionally, a certain sense of varying "quality" of flexibility of thought was "evident" in the responses of "capable" as compared with "average" or "incapable" subjects. Krutetskii gathered thinking-aloud protocols and provided

Table 5.4 *Krutetskii's System of Experimental Problems for Investigating*
*Schoolchildren's Mathematical Abilities**

Category	Group	Series
Information gathering	Perception (interpretation of a problem)	I. Problems with an unstated question II. Problems with incomplete information III. Problems with surplus information IV. Problems with interpenetrating elements
Information processing	Generalization	V. Systems of problems of a single type VI. Systems of problems of different types VII. Systems of problems with gradual transformation from concrete to abstract VIII. Composition of problems of a given type IX. Problems on proof X. Composition of equations using the terms of a problem XI. Unrealistic problems XII. Formation of artificial concepts
	Flexibility of thinking	XIII. Problems with several solutions XIV. Problems with changing content XV. Problems on reconstructing an operation XVI. Problems suggesting "self-restriction"
	Reversibility of mental processes	XVII. Direct and reverse problems
	Understanding; reasoning; logic	XVIII. Heuristic tasks XIX. Problems on comprehension and logical reasoning XX. Series problems XXI. Mathematical sophisms
Information retention	Mathematical memory	XXII. Problems with terms that are hard to remember
Typology	Types of mathematical ability	XXIII. Problems with varying degrees of visuality in their solution XXIV. Problems with verbal and visual formulations XXV. Problems related to spatial concepts XXVI. Problems that expose correlations between visual-pictorial and verbal-logical components of nonmathematical intellectual activi

*Krutetskii (1976, pp. 100-104), as abridged by Goldin (1977).

excerpts of these to illustrate the comparison of the existence and quality of this ability in various subjects.

The examples given here, as well as others in these series, are convincing evidence, upon at least minimal scrutiny, that the careful "engineering" of tasks is fruitful for evoking the desired behaviors. It is very plausible that a subject who can perform "many" of the following activities is more flexible in thought than one who can do "few" of them.

Refer to Problem *5.3:*

 (a) Note that 78 rubles is the same as (75 + 3) rubles or 15 five-ruble notes and 1 three-ruble note.

 (b) Note that 5 three-ruble notes are equal in value to 3 five-ruble notes; that 10 three-ruble notes equal 6 five-ruble notes, etc.

Refer to Problem *5.4:*

 (c) The weighted average of $\underline{4}$ x 15° and $\underline{3}$ x 36° is 24°.

 (d) The temperature will be 3/7 of the "distance" from 15° to 36°.

 (e)

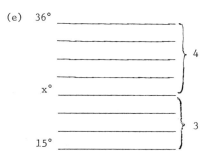

(see Krutetskii, 1976, p. 279)

Refer to Problems *5.5* and *5.6:*

 (f) The average speed in the problem is the average of the speeds, and by contrast in the second variant the average speed is the total distance divided by the total time.

 (g) The average speed in the second variant is independent of the length of the journey; whereas the average speed in the original problem is independent of the time.

A most fundamental assumption underlying this enormously involved
and fruitful complex of investigations is that problem tasks can be so
composed that they extract from the experimental subjects the varied
mental-psychological operations that characterize their mathematical
abilities. Throughout these studies, certain series of tasks were
administered to subjects classified as capable, average, and incapable
so as to analyze the thought and problem-solving processes and how
they relate to mathematical abilities. As another example, four or
five of the tasks were designed to extract from subjects their ability
to reverse their mental process. The fundamental assumption underlying
these problem tasks was that subjects who could reverse their mental
processes would be led to do so by these tasks and would be successful
in solving the problems of these series. On the other hand, subjects
who could not switch from one mental operation to its reverse would be
less able (or relatively less successful) in solving these problems due
to the underdevelopment of the ability (not due to the lack of an
appropriate type and intensity of stimulation from the task presentation or of inadequate content knowledge).

The basic connection of heuristic reasoning to the complex of
investigations carried out under the direction of Krutetskii is that
"heuristics--the study of the ways and means of problem solving, particularly the mental operations involved in it" (Polya, 1957)--focuses
upon the mental operations or mental activity. Similarly, Krutetskii
states that his work was intended ". . . to reflect the basic specific
character of mathematics within the framework of the demands it makes
on a person's mental activity." Krutetskii is, of course, interested
in the cognitive and psychological aspects--the mental operations--
required to characterize a "capable" mathematics student's thinking.

Although heuristic processes and mathematical abilities share the
common characteristic of being based in mental activity, thought and
operations of the mind related to and inferrable from these mathematical activities differ in rather significant ways. Heuristic processes
are volitionally related processes. As Polya indicated, his desire is
that ". . . the student may absorb a few of the questions . . . so well
that he is finally able to put to himself the right question at the
right time and perform the corresponding mental operation. . ." (1957,
p. 4); thus, he implies the deliberate, volitional nature of question-
based heuristic processes. In contrast, mathematical abilities are
more a product, a synthesis of mental processes. Krutetskii infers the
definition of mathematical abilities from his definition of ability to
learn mathematics. [He is, in context, making reference to abilities
in school mathematics.] The individual psychological traits undergird-
ing the creative mastery of mathematics, including the rapidity,
fluency, and thoroughness of mastery of mathematical knowledge, skills
and habits, are indicative of mathematical abilities in Krutetskii's
view (1976, pp. 74-75). He further emphasizes that abilities derive
from a synthesis or a combination of mental processes such as perception, memory, attention, imagination and thought, to mention a few
(p. 75).

Thus, heuristic processes are mental operations, activities and the like, *volitionally* controllable or initiatable, that direct, organize, plan, and conduct the problem-solving process. Mathematical abilities refer to the relatively more involuntary, more synthetic combinations of mental processes that assume a degree of success in all domains for which the particular ability or abilities are "suitable." Referring to the examples of "flexibility of thought" mentioned earlier, the evidence Krutetskii presents of capable students' activity in these examples is worthy of note. Their solutions demonstrated "mental freedom" to "look at" a problem one way, and solve it, then to "look at" it another way and produce a very different solution in terms of representation and process; to "know" how many solutions to expect in "multiple solutions" problems and rapidly to find all of them; to attack similar but contrasting variants of the same problem and to "cut through" the less relevant features and immediately abstract the contrasting features of problem structure, in a sense avoiding mental fixedness; *and* to avoid remaining "fixed" on certain possibilities to the exclusion of others.

Techniques for Coding and Scoring Problem-Solving Processes

Thinking Aloud, Retrospection, and Introspection

The definition of heuristic processes, be it related to Polya's idea of the mental operations typically useful in discovery and invention in problem solution or to the IPS ideas related to the techniques for selecting and ordering the search for solution, implies that the collection of data on which to base observation must be objective and undistorted and must be "externalized" and sequenced among the total set of problem-solving behaviors. In order to "see" the influence of the problem task on the heuristic processes employed in its solution, a *complete* record of problem-solving effort on the task must be captured.

In this country, Kilpatrick (1967) initiated the use of thinking aloud as the presently most appropriate "way for getting subjects to generate observable sequences of behavior" (p. 4) in the realm of processes used in mathematical problem solving. Drawing from available methods for collecting data related to "thought" and using Polya's problem-solving model, Kilpatrick saw the necessity for collecting as complete and undistorted a "motion picture" of the entire solution process as is possible in order to be able to analyze the temporal, behavioral manifestations of the mental operations involved in the problem-solving process.

Psychology has used four basic methods of gathering data on complex tasks. Retrospection, introspection, material/mechanical "choice" devices, and thinking aloud have all been used during this century to "get close to" thinking.

Retrospection is a self-reporting technique in which the subject who is asked to perform a task is also asked reflectively (after the fact) to describe his or her thinking as the task is performed. In problem solving the search for solution often involves false starts, following paths that lead to blind alleys, and exploration of widely differing alternatives. Hadamard (1945) and Poincaré (1908) both suggest that sudden inspiration and flashes of insight often precipitate a solution. The time sequencing, for example, of the occurrence of exploration of particular alternatives, the discovery of a blind alley, and flashes of insight, though particularly crucial for understanding the solution process, are subject to editing, reordering, and distortion from incomplete memory when retrospection is the source of data collection.

Introspection is also a self-reporting technique which is dependent upon the subject who is solving a problem *simultaneously* to solve the problem and report the internal (including mental) and external forces in operation along the entire solution path. Used by Binet (1903) in the early part of the twentieth century, introspection was successful in getting "thought" externalized, but it required much time both in preparing a subject to introspect and in collecting the data after the training and practice in the technique of introspecting had been completed. Consider the time consumption involved in tape-recording the solution of a complex problem. The relative amount of time involved in introspectively solving a problem can now be estimated by *adding* to the time of solving the problem the time one would take to explain carefully all aspects of the solution process (much like recording yourself solving the problem and then "teaching" another person to solve the problem). Two basic difficulties with the method of introspection as a tool for data collection are recognized and regarded as insurmountable difficulties. These are the disruption of thought by introspecting, along with the implied loss of temporal sequencing and the lack of observational reliability. The observational reliability difficulty (see Johnson, 1955) is basically that different interpreters (analyzers) of the introspectively collected data infer very different "qualities of thought" from the same data. The difficulty is, at least partially, a problem of attaching various levels of confidence to the introspective accounts and of inferring sequencing of processes and relationships among processes that are "clouded" by interruption caused by taking time out to introspect.

The use of material devices, such as the well-known "envelope test" of Lazerte (1933) and mechanical devices such as branched-program machines (the autotutor and the Problem-Solving Information Apparatus), is a third method for collecting data on processes involved in solving problems. These devices, though somewhat effective as tools to assess certain decision-making skills, have severe limitations as data-collecting methods for complex problem solving. The most obvious and most serious drawback is that the devices are "pre-programmed" with the options and as a result may lead the subject through a solution path rather than allow the subject to discover and/or devise a solution.

Thinking aloud is a method most commonly agreed upon (Taylor, 1966; Kantowski, 1974) as the most valid means available today for collecting data on problem-solving processes. As Kilpatrick states, "There is one method of getting subjects to produce sequentially-linked, observable behavior that requires neither skill in self-observation nor the manipulation of mechanical devices: have the subject think aloud as he works" (1967, p. 6). As Taylor pointed out, "The use of 'thinking aloud' has repeatedly proved fruitful in the analysis of process" (1966, p. 123). What makes it fruitful is that it eliminates or at least minimizes the shortcomings of retrospection, introspection, and material/mechanical devices. There is not the editing and distortion from incomplete memory as is potentially present in retrospection, since thinking aloud *reports* activity and thought in the time sequence of their occurrence. There is not the disruption of thought to introspect nor the loss of temporal sequencing of thought and activity associated with introspection, since thinking aloud does not require the subject to stop and interpret thought and activity; rather, it is reported as it occurs. Again, there is not the external imposition of a "structure" on the course of solution—a "pre-programming" of an externally imposed set of options as with the "envelope test" or the autotutor; rather, the solver is free to create and try whatever options, processes, actions, and activities he or she chooses in the attempt to devise a solution strategy. Additionally, the data arising from thinking aloud permit a full range of observations, including all verbalized and written attempts at solution as well as whatever notes an observer may wish to take as the subject is being observed.

Two categories of thinking aloud methods appear to be emerging in mathematical problem-solving process research. These relate to whether the subject is being observed by an investigator or is privately recording problem-solving episodes. The strength of each of these thinking-aloud methods may well be the weakness of the other. The presence of an observer allows "prodding" the student to talk in those moments when he or she may fall silent; also, the observer may make notes to provide a more complete "picture" of the problem-solving process (for example, noting what was written, in what order, related to what verbalization). An inherent difficulty with the presence of an observer is that the subject may be inhibited by the presence or verbal statements of the observer. Similarly, having someone physically present may cause a subject consciously to change his or her activity and verbalization. On the other hand, the more private recording of problem-solving episodes may lead to the opposite difficulty. Without the reminder and conscious awareness that objective data requires complete verbalization and complete outpouring of attempts, a subject may lapse into silence, provide only sketchy written supplements, or may even erase portions of the solution attempts.

Process-Sequence Codes and Process-Product Scores

Recent research related to the processes involved in
mathematical problem solving has necessitated the development of
coding schemes and scoring procedures for these processes. In 1967
Kilpatrick developed a coding system that subsequently was used, in
modified form, in several process-oriented research efforts. The
evolution of the Kilpatrick (1967) process sequence coding scheme
will be described together with the modifications by Lucas (1972)
and Kantowski (1974), as well as a somewhat different approach by
Blake (1976). Following this discussion, efforts to date to produce
a scoring system that includes process as well as products in the
evaluation will be presented.

The preliminary approach taken by Kilpatrick toward producing a
workable process coding system involved the creation of a checklist of
36 questions taken from Polya's "How to Solve It" list (see Chapter I).
Attempts to use this checklist led to the conclusion that large numbers
of these heuristic processes were not used by the pilot-study subjects
and the processes could not be reliably coded. Kilpatrick then reduced
the list to a set of "behaviors" (see Table 5.5). Those contained in
the reduced list were processes that could be coded reliably, were used
by the subjects, and were central to the purpose of the research.

This checklist allowed a counting of the number of heuristic processes used by a given subject as well as a comparison across problems.
Yet the amount of process-related information "lost" in its application
led Kilpatrick to construct other systems that incorporated the sequencing of behaviors. A preliminary system for process-sequence coding
that included 21 "terms" (problem elements, either completely specified
or unspecified), 67 "processes" grouped into 10 categories (e.g.,
recalling information, looking ahead), 11 "modifiers," and 8 "punc-
tuations" was found to be unwieldy due to its "size" and the requirement of "fine distinctions" of processes (for a complete description,
see Kilpatrick, 1967, pp. 48-50, 140-148).

Kilpatrick then evolved the coding system shown in Table 5.6,
together with a checklist that was used for recording a wider variety
of behaviors than those sequence-coded. A more complete description
of the use of the coding system and the checklist will occur as other
coding systems are discussed; however, a complete description of the
application of such coding systems will be reserved for Chapter VIII.B.

The analytic tools for examining processes involved in mathematical
problem solving that Kilpatrick developed were modified by Lucas and by
Kantowski in preparation for studies of problem solving in the content
areas of calculus and geometry, respectively. Each of these researchers
maintained (1) the checklist approach, (2) the process-sequence coding
approach, and (3) major portions of the process codes as well. They
did, however, modify several codes and introduced others so as to capture additional processes of geometry and calculus subjects, while at
the same time making finer distinctions in such processes as deduction,
use of diagrams, and use of standard processes (equations and algorithms).

Table 5.5 *Kilpatrick's Modified Checklist*

A. Understanding the Problem	C. Carrying out the Plan

A. Understanding the Problem

   1. Identifies unknown, data, or condition

   2. Draws figure

   3. Introduces notation

B. Devising a Plan

   1. Rephrases problem

   2. Considers a related problem (special cases or part of problem)

C. Carrying out the Plan

   1. Uses successive approximation

   2. Checks steps before finding results

D. Looking Back

   1. Checks that result is reasonable

   2. Checks that result satisfies condition

   3. Retraces steps of argument

   4. Derives results by another method

(Kilpatrick, 1967, p. 46)

Table 5.6 *Kilpatrick's Process-Sequence Coding System*

Process Symbols

Preparation

Production

    R = Reading and trying to understand problem
    D = Deduction
    E = Setting up equation
    T = Trial and Error

Evaluation

    C = Checking Solution

Number Following
Production Processes
Symbols

    1 = Incomplete
    2 = Impasse
    3 = Intermediate Result
    4 = Incorrect Result
    5 = Correct Result

Modifiers

    Bar over symbol = structural error in process (used only with symbols for production)

    Underlined symbol = Difficulty (hesitation, repetition) in process

Punctuation

    , inserted between successive processes

    / work stopped without solution

    . work stopped with solution

(Kilpatrick, 1967, pp. 154-155)

Table 5.7 *Lucas' Process-Sequence Coding System*

<u>Process Sequence Variables</u>

R   Reads the problem

S   Separates/Summarizes data

M_f Introduces model by means of a diagram

M_f' Modifies existing diagram

M_{f_c} Introduces diagram with coordinate system imposed

DS   Deduction by synthesis

DA   Deduction by analysis

T   Trial and error: successive approximation

An   Reasoning by analogy

Me   Model introduced by means of equation, expression, or other relationship

Alg   Algorithmic process

N   Not classifiable

C   Checks the result

V_s Varies the problem (by analogy; by changing conditions)

<u>Outcomes of DS, DA, T Processes</u>

1   Abandons process

2   Impasse

3   Incorrect final result

4   Correct final result

5   Intermediate result (correct or incorrect)

<u>Punctuation Marks</u>

- (dash) hesitation of approximately 2 units (30 seconds)

( )   scope of DS, DA, or T process

,   inserted between successive processes

/   stops without solution

.   stops with solution (correct or incorrect)

<u>Errors</u>

$\downarrow$ over process symbol = structural error in process

$\downarrow$ over process symbol = executive error in process

$\overset{*}{\downarrow}$ $\overset{*}{\downarrow}$ (asterisk over error symbol) = previous error of type indicated was corrected

(Lucas, 1972, pp. 443-444)

Table 5.8 *Kantowski's Process-Sequence Coding System*

Processes

R	Reads Problem
S_d	Separates or summarizes data or marks diagram
S_c	Summarizes conditions
Q	Rephrases question
F_d	Draws diagram
F_a	Adds auxiliary construction
P_p	Suggests plan for final goal
P_i	Suggests plan for intermediate goal
P_t	States theorem to use
P_o	States operation to use
$U_{t/o}$	States theorem/operation used
N	Suggests needed datum
$D_{a/s}$	Deduction (analysis/synthesis)
D_d	Deduction from diagram
O	Uses alternate concept implied by data
I	Uses induction
T_r	Uses random trial and error
T_a	Uses successive approximation trial and error
V	Introduces variable
E	Introduces equation
A	Uses algorithm
C	Checks solution
C_a	Introduces alternate procedure
C_s	Tries to simplify proof
C_n	Suggests new problem
X	Has forgotten or does not know how to do problem

Outcomes

1	Abandons process
2	Impasse
3	Correct final results
4	Correct intermediate result
5	Incorrect result

Punctuation

,	Inserted between successive processes
/	Stops without solution
.	Stops with solution

Error

↓	Structural
↓	Executive
*	Over symbol = corrected
___	(Underline) -- difficulty with process

(Kantowski, 1974, pp. 141-142)

Table 5.9 *Blake's Process-Sequence Coding System*

Reading problem					
Request definition of terms					
Recall same problem					
Recall related problem					
Recall problem type					
Recall related fact					
Draw diagram					
Modify diagram					
Identify variable					
Setting up equations					
Algorithms--algebraic					
Algorithms--arithmetic					
Guessing					
Smoothing					
Analysis					
Templation					
Cases--all					
Cases--random					
Cases--systematic					
Cases--critical					
Cases--sequential					
Deduction					
Inverse deduction					
Invariation					
Analogy					
Symmetry					
Obtain solution					
Checking part					
Checking solution					
by subst. in equation					
by retracing steps					
by reasonable/realistic					
uncodable					
Exp. concern--method					
Exp. concern--algorithm					
Exp. concern--equation					
Exp. concern--solution					
Work stopped--solution					
Work stopped--no solution					

(Blake, 1976, p. 142)

These more complex process-sequence coding schemes were built upon Kilpatrick's firm basis. These schemes, presented in Table 5.7 and Table 5.8, generalized the codable behaviors used by supposedly more sophisticated problem solvers than the pre-algebra subjects whose behaviors Kilpatrick analyzed, and were found by the researchers to be reliably usable and representative of their subjects' problem-solving behaviors. It should be noted, by point of contrast, that the Kilpatrick scheme focused on *production processes*, implying that each process ended with a product--correct or incorrect; intermediate or final; complete, incomplete, or uncompletable. By comparison, "reasons by analogy" and "varies the processes" (see Lucas) required more inference by the coder.

Further contrasts among the Kantowski, Lucas, and Kilpatrick coding schemes include:

(1) the addition of preparation processes such as (a) separating and summarizing data and (b) drawing and modifying diagrams;

(2) modifying "deduction" to include analytic and synthetic deduction as well as (for Kantowski) deduction from diagrams;

(3) use of equations, algorithms, and random as well as more systematic trial-and-error forms;

(4) more categories of recall (states theorems, operations, and so on by Kantowski);

(5) more looking-back categories (alternate procedures, simplifies proof, by Kantowski); and

(6) reasoning by analogy and varies the process (by Lucas).

In addition to these changes in the process sequence coding system, the checklists were correspondingly modified. These checklists were also reorganized to: (1) parallel more completely Polya's four-stage model and (2) separate out (physically) productive processes from more error-oriented processes.

Blake (1976) developed a coding system (see Table 5.9) that resembles, somewhat, the Flanders Interactional Analysis System in that behavioral categories are matrixed against a rectangular time-sequenced checking array. It differs from the other three coding schemes in that "core" (mathematical content knowledge), heuristic processes, and other processes such as checking work and expressing concern are made more distinct and are located together as clusters on the coding matrix. Further, the Blake scheme assumes a hierarchical relationship among heuristic processes with "smoothing" and analysis as least sophisticated and invariation and analogy as most sophisticated.

In terms of usage, the process sequence coding systems of Kilpatrick, Lucas, and Kantowski are a means of producing a string of symbols, with appropriate punctuation and modification, to indicate the major time-sequenced mental and concrete (written or spoken) actions of the problem solver. By comparison, the Blake system involves placing checks in the row-column blocks corresponding to the listed behaviors (row) and the order of occurrence of the behaviors (column).

Chapter VIII.B contains the complete description of a process-sequence coding system together with a definition of all terms, sample coded protocols, and applications of the system. Thus the general and abbreviated discussion above will be made more specific and concrete in that chapter.

Process-product scoring systems have been devised for the evaluation of problem-solving effectiveness. Lucas (1972) based a five-point per problem score on three factors. In this system, one point was possible for "approach," two points were possible for "plan," and two points were possible for "result." To qualify for the one point for "approach," a subject necessarily displayed an "understanding" of the problem; no misinterpretation of data, condition, or goal, and no structural errors due to misinterpretation, constituted additional criteria for the "approach" point. The two points for "plan" required the derivation of relationships or approximations sufficient to focus upon the correct result, provided no executive errors were committed. (One point of credit was possible for "plan" whenever all but one relationship necessary for solution were included.) "Result" points were judged on the basis of execution of plan. Whenever the processes for solution were free of executive error or whenever any errors were detected and corrected, two points were awarded for the "result" score. One point was awarded for "result" in such cases as correct numerical solution but possibly incorrect units, close but inexact approximations, and the like (pp. 178-180).

Webb (1975) also assigned a process-product score to the solution attempts of his subjects. Again, the approach, plan, and result categories were the basis of his five-point scoring system. "Approach" was defined in a manner similar to that of Lucas. For the "plan" points, Webb allowed two points for plans sufficiently complete to lead to correct solutions in the absence of executive error; one point for plans that might have worked, but were insufficiently carried out to be sure; and no points otherwise. For the two points possible under the "result" category, Webb assigned two points for correct answers, one point in cases where multiple answers were possible and the subject correctly produced some but not all of the multiple answers, and no points otherwise. Thus, for each problem attempted by each subject in these two studies, the solution attempt was given a score from zero to five (pp. 157-158).

Kantowski (1974) devised a process-product scoring system that included one point of credit for each of: (1) devising a plan, (2) absence of structural error and of superfluous syntheses, (3) persistence, (4) "looking back" strategies, and (5) seeking alternate solutions. Additionally, one or two points were awarded for products, depending on whether computation was or was not necessary for solution. The scores Kantowski assigned were decimal values of sixths or sevenths, depending upon the necessity or lack of necessity of computation (p. 144).

Analysis of Heuristic Processes

Figure 1.1 in Chapter I indicated heuristic processes are related to each stage of Polya's problem-solving model. It further indicated that heuristic processes relate to each type of task variable. However, heuristic processes are most vital in the "devising a plan" and the "looking back" stages of Polya's model. Content and context variables, and, to an extent, syntax variables, are more relevant to "understanding the problem;" structure variables are more essential to "carrying out the plan." The close relationship between problem structure and heuristic behaviors suggests the consolidation of these types of variables in the representation of the problem. It suggests that heuristic behaviors serve a central role in initiation and exploitation of behaviors that make for efficient "carrying out" of a plan. Thus, indirectly, the heuristic processes serve as a guiding force for the choice and implementation of algorithmic processes. As Schoenfeld will describe in Chapter X, keeping track of alternatives and monitoring success (components of his idea of "master control") require the effective use of processes during carrying out the plan.

Figure 1.1 also indicates that heuristic behaviors may lead to related problem statements and related problem representations. These may or may not relate back to the original problem; they may move toward generalization of the problem, the results, or the methods of the given problem; they may (as is the case with most heuristic processes) lead to a blind alley, or to an interesting but essentially unrelated problem.

Figure 5.1 indicates the consolidation of the *major* heuristic processes into an organized grouping with respect to the problem representation. It is clear from the literature that the problem representation is an important idea, both in the actual solution of a problem and in an analysis of solution processes and problem spaces. IPS essentially relates the analysis of problem spaces to representations, whether it be at a state-space level or at a problem-solver "imagery" level. The figure makes no attempt to include all processes potentially usable at any stage of representation development and use; it only suggests those more powerful and more plausibly usable processes in each stage. The figure also draws upon the work of Wickelgren as a means of describing the heuristic sources of creation of equivalent, similar, simpler, and more complex related problems.

Figure 5.1 *Problem Representation and Heuristic Processes*

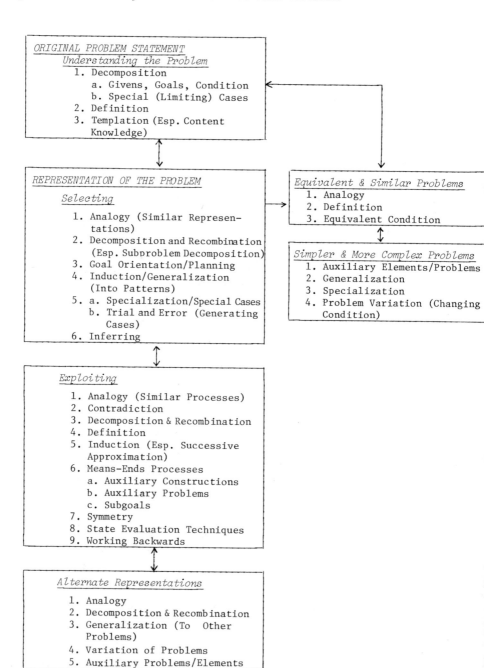

ORIGINAL PROBLEM STATEMENT
  Understanding the Problem
      1. Decomposition
          a. Givens, Goals, Condition
          b. Special (Limiting) Cases
      2. Definition
      3. Templation (Esp. Content
          Knowledge)

REPRESENTATION OF THE PROBLEM
  Selecting
      1. Analogy (Similar Represen-
          tations)
      2. Decomposition and Recombination
          (Esp. Subproblem Decomposition)
      3. Goal Orientation/Planning
      4. Induction/Generalization
          (Into Patterns)
      5. a. Specialization/Special Cases
         b. Trial and Error (Generating
            Cases)
      6. Inferring

Equivalent & Similar Problems
      1. Analogy
      2. Definition
      3. Equivalent Condition

Simpler & More Complex Problems
      1. Auxiliary Elements/Problems
      2. Generalization
      3. Specialization
      4. Problem Variation (Changing
          Condition)

Exploiting
      1. Analogy (Similar Processes)
      2. Contradiction
      3. Decomposition & Recombination
      4. Definition
      5. Induction (Esp. Successive
          Approximation)
      6. Means-Ends Processes
          a. Auxiliary Constructions
          b. Auxiliary Problems
          c. Subgoals
      7. Symmetry
      8. State Evaluation Techniques
      9. Working Backwards

Alternate Representations
      1. Analogy
      2. Decomposition & Recombination
      3. Generalization (To Other
          Problems)
      4. Variation of Problems
      5. Auxiliary Problems/Elements

It, like Figure 1.1, suggests the use of related problems for devising a plan, as well as the exploration (see Schoenfeld's Figure 10.4) of a variety of plausibly related problems, some of which may lead astray.

The processes in Figure 5.1 are discussed in the literature that was reviewed. The figure includes "templation" as described by Blake as a vital process of understanding the problem. His conclusion that this process is a much-used one by novice problem solvers places it squarely in the forefront as a heuristic process that initiates much of the exploration and selection of representations and processes. Except for the location in his model, Polya suggested a category of related processes called "templation." These appear as such heuristic advice as "try some related problem...recall a theorem...go back to definition..." Likewise, "inferring" as described by Wickelgren is a heuristic process recognized in the literature and accentuated in process research. For example, the form of deduction in the coding systems of Kantowski and of Lucas speak to the importance of this process. In fact, as Wickelgren suggests, this process (a heuristic approach because it requires a choice of the most likely useful inference from those possible) is the first one to use in an approach to representing a problem; Kantowski and Lucas also imply its importance by developing the category of deductions and by doing an analysis of the category.

Finally, the ideas from IPS about techniques for evaluating the progress one is making toward a solution (e.g., state evaluation techniques) play a prominent part in the exploitation of a problem representation. This evaluation process is analogous to the one made operational for problem solvers by Schoenfeld. It includes local as well as specific and general verification techniques. For exploitation of trial-and-error techniques, the successive approximation form of trial-and-error has a built-in verification process; it is based on evaluation of progress by checking at each stage of the guess as well as using the evaluated guess as a means of making more effective subsequent guesses. One notes that various forms of trial-and-error are apt to enter into the development and use of representations at different stages. In the development or selection of a representation, more rudimentary forms tend to dominate; they serve to explore the dimensions of the problem space. Following the existence of a representation, more goal-oriented and means-oriented forms of trial-and-error (successive approximation) are apt to occur.

In sum, the use of heuristic processes to develop and exploit a representation and to serve to create alternate representations is suggested by the literature. Figure 5.1 relates the two ideas. Its relationship to Figure 1.1, Figure 10.4, and Figure 8B.1 should be studied.

2. Problem Representation and Heuristic Processes

Processes for Understanding the Problem

Polya's stages of problem solving begin with the "Understanding the Problem" stage, as is the case with most problem-solving models. However, Polya took a very limited view of the processes useful in this stage. One might imply a somewhat larger class of heuristic processes as useful in understanding the problem. However, we assume that the more profound mental operations useful in problem solving occur after a surface level of understanding has been achieved. Since heuristic behaviors that extract meaning from the syntax features, content features, and context features of the problem statement are principally used to understand the problem, their initial position in the problem-solving process makes them necessary but not sufficient for successful problem solving.

Polya considers the processes of recognizing and of separating the unknown, the data, and the condition; separating the parts of the condition; determining the "fit" among the data, condition, and unknown; and drawing figures as well as introducing suitable notation, as those essential to understanding. Thus, he places "decomposition" of the syntax, content, and context features in the "understanding" category. Granted, it is virtually impossible to define the transition point between "understanding" and other stages (such as planning). Yet it would seem that other heuristic behaviors enter into the extraction of meaning and precede attempts to develop a plan. For example, recalling basic concepts and calling forth associations and semantic content are typically associated with syntax as well as content and context features of the problem and are a part of understanding the problem.

The use of definition also contributes to understanding. The complete sense in which Polya uses *definition* as a heuristic process does, indeed, go beyond understanding, but understanding of the problem depends upon knowledge of mathematical ideas. Consider the following problems:

5.7 *Find the smallest number that gives a remainder of*

    1 when divided by 3,
    2 when divided by 4,
    3 when divided by 5, and
    4 when divided by 6.   (Adapted from Krutetskii, 1976, p. 149.)

5.8a *Given four points in space, find the center of the circumscribing sphere.*

5.8b *Given three points in a plane, find the center of the circumscribing circle.*

*5.8c Given two points in a line, find the center of
the circumscribing "arc."*

Such words as "smallest number," "remainder," and "dividend" in
Problem *5.7*, as well as "center" and "circumscribing" in Problems
5.8a, *5.8b*, and *5.8c* are terms taken from mathematical content that
evoke recall from long-term memory necessary for understanding.
The heuristic aspect of *definition* in understanding a problem is
that of flexibility in exploration of the connotations of the words.
To derive the maximum information from the statement and to avoid a
fixed notion of the problem's principal parts necessitate heuristic
interpretation of the concepts in which the problem is embedded.

Now let us consider additional problems in terms of their syntax
and content.

5.9 What is the limiting sum of the infinite series

$$1 - \frac{1}{2} - \frac{1}{4} + \frac{1}{8} - \frac{1}{16} - \frac{1}{32} + \frac{1}{64} - \ldots ?$$

5.10 What is the limiting sum of the infinite series

$$\frac{1}{10} + \frac{2}{10^2} + \frac{3}{10^3} + \ldots ?$$

*5.11 The roots of the equation $x^3 + 4x^2 - 7x - 10 = 0$
are -5, -1, and 2. What are the roots of the
equation*

$$(x-3)^3 + 4(x-3)^2 - 7(x-3) - 10 = 0?$$ (Webb, 1975)

5.12 Find x, y, u, and v satisfying the four equations

$$x + 7y + 3v + 5u = 16$$
$$8x + 4y + 6v + 2u = -16$$
$$2x + 6y + 4v + 8u = 16$$
$$5x + 3y + 7v + u = -16$$

(This may look long and boring; look for a shortcut.)

(Polya and Kilpatrick, 1974, p. 12)

The repeated phrases and patterns in Problem *5.7* as well as Problems
5.9 through *5.12* represent syntax features and content features of
significance for processes related to understanding. Definitions and
meanings of symbols make the repeated phrases and symbol patterns take
on meaning. It is insufficient to separate and categorize principal
parts of the problem, in the most strict sense of separating and categorizing. Polya undoubtedly associated related meanings of mathematical

content and syntax features with the principal parts of a problem. Yet, these task characteristics are so vital to problem solving that they need to be separated out and accentuated.

Finally, consider the problems that follow in terms of their semantic content.

> 5.13 *Twenty U.S. coins consisting of nickels, dimes, and quarters have a value of $2.00. How many coins of each type are there?*

> 5.14 *One solution is 15 percent insecticide and another is 40 percent insecticide. What amount of each solution is needed to form 25 pints of a 25 percent solution?*

The idea of semantic content is that there is more given in the problem statement than meets the eye. Understanding the problem implies that the problem solver recognizes the existence of this additional information and its implicitness in the problem statement. The fact that there is more implicit information than is necessary, causing the problem solver to deliberate and make choices that are plausible rather than "sure," is what makes this idea of semantic content heuristic-related. By and large, the major heuristic process involved is that of definition. For example, exploiting the meaning of the word "value" helps produce understanding for Problem *5.13;* similarly, exploiting the meaning of the word "solution" contributes to understanding for Problem *5.14.*

Processes for Selecting a Representation

As with "devising a plan," the processes for selecting a representation are among the most profound ones in the solution process. For example, the description and discussion given by Duncker about subproblem decomposition indicate his view that these processes are *the* major mental operations typically useful in problem solving. The goal-oriented heuristic processes of Kantowski, like the operative propositions of Talyzina, also exemplify techniques problem solvers use to *organize* the essential features of a problem to the exclusion of the inessential features.

A representation may be either internal or external. The development of an *internal representation* for a problem corresponds to a "second level of meaning" with respect to the problem-solving process. The *internal representation,* which is in a sense a visual, abstract, symbolic, or in some other form a "mental picture" of the problem, arises in part from content and context characteristics of the problem but brings together structure characteristics as well. It includes some of the following: the problem in its initial form, the desired end results, all initial transformed representations (deductions from the givens) and intermediate states, as well as ideas that describe and capsulize the stimulus to the problem solver.

For an example of an internal representation, consider the problem given by Paige and Simon (1966, pp. 100-109):

> 5.15 *A car radiator contains exactly one liter of a 90 percent alcohol-water mixture. What quantity of water will change the liter to an 80 percent alcohol mixture?*

An interesting account of a representation of this problem is described by Paige and Simon. They report that an experimenter drew the representation in Figure 5.2 privately after interviewing a subject solving the problem. The subject was asked to describe the "imagery" he used in solving the problem. When the interviewer disclosed his picture, the subject was amazed at the near-perfect correspondence between the representation and his "imagery."

A representation explicitly produced is an externalized, formalized form of an internal representation. It contains the same features, although their form may be inexact due to the necessity of symbolization.

Now we turn to the question: What mental operations (heuristic processes) have been found or are likely to be found useful in selecting a representation for a task? We start with the observation by Wickelgren:

> . . . we see that the role of generalization (of abstracting the essential properties from a problem) and the role of representation of information . . . are very closely linked and perhaps identical (p. 183).

Thus Wickelgren's statement places *generalization* clearly in the category of selecting a representation. Together with generalization, the specialization and inductive processes, including trial-and-error and successive approximation trial-and-error in particular, are essential to the development of a problem representation.

In the following problems trial-and-error may assist in creating a representation:

> 5.16 *A gum ball costs one penny. The gum balls come in 5 different colors. How many pennies do you need to make sure you get 3 gum balls of the same color?*

(Gibb, et al., 1975, p. 37)

Figure 5.2 *A Hypothetical Representation for the Mixture Problem (Problem 5.15)*

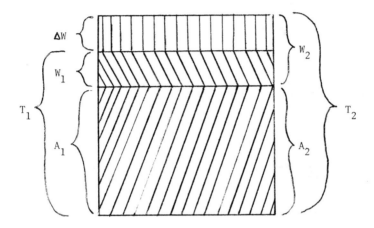

In this representation W_1, A_1, and T_1 represent the initial water, initial alcohol, and initial total mixture, respectively; W_2, A_2, and T_2 are the final water, final alcohol, and final total mixture; and ΔW is the change in the amount of water.

5.17 A gang of 13 thieves stole a sack of silver dollars.
When they tried to divide the booty evenly, there
were 3 dollars left over. In a fight over the extra
dollars, 2 thieves were killed. The money was dis-
tributed again, but this time there were 5 dollars
left over. Another argument ensued and 1 more thief
was killed. The money could now be divided evenly
among the remaining thieves. What is the least
possible amount of money that could have been stolen?

Analogy is a useful heuristic process for selecting a representation. Although it is more generally useful in exploiting a representation (the more complete discussion and exemplication will
be given below, the similarity between two problems is
generally based in problem structure and as such would reflect itself
in a representation of the problem. Thus, it is frequently beneficial
to attempt to develop a problem representation similar to a known or
given one if the problem under consideration has apparent structural
similarity to the problem with the known or given representation.

One could attempt the development of an analogous representation
whenever (1) a geometric task is a higher-dimensional analog of another
task of known representation, (2) the condition of one task is a part
of the condition of another or similar to the condition of another, or
(3) the goal of one task is the same as the goal of another.

To illustrate the use of analogy in the development of representations of problems, consider first Problems *5.8a*, *5.8b*, and *5.8c*.
The similarity across dimensions of (a) four points in space and a
circumscribing sphere, (b) three points in a plane and a circumscribing circle, and (c) two points in a line and a circumscribing "arc"
suggests that whatever representation--be it geometric, analytic, or
otherwise--is used for one would likely be useful for the other.

As a second example, consider the tasks given in Problems *5.7* and
5.19. The similarity of the condition of Problem *5.7* to that of *5.19*
indicates that the representation of one would serve as a guide in
forming the representation of the other. Since various representations
of Problem *5.19* are given later, the analogous representations may then
be observed.

Duncker (1945) and Kantowski (1974) (among others) have observed
that decomposition and recombination, particularly in the form of subproblem decomposition, appear to be fundamentally related to "visual-
izing" a path to the goal. The occurrence of goal-oriented heuristic
processes immediately before regular patterns of analysis and synthesis,
and the successive phases, with each phase viewed as a problem in prospect and a solution in retrospect, are ways these researchers described
their subjects' solution processes. These were the internal representations of the problems for the subjects. The processes for selecting
the subgoals for Duncker's subjects and the goal-oriented heuristic
processes for Kantowski's subjects were, therefore, heuristic processes

Figure 5.3 *Diagram for Problem 5.18*

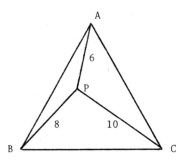

Figure 5.4 *Rearrangement of Figure 5.3, Preserving the Area*

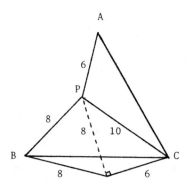

for selecting representations. In the case of Duncker, "meaningful"
variation of the problem was recognized as leading to a representation.
For Kantowski, *auxiliary elements* and *auxiliary problems*, as well as
variation of the problem, tended to lead to the selection of a representation.

There are several ways one may accomplish *variation of a problem*.
Since those that are most usually successful are analogy, decomposition
and recombination, generalization, and specialization, they constitute
secondary means of creating a representation for a problem. We keep in
mind, however, that these processes are simply means to the end of
variation of the problem, *auxiliary elements*, and *auxiliary problems*
insofar as they contribute to selection of a representation.

Processes for Exploiting a Representation

The second major part of creating a plan draws from content and particularly structure characteristics of a problem. The representation of a
problem corresponds to the structuring of the information available to
the solver and includes, as Bruner (1973) has described it:

> . . . visualization or some other shorthand way of summariz-
> ing the connections made in a set of givens . . . reduces the
> range of things to which he (the problem solver) attends.
> This narrowing of focus involves a bit of risk taking . . . a
> kind of implicit rule for ignoring certain information
> [involving] the nature of the solution or the kind of goal
> one is looking for. (p. 85)

The reduction of range to which Bruner refers generally is guided by
the structure characteristics of a problem. From the point of selection of an appropriate representation, the plan constitutes an outline
of the movement from givens to the goal through the structure of the
representation. Wilson (1967), as well as Newell, Shaw, and Simon
(1959), suggest means-ends analysis as a means of accomplishment of
subgoals, while Kantowski notes regular patterns of analysis and
synthesis (a decomposition and recombination process) for effective
movement within the representation.

Let us now consider the following problem:

> 5.18 *Located inside an equilateral triangle ABC is a
> point P in such a way that PA=6, PB=8 and PC=10.
> What is the area of triangle ABC?*

Consider as the representation the geometric figure described by the
problem (see Figures 5.3 and 5.4). By decomposing and recombining
the constituent triangles of triangle ABC, the exploitation begins
to occur. Further decomposition and recombination following that
shown in Figure 5.4 leads to an elegant problem solution, thus showing how, by decomposition and recombination, the pictorial representation leads to an exploitation of the information of the task.

Recall now the problem of the limiting sum (Problem *5.9*):

$$1 - \frac{1}{2} - \frac{1}{4} + \frac{1}{8} - \frac{1}{16} - \frac{1}{32} + \frac{1}{64} - \frac{1}{128} - \cdots$$

By decomposing and recombining the given representation, the information and hence the representation is organized for efficient processing:

$$(1 + \frac{1}{8} + \frac{1}{64} + \cdots) - (\frac{1}{2} + \frac{1}{16} + \frac{1}{128} + \cdots) - (\frac{1}{4} + \frac{1}{32} + \frac{1}{256} + \cdots).$$

Definition may be viewed as a heuristic process of usefulness under a variety of circumstances. It potentially transforms a problem into an equivalent problem, but gives no assurance that the resulting problem is more tractable than the original problem. It is a technique worth attempting whenever one operation or relation is defined in terms of another operation or relation. As a transformation on "terms," it represents an exploitation of a metalinguistic representation.

Problems that illustrate the use of *definition* are given below. Schoenfeld further illustrates the use of this heuristic process in cases in which a concept is defined in terms of the negation of another.

5.19   *What is the smallest number that leaves a remainder*
       of 9 when divided by 10, 8 when divided by 9, 7 when
       divided by 8, ..., 2 when divided by 3, and 1 when
       divided by 2?

5.20   *Tom drove from his home in Washington to a location*
       in Philadelphia at 40 miles per hour. His return
       trip from the location to his home in Washington was
       at a rate of 50 miles per hour. What was his rate
       for the total trip?

By representing the parallel phrases in terms of multiples of the respective integers and by replacing the nine phrases by a single phrase involving "common multiple," an insightful solution becomes apparent. Note how completely the statement of Problem *5.19* cues the use of this heuristic process. Definition not only transforms a problem into an equivalent problem; it also serves to characterize the invariants in a situation. In Problem *5.20*, the definition of "rate" is exploited as a source of avoiding an "obvious" pitfall.

Given a representation for a problem, it is frequently profitable to attempt the heuristic process involving the use of symmetry. This heuristic process is particularly fruitful for certain geometry problems, but it has potential in non-geometric (algebraic, number theoretic, and probabilistic) tasks as well. A clue that exploiting symmetry is apt to be of value for a given problem is the existence of some form of symmetry in the problem givens or condition. For example, if a part of the givens or condition in a geometric task is that the figure is a symmetric one (e.g., equilateral triangle, square, circle, rectangle), the use of symmetry-preserving transformations such as rotation or reflection are worth considering (Goldin and McClintock, in press).

Many tasks contain "hidden symmetries" that, when recognized, lead to elegant or insightful solutions. Several tasks with structures containing symmetry have already been discussed. For example, in Chapter IV the state-space representations for the Tower of Hanoi and the various isomorphic forms of tick-tack-toe demonstrate symmetry in solutions. These symmetries actually reflect symmetries in the givens of the problems themselves. It is frequently the case, as in these two examples, that solution processes (and end-results) involve symmetry in some way when givens or condition have symmetry properties.

Further examples of this reflection of symmetry of givens or condition in the solution occur in Problems *5.12*, *5.18*, and *5.33*. The symmetric pattern of coefficients in Problem *5.12* can be exploited to produce a problem solution short-cut. The symmetric properties of the geometric figures in both Problems *5.18* and *5.33* illustrate underlying structure features that can be preserved by symmetry-preserving transformations; further, these transformations lead to efficient and insightful solutions.

Empirical evidence does not suggest the use of symmetry in protocols of novice problem solvers. Neither of the researchers discussed in the review found evidence of even limited use of symmetry. This absence of evidence occurred in spite of the explicit selection of tasks that were conducive to the use of this process and in spite of instruction designed to suggest the usefulness of this process. It is important to note that both Lucas (1972) and Webb (1975) considered symmetry as a form of evaluation for correctness of solution (the invariance of symmetry following transformations used in the solution), whereas Blake defined it more in accordance with Polya.

Working backward is another heuristic process that serves to exploit a representation. The process identified by Pappus as analysis, *working backward* is a much-overlooked but powerful problem-solving technique. Wickelgren (1974) has characterized the conditions under which this process is likely to be useful. He suggests that (1) a uniquely specified goal and (2) unary (a single input statement yields a single output statement) and one-to-one (the input is uniquely determined by the output) operations constitute these conditions. One can see that large classes of problems, such as many geometric proofs as well as trigonometric and algebraic relations, satisfy these conditions and are, therefore, plausibly solvable through working backward.

Empirical research has demonstrated some use of the working-backward technique among non-mathematician subjects; the use of this technique has been repeatedly confirmed by mathematicians. In contrast to the frequent occurrence of working backward in the process sequence of Webb's (1975) subjects (approximately 100 instances), Blake (1975) found the process used by only four subjects on only one problem. Lucas (1972), on the other hand, found it occurring rather frequently (6 or more times) in the protocols of 17 subjects out of 30; Lucas' conclusion was that *reasoning by analysis* develops as a technique subjects use following heuristic-oriented instruction.

The use of analogy in mathematical problem solving is a means of exploiting the information in a representation by virtue of its similarity to another problem (together with the information of the second problem and its similar representation). Analogy has been described as a quasi-isomorphism between problems and as structure similarity. This contrasts with equivalent problems, which would be classified as *completely* analogous or isomorphic. Examples of analogous problems that have been described earlier are the four-ring Tower of Hanoi problem in comparison to the three-ring Tower of Hanoi problem, or the different versions of the missionary-cannibal problems. In addition, Problems *5.8a*, *5.8b* and *5.8c* are examples of mutually analogous problems. As is evident from examining these examples of analogous problems, the relationship between analogy and generalization is, at times, a close one. In fact, the related sets of problems given here are either special cases of a more general problem, or one task is a generalization of another.

Researchers who have deliberately attempted to observe the use of analogy have generally not found it present in problem-solving protocols. For example, the exploratory studies of Blake and Webb did not find analogy used by subjects sufficiently often to justify analysis. Similarly, Lucas found analogy occurring, even after heuristic-oriented instruction, in no more than a single isolated instance of less than 10 percent of his subjects. Thus, the extent to which analogy is inducible in the processes of novice problem solvers seems very small, but is basically non-tested.

Processes for Utilizing Alternate Representations

Alternate representations will be considered here as representations that adjust for difficulties inherent in the initial representation or that lead to a second, possibly more elegant or more general solution. In a sense, alternate representations lead to a more complete view of a problem space, possibly to the creation of a larger portion of a state-space representation. They relate closely to processes of evaluation and include "looking back" processes, particularly those that involve attempts to solve the problem another way. Likewise, processes that simplify the solution, that is, processes that produce a clear, more compact "imagery" of the problem and its solution, are relevant for alternate representations.

Consider Problem *5.18* as it may be represented in an analytic form (superimpose a well-chosen coordinatization). This alternate representation allows a problem solver not only to solve the problem as stated, but also provides a means of solving a more general problem. The solution to the problem through analytic geometry produces a quadratic surd pair, one member of which is the solution to the original problem and the other a solution to the analogous problem with "P" outside rather than inside the equilateral triangle.

The Tower of Hanoi problem(s) as discussed in Chapter IV are generalizable to n rings. A question frequently asked (an associated task) is that of the minimum number of moves in the n-ring version. Inductive processes, involving the solutions of the 2-ring, the 3-ring, and so on versions of the Tower of Hanoi puzzle, and the inherent structure of mathematical induction that it represents, will lead one to an algebraic expression that "solves" the general problem.

In contrast, but in the same inductive vein, consider again Problem 5.17. Initial attempts (and successes) in solving this problem may involve the search of a number sequence such as "three more than the multiples of 13" for a number that leaves a remainder of 5 when divided by 11 and that is divisible by 10. However, $13n + 3$ and $11m + 5$--representing 3 more than a multiple of 13 and 5 more than a multiple of 11, respectively--(or their number sequence analog) may be synthesized into $143k + 16$ (or its number sequence analog). In essence, this process is a restatement of a part of the condition (using other essential notions) and is an alternate representation for the problem.

Now let us consider the problem:

5.21 *A club with x members is organized into four committees in accordance with these two rules:*

    a. *Each member belongs to two and only two committees.*

    b. *Each pair of committees has one and only one member in common.*

How many members has this club?

Suppose that this problem has already been solved by a combinatorial means. In an attempt to produce a more concrete imagery of the problem, a problem solver conceivably would note the similarity among the parts of the condition and postulates of geometry. Specifically, note the analogy between: (a) each member belongs to two and only two committees and "each point belongs to two and only two intersecting lines," and (b) each pair of committees has one and only one member in common and "each pair of intersecting lines has one and only one point in common." This analogy suggests a geometric representation, as given in Figure 5.5, in which the lines represent committees and the points of intersection represent club members.

For one who does not observe the analogy to geometric elements, other forms of representation may be suggested. For example, a diagram

Figure 5.5 *Geometric Representation for Problem 5.21*

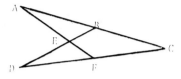

Figure 5.6 *Matrix Representation for Problem 5.21*

	A	B	C	D
A		x	y	z
B			u	v
C				w
D				

or chart will allow a problem solver to display the parts of the
condition in a visual, concrete form. Suppose the four committees
are represented as in the matrix in Figure 5.6 (the committees are
labeled A, B, C, and D). Since the condition hints at the member in
common to a pair of committees, the matrixing of committees across
committees is suggested. One then notes that the representation provides an immediate, concrete means of satisfying the problem condition and reduces the solution to a counting process.

The utilization of alternate representations parallels the
production and exploitation of initial representations. The combined
processes of these categories apply to utilizing alternate representations as well. The major difference is the purpose alternate
representations serve. A generalized solution, a clearer and more
completely justified solution, and a more elegant solution are results
that are more easily recalled from memory and that are more transfer-
rable.

3. Associating Heuristic Processes with Tasks

The idea of associating heuristic processes with tasks is a much-
used one. Separating heuristic variables as task variables from
subject variables is a difficult one for complete analysis. If one
views heuristic processes as choices a problem solver makes or as
"rules of thumb" that guide choices, then one class of heuristic
processes derive meaning from the number and nature of the decision
points.

In general, problem solvers may make deliberate or "forced"
choices at the point of representation of a problem. The knowledge
of mathematical content (definitions, theorems, etc.) and the skill
in performing algorithms may determine the extent and nature of the
choices a problem solver has as he or she develops the representation
of the task. For example, the problem given by Blake (1975) will
demonstrate the possible representations and the possibility of
deliberation as opposed to the predetermination of choice.

5.22 *A yacht is moored at A, 50 meters
away from a straight sea wall, CD.
The captain of the yacht wishes to
row to the sea wall to collect a
passenger and then row to a speed-
boat moored at B, 80 meters from
the wall. Where should the
passenger meet the captain to make
the route as short as possible?*

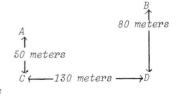

A knowledge of the Pythagorean Theorem would allow a problem solver
to derive a function that, when minimized, would solve the problem:

$$f(x) = \sqrt{(130-x)^2 + (50)^2} + \sqrt{x^2 + (80)^2}$$

Add to this content knowledge the skill of taking derivatives of radical functions and the skill of solving radical equations, and one has a solution strategy.

In contrast, using a knowledge of theorems of proportionality and the heuristic processes of auxiliary constructions and symmetry yields a proportion--$\frac{50}{130-x} = \frac{80}{x}$--that also leads to the minimum required in the problem. As a third option, for one who has the content knowledge (of physics) that "the angle of incidence is equal to the angle of reflection" and its connection to minimum paths (along with analogy), one can deduce an equation which also leads to the location the passenger should assume and to the minimum path.

The three choices of algebraic representation of this task are but a few of the possibilities. The point to be made is that inherent in the task are a number of heuristic processes and strategies. However, the association of these processes with the task is much dependent upon the content (and context) knowledge of the subject. Thus, certain task variables that derive meaning from the intrinsic problem structure lead to certain choices for some problem solvers. Yet for other problem solvers the choices are more delineated. For example, for a student of algebra who has insufficient geometry and physics content at his or her disposal, the Pythagorean Theorem is essentially the only "hunch" as to an approach. For a student with a mastery of geometry and a knowledge of physics, processes other than the solution through calculus are afforded. Theoretically, the student of calculus has at least the one additional strategy not available to other students. Thus, the number and nature of the ways in which a subject can represent the problem are variables.

There is a wide variety of ways one can associate heuristic processes with tasks. Two of the most commonly used associations are (1) the association of single heuristic processes and (2) the association of multiple heuristic processes. The illustration given above is one category of multiple heuristic processes association. What follows will illustrate these two ways of associating heuristic processes with tasks.

Single Heuristic Processes

It is clear that more than one heuristic process would be useful for almost all mathematical problem tasks imaginable. Yet, the easy, the most elegant, or the most common solution of a problem frequently features a particular heuristic process. The writings of Polya and particularly Wickelgren, among others, generally indicate solution processes of their examples as if a *single* heuristic process were the one appropriate to the solution. In general, however, associating multiple heuristic processes with a task is more natural. Either multiple solution paths require multiple processes, or multiple processes lead to a more efficient single solution. However, it is useful to focus on single heuristic processes for instructional and coding purposes.

In developing the concept of a particular heuristic process, it is customary to select a problem to "illustrate" that process. In essence, whenever this is done, the author is implying that the heuristic process is *the* essential process for solving the problem. For example, Wickelgren (1974) suggests that "working backward" is the appropriate heuristic process for "Nim" tasks.

> 5.23 *Fifteen pennies are placed on a table in front of two players. Each player is allowed to remove at least one penny but no more than five pennies at his turn. The players alternate turns, until one player takes the last penny on the table, and wins all 15 pennies. Is there a method of play that will guarantee victory?* (p. 142)

This association of "working backward" with "Nim" is accomplished in several ways. For the researcher a theoretical analysis of "Nim" in the sense developed in Chapter IV, or an empirical analysis based on success in solving the "Nim" problem, are two fruitful ways of making such an association.

Although we speak of "single heuristic processes" as if they were unitary ideas, the actual use of one such process is quite varied. Even when a single process is very specific, such as "try factoring" as opposed to very general, such as "try to use special cases" or try to break the problem into subproblems," the way in which it is applied can be quite varied. In essence, a heuristic process is a name given to a class of similar rules for selecting search paths through a problem space. This point should be kept in mind in teaching heuristic processes and in evaluating the acquisition of such processes.

We shall illustrate the variety, across a set of problems, in the use of a rather specific heuristic process. Chapter X.B contains several examples to make the same point for more general heuristic processes. Consider now the following set of five problems:

> 5.24 *What is the fractional form of the repeating decimal .363636...?*

> 5.25 *A six place number is formed by repeating a three place number; for example, 256,256 and 678,678. What is the largest integer that divides all six place numbers of this form?*

*5.26 If $N=1\cdot2\cdot3\cdot\ \cdot\cdot\ 1,000$ (more conveniently, 1000!), find
the number of terminating zeros when the multiplica-
tion is carried out.*

*5.27 Determine the number represented by the words HATBOX
and BOXHAT if it is known that:*

$$9\cdot HATBOX = 4\cdot BOXHAT.$$

*5.28 How old is the captain, how many children has he, and
how long is his boat if 32,118 is the product of the
three numbers (integers); the length of the boat as
given in feet; the captain has both sons and daughters;
he has more years in age than children, but he is not
yet 100 years old.*

For each of these problems, a single heuristic process (used in different ways) may be fruitfully applied. Yet, in some cases other problem-
solving procedures (including algorithms) may occur to the problem
solver. To single out a particular process and show its applicability
(or allow for the discovery of its applicability) should serve both to
motivate and to increase the transfer potential for that process.
Herein lies a major virtue of examining single heuristic processes.

Multiple Heuristic Processes

Problem solving involves the use of heuristic processes in combination. Research and theory to date, however, only hint at the
combinations that are effective. For example, Wilson (1967) suggested
that the combination of general and task specific heuristic processes
complement each other in the problem-solving process. Kantowski (1974)
indicated that progress toward the goal of a problem tended to take
the form of goal-oriented processes immediately followed by patterns
of analysis and synthesis. In addition, Krutetskii (1976) noted that
problem solutions of very capable subjects were characterized by
clearly segmented, sequential logical "chunks" toward the goal.

Multiple heuristic processes may occur as sequenced, complementary
processes. Yet they may occur in other combinations as well. We shall
limit the discussion of other combinations to only two types, although
it is clearly recognized that the reality of problem solving is not so
limited.

Polya (1957) has suggested a sense of "embedded" combinations of
heuristic processes. For example, the heuristic process known as
variation of the problem may be accomplished through such processes as
generalization, specialization, analogy, or *decomposition and recombination* (p. 65). As another example of "embedded" combinations of
processes, Polya and Kilpatrick (1974) suggest that "induction requires
observation," an implication that repeated use of special cases and

pattern search underlies the induction process. In a similar sense, generalization may be conceptualized as "containing" inductive processes.

In associating multiple heuristic processes with a task, we will discuss two basic classification schemes. First we suggest alternate processes that lead to distinct solution paths. In contrast with this, we suggest multiple heuristic processes representing a sequenced set of behaviors along a single solution path. "Looking back" may uncover the first of these, while "planning" suggests the second. In either case, state-space analysis of a task is a means of identifying the multiple heuristic processes of a task regardless of the classification scheme used.

It seems reasonable to assume that the likelihood for successful solution of a problem increases with an increase in the number of alternatives at any decision point in the solution. Of course, this is an oversimplification, but availability of alternate means of successful solution, all other things being equal, is a plausible factor in problem difficulty. Likewise, "getting started" on a solution is a necessity for successful solution. Thus, multiple "approach" processes may plausibly relate to success in problem solving.

Let us consider Problem 5.19. There is a variety of distinct heuristic approaches to this problem. In addition to using the method of the related problem (Problem 5.7), we could try "definition." How does the solution to his problem relate to the definition of "least common multiple" of 10, 9, 8, ..., 2?

One could also consider "variation of the problem" in the form of dropping a part of the condition and maybe its use in combination with induction. For example, induction may involve searching the sequence of answers to

5.29a *What is the smallest number that leaves a remainder*
       of 1 when divided by 2?

5.29b *What is the smallest number that leaves a remainder*
       of 1 when divided by 2 and leaves a remainder of 2
       when divided by 3?

and so on, for a pattern.

Finally, one could use successive approximation trial-and-error by testing numbers that end in 9 to determine the members of that set that leave the proper remainders when divided by 9, 8, 7, ..., 3, and 2, respectively. Successive approximation becomes relevant by noting patterns in the set of numbers ending in 19.

Multiple heuristic processes for key approaches to solutions to Problem 5.22 were given. As another example of the use of multiple heuristic processes, consider the following set of three problems.

5.30 In the figure AB=AC, angle BAD=30°, and AE=AD. Find the measure of angle EDC. (Adapted from The Contest Problem Book II, 1961, p. 45.)

5.31 In the figure, AC=CD and angle CAB - angle ABC = 30°. Find the measure of angle BAD. (Adapted from The Contest Problem Book II, 1961, p. 54.)

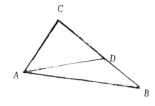

5.32 Triangle ABC has AB=AC, and angle A=20°. D is a point on AC such that BD=AD. E is a point on AB such that BE=BC. Find (and prove!) the measure of angle BDE.

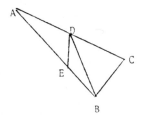

One representation for Problem 5.30 is in the form of a set of linear equations in unknowns (such as 30° + ∠DAC + 2 ACB = 180°; ∠DAC + 2∠DEA = 180°; and x° + ∠ACB = ∠DEA). An alternate heuristic process that is productive is to observe that ∠DAE is not of fixed size; therefore, the implication is that the solution is independent of the size of that angle. Specialization, choosing a special case, such as ∠DAC = 30°, could be productively explored.

Now we consider Problem 5.31. For one who has solved Problem 5.30, the use of an auxiliary construction--construct CE = CB for a point E on BA extended through A--would be plausible toward the means of "using the result" of Problem 5.30. As an alternate for one who notes the symmetry implicit in the isosceles triangle ACD, the reflection of the figure about the perpendicular from C to AD is another plausible approach. These two problems exemplify tasks for which multiple heuristic processes may initiate alternate, distinct solution paths.

Is Problem 5.32 sufficiently related to Problems 5.30 and 5.31 for the use of the results of a related problem or the use of the method of a related problem to be justified? Is an auxiliary line suggested? Whether or not the method of "consider a related problem" is helpful, such other approaches as "consider using (constructing through extended line segments) a triangle that can be proved

congruent to triangle ADE" are fruitful. Also, approaching the problem
through the use of a trigonometric relation is productive; this
suggests multiple heuristic processes.

There are, of course, numerous examples in which a heuristic
process may be "embedded" in another. A particularly frequently
occurring combination is that of a task-specific heuristic process
being embedded in a general process, such as means-ends analysis or
planning.

Heuristic processes may also be sequentially linked in the solution. One general pattern of such sequencing suggested by Kantowski
(1974) was that of a goal-oriented process, followed by analysis and
synthesis, followed by a goal-oriented process, and so on. This
suggests heuristic processes for accomplishing a subgoal in sequence
with those for accomplishing successive subgoals, and so on, similar
to Duncker's (1945) view of problem solving.

*Interaction of Other Task Variable Cate-
gories with Heuristic Behavior Variables*

The model of Figure 1.1 suggests that syntax variables as well
as content and context variables may initiate heuristic behaviors,
and vice-versa. We have seen several examples of this interaction
already. Consider also the problem:

5.33 *In circle O of radius 5, OABC
is a rectangle. Side OA=3 units,
and the segment AD of the radius
is 2 units. What is the length
of AC?*

Content knowledge will serve to suggest alternate solution paths.
For example, the length of AB may be found by using the fact that
"whenever two chords intersect in a circle, the product of the segments of one of them is equal to the product of the segments of the
other." By using chord (diameter) DF in conjunction with BA (extended
to form a chord), one obtains BA = 4. However, this result is obviated
if one recognizes the applicability of "the diagonals of a rectangle
are equal." The use of this fact may require "insight" of the naive
problem solver. Yet, the structural features of the givens and condition imply the applicability of "problem symmetry" and the use of a
symmetry-preserving transformation (reflection of the rectangle about
either of its axes of symmetry).

Problems *5.7*, *5.9*, and *5.19* represent examples of problems in
which syntax features potentially clue heuristic processes. The
"parallel" nature of the phrases in Problem *5.7* implies a need to

"rephrase the problem," which suggests the possible use of definition. The pattern of signs in Problem 5.9 suggests regrouping according to this pattern; hence, a decomposition-recombination process is suggested. Likewise, the pattern of phrases in Problem 5.19 should again lead the observant problem solver to rephrase, or possibly to produce a simpler related problem. In any event, the syntax features of the problem potentially cue the heuristic process useful in problem solution.

Problems 5.5, 5.10, and 5.18, as well as Problem 5.33, connect content variables and heuristic processes. For example, Problem 5.10 is recognizable as a place-value-related problem and as such suggests again the process of decomposing and recombining. Problem 5.18 recalls the Pythagorean triple, 6-8-10, and cues the problem solver to the decompose-recombine heuristic possibilities inherent in the problem by virtue of this content knowledge. Finally, Problem 5.5 recalls the "rate" problem type and possibly the process of constructing a table. It may also suggest "variation of the problem" or "go back to definition" in light of the fact that two seemingly very closely related problems are so structurally dissimilar. The apparent inconsistency of results in Problems 5.5 and 5.6 will cue such behaviors.

For the very observant problem solver, analogy may be a heuristic approach of relating Problem 5.22 to the physics content mentioned earlier as a third solution option. The contextual clues of the problem, together with the physics content knowledge, may allow a problem solver, by making insightful use of analogy, to derive a solution with little effort (compared with the effort of the calculus solution process.)

4. Conclusions

Although a notable increase of interest in heuristic processes has occurred since Polya's reintroduction of the concept, inquiry into the ramifications of this form of reasoning is still in its infancy. We have seen some of the impact of heuristic reasoning in computer programming and in psychology. Experimental and exploratory studies related to mathematics have begun to probe the "natural existence" as well as the "instructed development" of heuristic processes, and to study their effects on problem-solving success.

As research hypotheses evolve from exploratory investigations, much work is needed to substantiate or reject them by means of rigorous experimental studies. Some topics are still in need of hypothesis-generating exploration. What heuristic techniques are useful for what subject population, what processes can be developed by specified forms of instruction, and how these affect success in solving non-routine problems, are all virtually untouched areas. An understanding of the properties of problem tasks with respect to heuristic behavior is fundamental to the success of future research.

VI.

Syntax, Content, and Context Variables Examined
in a Research Study

by

Gerald A. Goldin
Northern Illinois University
De Kalb, Illinois

and

Janet H. Caldwell
Research for Better Schools
Philadelphia, Pennsylvania

In this chapter the relative difficulties of four kinds of verbal problems are compared with respect to student populations in different grades. The experimental problem characteristics, defined below, are: abstract factual (AF), abstract hypothetical (AH), concrete factual (CF), and concrete hypothetical (CH). These variables were selected for study because of their possible importance from the standpoint of cognitive-developmental theory. At the stage of formal operational thought, the adolescent can construct systems and theories, drawing conclusions from pure hypotheses as well as from actual observations. Two of the main characteristics of this stage, in contrast to the concrete operational stage which precedes it, are the ability to handle abstract situations, and the capability of thinking in a hypothetical-deductive manner (Johannot, 1947; Piaget, 1968). Thus, a strictly developmental model might suggest that concrete problems and factual problems would be less difficult than abstract problems and hypothetical problems for elementary school children, while for older subjects the differences would tend to disappear.

The process of solving verbal problems in mathematics has often been described as consisting of two general stages—translation and computation (Jerman, 1973; Kinsella, 1970; Paige and Simon, 1966). This point of view has been adopted for the model underlying the present book (see Figures 1.1 and 2.1). In Chapter I, syntax, content, and context variables are associated with the problem *statement*, and thus are expected to affect problem difficulty principally during the translation stage. In Chapter II, Barnett provides a more detailed model for the influence of syntax variables on the translation stage of a verbal problem, and in Chapter X.B, Schoenfeld urges the teaching of heuristic processes by means of the particular stages with which they are associated.

For the verbal problems in the present study, the translation stage corresponds to the "setting up" of the verbal problem statement as a system of mathematical expressions or equations. During the computation stage, the problem solver performs the algebraic operations necessary to obtain the solution. The kind of situation (abstract or concrete, factual or hypothetical) described by the problem statement (i.e., its verbal *context*) may be expected to affect the difficulty of translating the problem into mathematical expressions, and consequently the overall difficulty of the problem.

Interest in the field of information processing has stimulated the creation of computer programs which can solve verbal problems in mathematics through the above two-stage process; for example, Bobrow's STUDENT program (Bobrow, 1968). Paige and Simon used Bobrow's program as the basis for a model of human behavior in solving verbal problems, comparing the protocols of subjects instructed to "think aloud" with STUDENT's direct translation of algebra word problems (Paige and Simon, 1966). In order to determine the implications of such a model for the relative difficulties of abstract *vs.* concrete and factual *vs.* hypothetical problems, we here utilize the STUDENT program procedure to analyze problems of the four types AF, AH, CF, and CH. The analysis modifies STUDENT only by broadening its vocabulary in a consistent manner. It is concluded that concrete problems are more complicated for STUDENT than abstract problems, since concrete problems must undergo additional idiomatic substitutions in order to reference the *number* or *quantity* of objects described in the problem, rather than the objects themselves. Likewise, hypothetical problems require procedures considerably more complex than do factual problems (see below).

Thus in contrast to a strictly developmental theory, the STUDENT-type information processing model would suggest that AF problems are the easiest and CH the most difficult.

The purpose of the present chapter is to describe in detail the methods used in the construction of the problem instruments used in the study. An effort was made to address systematically each of the categories of task variables described in this book, so that parallel forms of verbal problems could be constructed—forms which held constant as many task variables which were *not* of experimental interest as possible, while varying those which were of interest. Often it was most difficult to ensure that variables were held constant, and the reader will be able to observe the extent of our success or lack of success for each variable.

Before proceeding with the detailed description and analysis of the problem instruments, a brief overall description of the study will be given.

1. Description of the Study

The population for this study consisted of students in grades 4 through 12 in a predominantly white middle- and upper-middle class school district in suburban Philadelphia. The school district contains seven elementary schools, one junior high school, and one senior high school. Two elementary schools deemed to be the most representative in mathematics achievement were selected; the tests were administered to all children in grades 4 through 6 in the elementary schools. Junior high classes were selected randomly from the three achievement levels in grades 7 through 9, and senior high classes were selected at random to obtain a representative cross-section of mathematics achievement in grades 10 through 12. A total of 399 elementary school children, 813 junior high students, and 274 senior high students completed the problem sets in the study.

The word-problem tests used in the study consisted of five sets of four problems each, for a total of 20 problems. Each set of four problems contained one problem each of the type AF, AH, CF, and CH. Three different tests were used: an elementary test for grades 4 through 6, an intermediate test for grades 7 through 9, and an advanced test for grades 10 through 12. There were three problem sets common to both the elementary and intermediate tests, four problem sets common to both the intermediate and the advanced tests, and two problem sets common to all three tests. (No problems were uniquely used with grades 7 through 9.) In general, the computationally more complex problems were retained for the higher grade levels.

In addition three different computational skills tests were developed: elementary, intermediate, and advanced. The computational skills tests consisted of five sets of two problems each, testing the computational algorithms necessary to solve the corresponding sets of verbal problems.

A researcher met with all teachers in the elementary schools and the junior high school prior to the testing to explain procedures. In the senior high school, the department chairperson explained the procedures to the participating teachers after meeting with the researcher. Instruction sheets and record forms were distributed at that time. The tests themselves were administered to all of the students on two consecutive days in September 1976. Each day the students were first asked to solve ten word problems in 30 minutes. These tests were collected, and a computational test consisting of five problems was distributed for completion in a ten-minute period. On the first day, half of the students received Part I and half received Part II of the word problem tests; on the second day, these were reversed. Testing order was assigned randomly within each class. The analysis included only data for students who completed the entire test.

The basic experimental design was a multifactorial analysis of variance with repeated measures on two experimental factors (Winer, 1971, pp. 599-603). Factors included in the analysis were: (a) grade level, (b) sex, (c) test order (Part I first or Part II first), (d) performance on the computational skills test (pass or fail), (e) first experimental factor—abstract or concrete, and (f) second experimental factor--factual or hypothetical. Six different analyses of variance were performed in accordance with the above design: (1) elementary school students, all problems; (2) junior high school students, all problems; (3) senior high school students, all problems; (4) elementary and junior high students, problems common to both tests; (5) junior high and senior high students, problems common to both tests; and (6) all students, problems common to all three tests.

More detail on the study itself may be found in the dissertation of one of the authors, and is to appear in the literature (Caldwell, 1977; Caldwell and Goldin, 1979). Some of the findings are summarized at the end of this chapter, but first we shall examine the construction of the problem instruments.

2. The Experimental Variables

The classification of problems as concrete or abstract, and as factual or hypothetical, was based on the following definitions (see also Chapter III). An *abstract* word problem involves a situation which describes abstract or symbolic objects, while a *concrete* word problem describes a real situation dealing with real objects. For example, a problem about digits in a number would be abstract, while a problem about baseballs would be concrete. A *factual* problem describes a situation. A *hypothetical* problem not only describes a situation, but also describes a possible change in the situation. This change does not really occur within the context of the problem. In solving the hypothetical problem, the problem-solver must consider not only the situation which occurs within the context of the problem, but also the described alteration which does not occur.

It was desired that the classification of problems as abstract or concrete, factual or hypothetical, be both a valid and reliable process. Consequently each problem was first classified by consensus of the participants in the mathematics education doctoral seminar at the University of Pennsylvania. Where there was not unanimous agreement of the five participants, a problem was reworded until agreement was achieved. In a final validation procedure, a *validation instrument* was given to five faculty members and graduate students in education, none of whom had participated in the doctoral seminar. After some experimentation, it was determined most reliable to use separate questionnaires for the abstract/concrete and the factual/hypothetical classifications.

Thus on the "Abstract/Concrete Validation Instrument," there were these instructions: "Please decide whether each of the following problems is *abstract* or *concrete* according to the following definitions and circle the appropriate adjective below." The above definitions of abstract and concrete problems were then stated, followed by 44 problems to be classified as one or the other. The

"Factual/Hypothetical Validation Instrument" contained similar instructions followed by the definitions; but on this instrument it was deemed
advisable to include four examples. These were as follows:

6.1 *There is a certain given number. Three more than twice
this given number is equal to fifteen. What is the
value of the given number?*

(Factual. No change is described.)

6.2 *There is a certain number. If this number were four
more than twice as large, it would be equal to eighteen.
What is the number?*

(Hypothetical. The number is not really four more than
twice as large.)

6.3 *Susan has some dolls. Jane has five more than twice
as many, so she has seventeen dolls. How many dolls
does Susan have?*

(Factual. No change is described.)

6.4 *Susan has some dolls. If she had four more than twice
as many, she would have fourteen dolls. How many dolls
does Susan really have?*

(Hypothetical. Susan does not really have four more
than twice as many dolls.)

It will be noted that of the example problems given, the first two
are abstract and the last two are concrete, although this was not
explicitly pointed out on the "Factual/Hypothetical Validation
Instrument."

In order to include a problem in the experiment, it was required
that four of the five validators *independently* classify the problem
as abstract or concrete, factual or hypothetical, in agreement with
the consensus of the doctoral seminar. This stringent requirement
was imposed in order that there be little doubt in the interpretation
of the definitions of the experimental variables. The underlying
consideration was to obtain a degree of precision which would ensure
the *reproducibility* of the results of the study; or alternatively,
which would permit further studies of the *same* abstract/concrete and
factual/hypothetical variables. The experimental problems are listed
by sets in Table 6.1.

Of the 44 problems listed on the "Abstract/Concrete Validation
Instrument," there was *unanimous* agreement of the five validators on
37 problems. One validator classified the four problems involving
age as abstract (including Problems *5(a)*, *5(b)* and *6(a)* in Table 6.1);
one classified a problem about camels' loads as abstract (Problem

Table 6.1 *The Experimental Problems Arranged by Sets*

Set 1 (a) Jane has 32 gumdrops. Her older sister Sarah has three   *CF*
times as many gumdrops as Jane has. How many gumdrops
does Sarah have?

(b) George has 34 marbles. Suppose that he had two times as   *CH*
many marbles as he really has. How many marbles would
George have then?

(c) The number 33 is given. A second number is three times   *AF*
as large as the first number is. What is the value of
this second number?

(d) The number 34 is given. Suppose that this number were   *AH*
two times as large as it really is. What would the value
of the number be then?

Set 2 (a) Julie has seven more books than Bob. Bob loses four   *CF*
books, so that now he has fifteen left. How many books
does Julie have?

(b) Charlie has eight more records than Amanda has. If   *CH*
Amanda lost three records, then she would have sixteen
left. How many records does Charlie have?

(c) A number is six larger than a second number. The second   *AF*
number is changed so that it is five smaller, and now
it equals sixteen. What is the first number?

(d) A number is nine larger than a second number. If the   *AH*
second number were three smaller, then it would equal
seventeen. What is the value of the first number?

Set 3 (a) Phil has seven more than three times as many toys as he   *CF*
had last year, and he has 31 toys. How many toys did
he have last year?

(b) If Sally had nine more than twice as many records as   *CH*
she really has, she would have 25 records. How many
records does she really have?

(c) The value of eight more than six times a given number is   *AF*
known to be equal to 44. What is the value of the given
number that is described here?

(d) If an unknown number were eight more than five times as   *AH*
large as it is now, then it would be equal to 33. What
is this unknown number?

continued

Table 6.1 *(continued)*

Set 4 (a) Alan bought an equal number of plants and flowerpots.   *CF*
           Each plant cost three dollars and each flowerpot cost
           five dollars, so that he spent 48 dollars in all. How
           many plants did Alan buy?

       (b) Jane has an equal number of dogs and cats. If she had   *CH*
           twice as many dogs and four times as many cats, she
           would have 42 pets in all. How many dogs does Jane
           have?

       (c) A number Δ is equal to a number $\bigcirc$. The sum of   *AF*
           three times the first number and four times the second
           number is known to be equal to 56. What is the value
           of Δ in this question?

       (d) The numbers Δ and $\bigcirc$ are equal. If Δ were twice   *AH*
           as large as it is and $\bigcirc$ were five times as large,
           then the sum of the new numbers would be 49. What is
           the value of Δ ?

   Note: On the validation instruments, problems *4(c)* and *4(d)*
         appeared with an X in place of the triangle and a Y
         in place of the circle. The change was made in order
         to permit these problems to be used with all three groups
         of subjects.

Set 5 (a) Jenny is a girl. Jenny's father is three times as old   *CF*
           as Jenny is, and he is 39 years old. How old is Jenny?

       (b) Eddie is a boy. If Eddie were four times as old as he   *CH*
           really is, then he would be 48 years old. How old is
           Eddie?

       (c) There is a number. A second number is five times as   *AF*
           large as the first number, and the second number is 55.
           What is the value of the first number?

       (d) There is a number. If this number were two times as   *AH*
           large as it really is, then it would be equal to 28.
           What is the number?

continued

Table 6.1 *(continued)*

Set 6 *(a)* There are four people in the Smith family. Mary Smith   *CF*
is the youngest, her sister Rose is two years older
than Mary, her sister Ann is two years older than Rose,
and her sister Louise is two years older than Ann. The
sum of all four ages is equal to 132. How old is Mary?

(b) Four camels are carrying equal loads. Suppose the first   *CH*
camel were carrying the same load, the second were carrying
six pounds more than the first, the third were carrying
six pounds more than the second, and the fourth were
carrying six pounds more than the third. The sum of the
four loads would be 156 pounds. How many pounds is the
first camel carrying?

(c) There are four numbers in a given list. The first number   *AF*
is the smallest, the second number is four more than the
first number, the third number is four more than the
second number, and the fourth number is four more than
the third number. The sum of all four numbers is 184.
What is the first number in the list?

(d) There are four equal numbers in a given list. Suppose   *AH*
the first number were the same, the second number were
three more than the first, the third number were three
more than the second, and the fourth number were three
more than the third. The sum of all four numbers would be
178. What is the value of the first number?

Set 7 *(a)* In a certain school in Pennsylvania, one-fourth of the   *CF*
pupils are boys, and there are 43 boys in the school.
How many pupils are there?

(b) If John were able to work only one-third as much, he   *CH*
would receive 35 dollars a week. How much does he
receive a week?

(c) It is known that one-fifth of a given number has a value   *AF*
equal to 42. What is the given number that is described
here?

(d) If a certain number were only one-fourth as large as it   *AH*
is, it would be equal to 28. What is this number?

continued

Table 6.1 *(continued)*

Set 8 *(a)* A young farmer has eight more hens than dogs. Since   *CF*
hens have two legs each, but dogs have four legs each,
all together the animals have 118 legs. How many dogs
does the young farmer own?

(b) There are four more girls in an English class than boys.   *CH*
If there were six times as many girls and twice as many
boys, there would be 136 pupils. How many boys are
there?

(c) The value of a given number is six more than the value   *AF*
of a second number. The sum of two times the first
number and four times the second number is 126. What is
the value of the second number?

(d) A given number is six more than a second number. If the   *AH*
first number were four times as large and the second
two times as large, their sum would be 126. What is
the second number?

The *elementary* word problem test consisted of *Sets 1-5* above; the
intermediate test consisted of *Sets 2-4* and *6-7*; and the *advanced* test
included *Sets 3-4* and *6-8*.

6(b) in Table 6.1); and one classified a salary problem as abstract
(Problem *7(b)* in Table 6.1). Only one problem did not receive the
required agreement of four validators; that problem was rewritten
and classified by the same group of validators with unanimous agreement. Of the 44 problems listed on the "Factual/Hypothetical
Validation Instrument," there was unanimous agreement of the five
validators on all of them. The rewritten problem was resubmitted
to the same validators, and agreement was again unanimous. In short,
it was not overly difficult to obtain independent agreement on the
classification of verbal problems with respect to the experimental
variables. Greater unanimity might have been achieved for the
abstract/concrete variable had illustrative examples been provided
the validators, as they were for the factual/hypothetical variable.

Let us discuss somewhat further the interpretations of the
experimental variables with respect to cognitive-developmental theory,
and with respect to Bobrow's STUDENT program. Our most important
remark is that both the abstract/concrete and factual/hypothetical
variables describe the problem's *verbal* context. Making reference
to the context variables discussed in Chapter III (Table 3.2),
variables describing a verbal context are distinguished from those
describing differences among problem embodiments (e.g., verbal problems *vs.* manipulative problems). Thus the "concrete" problems that
we study are only "concrete" in the sense that the problem statements
discuss "real objects" or "real situations," not in the sense of being
embodied in a manipulative task environment. This is a step removed
from the meaning of "concrete" as it is often interpreted in developmental theory. Nevertheless, there is a widespread assumption among
elementary educators that concrete verbal problems (in our sense) are
more appropriate for younger children, and therefore this represents
an important variable to study.

We have been considering the experimental variables to be *context*
variables, because they characterize different kinds of situations
which are described when the meanings of the problem statements are
interpreted. However, each of these variables has a *syntactic* component as well, which becomes very apparent when our problems are
examined with reference to the STUDENT program.

The input for STUDENT consists of a restricted subset of English
words which can be used to express a variety of algebra and arithmetic word problems. The program sets up a corresponding set of
equations and solves for the requested unknowns. A store of "global"
information, not specific to any one problem, enables the program to
identify equivalent terms. The language-processing system proceeds
by transforming statements into semantically equivalent sequences of
simpler sentences which can be directly interpreted. The first step
is to make "mandatory substitutions," which reduce certain words or
phrases to their standard equivalent or canonical forms. This is
accomplished by means of a simple dictionary of synonyms which is
part of the global information. The next step, "tagging words by
function," applies labels to some of the words in the text, indicating

Figure 6.1 *Flowchart for STUDENT (Adapted from Bobrow, 1968)*

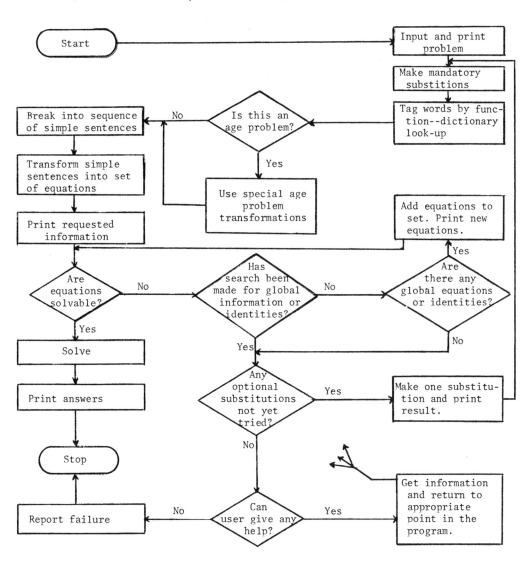

Table 6.2 *Example of a Problem Solved by STUDENT (Adapted from Bobrow, 1968)*

The problem to be solved is:

> If the number of customers Tom gets is twice the square of 20 percent
> of the number of advertisements he runs, and the number of advertisements
> he runs is 45, what is the number of customers Tom gets?

With mandatory substitutions the problem is:

> If the number of customers Tom gets is 2 times the square 20 percent
> of the number of advertisements he runs, and the number of advertisements
> he runs is 45, what is the number of customers Tom gets?

With words tagged by function the problem is:

> If the number (of/op) customers Tom (gets/verb) is 2 (times/op 1) the
> (square/op 2) 20 (percent/op 2) (of/op) the number (of/op) advertisements
> (he/pro) runs, and the number (of/op) advertisements (he/pro) runs is
> 45, (what/Q word) is the number (of/op) customers Tom·(gets/verb) (?/DLM

The function tags have the following meanings:

op   This tag designates a possible arithmetic operation.

op 1,2 The tags op 1 and op 2 also designate operations; the
        number indicates the order of operations.

verb   This tag is used to designate a verb.

pro   This tag is used with pronouns.

Q word This designates question words, such as "what" or "how many."

DLM   This abbreviation is used for the tag "delimiter." These
        are punctuation marks indicating the end of a sentence.

The simple sentences are:

> The number (of/op) customers Tom (gets/verb) is 2 (times/op 1) the
> (square/op 1) 20 (percent/op 2) (of/op) the number (of/op) advertisements
> (he/pro) runs (period/DLM)
>
> The number (of/op) advertisements (he/pro) runs is 45 (period/DLM)
>
> (What/Q word) is the number (of/op) customers Tom (gets/verb) (?/DLM)

continued

Table 6.2 *(continued)*

The equations to be solved are:

   Equal X (number of customers Tom (gets/verb))

   Equal (number of advertisements (he/pro) runs) 45

   Equal (number of customers Tom (gets/verb)) (times 2 (expt (times .2000 (number of advertisements (he/pro) runs)) 2))

   Prefix notation is used in setting up these equations; the operation is indicated first and then the two operands.

   The operation "expt" has two operands and indicates exponentiation; the first operand is the base and the second the exponent.

The solution is:

   The number of customers Tom gets is 162.

their grammatical function. This is also accomplished by means of a
dictionary classifying certain words as operators, verbs, and
delimiters. The text is then divided into a sequence of simple
sentences, and these are translated into equations by assigning
variable names to question words and noun phrases. Figure 6.1 outlines STUDENT's operation, and Table 6.2 gives an example adapted
from Bobrow of a problem solved by STUDENT.

We shall use the STUDENT procedure to analyze Problems *6.1*
through *6.4*. The first problem (*6.1*) is abstract and factual.

*There is a certain given number. Three more than twice
this given number is equal to fifteen. What is the
value of the given number?*

With the mandatory substitutions, the problem becomes:

There is a certain given number, 3 plus 2 times the given
number is 15. What is the value of the given number?

The next step involves tagging the words by function:

There is a certain given number (period/DLM) 3 (plus/op 2)
2 (times/op 1) the given number is 15 (period/DLM) (What/
Q word) is the value (of/op) the given number (?/DLM)

When the problem is divided into simple sentences, we have:

There is a certain given number (period/DLM)

3 (plus/op 2) 2 (times/op 1) the given number is 15 (period/DLM)

(What/Q word) is the value (of/op) the given number (?/DLM)

The problem is now translated into equations. The first sentence is
redundant, since it is the question sentence which identifies the
unknown.

Equal X (given number)

Equal (plus 3 (times 2 (given number))) 15

The program now solves the problem by solving the equations X = given
number, and 3 + 2X = 15. No significant alterations in the program
have been required for this problem, and no optional or idiomatic
substitutions were made.

Problem *6.2* is abstract and hypothetical.

*There is a certain number. If this number were four more
than twice as large, it would be equal to eighteen. What
is the number?*

With mandatory substitutions, the problem becomes:

> There is a certain number. If the number were 4 plus
> 2 times as large, it would be 18. What is the number?

With words tagged by function:

> There is a certain number (period/DLM) If the number
> were 4 (plus/op 2) 2 (times/op 1) as large, (it/pro)
> would be 18 (period/DLM) (What/Q word) is the number
> (?/DLM)

The simple sentences are:

> There is a certain number (period/DLM)
>
> The number were 4 (plus/op2) 2 (times/op 1) as large (period/DLM)
>
> (It/pro) would be 18 (period/DLM)
>
> (What/Q word) is the number (?/DLM)

As in Problem 6.1 the first sentence is redundant, and the last sentence translates to the equation "Equal X (number)." However, the middle sentences require additional elaboration of the processing system. In the second sentence, the comma is automatically replaced by (period/DLM), because it has been preceded by a subject and a predicate. In the third sentence, there is ambiguity as to the antecedent of the pronoun "it;" "(it/pro)" refers to the hypothetical number rather than the real one which is to be found, but it is not clear that STUDENT could handle this distinction. The comparison "as large" also involves some ambiguity; the insertion of the phrase "as it is" to complete the comparison helps somewhat, after which the comparison "as large as ... is" must be omitted, leaving only the "it." Then, in order to specify the antecedents of the pronouns, the noun phrases associated with the subjunctive tense verbs must be distinguished from those associated with the present-tense verbs. The second and third sentences thus become:

> (The number/different tense) is 4 (plus/op 2) 2 (times/
> op 1) (it/pro) (period/DLM)
>
> (It/pro, different tense) is 18 (period/DLM)

Translated into equations, the problem now becomes:

> Equal X (number)
>
> Equal Y (number, different tense)
>
> Equal (number, different tense) (plus 4 (times 2 (it/pro)))
>
> Equal (it/pro, different tense) 18

where (it/pro) refers to (number) and (it/pro, different tense) refers to (number, different tense).

Thus, many more steps are required for STUDENT to process a hypothetical problem than are required for a factual problem. The difficulties are difficulties of *syntax*, and may be expected to occur similarly in all of the hypothetical problems. We wish to contrast this purely syntactic analysis with the view that the factual/hypothetical distinction has an important *semantic* component --that hypothetical contexts might be more difficult (for a human being) to *visualize* or *imagine* (on a level that is not exclusively verbal).

Next we consider the processing of a concrete problem *(6.3)* by STUDENT.

> *Susan has some dolls. Jane has five more than twice as many, so she has seventeen dolls. How many dolls does Susan have?*

With mandatory substitutions, the problem becomes:

> Susan has some dolls. Jane has 5 plus 2 times as many, so she has 17 dolls. How many dolls does Susan have?

With words tagged by function, we obtain:

> (Susan/person) (has/verb) some dolls (period/DLM) (Jane/person) (has/verb) 5 (plus/op 2) 2 (times/op 1) as many, so (she/pro) (has/verb) 17 dolls (period/DLM) (How many/Q word) dolls does (Susan/person) (have/verb) (?/DLM)

The simple sentences are:

> (Susan/person) (has/verb) some dolls (period/DLM)
>
> (Jane/person) (has/verb) 5 (plus/op 2) 2 (times/op 1) as many
>
> (She/pro) (has/verb) 17 dolls (period/DLM)
>
> (How many/Q word) dolls does (Susan/person) (have/verb) (?/DLM)

An idiomatic substitution must now be made throughout the problem, changing "Susan has some dolls" to "There is a number of dolls Susan has;" "Jane has ..." to "The number of dolls Jane has...;" and so forth. For example, the last sentence becomes:

> (What/Q word) is the number (of/op) dolls (Susan/person) (has/verb) (?/DLM)

The first sentence is again redundant. "(She/pro)" in the third simple sentence refers to the person named last, thus posing no difficulty. The comparison "as many" must be processed by inserting its completion "as Susan has," which then undergoes idiomatic substitution. The equations which result are:

Equal X (number of dolls (Susan/person) (has/verb))

Equal Y (number of dolls (Jane/person) (has/verb))

Equal (number of dolls (Jane/person) (has/verb)) (plus 5
(times 2 (number of dolls (Susan/person) (has/verb))))

Equal (number of dolls (Jane/person) (has/verb)) 17

We see that more steps are required for a concrete problem than
for an abstract problem; the language processing for the concrete
problem requires additional idiomatic substitutions in order to refer
to the *number* of objects of each kind, rather than to the objects
themselves. Again, the differences in processing by STUDENT are due
solely to the *syntax* differences associated with the abstract/concrete
variable. In contrast, regarding this variable as a *context* variable
emphasizes the differences in the *actual situations* described by the
problem statements, leaving open, for example, the possibility that
(for a human being) concrete situations might be easier to visualize
or imagine than abstract situations.

Problem *6.4*, being both concrete and hypothetical, is the most
complicated for STUDENT to process.

To summarize, the abstract/concrete and factual/hypothetical
classifications may be thought of as context variables, for which a
developmental theory might predict concrete factual problems to be
the easiest and abstract hypothetical problems the hardest, with the
differences tending to disappear for older children. However, each
of these variables has a syntactic component, for which a STUDENT-
type information-processing model might predict abstract factual
problems to be the easiest and concrete hypothetical problems the
most difficult.

Next, we return to the discussion of the system of experimental
problems in Table 6.1. The problem sets were designed to hold constant within each set a list of task variables which were not of
experimental interest; we shall describe how this was done.

3. Controlling for Syntax Variables

Problem Length

The length of each problem is described by the number of words,
counting each numeral as one word, and not counting articles. The
number of sentences is held constant for all problems within a set,
while the number of words varies by no more than 10 percent of the
number of words in the shortest problem in the set. The values of
these variables are objectively determined and easily re-checked;
thus no additional validation was considered necessary (see Table 6.3).

Table 6.3 *Characteristics of the Experimental Problems*

Set	Problem	Type	Length	Number of Sentences	Numerical Data v = verbal, n = numeral	Syntactic Complexity
1	(a)	CF	23	3	32(n),3(v)	3.33
	(b)	CH	24	3	34(n),2(v)	4.33
	(c)	AF	22	3	33(n),3(v)	3.33
	(d)	AH	24	3	34(n),2(v)	4.00
2	(a)	CF	24	3	7(v),4(v),15(v)	3.33
	(b)	CH	25	3	8(v),3(v),16(v)	3.33
	(c)	AF	26	3	6(v),5(v),16(v)	3.33
	(d)	AH	24	3	9(v),3(v),17(v)	3.67
3	(a)	CF	28	2	7(v),3(v),31(n)	7.00
	(b)	CH	26	2	9(v),2(v),25(n)	6.50
	(c)	AF	26	2	8(v),6(v),44(n)	7.50
	(d)	AH	27	2	8(v),5(v),33(n)	7.00
4	(a)	CF	33	3	3(v),5(v),48(n)	5.00
	(b)	CH	34	3	2(v),4(v),42(n)	6.00
	(c)	AF	33	3	3(v),4(v),56(n)	6.00
	(d)	AH	35	3	2(v),5(v),49(n)	5.00
5	(a)	CF	23	3	3(v),39(n)	3.00
	(b)	CH	24	3	4(v),48(n)	4.00
	(c)	AF	24	3	5(v),55(n)	3.33
	(d)	AH	25	3	2(v),28(n)	3.67
6	(a)	CF	52	4	4(v),2(v),2(v),2(v),4(v),132(n)	6.00
	(b)	CH	53	4	4(v),6(v),6(v),6(v),4(v),156(n)	6.75
	(c)	AF	49	4	4(v),4(v),4(v),4(v),4(v),184(n)	6.00
	(d)	AH	49	4	4(v),3(v),3(v),3(v),4(v),178(n)	7.00
7	(a)	CF	22	2	1/4(v),43(n)	4.00
	(b)	CH	22	2	1/3(v),35(n)	4.50
	(c)	AF	21	2	1/5(v),42(n)	5.00
	(d)	AH	21	2	1/4(v),28(n)	5.00
8	(a)	CF	32	3	8(v),2(v),4(v),118(n)	5.67
	(b)	CH	33	3	4(v),6(v),2(v),136(n)	6.67
	(c)	AF	32	3	6(v),2(v),4(v),126(n)	6.33
	(d)	AH	31	3	6(v),4(v),2(v),126(n)	6.33

Sequencing of Information

Within each set of problems, corresponding problem elements are presented in the same sequence. The order in which the numerical information appears is the same, and the question appears at the end of each problem. For example, all problems in *Set 5* have the underlying equation $ax = b$, where a and b are given and x is unknown. In each problem a is given first, then the operation of multiplication is indicated, then a phrase occurs describing the unknown quantity, then equality is asserted to a given value of b, and finally the unknown quantity is asked for.

No extraneous numerical information is needed to solve any problem. For example, in Problem *8(a)* it is not assumed but stated explicitly that hens have two legs and dogs have four. Likewise, there are no coin problems in which the values of coins are assumed.

Where there is irrelevant numerical information, the same data are included in all problems within the set. For example, in *Set 6* the *same* number "four" in the first sentence of each problem does not enter into numerical computation. However, this rule was *not* enforced for *ordinals* (first, second, third, etc.) which were treated as ordinary English adjectives. Thus Problem *6(b)* mentions "the first camel," "the second," and so forth, while in Problem *6(a)* the members of the Smith family are described by name. In retrospect it might not have been too difficult to change this particular problem set so that the ordinal numbers were the same in all four problems--we might have described four "sisters" in the Smith family, and referred to them as "the first sister," "the second," and so forth. However, in many of the abstract problems it was necessary to refer to "a number" and "a second number;" this wording would have become awkward if it had been used in the corresponding concrete problems (e.g., "a student" and "a second student" instead of "Charlie" and "Amanda" in Problem *2(b)*).

Participants in the mathematics education doctoral seminar verified as a group that the sequencing of the data was the same for all problems within each set. Unanimous agreement was obtained without any difficulty.

Numerals and Mathematical Symbols

Within each set of problems, the corresponding numbers have the same number of digits and are of the same type--whole numbers or fractions. Corresponding numbers are also of the same written form-- either words or numerals. No special mathematical symbols appear in any of the problems.

The numbers and the forms of the numbers appearing in each problem are listed in Table 6.3. It was not deemed necessary to validate these variables.

Table 6.4 *Assigned Counts for Computing the Syntactic Complexity Coefficient (based on Botel, Dawkins and Granowsky, 1973)*

0-count Structures

The most frequently used simple sentences

Subject-Verb (Adverbial)	SV (Adv)
Subject-Verb-Object	SVO
Subject-Verb-be-Complement	SVbeC

> The complement may be an adjective, as in "He
> is big," a noun as in "He is a clown," or an
> adverb as in "He is there."

Subject-Verb-Infinitive	SVInf

Simple transformations, such as interrogatives (simple questions and
tag-end questions), exclamations, and imperatives,

Coordinate clauses joined by "and"

Non-sentence expressions, such as nouns of direct address,
greetings, calls and attention-getters, interjections,
responses, empty phrases, and sentence openers

There is no extra count for verb expansions using auxiliary verbs
such as "be," "have," "do," "will," and "can," intensifier expansions
such as "very," or determiner expansions such as articles, demonstrative
pronouns and possessive pronouns.

1-count structures

Less frequently used sentence patterns

Subject-Verb-Indirect Object-Direct Object	SVIO
Subject-Verb-Object-Object Complement	SVOC

Any prepositional phrase added to any of the 0-count structures

Noun modifiers, such as adjectives, nouns, predeterminers (e.g.
"all of," "one of,"), possessive nouns, adjectival participles
(-ed and -ing forms)

Other modifiers, such as adverbial additions to the 0-count
structures, modals, and negatives (however, adverbial structures
which begin a sentence are 2-count structures)

continued

Table 6.4 *(continued)*

1-count structures *(continued)*

Familiar idiomatic expressions such as "once in a while," "_____ years old," "more or less," etc.

Infinitives not immediately following the verb

Gerunds used as subjects

Clauses joined by coordinating conjunctions other than "and"

Deletion in coordinate clauses (or compound objects of prepositions, as interpreted by the present authors)

The paired conjunction "both ... and"

2-count structures

Passive transformations

Paired conjunctions ("either ... or ...," "not ... but ...," etc.)

Comparatives ("as ... as," "same ... as," "more ... than," etc.)

Dependent clauses (adjectival clauses, adverbial clauses, nominal clauses)

Participles appearing after a noun, or separated from it by commas

The infinitive as a subject

Appositives

Conjunctive adverbs (e.g. "thus," "however," "therefore")

3-count structures

Clauses used as subjects

Absolutes

Syntactic Complexity

In order to control for syntactic complexity, the system developed by Botel, Dawkins, and Granowsky (see Chapter II) was adapted to mathematics word problems (Botel, Dawkins, and Granowsky, 1973). The system takes into account many of the grammatical structure variables described by Barnett in Chapter II. For each problem, a *syntactic complexity coefficient* is computed. This coefficient ranges from 3.00 to 7.50 for the entire system of experimental problems, but within each set its range varies by no more than 1.00. (A primary reading program would typically include sentences having an average complexity of three or four points.) Thus, while the syntactic complexity varied from set to set, it remained relatively constant within each set of four problems (see Table 6.3).

The syntactic complexity coefficient is based on a theory of transformational grammar suggesting that complex sentences are derived from changing and combining structures such as simple sentences. The formula was originally developed and tested with school children in the primary grades. Its use is described as follows:

> To apply the syntactic complexity formula to any passage, each sentence in the passage is assigned a complexity rating. These ratings are then averaged to obtain the complexity rating for the entire passage. The complexity rating for a sentence is determined by comparing the structure of the sentence to the structures described and illustrated... The basic structure of the main clause of the sentence is assigned a count of 0, 1, or 2 and counts are added for additional features or structures that add complexity. For example, the sentence "His vacation over, the tired doctor drove home" has a complexity count of four: The basic structure ... ("The doctor drove home") gets a count of 0 ... Since the subject ("doctor") is modified by an adjective ("tired") a count of 1 is added ... The absolute ("His vacation over") at the beginning of the sentence adds an additional count of 3 ... The whole sentence thus receives a count of 0 + 1 + 3 = 4. (Botel, Dawkins, and Granowsky, 1973)

Table 6.4 lists the 0-count, 1-count, 2-count, and 3-count structures according to Botel, Dawkins, and Granowsky.

The analysis of several structures common in mathematical word problems was not made explicit in the original system. The following sentences illustrate these structures, and display the interpretations we have made:

(1) "One number is three more than a second number." The basic sentence here is "number is more," a Subject-Verb-be-Complement pattern (SVbeC), which counts 0 points. The adjectives "one," "three," and "second" each receive 1

point, and the comparison "more than," together with its object "a number," receives 2 points. Thus, the total for this sentence is 5.

(2) "A number is five more than three times a second number." The basic sentence is "number is more." The adjectives "five," "three," and "second" each receive 1 point. The comparison "more than" and the relational expression "times" each receive 2 points. The sentence total is thus 7.

(3) "Five times six is 30." The subject of the sentence is itself a phrase; thus 1 point is initially added to the count. The relational expression "times" receives 2 points, so that the total is 3.

(4) "A number is five more than three times as large as a second number." The basic sentence is "number is more." The adjectives "five," "three," and "second" count 1 point each; the comparisons "more than" and "as large as" and the relational expression "times" count 2 points each, for a total of 9.

(5) "The sum of five and a number is fifteen." The basic sentence is "sum is fifteen." The prepositional phrase "of five and a number" counts 2 points: 1 point for the prepositional phrase *per se*, and 1 point for the compound object of the phrase. The sentence total is 2.

(6) "John is two years older than Mary." The basic sentence is "John is older." The comparison "older than" receives 2 points, and the adjective "two" receives 1 point. In addition, since the phrase "two years" modifies "older," it receives 1 more point. The total number of points is 4.

(7) "One number is twice as large as a second number." The basic sentence is "number is large." The adjectives "one" and "second" and the adverb "twice" each receive 1 point. The comparison "as large as" receives 2 points, for a total of 5.

We shall indicate the computation of the syntactic complexity coefficients for just one set of experimental problems. The computations for the full set of problems may be found in the second author's dissertation (Caldwell, 1977).

Set 8 (a) "A young farmer has eight more hens than dogs."   5

    1-count structures: Adjectives ("young"; "eight"; "eight more" modifies "hens") 3

    2-count structures: Comparison ("more ... than") 2

"Since hens have two legs each, but dogs have four   10
legs each, all together the animals have 118 legs."

1-count structures: Adjectives ("two"; "each"; "four";
  "each"; "118") 5, Coordinating conjunction ("but") 1,
  Adverbs ("all"; "together") 2

2-count structures: Dependent clause ("Since ...") 2

"How many dogs does the young farmer own?"   2

1-count structures: Adjectives ("How many"; "young") 2   —

                                                           17

  (b) "There are four more girls in an English class
       than boys."   6

1-count structures: Adjectives ("four"; "four more"
  modifies "girls"; "English") 3, Prepositional phrase
  ("in an English class") 1

2-count structures: Comparison ("more ... than") 2

"If there were six times as many girls and twice as   13
many boys, there would be 136 pupils."

1-count structures: Adjectives ("six"; "twice"; "136")
  3, Coordinate clause deletion ("and [there were] twice
  as many ...") 1, Modal (" ... were ..., ... would be
  ...") 1

2-count structures: Dependent clause ("If ...,") 2,
  Comparisons ("times"; "as many"; "as many") 6

"How many boys are there?"   1

1-count structures: Adjective ("How many") 1   —

                                                           20

  (c) "The value of a given number is six more than the   7
       value of a second number."

1-count structures: Adjectives ("given"; "six"; "second")
  3, Prepositional phrases ("of a given number"; "of a
  second number") 2

2-count structures: Comparison ("more than") 2

"The sum of two times the first number and four times   10
the second number is 126."

1-count structures: Adjectives ("two"; "first"; "four"; "second") 4, Prepositional phrase ("of ... second number") 1, compound object of preposition ("of ... and ...") 1

2-count structures: Comparisons ("times"; "times") 4

"What is the value of the second number?"   2

1-count structures: Adjective ("second") 1, Prepositional phrase ("of the second number") 1   ___

      19

(d) "A given number is six more than a second number."   5

1-count structures: Adjectives ("given"; "six"; "second") 3

2-count structures: Comparison ("more than") 2

"If the first number were four times as large and the second two times as large, their sum would be 126."   13

1-count structures: Adjectives ("first"; "four"; "second"; "two"; "their") 5, Coordinate clause deletion ("and the second [were] two ...") 1, Modal ("... were ..., ... would be") 1

2-count structures: Dependent clause ("If ...,") 2, Comparisons ("times as large"; "times as large") 4

"What is the second number?"   1

1-count structures: Adjective ("second") 1   ___

      19

Since each of the above problem statements contains three sentences, the syntactic complexity coefficients are, respectively, $17 \div 3 = 5.67$, $20 \div 3 = 6.67$, $19 \div 3 = 6.33$, and $19 \div 3 = 6.33$. These values are entered in Table 6.3.

Computation of the syntactic complexity coefficients requires some degree of expertise, and no formal check of inter-coder reliability was performed. As the study progressed and we gained familiarity with the system, some values were recomputed; in fact, the values for *Set 8* above differ slightly from the values originally listed by Caldwell (1977). However, such disagreements as did occur were minor, and did not challenge the correctness of the main assertion that the problems within each set are of approximately the same level of syntactic complexity.

Another limitation of our use of the syntactic complexity coefficient is the fact that pronouns *per se* represent 0-count structures. In Chapter II it was pointed out that pronouns could sometimes be expected to increase problem difficulty; and the STUDENT program, as we have seen, encounters complexities due to the use of pronouns in hypothetical problems. Nevertheless, they are not counted in our measure of syntactic complexity. Table 6.5 lists the number of pronouns in each problem.

4. Controlling for Content and Context Variables

Vocabulary

Each problem uses only vocabulary which is appropriate for a fourth-grade reading level, as given by the Dale List of 3000 Familiar Words (Dale and Chall, 1948). The list is augmented by numbers, proper names in common use, verb forms (-ed, -ing, -s), plurals, and comparisons (larger, older, etc.) which are not explicitly listed. These are assumed to be at the same reading level. Technical mathematical vocabulary is avoided.

Key Words

Key words (that is, English words which generally indicate specific mathematical operations) were not controlled as carefully as they might have been within each problem set. Table 6.5 lists the key words which appear in each problem. Included in the table are terms which, although commonly functioning as key words, do not indicate the usual operation in the problem at hand. For example, the word "older" frequently suggests addition or subtraction (as in Problem *6(a)*); but in Problem *1(a)* it is an irrelevant adjective.

The key words in Table 6.5 have further been arranged so that words which indicate corresponding operations within each set are directly beneath each other. This permits us to observe the extent to which parallelism among the key words has been maintained. The following stand out as discrepancies which might have been avoided: Problem *1(a)*, the adjective "older"; Problem *3(c)*, the term "equal" and Problem *3(d)*, the terms "unknown" and "equal"; Problem *4(a)*, the word "spent" (which often indicates subtraction but in this problem indicates no operation); Problem *5(d)*, the term "equal"; Problem *6(a)*, the term "equal" and Problem *6(b)*, the missing term "all," as well as the terms appearing at the beginning of Problems *6(a)-(d)*; Problem *7(b)*, the word "receive" (which often indicates addition but does not do so here); Problems *7(c)-(d)*, the word "equal"; and Problem *8(b)*, the absence of a key word to suggest addition. Furthermore, it is apparent from Table 6.5 that the *sequencing* of key words which indicate operations is discrepant in Problems *4(c)* and *8(c)*--although as we saw above the sequencing of numerical information is the same for all problems within each set.

Table 6.5 Additional Characteristics of the Experimental Problems

Set	Problem	Number of Pronouns	Key Words				
1	(a)	1	older	times as many			How many
	(b)	2		times as many			How many
	(c)	0		times as large			What
	(d)	1		times as large			What
2	(a)	1	more ... than	loses	left		How many
	(b)	1	more ... than	lost	left		How many
	(c)	2	larger than	smaller	equals		What
	(d)	1	larger than	smaller	equal		What
3	(a)	3		more than	times as many		How many
	(b)	3		more than	twice as many		How many
	(c)	0		more than	times	equal	What
	(d)	2	unknown	more than	times as large	equal	unknown What
4	(a)	1	equal	Each ... cost	spent	in all	How many
	(b)	2	equal	twice as many	times as many	in all	How many
	(c)	0	equal	sum	times	equal	What
	(d)	1	equal	twice as large	times as large	sum	What
5	(a)	1	times as old	How old	How old		
	(b)	2	times as old	How old	How old		
	(c)	0	times as large	What	What		
	(d)	2	times as large	equal	What		
6	(a)	3		youngest	older than	older than	sum all
	(b)	0	equal	same	more than	more than	sum all
	(c)	0		smallest	more than	more than	sum all
	(d)	0	equal	same	more than	more than	sum all
7	(a)	0	[fraction] of		How many	receive	
	(b)	2	[fraction] as much		How much	receive	
	(c)	0	[fraction] of	equal	What		
	(d)	2	[fraction] as large	equal	What		
8	(a)	0	more ... than	each	each	all together	How many
	(b)	0	more ... than	times as many	twice as many		How many
	(c)	0	more than	sum	times	times	What
	(d)	0	more than	times as large	times as large	sum	What

It is certainly to be hoped that the discrepancies noted here in key words are not sufficiently great to interfere with the effects of the experimental variables. However, they are pointed out as limitations in the achievement of our goal of holding constant each major task variable except those which are deliberately varied for experimental effect.

Mathematical Content and "Problem Types"

The problems within each set have been made as nearly identical as possible with respect to mathematical content. *Sets 1-5* contain arithmetic problems with whole number givens and whole number solutions. Within each set, the needed arithmetic operations are the same for all problems. *Sets 6-8* contain elementary algebra problems. In *Set 7,* one of the givens in each problem is a fraction; otherwise all of the givens and all of the solutions are whole numbers. Again, within each set the needed algebraic and arithmetic operations are the same for all problems. Thus it appears reasonable to assert that the mathematical *content* of the problems within each set is the same.

Some of the problems fall into categories of familiar "problem types" such as those discussed in Chapter III. These are: Problem *4(a)*, a "money problem"; Problems *5(a)*, *5(b)* and *6(a)*, "age problems"; and Problem *7(b)*, a "work problem." Of course, none of the abstract problems fall into these categories. It was felt that this fact was to some extent a natural consequence of the abstract/concrete dichotomy as it was defined; therefore problems of such "types" were not entirely avoided in constructing the experimental instruments. However, it was considered important that none of the problems rely on mathematical relationships which were not explicitly stated, as often occurs with these "problem types." Thus the "money problem" does not assume the values of coins or the conversion of cents to dollars, and the "age problems" do not employ expressions such as "four years from now" to imply that four should be added to all of the ages. The "work problem" does not entail use of the proportionality of wages to rate of pay and time worked; however, it does (unfortunately) assume that what John "earns" *is* proportional to the amount he "works." Thus Problem *7(b)* could have been improved by changing the phrase "If John were able to work only one-third as much," to "If John were able to earn only one-third as much."

The variation in "problem types" which occurs within problem sets is thus interpreted as a *contextual* consequence of the abstract/concrete experimental factor, not affecting the mathematical *content* in any important way. Nevertheless, in order to minimize any possible interaction with the factual/hypothetical variable, it would have been better for Problems *4(b)*, *6(b)* and *7(b)* to have been of the same "types" as *4(a)*, *6(a)*, and *7(a)* respectively. We shall return to this point later, in the discussion of the findings for *Set 4*.

Context Familiarity

All of the experimental problems are conventional rather than imaginative in style, and the concrete problems all describe relatively familiar objects for the subject population. However, apart from the use of the Dale List of 3000 Familiar Words, no attempt was made to validate these assertions.

More importantly, it is to be expected that concrete and factual problems are in general more familiar to the subjects than abstract and hypothetical problems. A classification was performed for the word problems in several current texts: in *Modern School Mathematics: Structure and Use*, *K-6*, more than 80 percent of the word problems were found to be concrete and factual (CF), and less than 1 percent were hypothetical (Duncan et al., 1972). In *Mathematics for Individual Achievement*, *Books 7-8*, for junior high school, 75 percent of the word problems were CF and less than 2 percent were hypothetical (Denholm et al., 1975). In one of the algebra texts by the same publisher, the classification was 74 percent CF, 20 percent AF, and 2 percent hypothetical (Dolciani and Wooton, 1973); in the second-year algebra text, the distribution was 75 percent CF, 19 percent AF, and 4 percent hypothetical (Dolciani, Berman, and Wooton, 1973).

Thus in interpreting our findings we must be aware that there may be effects due solely to the greater familiarity of concrete, factual word problems.

5. Controlling for Structure Variables and the Effects of Problem Sequence

Mathematical Algorithm

As has been pointed out in Chapter IV, the complexity of the algorithm needed to solve a verbal problem may strongly affect the problem's difficulty. Thus, it was extremely important that the four problems within each set require the same algorithm for their solution. This is a particularly difficult variable to control, because it is possible that different individuals may use somewhat different algorithms to solve the same problem--that is, it is not really possible to say that a given problem "requires" a uniquely specified algorithmic procedure. Taking Problem *6.3* as an example, most people would probably write the equation $5 + 2X = 17$ and solve for X. However, we saw that the STUDENT-type analysis yielded in effect the equations $Y = 5 + 2X$ and $Y = 17$; equations which require a *different* algorithm (and an additional step) for solution. In short, our actual goal was to create problems within each set which were *isomorphic* in the sense of Chapter IV--so that *any* algorithm appropriate for one problem in a set would be appropriate for the others.

Each problem set was first examined by participants in the mathematics education doctoral seminar at the University of Pennsylvania. Where necessary, problems were reworded or reconstructed until unanimous agreement was achieved that the problems were of identical algorithmic structure. Two "Algorithm Validation Instruments" were then constructed, with these instructions:

Each of the following groups contains four word problems. If one of the problems differs from the rest in regard to the algorithm which will be used to solve it, then circle the letter corresponding to that problem on the answer sheet. Different numerical constants do not indicate that two word problems are different. For example, a problem using the equation $2x + 5 = 9$ and one using the equation $3x + 7 = 28$ are considered to be equivalent. If the underlying equation for all four problems is the same, then circle "E" (None of the above).

One version of the "Algorithm Validation Instrument" included the elementary word problems, and a second version included the high school word problems. Each version actually consisted of *ten* sets of four problems each. Three of the sets on each instrument included one problem which was clearly solved by a different algorithm from the others; these sets were included so as to eliminate the possibility of a "set" response among the validators and to confirm that the validators understood the instructions. These "distractor" sets of problems were developed according to the same criteria as the experimental problems, with the exception of the difference in structure, so that no additional cues would be available to the validators. An example of a "distractor" set of problems is given in Table 6.6.

The "Algorithm Validation Instruments" were designed to validate eleven sets of experimental problems in all, with some of the sets appearing on both versions of the instrument. The elementary word problems were validated by four secondary school mathematics teachers and two preservice teachers; the high school word problems were validated by a different group of four secondary school mathematics teachers and two preservice teachers. Agreement was unanimous on the eight problem sets eventually included in the study that the underlying equation for all four problems within each set is the same.

In Table 6.7, the equations needed to solve each problem are tabulated. While the numerical constants which appear may differ from problem to problem within each set, it is important that the *path through the computational algorithm* be the same for all problems within a set. Thus if one problem requires a "carrying" or "regrouping" operation in the course of a numerical computation, the other problems should as well. Table 6.7 thus characterizes the computational procedure required for each problem set. There was no independent validation carried out for the identity of paths through the computational algorithm; evidently *Set 6* has some imperfections in this respect.

Table 6.6 *A "Distractor" Set of Problems Used in the "Algorithm Validation Instrument"*

Set D1 *(a)* The Jones family has two children, Sarah and Jeff. CF
Sarah is twelve years older than her brother Jeff
and the sum of their ages is equal to 22. How old
is Jeff?

(b) A square field has four equal sides. If the field CH
were fourteen feet wider than it is, the product
of the length and the width would be 72. How long
is the field?

(c) Two numbers are given. The first given number is AF
twelve larger than the second given number, and
their product is equal to 64. What is the value
of the second given number?

(d) $\square$ and $\triangle$ are two equal numbers. If $\square$ were AH
thirteen larger than it is, then the product of
the new numbers would be 48. What is the value of
$\triangle$?

Table 6.7 *Mathematical Equations and Computational Procedures for the Experimental Problems*

Set	Problem	Equation(s)	Computational Procedure
1	(a)	$3 \cdot 32 = X$	$3 \cdot 32$ short multiplication, no carrying
	(b)	$2 \cdot 34 = X$	$2 \cdot 34$
	(c)	$3 \cdot 33 = X$	$3 \cdot 33$
	(d)	$2 \cdot 34 = X$	$2 \cdot 34$
2	(a)	$X = 7+Y;\ Y-4 = 15$	$15+4+7$ three addends, single carry
	(b)	$X = 8+Y;\ Y-3 = 16$	$16+3+8$
	(c)	$X = 6+Y;\ Y-5 = 16$	$16+5+6$
	(d)	$X = 9+Y;\ Y-3 = 17$	$17+3+9$
3	(a)	$7 + 3X = 31$	$(31-7)/3$ simple borrow; division fact
	(b)	$9 + 2X = 25$	$(25-9)/2$
	(c)	$8 + 6X = 44$	$(44-8)/6$
	(d)	$8 + 5X = 33$	$(33-8)/5$
4	(a)	$X = Y;\ 3X + 5Y = 48$	$48/(3+5)$ addition fact; division fact
	(b)	$X = Y;\ 2X + 4Y = 42$	$42/(2+4)$
	(c)	$X = Y;\ 3X + 4Y = 56$	$56/(3+4)$
	(d)	$X = Y;\ 2X + 5Y = 49$	$49/(2+5)$
5	(a)	$3X = 39$	$39/3$ short division, no remainders
	(b)	$4X = 48$	$48/4$
	(c)	$5X = 55$	$55/5$
	(d)	$2X = 28$	$28/2$
6	(a)	$Y = X+2;\ Z = Y+2;\ W = Z+2;\ X+Y+Z+W = 132$	$(132-(2+(2+2)+(2+2+2)))/4$ see below
	(b)	$Y = X+6;\ Z = Y+6;\ W = Z+6;\ X+Y+Z+W = 156$	$(156-(6+(6+6)+(6+6+6)))/4$
	(c)	$Y = X+4;\ Z = Y+4;\ W = Z+4;\ X+Y+Z+W = 184$	$(184-(4+(4+4)+(4+4+4)))/4$
	(d)	$Y = X+3;\ Z = Y+3;\ W = Z+3;\ X+Y+Z+W = 178$	$(178-(3+(3+3)+(3+3+3)))/4$

The repeated additions in Set 6 require varying columns and carries; however each of these may be replaced by a multiplication fact. Subtraction without borrowing; short division, no remainders.

Set	Problem	Equation(s)	Computational Procedure
7	(a)	$(1/4)X = 43$	$4 \cdot 43$ short multiplication, single carry
	(b)	$(1/3)X = 35$	$3 \cdot 35$
	(c)	$(1/5)X = 42$	$5 \cdot 42$
	(d)	$(1/4)X = 28$	$4 \cdot 28$
8	(a)	$X = Y+8;\ 2X + 4Y = 118$	$(118-2 \cdot 8)/(2+4)$ multiplication fact; subtraction
	(b)	$X = Y+4;\ 6X + 2Y = 136$	$(136-6 \cdot 4)/(6+2)$ without borrowing; short divisio
	(c)	$X = Y+6;\ 2X + 4Y = 126$	$(126-2 \cdot 6)/(2+4)$ one intermediate remainder
	(d)	$X = Y+6;\ 4X + 2Y = 126$	$(126-4 \cdot 6)/(4+2)$

Computational Skills Test

Since the purpose of the study was to examine the effects of certain syntax and/or context variables, it was desired to separate out in some way the possible effects of limitations in computational skills among the students taking the tests. That is, we wished to verify that any differences in difficulty which might emerge among the CF, CH, AF, and AH problems would continue to appear even among students who evidenced all of the computational skills necessary to solve all of the verbal problems.

Accordingly, a computational skills test was devised at the elementary, intermediate, and advanced levels. Each computational skills test consisted of five sets of two problems each, testing the computational algorithms necessary to solve the corresponding word problem sets. The computational skills test items are listed by sets in Table 6.8. A subject was defined to "pass" the computational skills test if he or she answered correctly at least one of each pair of items, thus providing some evidence of being able to perform satisfactorily on each computational algorithm.

Problem Sequence

The order in which the problems are presented may affect their difficulty; therefore it was necessary to consider the sequencing of problems very carefully. Sequences of problems were constructed which (a) separated the four problems within each set from each other; (b) avoided successive problems of the same experimental type (CF, CH, AF, or AH), and (c) placed problems with shorter computational procedures both near the beginning and near the end. This scheme is illustrated in Table 6.9 for the elementary test; the other two tests were sequenced similarly. The position of each problem on each test may be determined from Table 6.10.

The experimental problems were administered in two parts (I and II), with two forms (A and B) of each part. Form I-A contained problem sequences 1 and 2; form I-B contained sequences 2 and 1; form II-A contained sequences 3 and 4; form II-B contained sequences 4 and 3. Test order (Part I first or Part II first) was one of the factors in the experimental design; but within the Part I first group, half of the subjects (randomly selected) received form A and half received form B. Thus, within each set of problems, all four problems occupied the same position on the test equally often.

The computational skills test was likewise administered in two parts consisting of five problems each, one from the pair testing each computational algorithm.

Table 6.8 *Computational Skills Test Items Arranged by Sets*

Set 1   32 x 2 = ☐

       33 x 3 = ☐

Set 2   8 + 4 + 15 = ☐

       9 + 3 + 15 = ☐

Set 3   9 + (5 x ☐) = 34

       7 + (3 x ☐) = 34

Set 4   (3 x ☐) + (6 x ☐) = 54

       (5 x ☐) + (3 x ☐) = 56

Set 5   3 x ☐ = 36

       4 x ☐ = 44

Set 6   ☐ + (☐ + 2) + (☐ + 4) + (☐ + 6) = 172

       ☐ + (☐ + 3) + (☐ + 6) + (☐ + 9) = 138

Set 7 $\frac{1}{5}$ x ☐ = 28

       $\frac{1}{3}$ x ☐ = 27

On the advanced test, algebraic notation was used; thus the items for Set 3 were written "9 + 5x = 34" and "7 + 3x = 34," on the advanced test.

Set 8 $4x + 3(x + 4) = 124$

       $5x + 3(x + 7) = 133$

Table 6.9 *Four Sequences of Problems Constructed in Order to Separate*
Problems from the Same Set (Elementary Test)

		Set 1	Set 2	Set 3	Set 4	Set 5
Part I:	Sequence 1	CH	AF	CF	AF	AH
	Sequence 2	AF	CF	CH	AH	CF
Part II:	Sequence 3	CF	AH	AF	CH	AF
	Sequence 4	AH	CH	AH	CF	CH
		shorter computations		longer computations		shorter computations

Table 6.10 *Position of Each Problem on Each Test*

Set	Problem	Part I (Form A) Elem.	Int.	Adv.	Part I (Form B) Elem.	Int.	Adv.	Part II (Form A) Elem.	Int.	Adv.	Part II (Form B) Elem.	Int.	Adv.
1	(a)							1			6		
	(b)	1			6								
	(c)	6			1								
	(d)							6			1		
2	(a)	7	7		2	2							
	(b)							7	7		2	2	
	(c)	2	2		7	7							
	(d)							2	2		7	7	
3	(a)	3	3	3	8	8	8						
	(b)	8	8	8	3	3	3						
	(c)							3	3	3	8	8	8
	(d)							8	8	8	3	3	3
4	(a)							9	9	9	4	4	4
	(b)							4	4	4	9	9	9
	(c)	4	4	4	9	9	9						
	(d)	9	9	9	4	4	4						
5	(a)	10			5								
	(b)							10			5		
	(c)							5			10		
	(d)	5			10								
6	(a)		10	10		5	5						
	(b)								10	10		5	5
	(c)								5	5		10	10
	(d)		5	5		10	10						
7	(a)								1	1		6	6
	(b)		1	1		6	6						
	(c)		6	6		1	1						
	(d)								6	6		1	1
8	(a)			7			2						
	(b)									7			2
	(c)			2			7						
	(d)									2			7

6. Experimental Findings

The number of correct solutions to each verbal problem among the various subject populations is tabulated in Tables 6.11 through 6.16. It is intended that the results of the multivariate analyses, levels of significance, and interactions among the factors be reported elsewhere. Here we shall summarize only the main effects for the concrete-abstract and factual-hypothetical factors, and look once more at the experimental problems.

For the elementary test, significantly more concrete problems than abstract problems were solved by the subject population ($p < .01$). Perhaps surprisingly, significantly more hypothetical problems were solved than factual problems ($p < .01$). However, there was a significant interaction between the two experimental factors ($p < .01$). For concrete problems, the factual and hypothetical versions differed little in their level of difficulty, with the exception of Problems *4(a)* and *4(b)*; Problem *4(a)*, the factual problem, is considerably less difficult. For abstract problems, the factual versions were consistently more difficult than the hypothetical versions.

For the intermediate test, significantly more concrete problems than abstract problems were solved ($p < .01$), and significantly more factual problems than hypothetical problems were solved ($p < .01$). There was again a significant interaction between the two experimental factors ($p < .01$). For concrete problems, the factual versions were less difficult than the hypothetical versions. For abstract problems, the factual and hypothetical versions differed little in their level of difficulty. Again *Set 4* makes a large contribution to the lesser difficulty of CF as compared with CH problems. *Set 7* also makes a large contribution to this effect. In addition, Problem *7(d)* is substantially more difficult than Problem *7(c)*, although most other AH problems are less difficult than the corresponding AF problems.

For the advanced test, concrete problems are again significantly less difficult than abstract problems ($p < .01$), but the magnitude of the effect is smaller than for the elementary or intermediate tests. In addition, factual problems are less difficult than hypothetical problems ($p < .01$). For this test there was no significant interaction between the concrete-abstract and factual-hypothetical factors.

For the three analyses of variance on problems common to two or more tests, concrete problems are again significantly less difficult than abstract problems, and there is a significant interaction between the two experimental factors. For concrete problems, the hypothetical versions are more difficult, while for abstract problems the factual and hypothetical versions differ little in their level of difficulty.

The above results continue to hold when attention is restricted to students who passed the computational skills test. While there are significant interactions with the "test order" factor in some of the

analyses, the interactions do not change the relative order of difficulty of the CF, CH, AF, and AH problems.

There are many interesting points which can be made in interpretation of the above findings, which are beyond the scope of this
chapter. Since we are principally interested in the use of the
"task variables" approach to design the system of experimental problems, let us look back once more at the problems which seemed to
produce effects different from other problems of the same types--as
mentioned above, 4(a) and 4(b), and Set 7.

None of the task variables which we have examined in such pains-
taking detail seem to account for the fact that Problem 4(a) is
substantially easier than Problem 4(b) for every population of
subjects (see Tables 6.3, 6.5, and 6.7 for tabulation of the variables). If this were due exclusively to the factual-hypothetical
variable, we would expect to see a similar strong effect in other
problems, which we do not. Could it be due solely to the "problem
type" classification of Problem 4(a) as a "money problem?" There is
another possible explanation, one which was overlooked in the construction of Problem 4(a). Referring to the statement of the problem,
we see that it is possible to reason as follows: "Each plant cost
three dollars and each flowerpot cost five dollars, so that the pair
cost eight dollars. Since Alan spent 48 dollars in all, he must have
bought six plants." The analogous line of reasoning is almost impossi-
bly awkward to state for Problem 4(b), despite the fact that the problems have identical or isomorphic structures. This is due to an
unintentional interaction between context and structure--the fact that
plants and flowerpots are naturally paired, especially for purchase,
facilitates a certain chain of reasoning in Problem 4(a) which is not
equally facilitated in Problem 4(b). Problem 4(a) could thus have
been improved, for purposes of this study, by having Alan buy an
equal number of plants and baseballs.

Of course we do not know if the above is a correct explanation of
the lesser difficulty of Problem 4(a). But this instance points out
the extreme sensitivity which may exist towards minor wording changes
in a verbal problem, and the extraordinary difficulty of controlling
for every task variable which may affect an experimental outcome.

In Set 7, we have already noted that Problem 7(b) entails the
assumption of a proportionality between the amount John works and the
amount he earns, which is not explicitly stated in the problem. This
may be causing Problem 7(a) to be less difficult than Problem 7(b) for
the junior high school students. Finally, Problem 7(d) may be more
difficult than Problem 7(c) for an unanticipated reason. In Problem
7(d), the underlying equation is $(1/4)X = 28$. The student who erro-
neously divides 28 by 4 will arrive at a whole number answer. In
Problem 7(c), however, the underlying equation is $(1/5)X = 42$, and the
temptation may not be so great to divide 42 by 5, since the answer
would in this case be a mixed number. Although Problems 7(c) and 7(d)
are of identical structure with respect to the correct arithmetic

Table 6.11 *Number of Correct Solutions to Each Problem by All Elementary School Subjects*

Set	CF	CH	AF	AH	
1	324	320	271	302	N = 399
2	211	199	66	88	
3	49	65	39	62	
4	129	74	49	62	
5	245	249	165	249	
Tot.	958	907	590	763	

Table 6.12 *Number of Correct Solutions to Each Problem by Elementary School Subjects Meeting the Computational Skills Criterion*

Set	CF	CH	AF	AH	
1	104	104	92	97	N = 112
2	71	77	31	38	
3	26	32	23	33	
4	55	33	19	28	
5	93	97	75	102	
Tot.	349	343	240	298	

Table 6.13 *Number of Correct Solutions to Each Problem by All Junior
High School Subjects*

Set	CF	CH	AF	AH	
					N = 813
2	609	621	287	361	
3	358	376	368	378	
4	530	357	321	326	
6	356	286	305	301	
7	541	458	440	397	
Tot.	2394	2098	1721	1763	

Table 6.14 *Number of Correct Solutions to Each Problem by Junior High
School Subjects Meeting the Computational Skills Criterion*

Set	CF	CH	AF	AH	
					N = 281
2	236	250	148	177	
3	213	195	208	214	
4	231	194	179	182	
6	206	175	188	189	
7	243	221	237	214	
Tot.	1129	1035	960	976	

Table 6.15 *Number of Correct Solutions to Each Problem by All High
School Subjects*

Set	CF	CH	AF	AH	
3	211	200	213	204	N = 274
4	213	171	187	176	
6	185	182	178	182	
7	223	213	215	206	
8	147	146	119	119	
Tot.	979	912	912	887	

Table 6.16 *Number of Correct Solutions to Each Problem by High School
Subjects Meeting the Computational Skills Criterion*

Set	CF	CH	AF	AH	
3	180	172	185	176	N = 197
4	179	157	169	157	
6	171	162	161	166	
7	179	178	184	172	
8	137	141	113	116	
Tot.	846	810	812	787	

operation, they are not of identical structure with respect to the (possibly most frequent) *incorrect* operation. Again, we are not sure if this feature accounts for the greater difficulty of Problem *7(d)*, but it illustrates the ease with which potentially important task variable differences can be overlooked.

7. Conclusion

In this chapter, we have shown in detail how the task variables discussed in the first half of this book entered into the construction of a verbal problem-solving instrument. The purpose was to control for all task variables which were not of direct experimental interest, in order to ensure that observed effects were due exclusively to the experimental factors. Such an undertaking would seem to be a prerequisite for obtaining reproducible and generalizable findings.

This effort was partially but not completely successful. The development of the problem instruments, together with the validation procedures described, took more than a year; and, even so, the control was not perfect. We have endeavored, however, to *establish a standard* for such studies by elaborating on the imperfections as well as the successful procedures. It is hoped that by making available the details of our approach to other researchers, the concept of systematically controlling for task variables will find other adherents, and the state of the art will advance beyond that which is described here.

VII.

Structure Variables in Problem-Solving Research

A.

Concept Acquisition Tasks

by

William Waters
W. Windsor-Plainsboro School District
Princeton Junction, New Jersey

1. Description of the Study

This study illustrates some of the effects which may be observed by controlling for structure variables across a series of tasks. Three tasks were developed for the purpose of studying *conjunctive concept acquisition* in a problem-solving framework. The principal independent variables in the tasks are context variables, and may be defined as (1) the degree of abstractness of the defining attributes of the conjunctive concepts, and (2) the degree of diversity of the universe of objects which do or do not exemplify the conjunctive concepts. A third independent variable, the order of presentation of the tasks, qualifies as a treatment variable. The purpose of the study was to measure the effects of these variables on overall task difficulty, the usage of particular strategies, and the efficiency of the strategies (Waters, 1979).

Background

In the literature on "concept acquisition" tasks, a concept is defined by means of some combination of *attributes* of the stimuli which are presented in the task. The goal of the problem solver is usually to learn which combination of attributes defines the concept. The book A Study of Thinking (Bruner, Goodnow, and Austin, 1956) was the pioneering work in this area, and many follow-up studies since then have concentrated on how subtle changes in the task itself may influence subjects' performance.

The basic task consists of an array of cards containing pictures of objects. These cards are "matrixed" over a number of attributes, with each attribute having several possible attribute values. The goal of the subject is to verbalize the particular combination of attribute values known to the experimenter as the goal concept. In the basic task, the experimenter begins by indicating a card which *is* an example of the goal concept. The subject then chooses cards one by one to test whether they are examples of the goal concept, and after each choice the experimenter indicates "yes" or "no." The subject may also make a hypothesis as to the identity of the goal concept after any card choice; the task terminates when the subject correctly identifies the goal concept.

Bruner and his associates investigate in detail the *strategies* employed by subjects in performing this task. The four main strategies identified are called conservative focusing, focus gambling, successive scanning, and simultaneous scanning. The existence of the focusing and scanning strategy groupings has been replicated many times, but objections have been raised to the methods employed by Bruner and his successors in scoring for the usage of these strategies. Chapter IV reviews some of the literature involving strategy scoring systems, and Laughlin (1973) provides a valuable review for concept acquisition tasks. In the present study, we propose new definitions of the scanning and focusing strategies to mirror more precisely the intent of the problem solver during the task performance.

In the literature it appears rather consistently that focusing strategies are more efficient in concept acquisition tasks than scanning strategies, with the implication that focusing strategies are therefore preferable for concept attainment in non-laboratory learning situations. However, we suggest that the usefulness of the focusing strategies may result principally from characteristics of the tasks which do not carry over into real-life situations. More specifically, most previous experiments utilize only attributes which are immediately identifiable by subjects, such as shape, size, and color, while in real-life problems, the possible relevant attributes may not be known ahead of time.

In order to investigate these ideas, new card tasks were developed, which are described in detail in the following sections. Task 1 is intended to replicate the basic task of Bruner and his associates, with immediately identifiable attributes. In Task 2 and Task 3, one attribute has been changed from an easily recognizable attribute to a more abstract attribute which may not be so easily discerned. In addition, Task 2 contains a greater diversity of objects than Task 1, and Task 3 a still greater diversity of objects.

General Design of the Study

The purpose of this study was to measure effects on (a) overall difficulty, (b) strategy usage, and (c) strategy efficiency for three tasks, which are structurally isomorphic yet differ in embodiment.

A 3x5 orthogonal factorial design was employed, with three task groups and five experimenters. Each group received two of the three tasks. Group A received Task 3 followed by Task 1; group B received

Task 2 followed by Task 1; and group C received Task 1 followed by Task 3. One-hundred-eight female college undergraduates were employed as subjects. Thirty-six subjects were assigned at random to each of the task groups. The five experimenters administered the tasks to 36, 24, 18, 18, and 12 subjects, respectively. Each experimenter's subjects were divided equally among the three task groups. For each subject on each of the two problems, five dependent variables were measured. These are: (1) number of card choices to solution, (2) time to solution, (3) problem solved (=1) versus problem not solved (=0), (4) *intended focusing index* (defined below to be the number of focusing choices/number of choices to solution), and (5) *intended scanning index* (defined below to be the number of scanning choices/number of choices to solution).

A summary of the results of this study will follow a more detailed description of the task variables.

2. Analysis of Task Structure

Structurally Isomorphic Tasks

Task 1 is essentially a replica of Bruner's basic task. Subjects are asked to identify a conjunctive concept which is defined by attributes which are "matrixed" on a board before them (see Figure 7A.1). In Task 1, four perceptual attributes are employed. These are: *shape* (circle, square, or triangle), *color* (red, green, or brown), *size* (large or small), and *number* (one object or two objects). The objects used as exemplars of attribute value combinations vary over only one dimension, the dimension of shape.

In Task 2 (see Figure 7A.2), the goal is also to identify a conjunctive concept. However, the dimension of shape has been replaced by a less perceptually apparent attribute, that of "animal life-plant life-inanimate object." Furthermore, there is a greater diversity of objects: objects vary over both this attribute and the attribute of color. Thus in Figure 7A.1, we have "one small red circle" and "one small green circle." In Figure 7A.2, however, we have "one small red apple" and "one small green cactus."

In Task 3, the same attributes are employed as in Task 2, but the objects used as concept exemplars vary over all four relevant dimensions (see Figure 7A.3).

The principal independent variables in the tasks are in the category of problem context and may be defined as the degree of perceptual immediacy in the defining attributes of the concepts, and the degree of object exemplar diversity employed in the representations of the combinations of attributes. The tasks are designed to measure the effects of these variables on the usage and efficiency of various strategies employed in solving the tasks.

Figure 7A.1. *Task 1, Conjunctive Concept Acquisition (Schematic)*

one small red circle	one small red triangle	one small red square	one large red circle	one large red triangle	one large red square	two small red circles	two small red triangles	two small red squares	two large red circles	two large red triangles	two large red squares
one small green square	one small green circle	one small green triangle	one large green square	one large green circle	one large green triangle	two small green squares	two small green circles	two small green triangles	two large green squares	two large green circles	two large green triangles
one small brown triangle	one small brown square	one small brown circle	one large brown triangle	one large brown square	one large brown circle	two small brown triangles	two small brown squares	two small brown circles	two large brown triangles	two large brown squares	two large brown circles

On the board presented to subjects are pictures of the objects described.

Figure 7A.2. *Task 2, Conjunctive Concept Acquisition.*

one small red apple	one small red bell	one small red fox	one large red apple	one large red bell	one large red fox	two small red apples	two small red bells	two small red foxes	two large red apples	two large red bells	two large red foxes
one small green snake	one small green cactus	one small green bottle	one large green snake	one large green cactus	one large green bottle	two small green snakes	two small green cacti	two small green bottles	two large green snakes	two large green cacti	two large green bottles
one small brown clock	one small brown bear	one small brown tree	one large brown clock	one large brown bear	one large brown tree	two small brown clocks	two small brown bears	two small brown trees	two large brown clocks	two large brown bears	two large brown trees

Figure 7A.3. *Task 3, Conjunctive Concept Acquisition.*

one small red cherry	one small red roller skate	one small red bug	one large red tomato	one large red fire truck	one large red horse	two small red straw-berries	two small red tele-phones	two small red birds	two large red flowers	two large red slides	two large red dogs
one small green frog	one small green bean	one small green pen	one large green dinosaur	one large green lettuce	one large green chalk-board	two small green fish	two small green leaves	two small green spoons	two large green alli-gators	two large green Christ-mas trees	two large green cars
one small brown penny	one small brown worm	one small brown pine cone	one large brown cannon	one large brown kangaroo	one large brown potato	two small brown combs	two small brown chip-munks	two small brown acorns	two large brown tractors	two large brown Indians	two large brown coconuts

For this purpose, an attempt has been made to make the tasks *isomorphic* from the point of view of task structure. Each task encompasses the same number of attributes and object exemplars which are matrixed on the boards. We can set up a one-to-one correspondence of attributes and values as follows:

Task 1		Task 2		Task 3
Circle	$\longleftrightarrow$	Plant Life	$\longleftrightarrow$	Plant Life
Square	$\longleftrightarrow$	Animal Life	$\longleftrightarrow$	Animal Life
Triangle	$\longleftrightarrow$	Inanimate Object	$\longleftrightarrow$	Inanimate Object

The attributes of color, number, and size correspond across all three tasks.

The correspondence of relevant attributes and attribute values is utilized throughout the administration of the tasks. Cards which exemplify isomorphic combinations of attribute values occupy the same relative positions on the problem boards. Thus "one small red cherry" and "one small red circle" are both situated in the upper left-hand corner. Likewise, the *goal concepts* to be attained are assigned isomorphically. That is, if "large squares" is the concept to be attained for a particular subject in Task 1, "large animals" would be the concept to be attained by corresponding subjects in Tasks 2 or 3. In addition, the *start card* (i.e., the initial positive instance of the concept which is shown to the subject) is assigned in each task according to the same isomorphism.

Task directions for the three problems are essentially the same. They differ only where the subject is asked to point to examples of a specific conjunctive concept on the board. In this case, however, care is taken not to include in the example any of the dimensions which are employed as goal concepts. A transcript of the task directions is included as an appendix to this chapter.

State-Space Analysis

Defining an isomorphism of structure through a one-to-one correspondence of the attributes, the attribute values, and the object exemplars, seems to be a reasonable approach in the case of concept acquisition tasks. In tasks where the number of moves is not too large, it is often useful to consider the task state-space, recording a subject's moves as a path through the state-space (see Chapter IV). Isomorphic tasks may then be defined as tasks whose *states* may be placed in one-to-one correspondence so as to preserve the structure of the permitted moves; or, alternatively, whose *moves* may be placed in one-to-one correspondence so as to establish a one-to-one correspondence of the states. Let us see how this definition applies to the present situation.

In the concept acquisition tasks, a *move* may be defined to be either (1) a choice of a card by a subject, together with the disclosure by the experimenter of whether or not the card exemplifies the goal concept; or (2) a hypothesis by the subject, together with the disclosure by the experimenter of whether or not the hypothesis is the correct goal concept. A *state* may then be defined as a finite sequence of moves; the goal state is a sequence terminating in the hypothesis of the goal concept. It is clear that there is a one-to-one correspondence between *card choices* in Task 1, Task 2, and Task 3. However, there is not a strict one-to-one correspondence between the hypotheses which are possible in Tasks 1, 2, and 3. Since Tasks 2 and 3 contain increasingly wide varieties of object exemplars, there are attributes in these tasks, irrelevant to the goal concept, which are not present in Task 1; and these irrelevant attributes suggest possible hypotheses which would not be present for Task 1. There is, of course, a one-to-one correspondence across Tasks 1, 2, and 3 of the hypotheses incorporating only the attributes across which the tasks have been "matrixed." In the language of Chapter IV, there is a state-space homomorphism from Task 1 to Task 2 and from Task 1 to Task 3, and there are *subspaces* of Tasks 2 and 3 for which the homomorphism defines an isomorphism.

Analysis and Scoring of Strategies

Another method of describing problem structure discussed in Chapter IV is by means of the strategies which may be employed in problem solving. In that chapter, Goldin has characterized a *strategy* as a rule which associates to each state of the problem a specified *subset* of the set of possible moves. Thus an algorithm is a strategy in which each specified subset contains no more than one move, and the sequence of moves leads to the goal state in finitely many steps.

For concept acquisition tasks such as Task 1 in the present study, researchers have been interested in characterizing the strategies used by subjects by means of the sequences of moves made. Four ideal strategies observed by Bruner, Goodnow, and Austin are defined as follows:

In the *simultaneous scanning* strategy, the subject simultaneously considers all possible concepts which could serve as outcomes, and at each stage makes that card choice which logically eliminates the most possible concepts.

In *successive scanning*, the subject attempts to discover several positive instances of the concept involved, observes particular attribute values which these instances have in common, and then hypothesizes that these attribute values define the concept.

In *conservative focusing*, the subject considers the particular attributes of a single positive instance of the concept. The subject then holds constant the values of all of the attributes *except for one*, which is varied in order to determine whether that attribute is a defining attribute for the concept.

Focus gambling involves basically the same procedure as conservative focusing, except that two or more attributes are varied simultaneously in the hope of eliminating two or more possible attributes as defining attributes of the concept in one trial.

Due to the isomorphism across Tasks 1, 2, and 3, each of the four ideal strategies has identical application to the three tasks. In order to exemplify more fully these strategies, let us suppose that a hypothetical subject is attempting to solve Task 1. Two of the attributes are bi-valued (number and size), while the other two attributes are tri-valued (shape and color), as in Figure 7A.1.

Suppose that the goal concept is "all cards containing one triangle" and the initial positive instance shown to the subject is the card in the lower left-hand corner of the problem board, one small brown triangle.

The subject at the outset reasons: "I see that the initial card contains something small and brown. Maybe the concept is all small brown things. To see if I'm right, I'll choose the card right next to it, since that's small and brown, too." The subject chooses one small brown square and receives a negative response from the experimenter.

This would be classified as a *successive scanning* choice. The subject made a tentative hypothesis as to the identity of the concept and chose a card containing the values of the hypothesis in order to attempt to verify the hypothesis.

The subject then reasons: "I see that one thing which is changing is the shape of the objects on the cards. Therefore, I'll choose a card which is exactly like the one given except for the shape. If I get a *no*, then shape is involved. If I get a *yes*, then shape is not involved." The subject chooses one small brown circle and receives a negative response.

This choice would be classified as a *conservative focusing* choice. The subject held constant all values of all attributes except for one, which was varied in order to test for inclusion in the concept.

The subject then reasons: "I know from my last choice that *triangle* is included in the concept. Two other things which are changing on the cards are the color of the objects and also the size of the objects. I will try to test these attributes for inclusion in the concept by choosing a card which differs from the first card by these two attributes only. A *yes* would mean that neither color nor size is included, while a *no* would mean that at least one of color or size is included." The subject chooses one large green triangle and receives a positive response.

This choice would be classified as a *focus gambling* choice (where the gamble paid off). Two attributes were varied while all others were held constant. A *yes* response indicated that changing the value of these attributes did not affect the concept status, so that neither color nor size was included.

The subject now reasons: "I know at this point that shape is included and that neither color nor size is included. Therefore, there are two possible hypotheses which remain for the concept. These are 'all cards with triangles' and 'all cards with one triangle.' I will therefore make a card choice which will eliminate one of these outcomes. Any card with two triangles will satisfy the requirement, since a *yes* eliminates the concept 'one triangle' and a *no* eliminates the concept 'triangles'." The subject chooses two, large, red triangles and receives a negative response.

This would be classified as a *simultaneous scanning* choice, since the subject simultaneously considered all possible outcomes and chose a card which would eliminate the most possible outcomes at that stage.

With this information, the subject can successfully guess that the goal concept is "all cards with one triangle." While this "inner protocol" is highly fictionalized, it should give some flavor for the qualitative distinctions which are intended by the definitions of these ideal strategies. It should also illustrate that the *same card choice* might exemplify different strategies, depending on the line of reasoning being followed.

However, there are problems with the measurement of these strategies, which we now mention. We shall discuss four methods of measuring strategy use: (a) protocol analysis, (b) behavioral measures, (c) retrospective accounts, and (d) structured questions.

In initially developing these strategies, Bruner and his associates essentially employed a technique of "protocol analysis," in which the experimenter may conduct a dialogue with the subject during problem solving, but tries to limit his or her own remarks to those designed to elicit responses from the subject describing the approach to the problem. After the session is completed, the experimenter then analyzes the subject's protocol in an attempt to discern methods of approach, attempting to arrive at a description of the strategy used. This analysis might take the form of a comparison with "ideal" methods of problem solution. Such an analysis is particularly useful if one is at the beginning stages of experimentation, and is trying to define the ideal strategies which may be employed on a set of related tasks. One disadvantage of this technique is that the risk of giving hints is relatively high.

One way to preclude the interference of verbal discourse with problem solving is simply to prohibit it; that is, to rely totally on nonverbal behavioral measures of strategy usage. This technique has been widely employed in the case of selection strategies in concept attainment. For example, the focusing index of Laughlin (1965) defines behavioral rules for scoring the focusing strategy. This technique has several advantages: it produces reliable measures since these are objectively determined, and verbal intercourse does not vary over different subjects. However, these *strategy scores* must satisfy several criteria if they are to be valid.

Strategy scores are based on the concept of partitioning the set of possible moves into mutually disjoint subsets, and associating each subset with a particular strategy. However, in the case of the focusing and scanning strategies in concept attainment, some of the early behavioral definitions of these strategies in terms of card choices and hypotheses were found to be imprecise in that certain choices could be associated with either focusing or scanning by these definitions. Thus the definitions had to be modified to eliminate these ambiguities.

In obtaining mutually exclusive categories of moves, however, the researcher must also be careful to preserve the validity of the definitions. In other words, it must be arguable that the "behavioral strategies" measure the ways in which subjects approach the problem.

In addition, it is important to realize that a purely behavioral approach to the measurement of strategies makes inferences about strategies from what the subject *does*, and not from what was *intended*. In the case of our concept attainment tasks, the strategies of focusing and scanning impose a heavy load on memory, and assume the understanding of rather complex logical inferences. The complexity of the tasks and of the strategies involved casts doubt on the assumption that a behavioral strategy score based only on a subject's card choices and hypotheses can totally reflect the *intended* approach to the problem.

Another technique of ascertaining a subject's *intended* strategy (as opposed to the behavioral implementation of that strategy) is through retrospective accounts. First, the subject performs the task without interference. Then, at the conclusion of the task, the experimenter asks the subject a series of detailed questions designed to ascertain the subject's method of approach to different problem configurations. Based on the answers to these questions, the strategy usage is scored.

One advantage of this technique is that the original task is unaffected by verbal discourse during problem solution. In addition, a greater emphasis is placed on the subject's intended strategy than on actual moves. Dienes and Jeeves (1965) and Branca and Kilpatrick (1972) have performed experiments involving the learning of mathematical group structures using the technique of retrospective accounts. According to Branca and Kilpatrick's results, a subject's retrospective account may not be consistent with what was intended at the time he or she was solving the problem. Retrospective accounts may reflect approaches which ultimately produced success rather than those which were unfruitful and fell by the wayside.

For the concept acquisition tasks in this study, we are interested in how certain variables of the task embodiment (i.e., the presence of an abstract attribute and the increase in object exemplar diversity) affect strategy selection and efficiency. For this purpose, we choose to employ the technique of structured questions.

In utilizing this technique, the first step, as with behavioral strategy scores, is to develop definitions of the ideal problem-solving strategies. The difference, however, is that these definitions now depend to some extent on things the subject *says* about what is done, in addition to his or her actions in solving the problem. After these definitions are formulated, the experimenter develops a short series of questions aimed at eliciting the information necessary for strategy classification according to these definitions. These questions are asked of the subject after each move or play in the task and should constitute almost the entirety of the experimenter's dialogue with the subject.

For our concept acquisition instruments, the structured questions technique is employed by first setting up mutually exclusive definitions of "intended" focusing and "intended" scanning as follows:

Intended focusing - The subject expresses concern with one or more attributes, and *changes* the values in his or her card choice of one or more of these attributes from its value on the original card.

Intended scanning - The subject either (1) expresses no hypothesis and chooses a card or (2) expresses a partial hypothesis and *holds constant* in his or her card choice all of the attributes involved in that hypothesis, making reference in the response to none of the changed attributes.

For experimental purposes, we define an *intended focusing index* to be the number of intended focusing choices divided by the total number of choices, and likewise an *intended scanning index*.

These definitions are theoretically mutually exclusive. Either a subject expresses a reason for a card choice or does not. If the subject does state a reason, either reference is made to changed attributes, or no such reference is made. However, in actual practice, the two indices do not necessarily add exactly to 1, due to the occasional occurrence of a completely different type of justification being offered by the subject. In such cases, the response counts in the denominator, but not in the numerator of either index.

Since our purpose in these tasks is essentially to find out *why* the subject made each particular choice, a short series of questions

which is designed to elicit this information is asked of each
subject. Immediately after each choice, the experimenter
asks the subject, "Why did you choose that card?" If the
subject states a clear reason for the choice, no further questions
are asked. If a clear reason is not stated, the experimenter asks,
"Did you have any particular concept in mind when you made that
choice?" If the subject answers "no," nothing else is said. If
the subject answers "yes," the experimenter asks, "What was your
concept?" It is important to note that these questions are asked
in the same way of *all* subjects after *every* card choice. In addition,
a series of allowable comments from the experimenter concerning the
rules of the game, etc., was developed. These questions and comments
constitute the experimenter's entire portion of the dialogue during
the task, and are given under the same conditions to all subjects.
Experimenters are strongly discouraged from making any other comments
during the administration of the task. By structuring questions and
comments in this way, the chances of hints are minimized, and what
hints may be given are given in a similar manner to all subjects.

It should be pointed out that the asking of this series of questions *does* change the task from one in which no dialogue is allowed.
In effect, the mere asking of the questions may cause subjects to view
the tasks differently than if no questions had been asked. However,
an important feature of the structured questioning technique is that
exactly the same series of questions is employed in the same order for
all subjects on all three versions of the task. Thus for the three
concept acquisition tasks, the structural isomorphism is preserved.

The use of "intended focusing" and "intended scanning" indexes in
measuring strategy use avoids another pitfall of the behavioral
"strategy scores" used by Bruner, Laughlin, and others. As these
strategy scores are frequently defined in the literature, card choices
which are "focus" choices are often those which are non-redundant in a
logical sense and yield new information; while card choices which are
"scanning" choices are often those which are repetitive or yield no
new information. (See Laughlin, 1965, for one such definition of
"focusing strategy.") Given these properties which hold *by definition*
of the choice categories, the reported findings that focusing is the
more efficient strategy must be viewed with great reservation--surely
this is more a consequence of the *logical* structure of the *definitions*, than of the psychological nature of the focusing and scanning
strategies. "Intended" focusing and scanning, on the other hand, are
defined with reference to subjects' statements about the reasons for
their choices; there is no *a priori* association of focusing with efficiency or scanning with inefficiency.

In the study itself, we shall observe how the task embodiment
influences the choice of strategy, and how the choice of strategy
influences the efficiency of solution.

3. Summary of Findings

The Hotelling-Lawley MANOVA Test was highly significant for over-all group differences ($p < .0001$), but was not significant for either experimenter differences or experimenter x group interactions. The latter result provides an important cross-check on inter-experimenter reliability, in view of the "structured questions" nature of the task and the extensive experimenter training which took place in preparation for the structured questions format. All experimenter groups are pooled in reporting the data below.

Table 7A.1 lists the means by group and by task on each of the dependent variables.

Table 7A.2 shows the main effects and differences between groups on dependent variables from the first problem. These effects were calculated using univariate analysis of variance and Duncan's Multiple Range Test.

From Tables 7A.1 and 7A.2, it can be seen that with respect to overall task difficulty, the introduction of the more abstract attribute and the increase in object exemplar diversity from Task 1 to Task 2 had a detrimental effect on performance, whereas the further increase in object exemplar diversity from Task 2 to Task 3 did not significantly worsen performance from Task 2 (although the three task difficulty variables of the number of choices to solution, the time to solution, and the percentage of subjects solving the problem, all showed slightly but not significantly greater difficulty for Task 3 than for Task 2).

With regard to the strategies for problem solution, it can be seen that each change in the task embodiment significantly affected subjects' intended strategies. Subjects intended to scan the most and focus the least on Task 3; they scanned the least and focused the most on Task 1; and they scanned and focused to an intermediate degree on Task 2.

In addition to the above results, some interesting effects of the change in problem embodiments on *transfer* of learning from the first task to the second were observed. For example, in comparing groups A and C, overall performance on the second problem was facili-tated only when the more difficult problem was presented first. In other words, group A significantly outperformed group C on Task 1, but group C did not significantly outperform group A on Task 3, even though group C subjects had the prior experience of Task 1. This result is consistent with the "deep end" hypothesis of Dienes and Jeeves (1970), discussed in Chapter IV.

In addition, the intended strategies which predominated on the first problem were carried over to increased usage on the second problem. For example, group A scanned more and focused less on

Table 7A.1 *Means by Group and by Task for Dependent Variables*

Dependent Variable			Group		
			A	B	C
			Task 3 First	Task 2 First	Task 1 Second
F P i r r o s b t l e m		Number of Choices to Solution	14.47	13.75	8.67
		Time to Solution	16.32	13.26	7.18
		Solved – Not Solved	.36	.56	.97
		Intended Focusing Index	.06	.20	.39
		Intended Scanning Index	.87	.75	.61
			Task 1 Second	Task 1 Second	Task 3 Second
S P e r c o o b n l d e m		Number of Choices to Solution	5.28	6.97	14.53
		Time to Solution	3.40	4.86	13.60
		Solved – Not Solved	1.00	.97	.53
		Intended Focusing Index	.15	.27	.19
		Intended Scanning Index	.84	.73	.78

Table 7A.2. *Main Effects and Differences Among Groups for the First Problem*

Dependent Variable	SS	df	MS	F	p	Differences
Number of Choices to Solution	720.80	2	360.40	8.57	.0004	Task 1 < Task 2 = Task 3
Time to Solution	155794.89	2	77893.44	18.08	.0001	Task 1 < Task 2 = Task 3
Solved - Not Solved	7.02	2	3.51	19.06	.0001	Task 1 > Task 2 = Task 3
Intended Focusing Index	19613.63	2	9806.82	23.91	.0001	Task 1 > Task 2 > Task 3
Intended Scanning Index	12217.35	2	6108.68	13.07	.0001	Task 1 < Task 2 < Task 3

Task 1 than did group C; group C focused more and scanned less on Task 3 than did group A. Also, on Tasks 1 and 3 combined, group A scanned more and focused less than did group C.

Table 7A.3 shows Pearson product-moment correlations between measures of overall performance and measures of intended strategy usage by task groups on the first problem. It can be seen from the table that these correlations are all quite low. In fact, none of the correlations, even for Task 1 (which employed all perceptual attributes), was significant at the .05 level. Thus the presumed superior efficiency of the focusing strategy was not substantiated at the level of intended strategy usage for any of the tasks.

The aforementioned results are illustrative of some of the interesting effects which can be observed through the variation of task structure and embodiments. In this study, care was taken on every level to preserve not only the structural isomorphism of the three tasks, but also to hold constant variables of embodiment which were not under consideration. The technique of asking subjects a structured series of questions after each card choice was used. This series of questions assessed process variables relating to the intended strategy, while at the same time preserving the isomorphic nature of the three tasks.

It can be concluded with a high degree of confidence that variations in the embodiment of a concept acquisition task may not only affect the overall difficulty of the task, but also induce subjects to employ different strategies for solution, even though the structure of the task remains unchanged. This is not to say that problem-solving strategies are totally task-specific. However, given that several different strategies can be employed on all problems having a certain structure, slight variations in the problem embodiment may induce subjects to solve the task using one strategy rather than another.

The variations in problem embodiment introduced in Tasks 2 and 3 have the effect of transforming these tasks into more "real-life" problem-solving situations. The results indicate that under these conditions, neither focusing nor scanning strategy usage was significantly associated with superior performance, but that the vast majority of subjects preferred to employ a scanning strategy to discern the concept. These results call into question some of the inferences regarding concept acquisition made by Bruner and his followers. The results support the assertion that the focusing strategy cannot be assumed to be the better strategy to employ in the attainment of "real-life" concepts. In cases where the possibly relevant attributes of the concept are unknown at the outset and where the diversity of examples of the concept is great, it may be preferable to adopt a scanning strategy.

Table 7A.3. *Pearson Product-Moment Correlations Between Measures of Overall Performance and Measures of Intended Strategy Usage by Task Groups on the First Problem*

Task 1	Solved – Not Solved	Number of Choices to Solution	Time to Solution
Intended Focusing Index	−.20167	.17445	.14228
Intended Scanning Index	.20091	−.18093	−.15403
Task 2			
Intended Focusing Index	.04363	−.28902	−.01605
Intended Scanning Index	.16342	.23752	−.16975
Task 3			
Intended Focusing Index	.31059	.07415	.01420
Intended Scanning Index	.11118	−.26416	−.30660

Appendix:

Directions Given to Subjects Prior to Task Administration

First Problem

Before we begin the experiment, I would like to ask you if you are familiar with the name Jerome Bruner? Have you ever heard of the phrase "concept attainment"?

This experiment contains two problems for you to solve. Your job in the problems is to find what is called a conjunctive concept. By a conjunctive concept, I mean a way of grouping things in terms of some shared characteristic or characteristics. For example, look at the pictures I am placing before you. If I were to ask you to name a property shared by pictures 1, 2, 3, and 4, you might say "people." People is an example of a conjunctive concept. If I were to ask you to name some characteristics shared by pictures 1 and 2, you might say "young people." Young and people are two characteristics which are shared by pictures 1 and 2, so young people is a conjunctive concept which is shown on pictures 1 and 2. However, picture 5 is not an example of the conjunctive concept young people, since there is no young person shown on picture 5. Do you have any questions on what a conjunctive concept is?

Can you give me an example of another conjunctive concept?

Would all things that are old be a conjunctive concept?

Would all things that are gray be a conjunctive concept?

Would all things that are both old and gray be a conjunctive concept?

Would all things that are either old or gray be a conjunctive concept?

Would all things that are old, gray, and wrinkled be a conjunctive concept?

Now in the first problem you are going to be finding a conjunctive concept which is shown on some of these cards but not on others. As you can see, I have typed the names of the objects in the lower right-hand corner to help you identify them, but the labels have nothing to do with the problem. Just for practice, I'll give you a sample conjunctive concept, and you show me all cards which are examples of the concept. How about all cards with objects which are red and make noise (all cards with objects that are red and have corners)?

Now we are ready to start the problem. I am thinking of a certain conjunctive concept. The concept is shown on some of the cards before you, and on others it is not. It is your job to describe which cards illustrate the concept. I will start by showing you a card which is an example of my concept. For example, if I were thinking of <u>all cards</u> <u>with objects which are red and make noise</u> (<u>all cards with objects</u> <u>that are red and have corners</u>), I might show you this card. Your job is to choose cards one by one to test whether they are examples of the concept I am thinking of, and after each choice, I will tell you whether or not the card you have chosen is an example of my concept. When you think you know the concept, you can make a guess, and I will tell you whether you are right or wrong. You can make a guess after any choice, but you can't make more than one guess after any particular choice without choosing another card for testing. Also, when you make a guess, please say something like, "I think it's all cards which..." and then say the concept.

The problem is solved when you have correctly described the cards which illustrate the concept. Do you have any questions?

Try to arrive at the concept as efficiently as possible. As you go along, I'd like you to think out loud and tell me why you are choosing each particular card. Are you ready to begin? Here is an example of the concept I am thinking of.

Second Problem

In the second problem, the rules will be exactly the same as in problem one except that we will be using a different set of cards. Before we begin, do you have any questions as to the rules of the game?

Here is an example of the concept I am thinking of.

VII.

Structure Variables in Problem-Solving Research

B.

Classifying Algebra Problems According to the Complexity of
Their Mathematical Representations

by

Harold C. Days
Fort Valley State College
Fort Valley, Georgia

1. Description of the Study

This section presents a scheme which can be used to classify a
variety of algebraic problems according to the complexity of their
structure. The particular scheme is designed to classify problems
which can be solved using one or more linear equations. Although
problems requiring the use of quadratic, cubic, or other equations
were not considered in the development, a few minor modifications of
the classification scheme will make it applicable to such problems
as well.

The procedure is based entirely on the mathematical representation obtained by translating the problem statement into symbols (i.e.,
on the algebraic structure of the problem). Although in this study it
is used to place problems into two categories (simple structure or
complex structure), it can easily be adapted to a more detailed classification.

The purpose of the study was to examine the effects of problem
complexity, together with the cognitive level of the subjects, on the
processes used in solving verbal problems (Days, 1977). Two eighth-
grade general mathematics classes were randomly selected from each of
three junior high schools. Sheehan's modified version of the Longeot
Test was administered to each class, in order to classify the students
as concrete operational or formal operational (Longeot, 1964; Sheehan,
1970). Ten subjects per school were then randomly selected from each
of the two cognitive groups; each of these 60 subjects was scheduled
for a two-hour interview.

In the interview, the student was asked to solve ten word problems while "thinking aloud." Two of these problems served as practice
problems and eight as experimental problems. Four of the experimental
problems were defined as having simple structures and four were defined

as having complex structures. The interviews were audiotape-recorded, and a written record was also kept of selected responses. The protocols obtained in the interviews were used as the basis for determining the processes employed by the subjects.

Coding of Protocols

A modified version of the coding system devised by Kilpatrick (1967) was used to code the tape-recorded protocols. The checklist variables were included on the coding form under the following eight categories:

(1) Understanding Processes -- (a) rereads, (b) restates, (c) separates.

(2) Representational Processes -- (d) performs exploratory manipulations, (e) draws a diagram, (f) uses mnemonic notation.

(3) Recall Processes -- (g) recalls related problems, (h) recalls related concepts, (i) uses method or results of related problem.

(4) Production Processes -- (j) reasons deductively, (k) uses successive approximations, (l) estimates.

(5) Evaluation Processes -- (m) checks manipulations, (n) checks conditions, (o) checks by retracing steps.

(6) Comments About Solution -- questions uniqueness or existence of solution, questions relevance of information, says he or she cannot solve problem.

(7) Executive Error -- makes counting or computational error while solving the problem.

(8) Strategies -- (i) uses deductive algorithmic approach (subject uses reasoning and an algorithm or a sequence of algorithms to obtain solution), (ii) uses systematic trial-and-error approach (trial-and-error in which successive trials are modified on the basis of former trials and trial-and-error in which some type of system is used to generate the numbers tried), and (iii) uses random trial-and-error approach (trial-and-error which is not systematic).

One coding form was completed for each problem. Only explicit behavior was coded. The checklist variables were recorded (with the exception of executive error and strategy variables) at the *first* observance of the process in a given solution attempt. The sequence of processes was coded at the bottom of the checklist. This sequence included the total number of times each process was used and the order

in which the processes occurred. The sequence of the solution processes was used to classify the solution attempt with respect to the
"strategy" variable. Further data collected included the number of
executive errors, the number of structural errors, and the total time
for each problem's solution.

Scoring

Two process scores were computed for each student for each of
the 15 processes (a) - (o) listed above, which were chosen for analysis.
Two strategy scores for each of the three strategies (i) - (iii)
listed above were also computed for each student. A score
was assigned to a given process on the *simple* structure problems by
counting the number of simple structure problems (0-4) on which the
student was observed using the process. Similarly a student's score
for a given process on the *complex* structure problems was the number
of complex structure problems (0-4) on which the student was observed
using the process. For example, a "draws-a-diagram" score of 3 on the
complex structure problems implies that the subject drew a diagram in
solving three of the four complex structure problems. The scores for
"systematic trial-and-error," "random trial-and-error," and "deductive
algorithmic" strategies were assigned in a similar manner.

The *range score* for each problem set was a measure of the *variety*
of processes used on the set. The range score was obtained by counting the number of different processes used to solve the problems in
the given problem set. For example, a range score of 6 on the simple
structure problems implied that six different processes were used
while attempting to solve the four simple structure problems. The
(1) understanding, (2) representational, (3) recall, (4) production,
and (5) evaluation scores were obtained by summing the process scores
which fell under the respective categories. For example, the "understanding" score was obtained by summing the scores for "rereads,"
"restates," and "separates."

The experimental design was a 2x2 factorial design with repeated
measures on problem structure. The factors were (A) cognitive level
(concrete or formal) and (B) problem structure (simple or complex).
Analysis of variance was used to analyze those scores which satisfied
the ANOVA assumptions, and Wilson's two-way analysis of variance based
on medians was used to analyze those scores which did not satisfy the
ANOVA assumptions (Wilson, 1956).

Before summarizing the findings, the classification scheme for
problem complexity, used to establish factor (B) in the study, will
be described in detail.

2. Definitions

Mathematical Representation of the Problem Statement

The mathematical representation of a problem statement was considered to consist of symbols representing known and unknown quantities, mathematical sentences involving these symbols, and the mathematical operations which were explicit in the mathematical sentences. A whole-number coefficient of a variable was considered to indicate the operation of multiplication, while a fractional or decimal coefficient was considered to indicate the operation of division. The mathematical sentences describe both the explicit and implicit relations found in the statement of the problem.

For example, consider the following problem:

> 7B.1 *Together Tom and John have 24 pennies. Tom has*
> *twice as many pennies as John. How many pennies*
> *does each boy have?*

A mathematical representation of this problem can be written as $T + J = 24$ and $T = 2J$. The mathematical representation consists of four different symbols, with two of them representing variables. The two variables are the number of pennies Tom has and the number of pennies John has. The mathematical representation also contains the operations of addition and of multiplication, but it does not contain any combination of the two operations. The symbols used in writing the mathematical representation of a problem are not unique. The above representation could have been written as $x + y = 24$ and $y = 2x$ just as well.

It should be pointed out that there may be more than one mathematical representation of some problems. However, in such cases either representation should give rise to the same classification of the problem. Consider the following problem:

> 7B.2 *There are some rabbits and some cages. When one*
> *rabbit is put into each cage, one rabbit will have*
> *no cage. When two rabbits are put into each cage*
> *there are two empty cages. How many rabbits and*
> *how many cages are there?*

One possible mathematical representation of the problem is: $R = C + 1$ and $\frac{1}{2}R = C - 2$. Another possible mathematical representation of the problem is: $C = R - 1$ and $C = \frac{1}{2}R + 2$. However, in both representations of the problem the numbers of variables and symbols are the same, and the operations involved are the same. Consequently, the use of either representation of the problem will give rise to the same classification. Thus, although there may be more than one mathematical representation of the same problem, for classification purposes the mathematical representations of a problem can be considered to be equivalent.

Other Terms and Expressions

Other terms and expressions important to the problem classification scheme were defined as follows:

1. *Variable.* A variable was defined as a symbol that represented an unknown quantity.

2. *An Expression Based on Explicitly Stated Relationships.* An expression is said to be based on explicitly stated relationships if that expression can be obtained by a direct translation of the verbal statement of the problem into a mathematical statement of the problem.

3. *An Expression Based on Implicit Relationships.* An expression is said to be based on implicit relationships if (a) the expression is based on relationships deduced from the information in the problem statement and (b) the expression cannot be obtained by a direct translation of the problem statement.

4. *Transformation.* A transformation was defined as an application of one of the following properties of real numbers: (a) the distributive property, (b) the addition property of equality, (c) the subtraction property of equality, (d) the multiplication property of equality, (e) the division property of equality, or (f) the substitution property of equality. Substitution was counted as a transformation only if an algebraic expression was substituted for a symbol. Consequently, substitution of a number for a variable was not counted as a transformation. The application of one of the order axioms was also included as a transformation. Due to the high frequency with which the associative and commutative properties are used in solving most problems, the application of these properties in the solution of a problem was not counted as a transformation.

5. *Conversion.* Conversion refers to changing one unit of measurement into another unit of measurement; for example, changing feet to inches, dollars to cents, or decimals to fractions.

3. The Classification Scheme

Simple Structure

A problem was said to have a "simple structure" if *at least four* of the following statements about the mathematical representation of the problem statement were true:

1. The mathematical representation contained at most four different symbols that represented either numbers of variables (i.e., the cardinal number of the set of numerals and letters in the mathematical representation was ≤ 4).

2. The mathematical representation of the problem statement contained only one variable.

3. The value(s) of the variable(s) in the mathematical representation could be obtained by substituting the given data into an expression that was based solely on explicitly stated relationships, and then performing the operations indicated by the expressions.

4. The mathematical representation of the problem statement could be written and the equations involved in the representation solved without any conversions.

5. The only operations or combinations of operations that were part of the mathematical representation were addition, multiplication (by a whole number), subtraction, or addition-subtraction. (The representation $2a + b = c$ implies a combination of multiplication and addition, whereas the representation $a + b + c = d$ implies only the one operation of addition.)

6. The portion of the mathematical representation that was based on a direct translation of the problem statement contained (a) one system of two or more linear equations in two variables and (b) one of these equations expressed a variable in terms of the other variables or it expressed one of the variables in terms of known quantities.

7. The minimum number of transformations necessary to reach a correct numerical solution to the number sentence in the mathematical representation of the problem statement was less than four. If the mathematical representation contained more than one linear equation, then the count of transformations was based on the substitution method of solution. (Consider the two linear equations $ax + by = c$, $y = dx$; it takes three transformations to solve this system of equation. First dx is substituted for y; then the distributive property is applied to obtain $(a + bd)x = c$; and finally, the division property of equality is used to get $x = \dfrac{c}{a + bd}$.

Complex Structure

A problem was said to have a "complex structure" if *at least five* of the following statements about the mathematical representation of the problem were true:

1. The mathematical representation contained at least five different symbols that represented either numbers or variables.

2. The mathematical representation contained at least three variables (unknowns).

3. The value(s) of the variable(s) in the mathematical representation could not be obtained by evaluating an expression that was based solely on explicitly stated relationships.

4. At least one conversion was necessary in order to write or solve the number sentences in the mathematical representation of the problem statement.

5. The mathematical representation contained at least one of the following combinations of operations: (a) multiplication-addition, (b) multiplication-subtraction, (c) division-multiplication, (d) division-addition, or (e) division-subtraction.

6. The mathematical representation contained a system of two or more linear equations in two or more variables. The portion of the mathematical representation that was based on a direct translation of the problem statement into mathematical sentences did not contain an equation which expressed one variable in terms of the other, nor did it contain an expression of one variable in terms of known quantities.

7. The minimum number of transformations necessary to reach a correct numerical solution to the number sentences in the mathematical representation was greater than four.

Problems which did not satisfy either of the above criteria were classified as neither simple nor complex; these problems have structures intermediate between simple and complex.

The mathematical representation of the problem statement was used solely for the purpose of classifying the problem as simple, intermediate, or complex. The subject was not necessarily aware of the underlying mathematical representation of the problems, nor necessarily expected to use the representation to obtain the solution.

To sum up, there are three steps required in the use of the above classification scheme. First, a mathematical representation for each problem must be written. Second, all equations or mathematical sentences should be simplified and solved. Finally, the properties in each set should be checked to determine if a given problem should be defined as having a simple, intermediate, or complex structure.

Reliability of the Classification Scheme

To check the reliability of the classification scheme, the author sent a set of 13 randomly selected verbal algebra problems, together with the problem classification definitions, to 13 mathematics educators at various universities. The respondents were instructed to use the definitions to classify each problem as having a simple structure, a complex structure, or neither. Of the 13 problem sets mailed, 10 were returned along with the classifications reached. Each respondent was considered as a judge, and analysis of variance was used to estimate the reliability of the problem classification procedure (Winer, 1962, p. 283).

For a given problem each judge assigned a "1" for a problem if it was classified as having a "simple structure," a "3" if it was classified as having a "complex structure," and a "2" if it was classified as "neither." These numbers were then used to compute the reliability of the classification procedure. The reliability of the mean of the ten judges was .94 and the reliability of a single judge was .63. Five of the ten judges were randomly chosen for a second analysis. The reliability of the mean of the five judges was .95 and the reliability of a single judge was .79. These statements mean that if the average of the numbers (rounded to the nearest whole number) assigned to a problem by the five judges was used to classify the problem, then the reliability of the classification was .95. But if the score of only one judge was used, the reliability was .79. Since the decisions of all judges were based on the problem classification definition, it was concluded that the procedure used to classify the problems was a reliable procedure.

Examples

To illustrate how problems can be classified according to complexity of structure, the above classification procedure is used to classify the following four problems into one of the three categories: (a) simple structure, (b) complex structure, or (c) neither.

7B.2. *There are some rabbits and cages. When one rabbit is put into each cage, one rabbit will have no cage. When two rabbits are put into each cage there are two empty cages. How many rabbits and how many cages are there?*

Representation
$$\begin{bmatrix} R = \text{number of rabbits} \\ C = \text{number of cages} \\ R = C + 1 \text{ (implicit in statement of problem)} \\ \tfrac{1}{2}R = C - 2 \text{ (implicit in statement of problem)} \end{bmatrix}$$

Solution to
Equations in
Representation
$$\begin{aligned}
&\tfrac{1}{2}(C+1) = C - 2 \text{ (substitution) Transformation 1} \\
&\tfrac{1}{2}C + \tfrac{1}{2} = C - 2 \text{ (distributive) Transformation 2} \\
&\tfrac{1}{2}C = C - 5/2 \text{ (addition property) Transformation 3} \\
&-\tfrac{1}{2}C = -5/2 \text{ (addition property) Transformation 4} \\
&C = 5 \text{ (multiplication property) Transformation 5}
\end{aligned}$$

7B.3 *A cow and pig together cost 56 dollars. The cow cost*
30 dollars more than the pig. How much does each
animal cost?

Representation
$$\begin{aligned}
&C = \text{cost of cow (unknown)} \\
&P = \text{cost of pig (unknown)} \\
&C + P = 56 \text{ (explicitly stated relation)} \\
&C = P + 30 \text{ (explicitly stated relation)}
\end{aligned}$$

Solution to
Equations in
Representation
$$\begin{aligned}
&(P + 30) + P = 56 \text{ (substitution) Transformation 1} \\
&2P + 30 = 56 \text{ (combining like terms)} \\
&2P = 26 \text{ (addition property of equality) Transformation 2} \\
&P = 13 \text{ (division property of equality) Transformation 3}
\end{aligned}$$

7B.4. *An apple and pear together cost 20 cents. Five apples*
and 10 pears cost $1.65. How much does one apple
cost? How much does one pear cost?

Representation
$$\begin{aligned}
&A = \text{cost of one apple (unknown)} \\
&P = \text{cost of one pear (unknown)} \\
&A + P = 20\textcent \text{ (explicitly stated)} \\
&5A + 10P = \$1.65 \text{ (explicitly stated)}
\end{aligned}$$

Solution to
Equations in
Representation
$$\begin{aligned}
&A + P = .20 \text{ (conversion)} \\
&A = .20 - P \text{ (addition property) Transformation 1} \\
&5(.20 - P) + 10P = 1.65 \text{ (substitution) Transformation 2} \\
&1.00 - 5P + 10P = 1.65 \text{ (distributive prop.) Transformation 3} \\
&1.00 + 5P = 1.65 \text{ (combining like terms)} \\
&5P = .65 \text{ (addition property) Transformation 4} \\
&P = .13 \text{ (division property) Transformation 5}
\end{aligned}$$

7B.5 *A housewife can buy sugar for 15¢ a pound and coffee*
for 80¢ a pound. If she buys the same number of pounds
of each and spends $5.70, how many pounds of each does
she buy?

Representation
$$\begin{aligned}
&S = \text{number of pounds of sugar (unknown)} \\
&C = \text{number of pounds of coffee (unknown)} \\
&C = S \text{ (explicitly stated)} \\
&15\textcent S + 80\textcent C = \$5.70 \text{ (implicit in problem statement)}
\end{aligned}$$

Solution to
Equations in
Representation
$$\begin{aligned}
&.15S + .80C = 5.70 \text{ (conversion)} \\
&.15S + .80S = 5.70 \text{ (substitution) Transformation 1} \\
&.95S = 5.70 \text{ (combining like terms)} \\
&S = 6 \text{ (division property of equality) Transformation 2}
\end{aligned}$$

Table 7B.1 *Properties of the Mathematical Representations of the Examples*

Simple Structure Properties Problems	7B.2	7B.3	7B.4	7B.5
1. Representation contains at most four different symbols.		✓		
2. Representation contains only one variable.				
3. Value of variable(s) can be obtained by substituting into expressions based on explicitly stated relationships.				
4. No conversions necessary.	✓	✓		
5. The only operations or combinations of operations are: addition, multiplication, subtraction, or addition-subtraction.		✓		
6. At least one variable is explicitly stated in terms of other variables or known quantities.		✓		✓
7. Minimum number of transformations less than four.		✓		✓

Complex Structure Properties Problems	7B.2	7B.3	7B.4	7B.5
1. Representation contains at least five different symbols.	✓		✓	✓
2. Representation contains at least three variables.				
3. Value of variable(s) cannot be obtained by substituting into expressions based on explicitly stated relationships.	✓	✓	✓	✓
4. At least one conversion necessary.			✓	✓
5. The operation of division or the combination multiplication-addition or multiplication-subtraction is contained in the representation.	✓		✓	✓
6. No variable is explicitly stated in terms of other variables or known quantities.	✓		✓	
7. Minimum number of transformations greater than four.	✓		✓	
Classification	complex	simple	complex	neither

Now let us consider Table 7B.1. If the mathematical representation of a problem satisfies a given property, a check is placed in the square which corresponds to that problem and property. Otherwise, the square is left blank. If at least four checks fall under the simple structure properties for a given problem, the problem is classified as having simple structure. If at least five of the complex structure properties are checked for a given problem, the problem is classified as having a complex structure. All other combinations of checks are classified as neither simple nor complex.

Note that Problem *7B.3* is classified as having a simple structure since five of the simple structure properties are satisfied. On the other hand, Problems *7B.2* and *7B.4* are classified as having complex structures since they both satisfy at least five of the complex structures properties. Since Problem *7B.5* satisfies only two simple structure properties and only four complex structures properties, it is placed in the "neither" category.

4. Empirical Results of the Study

Tables 7B.2 and 7B.3 contain a summary of the analyses performed on several of the process scores and strategy scores. The analysis of the range score reveals that both groups used a wider variety of processes on the complex structure problems than on the simple structure problems. In general, "understanding," "representational," "production," and "evaluation" processes were used on significantly more complex structure problems than simple structure problems. While problem structure had a significant effect on the use of "understanding" and "representational" processes, cognitive level did not significantly affect the use of these processes.

Of the three strategies studied, "systematic trial-and-error" was used on significantly more complex structure problems than simple structure problems, while "deductive algorithmic" approaches were used on significantly more simple structure problems than complex structure problems.

There was a significant interaction effect for the time score ($p < .05$). An analysis of the interaction revealed that the concrete and formal subjects did not differ significantly in the amount of time spent solving the complex structure problems ($p < .1$), but the concrete-operational subjects spent significantly more time solving the simple structure problems than did the formal-operational subjects ($p < .05$). As expected, both groups spent significantly more time solving the complex structure problems than they did solving the simple structure problems ($p < .001$).

There was a significant interaction between cognitive level and problem structure for the use of "evaluation" processes. Concrete- and formal-operational subjects did not differ significantly in their

Table 7B.2. *Analysis of Variance of the Range Score, the "Understanding,"" Score, the "Production" Score and the "Evaluation" Score*

Source	df	MS	F
Range Score			
Cognitive Level (A)	1	81.11	18.03**
Error	56	4.50	
Problem Structure (B)	1	110.08	28.79**
A X B	1	6.28	1.64
Error	56	3.82	
"Understanding" Score			
Cognitive Level (A)	1	.08	.02
Error	56	5.06	
Problem Structure (B)	1	48.49	27.83***
A X B	1	.42	.24
Error	56	1.74	
"Production" Score			
Cognitive Level (A)	1	147.94	60.49***
Error	56	2.43	
Problem Structure (B)	1	45.94	20.95***
A X B	1	10.00	4.79*
Error	56	2.19	
"Evaluation" Score			
Cognitive Level (A)	1	21.55	11.36**
Error	56	1.89	
Problem Structure (B)	1	37.55	21.75***
A X B	1	7.75	4.50*
Error	56	1.72	

*$p < .05$ **$p < .01$ ***$p < .001$

Table 7B.3 *Wilson's Two-way Analysis of Variance of "Representational,"*
"Recall," "Systematic Trial-and-Error" and Time Scores

Scores	df	χ^2
"Representational" Score		
Cognitive Level (A)	1	0.03
Problem Structure (B)	1	66.81**
A X B	1	0.52
"Recall" Score		
Cognitive Level (A)	1	1.01
Problem Structure (B)	1	1.01
A X B		
"Systematic Trial-and-Error" Score		
Cognitive Level (A)	1	20.05**
Problem Structure (B)	1	13.93**
A X B	1	0.00
Time		
Cognitive Level (A)	1	0.07
Problem Structure (B)	1	42.28**
A X B	1	4.14*

*$p < .05$ **$p < .001$

use of "evaluation" processes on the simple structure problems, but
the formal-operational subjects used "evaluation" processes on significantly more of the complex structure problems than did the concrete-
operational subjects. Similar results were found for the "production"
score.

Finally, the formal-operational subjects found the complex structure problems to be significantly more difficult than the simple
structure problems, while the concrete-operational subjects found the
simple structure problems to be as difficult as the complex structure
problems. This finding is supported in part by previous research.
Jerman and Mirman (1973) found that structural (task) variables which
were good predictors of problem difficulty for subjects in grades 4
through 9 were not as good predictors of problem difficulty for
college-level subjects. Similarly, Ingle (1975) found that certain
structural (task) variables were better predictors of problem difficulty for high-ability students than they were for low-ability students.

Thus, the structure variable has a significant effect on both
product variables and process variables in this study. It appears
that the classification procedure described in this chapter may be
fairly useful for studying algebra problems of varying levels of
complexity.

VII.

Structure Variables in Problem-Solving Research

C.

State-Space Representation of Problem-Solving Behavior

by

George F. Luger*
University of Edinburgh
Edinburgh, Scotland

In this section, the results of two empirical studies based on the state-space analysis of the Tower of Hanoi problem are summarized. The utilization of the state-space to represent problem-solving behavior has been discussed by Goldin in Chapter IV. Here our purpose is to illustrate how empirical research based on this kind of analysis of problem structure can be carried out.

1. Paths Through the Tower of Hanoi State-Space

The Tower of Hanoi (TOH) problem and its state-space have been described in Chapter IV (Problem 4.11, Figure 4.12). In the first study, the TOH state-space is used to describe the problem-solving behavior of subjects (Goldin and Luger, 1979; Luger, 1973, 1976). Fifty-one college students and college-educated adults solved the 4-ring TOH problem, and their behavior was recorded as sequences of paths through the state-space. The purpose of this study was to investigate a set of general hypotheses proposed by Goldin and Luger (1973, 1975), anticipating patterns which might be expected to occur in the paths generated by problem-solvers. These hypotheses are restated and extended in Chapter IV, Section 3 of the present book; we shall make reference to them by number as we go along.

Hypothesis 1. In order to test whether the subjects generate non-random, goal-directed paths through the state-space, a metric is defined on the state-space, with the distance between two states given by the number of moves along the shortest path between them. A *goal-directed path* is defined to be one for which the distance from the goal state is non-increasing; thus it is a path which does not "double back" within the state-space. *Subgoal-directed paths* are defined analogously for the 2-ring and 3-ring subspaces illustrated in Figure 4.12. In Figure

---

*Current address: Department of Computing and Information Science, University of New Mexico, Albuquerque, New Mexico.

Figure 7C.1 *Goal- and Subgoal-Directed Paths in the Tower of Hanoi State-Space*

(a) The Main 4-Ring State-Space

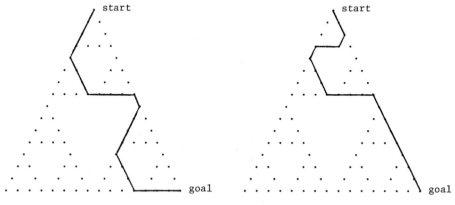

A goal-directed path.

A path that is weakly goal-directed but not goal-directed.

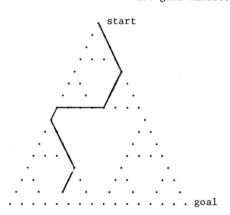

A path that is neither goal-directed nor weakly goal-directed.

Figure 7C.1 *continued*

(b) The 2-Ring Subspace (* = subgoals)

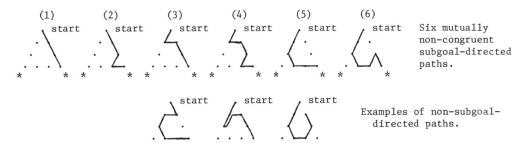

(1)   (2)   (3)   (4)   (5)   (6)   Six mutually
                                          non-congruent
                                          subgoal-directed
                                          paths.

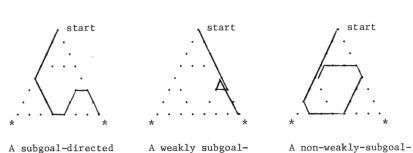

Examples of non-subgoal-
directed paths.

(c) The 3-Ring Subspace (* = subgoals)

A subgoal-directed   A weakly subgoal-   A non-weakly-subgoal-
      path.   directed path.   directed path.

Figure 7C.2 *The Exit Criterion for Subgoal States*

A path meeting the
criterion at the
subgoal state (*).

A path not meeting
the criterion at
the subgoal state (*).

7C.1, we have depicted goal- and subgoal-directed paths in the TOH state-space.

Every time a subject "starts over" in solving the TOH problem, a new "path" is said to begin. Thus a subject's problem solving consists of a sequence of attempts corresponding to a sequence of paths commencing with the initial problem state. When a subject arrived at the goal state, he or she was asked to solve the problem again in fewer moves. When a subject arrived at the goal state by means of the shortest possible path, the interview ended.

Six of the 51 subjects solved the problem on their first attempts in the minimum number of moves. These paths are, of course, goal- and subgoal-directed, by definition. For the remaining 45 subjects, Table 7C.1 summarizes the frequencies of occurrence of goal- and subgoal-directed paths.

For the sake of interest, a path is defined to be *weakly goal-directed* if it does not double back except within a 2-ring subspace of the main TOH state-space. A path through a 3-ring subspace is defined to be *weakly subgoal-directed* if it does not double back except within a 1-ring subspace. These definitions thus allow for slight deviations from strictly goal-directed paths. Table 7C.1 also summarizes the frequencies of occurrence for weakly goal- and subgoal-directed paths.

The frequencies of goal- and subgoal-directed paths in Table 7C.1 have been compared with those expected for randomly generated paths under various plausible sets of constraints (Luger, 1973). Not surprisingly, it turns out that in all cases subjects' frequencies of goal- and subgoal-directed paths substantially exceed the frequencies for randomly generated paths. (Under one set of constraints that is fairly rigorous, randomly generated paths through the 2-ring subspace are subgoal-directed 21 times in 32, or in 65.6 percent of the cases. Under the same set of constraints, randomly generated paths through the 4-ring state-space are determined experimentally to be goal-directed in approximately 9 percent of the cases. These figures compare with subjects' frequencies of 96 percent and 77 percent respectively.) Thus the goal- and subgoal-directedness of subjects' paths is *not automatic*, but is characteristic of problem-solving behavior for this problem.

Hypothesis 1 of Chapter IV further suggests that when a subgoal state is entered, the subject's path leaves the state in such a manner as to exit also from the subspace. This idea is illustrated for the TOH problem in Figure 7C.2. A randomly generated path would be expected to meet this criterion for exactly 50 percent of the subgoal states entered, assuming that reversals of single moves are totally disallowed. In fact, subjects' paths met the criterion for 96 percent of the 2-ring subgoal states entered and 98 percent of the 3-ring subgoal states, figures which seem to confirm a special role played by these states.

Table 7C.1 *Goal- and Subgoal-Directed Paths in the Tower of Hanoi State-Space*

(a) Paths Through the Main 4-Ring State-Space (<u>exclusive</u> of minimal solution
    paths)

	G	W	N	Tot.	G/Tot.	(G+W)/Tot.
Total 45 Subjects, All Trials	102	21	10	133	.77	.93
Total 45 Subjects, First Trial Only	33	6	6	45	.73	.87

G = goal-directed; W = weakly goal-directed (but not goal-directed);
N = neither goal-directed nor weakly goal-directed

(minimal solution paths are <u>not</u> included in the totals)

(b) Paths Through the 2-Ring Subspaces

	G								
	(1)	(2)	(3)	(4)	(5)	(6)	N	Tot.	G/Tot.
Total 45 Subjects, All Trials	563	8	29	2	53	3	27	685	.96

G = goal-directed; (1)-(6) = congruence class of goal-directed path,
see Fig. 7C.1; N = non-goal-directed

(minimal solution paths <u>are</u> included in these totals)

(c) Paths Through the 3-Ring Subspaces

	G	W	N	Tot.	G/Tot.	(G+W)/Tot.
Total 45 Subjects, All Trials	286	7	28	321	.89	.91

G = goal-directed; W = weakly goal-directed (but not goal-directed);
N = neither goal-directed nor weakly goal-directed

(minimal solution paths <u>are</u> included in these totals)

Hypothesis 2. The presence of the nested structure of subproblems in the TOH problem permits us to define *stages* during problem solving, in which the subproblems of a particular level are solved in the minimum number of moves. For each problem solver, a *2-ring stage* was defined to begin at the first point subsequent to which the solver's path through *more than half* of the 2-ring subspaces was congruent to the straight-line path [Path (1) in Figure 7C.1(b)]. During the period when *half or fewer* of the 2-ring subspaces were traversed by such minimal solution paths, the subject was said to be in a *1-ring stage*. Similarly, a *3-ring stage* was defined to begin at the first point subsequent to which the solver's path through more than half of the 3-ring subspaces was a minimal straight-line path. The first path in Figure 7C.1(a), for example, is characteristic of a 2-ring stage: in this path, six successive 2-ring subspaces are traversed by minimal straight-line paths, while two successive 3-ring subspaces are not.

Table 7C.2 shows how a subject's paths are analyzed with respect to the sequences of subspaces that are entered.

The sequence of stages is invariant by virtue of the way they are defined--in traversing a 3-ring subspace by means of a straight-line path, it is automatic that two 2-ring subspaces will be traversed by means of straight-line paths. However, it is not necessary that all stages occur for all subjects. For example, a subject may from the outset traverse more than 50 percent of the 2-ring subspaces by minimal paths; then that subject does not display the 1-ring stage as we have defined it. A subject may pass directly from a 1-ring stage to a 3-ring stage, bypassing the 2-ring stage, and so forth.

Of the 51 subjects in this study, six displayed no stages (these were the six who solved the main problem in their first attempts in the minimum number of moves); 16 displayed just one stage; 22 displayed just two stages; and seven displayed all three theoretically possible stages. The 1-ring stage was evident for 21 subjects and skipped by 30; the 2-ring stage was evident for 37 subjects and skipped by 14; and the 3-ring stage was evident for 23 subjects and skipped by 23, being undefined for five subjects who did not complete their minimal solution paths.

Although a 50 percent criterion was set *a priori* as the definition of the beginning of a new stage, the actual percentages of minimal solution paths prior to the beginning of a stage are substantially lower than 50 percent, while the actual percentages after the stage has begun are substantially higher. When these percentages are averaged over all subjects to whom they are applicable, it is found that during the 1-ring stage, the average subject traversed only 33 percent of the 2-ring subspaces by minimal solution paths; subsequent to the end of the 1-ring stage, the average subject traversed 91 percent of the 2-ring subspaces by minimal paths. Correspondingly, prior to the end of the 2-ring stage, the average subject traversed only 23 percent of the 3-ring subspaces by minimal solution paths; subsequent to the end of the 2-ring stage, the figure is 87 percent. These data seem to

Table 7C.2 *The Sequences of Subspaces Entered by Subjects' Paths*

Subject 1

	1-ring stage	2-ring stage	3-ring stage
2-ring	1 0 0 0 0 0 ⌐a	1 1 1 0 1 0 1 1 1 0 1 ⌐b	1 1 1 1 0 1 1 1 1 1 1 1 1
3-ring	0 0 0	1 0 1 0	1 1 0 1 1 0
4-ring	0	0	0 0 0

Subject 2

	2-ring stage	3-ring stage	minimal solution path
2-ring	a 1 0 1 1 0 1 ⌐b	1 1 ⌐c	1 1 1 1
3-ring	0 0	1	1 1
4-ring	0	0	1

Key: 1 = minimal straight-line path through a subspace
 2 = non-minimal path through a subspace

 a = beginning of 2-ring stage
 b = beginning of 3-ring stage
 c = end of 3-ring stage (beginning of minimal solution path)

Note that the 2-, 3-, and 4-ring subspaces are placed over each other so as to indicate the time-sequence (left to right) of subspaces entered.

indicate that a subject's acquisition of an n-ring subproblem structure, as evidenced by the production of minimal solution paths when
such subspaces are entered, is a fairly well-defined event.

Hypothesis 3. Since the n-ring subspaces at a particular level
are all mutually isomorphic, it was hypothesized that a subject's *non-*
minimal paths through the 2-ring (or 3-ring) subspaces might tend to
be congruent. For the 2-ring subspaces, a single congruence class of
non-minimal solution path was predominant for seven subjects (according to a pre-established criterion); for six subjects no single
congruence class was predominant; while for the remaining subjects,
no conclusion could be reached (because of insufficiently many non-
minimal paths, or an inconclusive distribution of these paths). For
the 3-ring subspaces, a single congruence class of non-minimal solution path was predominant for six subjects; for 21 subjects no single
congruence class was predominant; and for the remainder no conclusion
was possible.

These results appear inconclusive, and will not be elaborated
further in this section.

Hypothesis 4. The TOH problem state-space possesses a symmetry
automorphism. In the notation of Figure 4.12, the automorphism
exchanges the letters B and C in the description of any state, leaving
A fixed; for example, the image of state CCBA is BBCA. The automorphism thus maps the goal state CCCC into the state BBBB, which is not
a goal state in our presentation of the problem. Were the three pegs
of the TOH board to be arranged at the corners of an equilateral
triangle, the symmetry automorphism would represent the geometric
operation of reflection about the altitude of the triangle.

From the initial state AAAA, there are two possible first moves:
to BAAA, which is "towards" the goal state, and to CAAA, which is not.
As subjects begin to explore the TOH problem by moving rings from peg
to peg, we might expect that due to the reflection symmetry, approximately half of the subjects would generate paths leading towards the
goal state CCCC, and about half would generate paths leading towards
BBBB instead. The former group will not need to reorient the direction of their exploration during problem solving. Thus we would predict
that approximately half of the subjects will, at some point in their
problem solving, recognize that a transformation of their previous
steps is required in order to arrive at the correct goal state.

Figure 4.15 illustrates the occurrence of a pair of successive
paths which are *congruent modulo the symmetry automorphism.* In the
first path, the subject has commenced moving rings so as to approach
BBBB, but has apparently realized that the direction is wrong.
Starting over, the subject has generated an isomorphic image of the
previous path, state for state, but heading towards the goal state
CCCC. As illustrated in this figure, the second path in such a pair
of congruent paths is not necessarily the most direct solution path.
We conjecture that the interruption of a path, followed by the

generation of its conjugate path under the symmetry automorphism, corresponds to the acquisition of "insight" into the problem symmetry. Thus it may be hypothesized that a path which is the second path in such a congruent pair is more likely than other paths to be a minimal solution path.

For the 51 subjects discussed above, two successive paths by the same subject are defined to be a *congruent pair* if (a) the first path is at least four states long; (b) the second path is at least as long as the first; and (c) the second path is conjugate to the first, state for state, for the entire length of the first path. A path is classified as a minimal solution path if it connects the initial state to the goal state in exactly 15 or 16 steps (this definition allows for a 1-move deviation by the subject if it is immediately corrected).

The following hypotheses are investigated (Goldin and Luger, 1979):

(a) *Predicted randomness of initial move:* For subjects' very first moves, the frequency of moves to state BAAA rather than state CAAA does not differ significantly from .50.

(b) *Predicted frequency of the symmetry effect:* The proportion of subjects whose moves generate a congruent pair of paths does not differ significantly from .50.

(c) *Correlation between a subject's first move and subsequent occurrence of the symmetry effect:* Subjects whose first moves are to state CAAA are significantly more likely to generate congruent pairs of paths than subjects whose first moves are to state BAAA.

(d) *Association of the symmetry effect with successful problem solving:* A path which is the second path in a congruent pair is significantly more likely to be a minimal solution path than a path which is not the second path in a congruent pair.

Hypotheses (a) and (b) are tested using the binomial test; hypotheses (c) and (d) are tested using the chi-square test for two independent samples (Siegel, 1956). In the test of hypothesis (d), each *path* (commencing with the initial state) is treated as an independent event. This is not strictly correct, since two paths generated by the same subject can scarcely be considered independent of each other. However, there is no obvious way in which the lack of independence which is theoretically present should affect the outcome of the hypothesis; thus the chi-square test may be considered as a rough indication of statistical significance.

The outcomes are as follows:

(a) Among the 51 subjects there were 27 first moves to state CAAA and 24 first moves to state BAAA. N = 51 is sufficiently large to approximate the binomial distribution by means of a normal distribution with a correction for continuity. Then we obtain $z = .28$ or $p < .39$ even for a one-tailed test. The data are therefore consistent with the randomness of subjects' first moves.

(b) Of the 51 subjects, 22 generated at least one congruent pair of paths during the course of problem solving (one subject generated two such pairs), and 29 did not do so. Then $z = .84$ or $p < .20$ even for a one-tailed test. The data are therefore consistent with the hypothesis that congruent pairs will occur for 50 percent of the subjects.

(c) Table 7C.3 is a 2x2 contingency table, showing the distribution of *subjects* according to first move (state BAAA or CAAA) and according to the occurrence or non-occurrence of the symmetry effect during problem solving. For the data in Table 7C.3, chi-square = 4.76 (where a correction for continuity has been incorporated), df = 1, and $p < .05$ (for a one-tailed test) in confirmation of hypothesis (c). However, it should be noted that the significance of the effect lessens if the six subjects who solved the problem in the first trial are removed from the upper right cell. These subjects, by virtue of having solved the problem *via* a minimal path on the first trial, will not have the opportunity to generate the second path which would be necessary to observe the symmetry effect. It is simply assumed that, for these subjects, the effect is not present.

(d) Table 7C.4 is another 2x2 contingency table; but this table shows the distributions of *paths* (trials) according to whether or not each path is the second path in a congruent pair, and whether or not each path is a minimal solution path. Since each subject's first attempt cannot possibly be the second path in a congruent pair, first trials have been excluded from this table. For the data in Table 7C.4, chi-square = 10.59, df = 1, $p < .005$, and hypothesis (d) is confirmed. However, note the comment above concerning the use of chi-square here.

In short, it appears on balance that a symmetry effect can be defined using the concept of paths congruent under the symmetry automorphism (Hypothesis 4 of Chapter IV), and that the symmetry effect is associated with success in the problem task.

2. Transfer Between Isomorphic Problems

The second study discussed here (Luger and Bauer, 1978) examines transfer between the TOH problem and one of its isomorphs, the Tea Ceremony (TC) problem, which was first studied by Hayes and Simon (1974).

Table 7C.3 *Distribution of Subjects*

	congruent pair	no congruent pair	totals
first move to BAAA	6	18	24
first move to CAAA	16	11	27
totals	22	29	51

Table 7C.4 *Distribution of Paths (excluding first trials)*

	second path in a congruent pair	not the second path in a congruent pair	totals
minimal solution path	15	29	44
not a minimal solution path	8	80	88
totals	23	109	132

*7C.1 Three people, a host, an elder and a youth, partici-
pate in the ceremony. There are four tasks they
perform, listed in ascending order of importance:
feeding the fire, serving cakes, serving tea, and reading poetry. The host performs all the tasks at the
beginning of the ceremony, and the tasks are trans-
ferred back and forth among the participants until
all the tasks are performed by the youth, at which
time the ceremony is completed. There are two constraints on the transfer of tasks: only one task--the
least important a person is performing--may be moved,
and no person may receive a new task unless it is less
important than any task they perform at the time. The
object of the Tea Ceremony game is to transfer the
four tasks from the host to the youth in the fewest
number of moves.*

In the Tea Ceremony problem, each task is represented by a block with
a square base; the height of each block represents the relative importance of each task. The transfer of the blocks is constrained by
means of a track, thus allowing access only to the block representing
the least important task a person is performing.

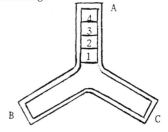

The three people--host, elder, and youth--correspond to the three
pegs in the TOH problem--A, B, and C respectively. The four tasks--
feeding the fire, serving cakes, serving tea, and reading poetry--
correspond to the four rings in the TOH problem--1, 2, 3, and 4
respectively. These labels have been introduced for convenience in
the above diagram.

Forty-eight subjects, all second-year psychology students at the
University of Edinburgh, volunteered for the study. These were randomly
assigned to two treatment groups: 24 solving the TOH problem first and
then the TC problem (TOH-1 and TC-2), and 24 solving the TC problem
first and then the TOH problem (TC-1 and TOH-2). Subjects were told
they were solving two different problems, and no reference was made
before or during the problem solving to any relationship between them.
Criterion for each problem consisted in performing the minimal sequence
of moves corresponding to the solution within a 90-second time period.
Although subjects were not explicitly informed of a time criterion,
they were if necessary told, "Your solution was in the fewest possible

number of moves. Now see if you can repeat this solution a little more quickly." The data for six subjects were not used, either because of prior experience with one of the problems (2), or inability to meet the criterion within a 45-minute time period (4). Data for the remaining 42 subjects are tabulated in Table 7C.5.

Hypothesis 6. This study provides a test of Hypothesis 6 of Chapter IV. TOH-1 is compared with TOH-2 and TC-1 with TC-2 with respect to the difficulty measures of total time required and total number of states entered. Table 7C.5 lists the medians (M) and interquartile ranges (IQR) for each group of subjects on each problem. The (one-tailed) Mann-Whitney U-test was used to determine the significance levels. There was a significant decrease both in total time to solution and the total number of states entered between TOH-1 and TOH-2 ($p < .001$ for both measures using a one-tailed test). There was also a significant decrease between TC-1 and TC-2 ($p < .02$ for the time, and $p < .05$ for the number of states entered, for a one-tailed test). Thus significant transfer occurred from one problem to the other, in either order of presentation.

An analysis of variance was also performed, indicating that the TC problem was more difficult than the TOH problem with respect to both measures, regardless of the order of presentation ($p < .01$).

Hypothesis 7. The evidence from this study is somewhat inconclusive with respect to the "deep end" hypothesis discussed in Chapter IV. From the fact that the level of significance for transfer from the TC problem to the TOH problem was greater than that for transfer from the TOH problem to the TC problem, one might infer that more transfer occurred when the TC problem was presented first. However, in the analysis of variance the problem order did not have a significant effect on either measure of difficulty: that is, the *total* number of moves and the *total* time required for solving *both* problems were not significantly influenced by the order of presentation.

Thus for these problems there may be a mild "deep end" effect (greater transfer when the more difficult problem is solved first) or none at all; additional evidence from more subjects is required.

To summarize, the above two studies have interpreted *Hypotheses 1-4* and *Hypotheses 6-7* from Chapter IV, Section 3 in a concrete fashion for the Tower of Hanoi problem and its isomorph, the Tea Ceremony problem. For the subject populations which were studied, confirming evidence was found for *Hypotheses 1, 2, 4,* and *6,* while the evidence for *Hypothesis 3* and *7* was scanty or inconclusive. More important than the details of the outcomes is the feasibility of this approach to the study of problem-solving behavior; namely, the graphing of behavior paths through the state-space, and the quantitative test of hypotheses concerning patterns in the observed paths.

Table 7C.5   *Measures of Difficulty for the Experimental Problems*

	TOH-1 (N = 23)		TOH-2 (N = 19)		TOH-1 = TOH-2
Time (seconds):	M = 307	IQR = 233	M = 79	IQR = 134	p < .001
Number of states:	M = 69	IQR = 26	M = 32	IQR = 30	p < .001

	TC-1 (N = 19)		TC-2 (N = 23)		TC-1 = TC-2
Time (seconds):	M = 386	IQR = 408	M = 242	IQR = 245	p < .02
Number of states:	M = 88	IQR = 114	M = 61	IQR = 68	p < .05(a)

M = median; IQR = interquartile-range. The Mann-Whitney (one-tailed) U-test was used to determine the significance levels.

(a) This corrects a typographical error which appeared in Luger and Bauer (1978), Table 1.

VIII.

Heuristic Behavior Variables in Research

A.

Heuristic Behaviors Associated with Problem Tasks

by

Fadia Harik*
Indiana University
Bloomington, Indiana

In Chapter V, the potential for heuristic behavior to be *inherent* in a task was discussed. We shall consider a heuristic process to be inherent in a problem when: (a) in a strictly logical sense, the process can be applied successfully to the problem; and (b) there exists a population of subjects of which a majority applies the process to the problem, independently of individual differences.

Establishing that a certain process is inherent in a particular task has important consequences for the study and teaching of problem solving. Being able to develop a task that will elicit a particular process enables the researcher to look more closely at that process, and to explore its characteristics in detail. It also enables the teacher to select appropriate tasks and to provide appropriate instruction in the improvement of the process.

In this chapter, these ideas are illustrated by describing and analyzing the heuristic process of *trial-and-error*. The tasks in the present study were originally developed for two reasons—first, to look at the influence of certain task variables on the difficulty of the task; and secondly, to elicit the heuristic process of trial-and-error as an "inherent" process, so that it could be closely examined. Here we shall discuss only the latter purpose.

Some of the criteria that were used in developing the tasks were the following: (a) the tasks should have a standard method of solution that permits methodical analysis by the researcher; (b) the standard method of solution should not have been previously taught to the solvers; (c) the task should be solvable using basic skills available to the solvers from previous learning, such as the operations of addition, subtraction, multiplication, and division of positive integers; (d) the tasks should vary systematically, to allow study of the effects of increasing complexity; in particular, how the process of trial-and-error might vary with the tasks while maintaining its major characteristics; (e) the solution process should require observable behavior that is repeated; that is to say, the tasks should be

---

*Current address: University of Maryland, College Park, Maryland.

sufficiently complicated so that several trials are needed before the
solution is found, and so that the trials have to be written rather
than oral.

Based on these criteria, sets of problems were constructed as
described below.

1. Definitions of Problem Characteristics

Story problems were developed which, when routinely translated,
yield two or more simultaneous equations. It is to be noted that the
subjects were untrained in algebra, and therefore were not expected
to be able to translate the problem statements into simultaneous
equations in the routine manner. The problems have different values
of three variables: the *number of unknowns,* the *number of conditions,*
and the *size of the search space.*

The following definitions were adopted. An *unknown* is a quantity
described in the problem statement for which the value is not expressly
given. A *condition* is a statement which translates to a linear equation involving at least two unknowns. The *number of conditions* in the
problem is the number of linear equations that are obtained by direct
translation of the verbal problem statement. The *search space of a
condition* of a problem with n unknowns is the set of all n-tuples of
positive integers that satisfy the condition. A *finite condition* is
a condition whose search space is finite. When all of the problem
conditions are finite, the *search space of the problem* is the union
of the search spaces of the conditions.

The idea of a search space is analogous to the corresponding
concept in information processing. It is based on the assumption
that trial-and-error is not completely random, and that in most cases
trials emerge from a domain of possibilities that satisfy some of the
conditions in a problem but not necessarily all of them.

Six systems of simultaneous equations were developed; two involving two equations and two unknowns, two involving two equations and
three unknowns, and two involving three equations and three unknowns.
Each pair of systems contained one example of a small search space,
and one example of a large one.

To illustrate what a search space is, let us consider the following problem:

> 8A.1 *A clothing factory makes blouses and dresses. A
> blouse takes 5 ft. of material, and a dress takes
> 25 ft. The factory uses a total of 160 ft. and
> produces 12 pieces of clothing. How many of each
> kind are produced daily?*

Table 8A.1   *Problem Sets Used in the Study*

There are a total of 36 problems, corresponding to six systems
of equations embodied in six stories. Each problem is labeled
by a pair of numbers (a,b); where <u>a</u> stands for the system of
equations and <u>b</u> stands for the story embodiment.

Problem Set 1

Equations:	$5x + 25z = 160$	Search space:	16 elements
	$x + z = 12$	Correct answer:	$(x,z) = (7,5)$

(1,1) Sam has $1.60 in nickels and quarters. He has 12 coins in all.
How many coins of each kind does Sam have?

(1,2) Jeff bought 5 jawbreakers and 25 candy canes for $1.60. A
candy cane and a jawbreaker together cost 12 cents. How much
did Jeff pay for each piece?

(1,3) Janet had a birthday party. She gave bags of candy to her
friends. Some bags had 5 lemon drops, other bags had 25 redhots.
Altogether there were 160 pieces of candy. There were 12 bags.
How many bags of each kind were there?

(1,4) A clothing factory makes blouses and dresses. A blouse takes
5 ft of material and a dress takes 25 ft. The factory uses a total
of 160 ft daily and produces 12 pieces of clothing. How many of
each kind are produced daily?

(1,5) Linda and David were on a walk for Mankind. Linda got pledges
of 5¢ for each mile she walked. David got pledges of 25¢ for each
mile he walked. Both walked for a total of 12 miles and got total
pledges for $1.60. How many miles did each one walk?

(1,6) Mrs. Robinson has a puzzle corner in her classroom. A kid scores
5 points for solving a picture puzzle and 25 points for solving a
block puzzle. Carol solved a total of 12 puzzles from both kinds
and scored 160 points. How many puzzles of each kind did she solve?

Table 8A.1 *continued*

Problem Set 2

Equations: $5x + 10y = 160$ Search space: 42 elements

                 $x + y = 29$ Correct answer: $(x,y) = (26,3)$

(2,1)   Sam has $1.60 in nickels and dimes. He has 29 coins in all. How many coins of each kind does Sam have?

(2,2)   Jeff bought 5 jawbreakers and 10 pieces of bubble gum for $1.60. A jawbreaker and a bubble gum together cost 29¢. How much did Jeff pay for each piece?

(2,3)   Janet had a birthday party. She gave bags of candy to her friends. Some bags had 5 lemon drops, other bags had 10 gumdrops. Altogether there were 160 pieces of candy. There were 29 bags. How many bags of each kind were there?

(2,4)   A clothing factory makes blouses and skirts. A blouse takes 5 ft of material and a skirt takes 10 ft. The factory uses a total of 160 ft daily and produces 29 pieces of clothing. How many of each kind are produced daily?

(2,5)   Linda and Jim were on a walk for Mankind. Linda got pledges of 5¢ for each mile she walked. Jim got pledges of 10¢ for each mile he walked. Both walked for a total of 29 miles and got total pledges for $1.60. How many miles did each one walk?

(2,6)   Mrs. Robinson has a puzzle corner in her classroom. A kid scores 5 points for solving a picture puzzle and 10 points for solving a story puzzle. Carol solved a total of 29 puzzles from both kinds and scored 160 points. How many puzzles of each kind did she solve?

Problem Set 3

Equations: $5x + 10y + 25z = 160$ Search space: 74 elements

                 $x + y + z = 10$ Correct answer: $(x,y,z) = (3,2,5)$

(3,1)   Sam has $1.60 in nickels, dimes and quarters. He has 10 coins in all. How many coins of each kind does he have?

Table 8A.1 *continued*

(3,2) Jeff bought 5 jawbreakers, 10 pieces of bubble gum, and 25
       candy canes for $1.60. A jawbreaker, a piece of bubble gum, and
       a candy cane together cost 10¢. How much did Jeff pay for each
       piece?

(3,3) Janet had a birthday party. She gave bags of candy to her friends.
       Some bags had 5 lemon drops, other bags had 10 gundrops, and the
       rest of the bags had 25 redhots. Altogether there were 160 pieces
       of candy. There were 10 bags. How many bags of each kind were
       there?

(3,4) A clothing factory makes blouses, skirts and dresses. A blouse
       takes 5 ft of material, a skirt takes 10 ft and a dress takes
       25 ft. The factory uses a total of 160 ft daily and produces
       10 pieces of clothing. How many of each kind are produced daily?

(3,5) Linda, Jim and David were on a walk for Mankind. Linda got pledges
       of 5¢ for each mile she walked. Jim got pledges of 10¢ for each
       mile he walked. David got pledges of 25¢ for each mile he walked.
       All walked a total of 10 miles and got total pledges for $1.60.
       How many miles did each one walk?

(3,6) Mrs. Robinson has a puzzle corner in her classroom. A kid scores
       5 points for solving a picture puzzle, 10 points for solving a story
       puzzle, and 25 points for solving a block puzzle. Carol solved
       a total of 10 puzzles from all 3 kinds and scored 160 points.
       How many puzzles of each kind did she solve?

Problem Set 4

Equations: $5x + 10y + 25z = 155$ Search space: 266 elements
             $x + y + z = 23$ Correct answer: $(x,y,z)=(18,4,1)$

(4,1) Sam has $1.55 in nickels, dimes and quarters. He has 23 coins in
       all. How many coins of each kind does Sam have?

(4,2) Jeff bought 5 jawbreakers, 10 pieces of bubble gum and 25 candy
       canes for $1.55. A jawbreaker, a piece of bubble gum and a candy
       cane together cost 23¢. How much did Jeff pay for each piece?

(4,3) Janet had a birthday party. She gave bags of candy to her friends.
       Some bags had 5 lemon drops, other bags had 10 gumdrops and the
       rest of the bags had 25 redhots. Altogether there were 155 pieces
       of candy. There were 23 bags. How many bags of each kind were
       there?

Table 8A.1 *continued*

(4,4) A clothing factory makes blouses, skirts and dresses. A blouse takes 5 ft of material, a skirt takes 10 ft, and a dress takes 25 ft. The factory uses a total of 155 ft daily and produces 23 pieces of clothing. How many of each kind are produced daily?

(4,5) Linda, Jim and David were on a walk for Mankind. Linda got pledges of 5¢ for each mile she walked. Jim got pledges of 10¢ for each mile he walked. David got pledges of 25¢ for each mile he walked. All walked a total of 23 miles and got total pledges of $1.55. How many miles did each one walk?

(4,6) Mrs. Robinson has a puzzle corner in her classroom. A kid scores 5 points for solving a picture puzzle, 10 points for solving a story puzzle and 25 points for solving a block puzzle. Carol solved a total of 23 puzzles from all 3 kinds and scored 155 points. How many puzzles of each kind did she solve?

Problem Set 5

$$5x + 10y + 25z = 155$$
$$x + y + z = 10$$
$$x + z = 9$$

Equation: Search space: 71

Correct answer: $(x,y,z)=(4,1,5)$

(5,1) Sam has $1.55 in nickels, dimes and quarters. He has 10 coins in all. Nine of these coins are nickels and quarters. How many coins of each kind does he have?

(5,2) Jeff bought 5 jawbreakers, 10 pieces of bubble gum and 25 candy canes for $1.55. A jawbreaker, a piece of bubble gum and a candy cane together cost 10¢. The cost of a jawbreaker and a candy cane is 9¢. How much did Jeff pay for each piece?

(5,3) Janet had a birthday party. She gave bags of candy to her friends. Some bags had 5 lemon drops, other bags had 10 gumdrops and the rest of the bags had 25 redhots. Altogether there were 155 pieces of candy. There were 10 bags. Nine of the bags were lemon drop bags and redhot bags. How many bags of each kind were there?

(5,4) A clothing factory makes blouses, skirts and dresses. A blouse takes 5 ft of material, a skirt takes 10 ft, and a dress takes 25 ft. The factory uses a total of 155 ft daily and produces 10 pieces of clothing. Nine of the pieces are blouses and dresses. How many of each kind are produced daily?

(5,5) Linda, Jim and David were on a walk for Mankind. Linda got pledges of 5¢ for each mile she walked. Jim got pledges of 10¢ for each mile he walked. David got pledges of 25¢ for each mile he walked. All walked a total of 10 miles and got total pledges of $1.55. Linda and David alone walked for a total of 9 miles. How many miles did each one walk?

Table 8A.1 *continued*

(5,6) Mrs. Robinson has a puzzle corner in her classroom. A kid scores 5 points for solving a picture puzzle, 10 points for solving a story puzzle and 25 points for solving a block puzzle. Carol solved a total of 10 puzzles from all 3 kinds and scored 155 points. 9 of the puzzles she solved were picture puzzles and block puzzles. How many puzzles of each kind did she solve?

Problem Set 6

Equations: $5x + 10y + 25z = 160$ Search Space: 248

$$x + y + z = 22$$ Correct answer: $(x,y,z)=(15,6,1)$

$$x + z = 16$$

(6,1) Sam has $1.60 in nickels, dimes and quarters. He has 22 coins in all. 16 of these coins are nickels and quarters. How many coins of each kind does he have?

(6,2) Jeff bought 5 jawbreakers, 10 pieces of bubble gum and 25 candy canes for $1.60. A jawbreaker, a piece of bubble gum and a candy cane together cost 22¢. The cost of a jawbreaker and a candy cane is 16¢. How much did Jeff pay for each piece?

(6,3) Janet had a birthday party. She gave bags of candy to her friends. Some bags had 5 lemon drops, other bags had 10 gumdrops and the rest of the bags had 25 redhots. Altogether there were 160 pieces of candy. There were 22 bags. 16 of the bags were lemon drop bags and redhot bags. How many bags of each kind were there?

(6,4) A clothing factory makes blouses, skirts and dresses. A blouse takes 5 ft of material, a skirt takes 10 ft and a dress takes 25 ft. The factory uses a total of 160 ft daily and produces 22 pieces of clothing. 16 of the pieces are blouses and dresses. How many of each kind are produced daily.?

(6,5) Linda, Jim and David were on a walk for Mankind. Linda got pledges of 5¢ for each mile whe walked. Jim got pledges of 10¢ for each mile he walked. David got pledges of 25¢ for each mile he walked. All walked a total of 22 miles and got total pledges of $1.60. Linda and David alone walked a total of 16 miles. How many miles did each one walk?

(6,6) Mrs. Robinson has a puzzle corner in her classroom. A kid scores 5 points for solving a picture puzzle, 10 points for solving a story puzzle, and 25 points for solving a block puzzle. Carol solved a total of 22 puzzles from all 3 kinds and scored 160 points. 16 of the puzzles she solved were picture puzzles and block puzzles. How many puzzles of each kind did she solve?

This problem can be expressed algebraically in the form of two equations and two unknowns:

$$5x + 25z = 160 \qquad \text{(i)}$$

$$x + z = 12 \qquad \text{(ii)}$$

If the subject is working towards satisfying equation (i) alone with positive integers, he or she will have the following possibilities for the values of x and z: (2,6) (7,5) (12,4) (17,3) (22,2) (27,1). However, if the subject chooses to satisfy equation (ii) alone, the possible values for x and z would be: (1,11) (2,10) (3,9) (4,8) (5,7) (6,6) (7,5) (8,4) (9,3) (10,2) (11,1). Looking at the two sets of pairs of possible values, we find that there is only one pair of possible values that they have in common.

It is assumed that the domain where the trial-and-error search for an answer will take place could be the union of these two sets. This union is referred to here as the search space.

Sizes of search spaces were varied with as little change in the coefficients of the equations as possible. Once the systems of equations were developed, six different stories were written in such a way that every story could be used to embody all six systems of equations. The stories are such that *only* positive integer solutions to the problems are suggested. Thus, six systems of equations embodied in six different stories produced a total of 36 problems. These problems are arranged by sets and listed in Table 8A.1.

2. The Analysis of Observed Processes

By observing subjects solving the above problems, four different kinds of "moves" by subjects were identified. The four kinds of moves fall into two categories, *guessing* moves and *deductive* moves. A guessing move is characterized by a series of actions as follows: (a) a guess is made that may be correct or incorrect, totally random or partially random; (b) calculations to test whether or not the guess satisfies one or more conditions of the problem are carried out; and (c) a conclusion is made as to the accuracy of the guess and the direction in which it should be modified. The two kinds of observed guessing moves are *guessing an answer* and *guessing an operation*. A deductive move is characterized by a series of actions as follows: (a) a deduction is made; (b) calculations that are consequent on the deduction are made; and (c) implications of the deduction for the rest of the problem are drawn. The two kinds of observed deductive moves are *deducing for an answer* and *deducing for an estimate*.

We shall illustrate these moves through sample solutions of the following problem:

8A.2 *Jeff bought 5 jawbreakers and 10 pieces of bubble*
gum for $1.60. A jawbreaker and a bubble gum
together cost 29¢. How much did Jeff pay for each
piece?

Guessing Moves

A. Guessing an Answer

"I'll try 10¢ for the jawbreaker and 19¢ for the bubble
gum. That makes 10 x 5 = 50; 19 x 10 = 190; 50 + 190 =
240. No, that is too much. The bubble gum should cost
less."

Here the subject of the guess is the values of the unknowns asked
for in the question. The calculations are to test whether or not the
guess satisfies the conditions stated in the problem.

B. Guessing an Operation

"29 ÷ 2 = 14 R1, 14¢ and a remainder of 1. No, I can't
have this. Try 10 + 5 = 15; 160 ÷ 15 = 10 R10. No, it
doesn't work."

Here the student has made two "guesses"; but the subjects of the
guesses are the operations that might provide a reasonable answer.

Deductive Moves

A. Deducing for an Answer

"Since the jawbreakers and the bubble gum together cost
29¢, I'll try 29 x 5 = 145. I'll figure how much 5 other
pieces of bubble gum cost: 160 - 145 = 15; 15 ÷ 5 = 3;
3¢ for each bubble gum and 26¢ for each jawbreaker."

This is an algorithmic deductive move that is structurally the
same as the algebraic approach to the solution of the system of two
simultaneous equations.

B. Deducing for an Estimate

"If a jawbreaker alone costs 29¢, 5 jawbreakers cost
29 x 5 = 145. If the bubble gum alone costs 29¢, 10
bubble gum pieces cost 29 x 10 = 290. 145 is closer
to 160. The bubble gum should cost less than the jawbreakers."

This hypothetico-deductive approach is used for the purpose of
estimating an answer more accurately.

Forms of "Guessing an Answer" Moves

The value of considering a heuristic process to be a *task* variable lies in the perspective of observing the changing characteristics of the process as elicited by variations in the task. Three groups of tasks will be used to describe the most common forms taken by the "guessing an answer" move in the present study.

The first group of tasks consists of the twelve story problems involving two equations and two unknowns. The only differences among the twelve problems are in the problem story context, and in the size of the search spaces. The equations representing the problems are:

(1) $5x + 25z = 160$ (i) Search space: 16 elements
$\quad\quad x + z = 12$ (ii) Correct answer: $(x,z) = (7,5)$

(2) $5x + 10y = 160$ (i) Search space: 42 elements
$\quad\quad x + y = 29$ (ii) Correct answer: $(x,y) = (26,3)$

The unknowns that can be guessed in each of the problems are four; for the first pair of equations, for example, they are x, z, $5x$, and $25z$. These variables have to satisfy two conditions, namely that $x + z = 12$ and that $5x + 25z = 160$.

The guessing moves that have been exhibited by the subjects solving the above twelve tasks can be classified into three forms. We will use Problem *8A.2* to illustrate each of the forms.

Form A:

"I will try 15¢ for the gum; 15 x 10 = 150; 160 - 150 = 10; 10¢ for 5 jawbreakers gives me 2¢ for each; 15 + 2 = 17. No, I need 29."

Graphically, the move can be represented as in Figure 8A.1(a). The subject makes a guess of the value of y, in this case the price of a piece of bubble gum; finds the value of $10y$; obtains a value of $5x$ that would satisfy the equation $5x + 10y = 160$; obtains a value for x; and checks to see if it satisfies $x + y = 29$. The arrows indicate the order in which the various values are obtained.

In the given example the initial guess was the value of y. However, subjects seem to start their guessing with any of the four variables, and still use the same "form" as in Figure 8A.1(a). Graphically, these variations of Form A appear in Figure 8A.1(b)-(d). The major difference among these diagrams is the starting point of the guess.

Form B:

"I will try 11¢ for each jawbreaker and 18¢ for each bubble gum; 11 x 5 = 55; 18 x 10 = 180; 180 + 55 is too much, I want 160."

Figure 8A.1 *A Form of Guessing Move for the First Twelve Problems*
(Sets 1 and 2)

(a)

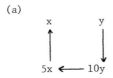

(b)

(c)

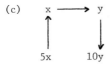

(d)

Figure 8A.2 *A Second Form of Guessing Move for the First Twelve Problems*

(a)

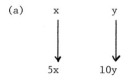

(b)

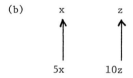

The graphic representation of Form B looks as in Figure 8A.2(a). The subject splits 29 into two values for x and y, finds 5x and 10y, them adds 5x and 10y to check if they amount to 160.

A move where 160 is split into two quantities and the values of x and y are checked is represented in Figure 8A.2(b) and has a form similar to the one above. The difference lies in the variables that are subject to the initial guess.

Form C:

"12¢ for a piece of bubble gum leaves 17¢ for a jawbreaker. 12¢ for one will make 120 for all the gum. That leaves 40¢ for jawbreakers; that means 40 ÷ 5 = 8¢ for one jawbreaker. It does not work, I need 17¢."

In both Forms A and B, one equation was satisfied, and the other equation was used to check if the guess worked. In Form C both equations are satisfied, and the subject looks to see if they lead to the same value. This protocol is depicted in Figure 8A.3(a).

As in Form A three variations of Figure 8A.3(a) appear in Figures 8A.3(b), (c), and (d).

The second group of tasks consists of the twelve story problems involving two equations and three unknowns. Again the only differences among the problems are in the problem story contexts and in the size of the search spaces. The equations representing the problems are:

(3) $5x + 10y + 25z = 160$ Search space: 74 elements
$\quad\quad x + y + z = 10$ Correct answer: $(x,y,z) = (3,2,5)$

(4) $5x + 10y + 25z = 155$ Search space: 266 elements
$\quad\quad x + y + z = 23$ Correct answer: $(x,y,z) = (18,4,1)$

Guessing moves that have been utilized by subjects can be classified into two forms, which will be illustrated using the following problem:

8A.3 *Sam has $1.60 in nickels, dimes and quarters. He has 10 coins in all. How many coins of each does he have?*

Form A:

"Ten coins; I'll try 2 quarters, 4 dimes and 4 nickels, that will make: 2 x 25 = 50; 4 x 10 = 40; 4 x 5 = 20; 50 + 40 + 20 = 110. No, I should have more."

Graphically, this can be represented as in Figure 8A.4. The subject splits "ten" into trial values for x, y, and z, finds 5x, 10y, and 25z, then adds them to verify whether or not they amount to 160.

Figure 8A.3 *A Third Form of Guessing Move for the First Twelve Problems*

(a)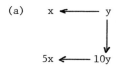

(b)

(c)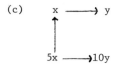

(d)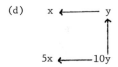

Figure 8A.4 *A Form of Guessing Move for the Second Group of Twelve Problems (Sets 3 and 4)*

Figure 8A.5 *A Second Form of Guessing Move for the Second Group of Twelve Problems*

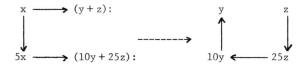

Form B:

"4 nickels make 20¢; 6 more coins and 160 - 20 = 140¢.
4 quarters make a dollar; that leaves 40 cents, it will
make 4 dimes. No, I need 2 dimes; I'll try less: 3
quarters...."

Graphically, this can be represented as in Figure 8A.5. Here the
subject allocates 20¢ for 4 nickels, reduces the problem to 6 coins
that are dimes and quarters totalling 140¢, and then proceeds to
attempt a two-unknown, two-condition problem. The essential characteristic of this form is that the subject has treated the three
unknowns by treating two unknowns at a time, and has utilized the
forms used in the problems with two unknowns. Thus Figures 8A.1(a) and
8A.3(b) are both components of Figure 8A.5. In effect, the associative property has been utilized.

Form C:

"2 nickels and 4 dimes will make 10 + 40 = 50; that leaves
110 for the quarters. No, it won't work."

Here the subject makes guesses on *two* unknowns, nickels and
dimes, and combines them into a single quantity to be coordinated
with the third unknown, quarters.

Figure 8A.6, like Figure 8A.5, is a composite of diagrams for
two-variable forms. The difference between Forms B and C can be
interpreted as in Figure 8A.7.

The third group of tasks consists of the twelve story problems
involving three equations and three unknowns:

(5) $\begin{aligned} 5x + 10y + 25z &= 155 \\ x + y + z &= 10 \\ x + y + z &= 9 \end{aligned}$ Search space: 71 elements
     Correct answer: $(x,y,z) = (4,1,5)$

(6) $\begin{aligned} 5x + 10y + 25z &= 160 \\ x + y + z &= 22 \\ x + z &= 16 \end{aligned}$ Search space: 248 elements
     Correct answer: $(x,y,z) = (15,6,1)$

Subjects who deduce a value for y from the second and third equations reduce these problems to two-variable, two-equation problems,
similar to the first group of tasks. This makes the *effective* search
spaces substantially smaller for those subjects. Under this condition, the search space for equations (5) has only 12 elements, and the
space for equations (6) only 17. Subjects who do not make such a deduction will have six quantities to guess, and their search spaces will be
very similar to the second group of problems.

A guessing move on the following problem illustrates how the problem is reduced to a simpler problem:

Figure 8A.6 *A Third Form of Guessing Move for the Second Group of Twelve Problems*

Figure 8A.7 *Comparison of Figures 8A.5 and 8A.6*

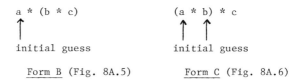

Figure 8A.8 *A Form of Guessing Move for the Third Group of Twelve Problems (Sets 5 and 6)*

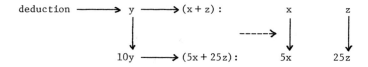

*8A.4 Mrs. Robinson has a puzzle corner in her classroom.
A kid scores 5 points for solving a picture puzzle,
10 points for solving a story puzzle, and 25 points
for solving a block puzzle. Carol solved 22 puzzles
and scored 160 points. 16 of the puzzles she solved
were either picture or block puzzles. How many
puzzles of each kind did she solve?*

Form A:

"16 puzzles were picture and block puzzles. That leaves
6 story puzzles; 60 points leaves 100 points; I'll try
10 picture puzzles and 6 block puzzles; that will make
10 x 5 = 50; 6 x 25 = 150. No, this is too much; I'll
try 15 and 1...."

As represented in Figure 8A.8, the subject is making a deduction
to obtain the number of story puzzles, and then reducing the problem
to a problem in two unknowns, picture and block puzzles, worth a
total of 100 points. The difference between the graphic representation of the move here and the moves associated with the second group
of problems is the fact that the first phase of the move here is a
deduction and not a guess. Thus there are only two variables that
require guessing.

Form B:

When subjects do not make the deduction, they are effectively solving a three-unknown, two-condition problem. The
guessing forms in that case are identical to those in Figures
8A.4, 8A.5, and 8A.6.

3. Empirical Findings

The subjects chosen were 60 average and above-average seventh-
grade students who had not had any formal instruction in algebra.
Of the 36 problems in Table 8A.1, six problems in random order were
presented to each subject, including one problem for each system of
equations. The purpose was to randomize any learning effects or
transmission of information among subjects. Each subject was interviewed for a period ranging from 45 minutes to two hours. Subjects
were asked to think aloud. Their written and oral work was recorded
and analyzed.

Information from all of the subjects was used in establishing
the classifications of heuristic processes; however, the preliminary
empirical data reported here are based on the detailed analysis of
just 20 randomly selected subjects.

It was hypothesized that the majority of the subjects would use
the heuristic process of "guessing an answer" at some point during

problem solving, and that, of those who successfully solved the problems, even a greater majority would have utilized the "guessing and
answer" process. In Table 8A.2, the data are displayed indicating
the use of the "guessing an answer" heuristic process by subjects
solving the six word problem embodiments of each of the six systems
of simultaneous equations.

On only two successful problem-solving attempts was the algebraic approach used rather than trial-and-error.

Comparing the frequencies of occurrence of all four kinds of
moves described, the "guessing an answer" moves were by far the most
frequent. During those problem-solving attempts which led to
successful solutions, this process occurred even more frequently
(see Table 8A.3).

The "deduction for an answer" moves occurred most frequently
in systems of equations 5 and 6. The deductive moves in these
problems occurred *in conjunction with* the guessing moves for
reasons inherent in the problem structure, as was discussed in
the previous section.

The above tables are purely descriptive, and the data have not
(yet) been subjected to statistical tests. However, it is apparent
that the "guessing an answer" process occurs more frequently than
the other processes when word problems involving simultaneous equations are given to students who have had no formal algebraic training.
Since this process seems to occur regardless of individual differences among the students, we can claim that the trial-and-error
heuristic process is "inherent" in the problems for this population
of subjects, and it can be studied as a task or problem variable.

A major theme emerges from observing the "guessing an answer"
moves; a theme which Polya calls "reducing the problem to a simpler
one." This tendency to reduce the problem takes several forms; from
large and permanent reductions to small and temporary ones. Some
reductions lead to a solution of the problem while others change
the problem.

We shall first look at problem reduction that results from lack
of coordination of simultaneous conditions. Such reduction is
exhibited by guesses that involve *one* of the conditions with *complete
disregard* for the other condition(s). A subject who is solving a
problem embodying the first system of equations, for example, would
guess a value for x and z that would satisfy $5x + 25z = 160$, with
complete disregard for the fact that $x + z$ has to be 12. Variations
on this guess would be guesses for the pair (x, z) or the pair $(5x, 25z)$
that would satisfy either $x + z = 12$ or $5x + 25z = 160$ but not both.
Of the 20 subjects considered in this report, 11 subjects failed to
coordinate the simultaneous conditions in at least one problem attempt.
Among the 91 problems attempted where coordination or lack of it could

Table 8A.2 (a) *Utilization of the Problem-Solving Process of "Guessing an Answer"*
by Subjects at Some Point During Problem Solving

System of Equations	1	2	3	4	5	6
Number of Subjects Attempting the Problem	20	19	18	16	16	19
Number of Subjects Using "Guessing an Answer"	18	14	14	13	16	14
Percentage of Subjects Using "Guessing an Answer"	90%	74%	78%	81%	100%	74%

(b) *Utilization of the Problem-Solving Process of "Guessing an Answer"*
by Successful Subjects at Some Point During Problem Solving

System of Equations	1	2	3	4	5	6
Number of Successful Subjects	10	9	5	8	10	8
Number of Successful Subjects Using "Guessing an Answer"	10	8	5	8	10	7
Percentage of Successful Subjects Using "Guessing an Answer"	100%	89%	100%	100%	100%	88%

Table 8A.3(a) *Frequencies of Types of Moves*

(The attempt of a subject on each problem may include one or more moves.)

System of Equations	1	2	3	4	5	6
Number of Subjects Attempting the Problem	20	19	18	16	16	19
Total Number of Moves	98	114	94	120	56	85
Number of GA Moves	77	87	88	103	39	59
Number of GO Moves	19	22	3	15	3	11
Number of DA Moves	0	2	2	0	14	15
Number of DE Moves	2	3	1	2	0	0
Percentage of GA Moves	79%	76%	94%	86%	70%	69%
Percentage of GO Moves	19%	19%	3%	12%	5%	13%
Percentage of DA Moves	0%	2%	2%	0%	25%	18%
Percentage of DE Moves	2%	3%	1%	2%	0%	0%

Key:

    GA = "Guessing an Answer"

    GO = "Guessing an Operation"

    DA = "Deducing for an Answer"

    DE = "Deducing for an Estimate"

Table 8A.3(b) *Frequencies of Types of Moves in Attempts Leading to Successful Solutions*

(The attempt of a subject on each problem may include one or more moves.)

System of Equations	1	2	3	4	5	6
Number of Successful Subjects	10	9	5	8	10	8
Total Number of Moves	69	67	24	86	36	44
Number of GA Moves	59	60	24	81	26	35
Number of GO Moves	10	4	0	4	1	0
Number of DA Moves	0	2	0	0	9	9
Number of DE Moves	0	1	0	1	0	0
Percentage of GA Moves	85%	90%	100%	94%	72%	80%
Percentage of GO Moves	15%	6%	0%	5%	3%	0%
Percentage of DA Moves	0%	3%	0%	0%	25%	20%
Percentage of DE Moves	0%	1%	0%	1%	0%	0%

be determined, 26 problem attempts exhibited lack of coordination of simultaneous conditions. It is worth noting here that the majority of the subjects who did not coordinate also did not exhibit a consistent lack of coordination. That is to say, a subject would coordinate conditions in one of the problems but not in another. Some exhibited lack of coordination in some of the guesses in a problem but not in all the guesses, an indication that their coordination ability had not been stabilized yet. In contrast to this situation, fifth-grade students given similar problems exhibited lack of coordination to a greater extent and in a more consistent manner (Harik, unpublished).

Preliminary observations across the variations in the tasks indicate no change in the degree of coordination (see Table 8A.4). This fact may lead us to consider the degree of coordination of the problem conditions as a consequence of individual development, rather than as a factor influenced by the limited variations in the task structures.

Another kind of problem reduction occurs when a deductive move is available such as in Problem Sets 5 and 6, where the problems have three unknowns and three conditions. A subject would make a deduction from the latter two equations in Table 8A.1, and reduce the problem to a two-unknown, two-condition problem. Of the 16 and 19 subjects who attempted problems from Sets 5 and 6 respectively, 14 subjects used a deductive move in the problems from each of these two sets. The numbers of subjects who followed the deductive move by guessing moves which led to correct solutions were 10 and 8 respectively. *All* those who solved problems from Sets 5 and 6 successfully used a deductive move to reduce the problem to a simpler one.

Preliminary observations of the interaction between deductive moves and guessing moves in Problem Sets 5 and 6 indicate that some subjects confuse the certainty of a deduction with the uncertainty of a guess. This confusion appears when a subject *deduces* the value of y in one move, then goes on to *guess* the value of y along with the values x and z in the next move. Of the 14 subjects who made the deduction in the problems from each of the Sets 5 and 6, four subjects solving problems from Set 5 and three subjects solving problems from Set 6 exhibited this behavior. However, two of the subjects for Set 5 and one subject for Set 6 subsequently resolved the confusion. All those who did not do so failed to solve the problem(s).

A third kind of problem reduction occurs when a subject uses "guessing an answer" moves with the three-unknown, two-condition problems such as those in Sets 3 and 4. In those problems, the form that the guessing move takes reduces the three unknowns to two through the associative law, as was shown graphically in the previous section. The data on this kind of problem reduction have not (yet) been analyzed.

Table 8A.4 *Degree of Coordination of the Problem Conditions*

System of Equations	$\underline{1}$	$\underline{2}$	$\underline{3}$	$\underline{4}$	$\underline{5}$	$\underline{6}$
Number of Subjects Attempting the Problem	20	19	18	16	16	19
Number of Attempts Exhibiting Coordination of the Problem Conditions	11	11	11	11	11	10
Number of Attempts Exhibiting Lack of Coordination of the Problem Conditions	5	3	5	2	4	7
Number of Attempts for which the Coordination of the Problem Conditions was Uncertain	4	5	2	3	1	2

4. <u>Summary</u>

Six sets of word problems were created, in which problem context
and structure were varied systematically. We have been able to define
a variety of available moves, and to observe that the process of
guessing an answer and modifying the guess is the most frequently
used process for these problems in the sample of seventh graders.
This process was the *only* process that led to successful solutions
in four of the six problem sets. It is interesting to note the
difference between the intuitive problem-solving process apparently
used *by* children, namely trial-and-error, and the problem-solving
algorithms taught *to* children, in this case the algebraic approach
to solving simultaneous equations.

We also observed three ways in which a problem is reduced to a
simpler one: (a) disregarding some of the conditions of the problem;
(b) making a deduction that reduces the number of conditions and
unknowns of the problem; and (c) reducing a three-unknown guess to
a two-unknown guess through the use of associativity. The first
reduction changes the original problem to another problem; the second
reduces the original problem to a subproblem; while the third reduces
the guessing moves to simpler guessing moves.

VIII.

Heuristic Behavior Variables in Research

B.

A Process-Sequence Coding System for Behavioral Analysis
of Mathematical Problem Solving

John F. Lucas
University of Wisconsin
Oshkosh, Wisconsin

Mary Grace Kantowski
University of Florida
Gainesville, Florida

Nicholas Branca
San Diego State University
San Diego, California

Howard Kellogg
LaGuardia College
New York, New York

Dorothy Goldberg
Kean College
Union, New Jersey

J. Philip Smith
Southern Connecticut
    State College
New Haven, Connecticut

The coding system described in this chapter was developed out
of a collaborative team research effort over a period of several
years. Its major objective was to study heuristic processes in
mathematical problem solving across varying developmental levels.
A secondary objective was to develop an instrument to organize and
record processes in their sequence of observed occurrence. The
coding system is a partial fulfillment of the secondary objective.
It represents, however, but one stage of refinement in a continuous
evolutionary process, since at the time of this writing the team is
still active.

1. Rationale

Clinical research in mathematical problem solving over the past
decade has concerned itself mainly with the *process of problem solving;* that is, the set of behaviors (actions, operations, decisions,
and rationale) which direct and characterize the search for a solution as an individual progresses from initial state to goal state of
a problem. It has become increasingly important to develop instruments which reflect and measure the problem-solving process as well
as the product. A process-sequence coding system has been developed
and will be presented here along with examples of its use. Our aim
in developing the coding system is to be able to describe a set of
behaviors and events through associated code symbols which can be
arranged in time-sequence of occurrence, so that a user of the system
can catch a glimpse of the entire problem-solving process and not
have his or her view restricted simply to the problem statement,
several written steps, and an outcome.

Three questions are suggested by the development of this coding system. They are:

(a) How might a researcher evoke observable and natural behaviors; that is, what is a feasible method for sampling genuine process behavior in problem solving?

(b) What manner of symbolic format best represents what actually happens during problem solving?

(c) Assuming there are behaviors sufficiently general to mathematical problem solving that can be identified within and across various developmental levels, can researchers be trained to identify these behaviors consistently?

The first question has been dealt with by researchers over the years in a number of ways; e.g., silent problem solving with paper-and-pencil testing, multiple-choice options, branching formats, retrospection, introspection, and simultaneous thinking-aloud. There is a growing body of literature on techniques for collecting and analyzing problem-solving behavior, but a discussion of the advantages and disadvantages of the various reporting styles will not be given here. Suffice it to say that the coding system described here was derived from data collected in the "simultaneous thinking-aloud" response style, where subjects of different ages and developmental levels solved problems and simultaneously verbalized thoughts during the solution. It is the opinion of the writers, therefore, that the coding system adapts best to data gathered in the same way.

With respect to validity of representation (question b), each thinking-aloud self-report was audiotaped, and the subject's written work, audiotape, and interviewer notes were synthesized to obtain a picture of the problem-solving process. In this manner, the authors collected samples of problem-solving behavior during pilot work taken from subjects across varying developmental levels. Using these samples together with Polya's writings on heuristics as a basis for discussion, the authors came to an agreement on the definitions for a set of constructs which were to represent observable, disjoint problem-solving behaviors and related phenomena. The constructs were selected and defined so as to capture each event in the problem-solving process. Each event was assigned a symbol, and the collection of events which comprised a problem-solving sequence of processes was recorded in a horizontal string of symbols corresponding to the chronological order of appearance during the actual problem solution. In this manner, a researcher could listen to a tape of a problem solution (in conjunction with observing written work, interviewer notes, and/or a verbatim transcript) and produce a string of symbols which represented a composite perception of the solution process. Conversely, examination of a given string of symbols could be used to provide a reasonably clear picture of what had happened during a problem-solving episode.

In the communication between problem solver and coder, there are four potentially different phenomena which must be recognized:

1. What the problem solver says and/or writes.

2. What the problem solver means (is thinking).

3. How the coder interprets what is perceived.

4. How the coder matches this interpretation with a category of behavior (symbolized).

If the analysis of problem-solving behavior were ideal, all four of these phenomena would be equivalent. Since this is not the case, we provide a discussion of relationships among the phenomena. Event 1, however, can be made invariant by keeping a record in the form of tapes and written work. Non-equivalence between events 1 and 2 is distortion. This can probably be reduced by maintaining an interview atmosphere in which the subject can "get into" the problem, forgetting the presence of the interviewer and making candid statements of thoughts as well as he or she can. In addition, a synthesis of written work, taped protocol, and notes made by the interviewer at the time of observation can be helpful. The degree of equivalence between events 2 and 3 or events 2 and 4 is not measurable, and one can only proceed on the assumption that event 2 can be replaced by event 1 and any non-equivalence between events 1 and 3 can be detected by intercoder reliability testing. Finally, non-equivalence between events 1 and 4 or 3 and 4 can be reduced by extensive practice in coding. Therefore, taking into account all the possible junction points in the channel of communication between problem solution by a problem solver and its final representation by a coder, it would be erroneous to believe that a method of behavioral analysis consisting of thinking-aloud protocols and symbolic coding is completely objective and valid. There is bound to be distortion or incompleteness on the part of the subject and drawing of erroneous inferences or inconsistency on the part of the coder. However, for the purpose of examining process behavior, this system represents a significant step in the search for improved methods. We take note of the obvious limitations of the system and temper our conclusions in light of them.

Questions (a) and (b) above were directed to the matters of coder objectivity and validity of the instrument in representing the solution process; question (c) is concerned with reliability. Usage of a coding system of the kind described herein requires considerable effort on the part of the researcher in concentration and practice. The diversity of potential behaviors and associated symbols, subscripts, and combinations requires carefully understood definitions of the behavioral constructs, ability to recognize cues from observed behavior, and quick recall of appropriate symbols from a memorized list. One would naturally anticipate, therefore, problems in maintaining both internal (to the coder) and external (among coders) consistency. Moreover, when a coding system arises out of the work of an individual researcher, it can be quite difficult to train other coders to have the same perception of various situations, and intercoder reliability suffers. This problem is at least partially resolved by producing a coding system through discussion and interaction of a group of persons familiar with both mathematics and the psychology of mathematical reasoning. It is precisely this feature which makes the coding system described here unique: it was developed and tested by a *team* of researchers which included several members who had previously worked with their own individual systems and who were now sharing their knowledge and experience to assist in the construction of a more effective and reliable system. The associated intercoder agreement and reliability (to be discussed in the final section of this chapter) has obvious implication for the feasibility of this coding system in problem-solving research.

It is significant to note that this coding system was developed in conjunction with a variety of teaching experiments, all of which shared, in instructional emphasis, a common set of heuristic processes. Therefore it was deliberately designed to be sensitive to the presence of heuristic-oriented actions as well as other problem-solving events. The schematic in Figure 8B.1, adapted from an earlier paper by Schoenfeld (1976), serves as an organizer of problem-solving and heuristic behavior (see also Chapter V and Chapter X.B of this book).

Figure 8B.1 incorporates Polya's four stages: *Understanding the Problem, Devising a Plan, Carrying Out the Plan, and Looking Back* (see also Figure 10B.4). Further, it includes the dimension of *Analogy* as an adjunct to problem approach and planning heuristics. As in the case of any model, this is an intentional oversimplification, presented here for the purpose of clarity and organization. Actual human problem solving does exhibit some or all of these characteristics, but they do not necessarily occur in order, and are frequently in a much more complex arrangement. There often occur such phenomena as problems nested within problems, fragmented plans, skipping back and forth from givens to goal, dead ends with reorganized efforts, and attempts at various points to build bridges connecting to prior information.

The production of a *Useful Formulation, Schematic Solution, Tentative Solution,* and *Verified Solution* suggests these as various points at which problem-solving performance can be measured. Such measurement focuses more on the process aspect of mathematical problem solving than on conventional measures of time, errors, difficulty, and final outcome (result).

Within each stage of the model, heuristic behaviors which generally characterize that stage are listed. Questions and suggestions such as

...draw a diagram...can you restate the problem in your own words?...can you find a related problem?...look for patterns...can you reduce the problem to a simpler case? ...separate conditions...is there any symmetry?...check your steps...try to derive the result differently... what if?...

Figure 8B.1 *Heuristic Problem Solving Model (Adapted from Schoenfeld, 1976)*

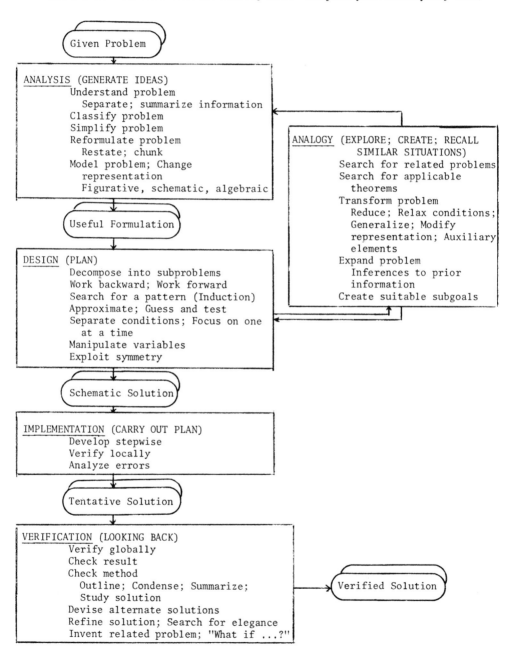

are generally recognized as cues for heuristic behavior.

According to Polya, a major goal in teaching mathematical problem solving is to make these questions and suggestions an integral part
of the problem-solving repertoire of the learner. Then a technique
(self-questioning) is available for cueing ideas, rather than rushing
headlong into the problem without a plan, or creating an impasse.
This goal of mathematics teaching is closely related to certain aims
of the problem-solving researcher. Some of these are: (1) to see if
such processes exist within and across subjects and problems, (2) to
examine the relationship between their presence and successful problem
solving, and (3) to suggest conditions for teaching and learning such
behavior. It is necessary, therefore, that the researcher be equipped
with a system which has the capability of recording the nature and
frequency of heuristic actions, their sequence in relation to other
processes, and judgments about intermediate and terminal outcomes.
With such an instrument, researchers or teams can reproduce a composite
picture of the problem solution for careful and detailed analysis.

Mathematical problem solving is like the action of a machine—the
input and output are clearly visible, but one does not really develop
a full appreciation for the machine until one has had a look inside to
see how it works. The system described next represents an attempt to
define some of the "internal moving parts" of the problem solver.

2. Code Symbols and Definitions

The code symbols which are presented and defined in this section
represent a consensus of agreement among six researchers with respect
to processes and phenomena that are likely to occur during mathematical
problem solving. They were derived from observational data gathered
from subjects of varying developmental levels and ranging in age from
10 to 27 years.

The coding system evolved organically through observation of
problem-solving behavior during initial pilot work. Although some
a priori assumptions about heuristic behavior may be made, a given
problem solution may involve complexities that do not conform to a
predetermined formal ordering or expected structure.

In the present system, observed behavior is coded in its order
of explicit appearance, and the coder makes judgments on the separation or clustering of processes from his or her perception of the
natural "pulse" of the problem solution. For example, the problem
solver may assert a plan or fragment thereof, perform some action or
sequence of actions to carry out the plan fully or partially, and
pause to evaluate the consequences of the actions in relation to the
plan, and/or the goal of that step, of the entire problem, or of some
subproblem. In the view of the coder, this brief sequence of
behaviors would constitute one step in the sense that symbols for

planning, execution process, and outcome would be placed in juxtaposition as one cluster, separated by commas from those referring to prior or subsequent behaviors. For example, the cluster of symbols "..., P_iD_a5E4, ..." refers to the following sequence of behaviors:

A plan for an intermediate goal (P_i), a deduction drawn from one piece of information (D_a) in a forward orientation from given information toward a goal (subscript 5), the production of an equation (E), and an outcome of the step in the form of correct intermediate result (4).

In several instances, variations among closely related behaviors are coded by using the same symbol but different subscripts. For example, "D_a" codes a deduction drawn from one piece of information (analysis) while "D_s" codes a deduction drawn from several pieces of information (synthesis). Also, processes that incorporate heuristic orientation are coded by using a process symbol for the behavior together with a numerical subscript referent to the list of fourteen commonly agreed-upon heuristic processes (see Table 8B.1). For example, "D_a5" codes analytic deduction in a forward orientation--working in the direction from given or derived information toward the goal (e.g., asking "What am I to deduce from this?"), whereas "D_a6" codes analytic deduction in a backward orientation--working in the direction from the goal toward given or derived information (e.g., asking "To obtain this result, what do I need to have?").

The preceding comments were intended to serve as examples illustrating the general nature of the code so that the reader might develop some feeling for the system prior to its introduction. A more thorough explanation with application to the analysis of a complete problem solution appears in the next section. The dictionary of code symbols and associated behaviors is given in Table 8B.2. All behavior is required to be explicit; otherwise, it is not coded.

Introduction of a coding system requires the use of a dictionary such as the one given in Table 8B.2 to define the meaning or interpretation of each symbol. However, it is difficult to appreciate the value of a system of communication by studying only from a dictionary--one obtains but a fractured view of "little pieces" of behavior. By using clusters of symbols to describe brief sequences of behavior, the system can be demonstrated in a more meaningful way, and finally, when these clusters are linked in horizontal strings to represent an entire problem solution, the utility of the system comes into full view. The next section is devoted entirely to a demonstration of how this coding system can be used to record a mathematical problem solution.

Table 8B.1 *List of Heuristic Processes (with Code Numbers)*

1   Draw a diagram (figure, schematic, table).

2   Test special cases.

3   Identify what is wanted and what is given.

4   Identify relevant or irrelevant data.
    Examine all the given information.

5   Work forward from what is given.

6   Work backward from the conclusion.

7   Search for a pattern. Find a generalization.

8   Search for a related problem (emphasis on
    similar structure).

9   Search for an applicable theorem,
    definition, operation or algorithm.

10 Solve part of the problem.

11 Check the solution

12 Is there another way to get the result?
    (alternate solutions)

13 Is there another result that could be obtained?
    (uniqueness)

14 Study the solution process.

3. Illustrative Applications of the Coding System

Sample Analyses of Problem-Solving Behavior

Several brief sequences of observed behavior appear below together with associated code clusters. Note that numerals representing heuristic processes appear as subscripts in the coding, while numerals which are outcome symbols are in line with the alphabetic symbols.

Sequence A: The problem solver reads the problem, hesitates, rereads part of the problem, says the problem resembles another problem and he will try to use the same method, then deduces correctly a piece of information from one of the given data.

Code A: $R, R, L_8 P_i D_{a5}4,$

Sequence B: During a problem solution, the problem solver says "to obtain the area of the circle, I need to find out what the radius is...how can I find the radius?" He then uses two points and applies the distance formula (an algorithmic calculation, but a mechanical error is made in the process) to arrive at an incorrect number for the radius of the circle.

Code B: $, P_i \sim \cdot D_{s6} \overset{\downarrow}{A}5,$

Sequence C: During a problem solution, the problem solver is searching for a pattern among the triangular numbers--testing three or four cases, then making a (correct) generalization. Next the subject decides to check one more special case as a test of the generalization.

Code C: $T_7, \ldots, I4, C_{11},$

Sequence D: The problem solver reads the problem, separates given information into three key conditions, states the intention to consider each condition separately, proceeds to translate the first condition into an inequality (correctly), focuses on the second condition but translates it incorrectly into an equation, checks back, discusses and corrects the error ...

Code D: $R, S_4, P_{p10} D_{a10} E4, D_{a10} \overset{\downarrow}{E}5, C_{11},$

Table 8B.2 *Dictionary*

R	Reads all or part of problem statement
S	Separates/summarizes information
S_3	Separates wanted from given information
S_4	Identifies relevant and/or irrelevant information
Q	Restates problem in other words or in another way
F_{d1}	Draws diagram, makes table, constructs schematic array (represents problem information in visual form)
F_{d10}	Using diagram(s), solves part of problem to exclusion of other parts
F_a	Adds auxiliary construction (used with geometric representation)
P	States plan
P_p	Suggests plan for final goal (goal orientation)
P_i	Suggests plan for intermediate goal (subgoal-orientation)
P_{p10}	States intention to solve part of the problem - part of larger, goal-oriented plan
P_{i10}	States intention to solve part of problem without reference to goal-oriented plan
G	States new goal or new subgoal
U_t	States theorem used
U_o	States operation carried out
N	Suggests needed information which could be helpful but is not apparently available
D_a	Makes deductive inference drawn from one piece of information, given or derived (analysis of information)
D_{a5}	D_a with forward orientation (working forward from initial or derived state toward subgoal or goal state)
D_{a6}	D_a with backward orientation (working backwards from goal or subgoal toward derived or initial state)
D_{a10}	D_a with emphasis on one part of the problem to the exclusion of others (e.g. imposing one condition at a time and examining variation in result)
D_s	Making deductive inference drawn from several pieces of information given or derived (synthesis of information)
D_{s5}	D_s with forward orientation
D_{s6}	D_s with backward orientation
D_{s10}	D_s with emphasis on one part of the problem to the exclusion of others
O	Using information in different way than originally given; renaming
I	States a generalization (inductive conclusion; conjecture)
T	Trial and error; successive approximation
T_2	Tests special case(s) as trial(s) to examine problem structure (not aimed at induction)

(continued)

Table 8B.2 *(continued)*

T_7 Tests special case(s) as trial(s) which form part of a pattern-
         search (aimed at induction)

V   Introduces variable or other notation

E   Introduces equation

A   Uses algorithm as routine calculation or technique

L   Reasons by analogy (notes similarity with another situation)

L_8 Recalls method of related problem or states related problem
         and uses its method

L_9 Recalls and states related definition, theorem, or problem;
         or does same and uses result

C_{11} Checks solution to problem or subproblem

C_{a12} Attempts alternate solution process

C_{s12} Attempts to simplify, condense solution or search for more
          elegant solution

C_n Suggests new problem

X   Has forgotten or does not know how to solve problem

B_{13} Searches for additional results that could be obtained

B_{14} Studies the solution

Outcome Symbols

    1   Abandons process
    2   at impasse
    3   Produces correct final result
    4   Produces correct intermediate result
    5   Produces incorrect result (final or intermediate)

Question Symbols

    ?   Subject asks investigator question
    ¿   Investigator asks subject question
    ↢·   Subject asks self question

Error Symbols

    ⊥   Structural error (misuse of information)
    ↓   Executive error (mechanical slip)
    *   Over error symbol means error has been corrected explicitly
    __   Underline process symbol means difficulty with that process

Punctuation Symbols

    ,   Inserted between successive steps
    /   End mark; stops without solution
    .   End mark; stops with solution
    ...   Iterated process (same process as last has been repeated
             at least once more)
    ○   Encircled process symbol means that process is exact
             repetition of some earlier process

Sequence E: Near the end of a frustrating problem episode, the
              problem solver is engaged in a series of trials, each
              using a new diagram which is not the solution but
              provides information which could potentially lead to
              the solution. The last trial leads to an impasse;
              the problem solver searches for an alternate way to
              do the problem but abandons his attempt, says he
              does not know how to solve the problem and gives up
              without the solution.

   Code E: $T \, F_{d1}4, \, \ldots, \, TF_{d1}2, \, C_{a12}1, \, X, \, /$

Analysis of a Problem-Solving Protocol

The remainder of this section is devoted to a single problem
solution executed by an adult subject in one of the individual
studies leading to the production of this system. The solution will
be presented here in three modes. These modes are: (1) a verbatim
transcript taken directly from the audiotaped protocol of the solution, (2) an analysis of various segments of the verbatim transcript
where code symbols and brief interpretations corresponding to these
segments are provided, and (3) the representation of the entire
problem solution using only horizontal strings of code symbols.

Verbatim Transcript

8B.1 *Two girls were selling candy. They had a dollar and seven
      cents in change to begin with. Their first customer said
      that before he could buy anything, he needed change for a
      half dollar. One of the girls looked into the change box
      and said they didn't have the change. The customer asked
      if they had change for a quarter; the reply was no. The
      customer asked if they had change for a dime; the answer
      was no again. The girls said that they had seven coins in
      all but could not change a nickel either. What were the
      coins that the girls had?*

OK, uh, the second last sentence came to my eye right away--
it says the girls said that they had seven coins in all but
could not change a nickel either... ah, which means they
have no pennies, theoretically.

What were the coins that the girls had? OK, they've got
seven coins in all...uhmm... OK, then I'm, I'm reading
backwards--they had no change for a nickel which says...
no pennies... ah, the customer asked if they had change
for a dime, the answer was no, which means they'd have to
have no nickels...customer has...ask if they had change
for a quarter...and the reply was no... Now, that doesn't
necessarily rule out dimes, because they could have dimes

...and just dimes, and then not be able to make change for the quarter, so it doesn't necessarily rule out dimes... because they could have dimes and still not make change for a quarter.

Needed change for a half-dollar... OK, assuming he's got dimes... assuming they have dimes... OK, if you want change for a half dollar you could have two quarters, or else five dimes--now they could have dimes and they could have quarters... but one thing they could not have, they could not have five dimes... and you could not have two quarters...

So, if "d" represents...the number of dimes, d cannot equal five at this point, and if "q" represents the number of quarters, q could not equal two.

All right, they had dollar and seven cents in change to begin with, OK, to get the dollar and seven cents, they're gonna have to have some pennies involved...and they... let "p" represent pennies, ...and p would have to equal two, or p could equal seven. OK, now, seven has to be ruled out, because they only had seven coins in all, and if they only had seven pennies, all right, that would take up all their coins and they certainly would not have a dollar and seven cents. So, they got two pennies, and that puts us down to a dollar and five cents, ah, with...five coins.

OK, five coins, dollar and five cents, ahm...and they have no nickels, they have absolutely no nickels...let's see... three quarters, that's seventy-five, and two dimes will only make it ninety-five--I'm short a dime...

All right, let's just try some possibilities, how about four quarters, ...uhm, ...one nickel, and two pennies... OK, I started the wrong way, I should have worked down... I should have started with the dollar and seven cents and said they'd have to have either seven or two pennies and then eliminate the seven cents right away and made it a simpler problem by saying a dollar and five cents and five pennies, or, and five coins. OK, if they had four quarters, one nickel, and two pennies; let's see if these conditions satisfy the conditions of the problem. He needed change for a half-dollar...now if he had, if they had four quarters, they could theoretically give him change for a half dollar...if that's what is meant by change...can I ask you that? [Interviewer...uh-huh]...Would two quarters be reasonable to say change for a half-dollar? [Interviewer...right] OK, so the four quarters would be ruled out ...'cause if they had four quarters, they could change a half-dollar, so that option is ruled out... [Interviewer ...could you say what you were thinking about now?]

Well, I'm just looking at the dollar and seven cents, and to get that dollar and seven cents, there's no other way about it except that they could have two pennies or seven pennies...and they can't have seven pennies, so they gotta have two pennies...

So, the problem is really now a dollar and five cents with five coins, and one of my options did not work...

OK, ...OK, I'm just trying one quarter now...that'll leave me with eighty cents, and four coins...that would be four twenty-cent pieces and they don't make those things yet...

A dollar and five cents with five coins...there can't be any nickels...well, maybe there's two nickels... Ah, these dumb problems!... Well, if they didn't have change for a quarter, and they only got two pennies there, there cannot be any nickels...and the same reasoning if they didn't have change for a dime...uhm... Am I interpreting the problem right that they have exactly seven coins to start with and they total to a dollar and seven cents? OK [Interviewer...uh-huh]

OK, so now, there cannot, there's two pennies and there are no nickels...or there could be one nickel and no dimes, and one dime--what if I have one nickel and one dime, that's a possibility because that still would not give them enough... change for a quarter...OK, that takes up...uh...fifteen cents, leaves me ninety cents with three coins...a half dollar,... OK, half-dollar...what if they had two half-dollars? One half dollar, one quarter...I'm just trying combinations...seems to be the best bet right now...I'm trying to find combinations that give me five coins 'n dollar and five cents. A half-dollar and one quarter, that's seventy-five cents and I've got...three coins left... OK, there it is...three dimes and two pennies, obviously...trial and error.

Just checking it out...fifty, seventy-five, three would be a dollar-five, a dollar-seven. Probably should have analyzed it something with algebra, but I didn't...OK?

Segmented Analysis of the Problem Solution

R,
(reads
problem)

Problem Two...Two girls were selling candy. They had a dollar and seven cents in change to begin with. Their first customer said that before he could buy anything, he needed change for a half dollar. One of the girls looked into the change box and said they didn't have the change. The customer asked if they had change for a quarter; the reply was no. The customer asked if they had change for a dime; the answer was no again. The

girls said that they had seven coins in all
but could not change a nickel either. What
were the coins that the girls had?

,S_4,
(identifies
relevant data)

OK, uh, the second last sentence came to my eye
right away--it says the girls said that they
had seven coins in all but could not change a
nickel either...

,$D_{a5}5$,
(deduction by
analysis; forward;
structural error;
outcome incorrect)

... ah, which means they have no pennies,
theoretically.

,$RD_{a5}5$,
(reads part;
repeats same
deduction by
analysis; forward;
structural error;
outcome incorrect)

What were the coins that the girls had? OK,
they've got seven coins in all...uhmm... OK,
then I'm, I'm reading backwards--they had no
change for a nickel which says...no pennies...

,$RD_{a5}5$,
(reads part;
deduction by anal-
ysis; forward;
structural error;
outcome incorrect)

... ah, the customer asked if they had change
for a dime, the answer was no, which means
they'd have to have no nickels...

,$RD_{a5}4$,
(reads part;
deduction by
analysis; forward;
outcome correct)

...customer has...ask if they had change for a
quarter...and the reply was no... Now, that
doesn't necessarily rule out dimes, because
they could have dimes...and just dimes, and
then not be able to make change for the quarter;

,$D_{a5}4$,
(deduction by
analysis; forward;
outcome correct)

so it doesn't necessarily rule out dimes...
because they could have dimes and still not
make change for a quarter.

,$RD_{a5}4$,
(reads part;
deduction by
analysis; forward;
outcome correct)

Needed change for a half-dollar... OK, assuming
he's got dimes...assuming they have dimes... OK
if you want change for a half dollar you could
have two quarters, or else five dimes--now they
could have dimes and they could have quarters...
but one thing they could not have, they could
not have five dimes...and you could not have
two quarters...

,V, —————————— So, if "d" represents...the number of dimes, d
(variables cannot equal five at this point, and if "q"
introduced d≠5 represents the number of quarters, q could not
and q≠2 are con- equal two.
sidered notation,
not equations)

,RD$_{a5}$4, —————————— All right, they had dollar and seven cents in
(reads part; change to begin with, OK, to get the dollar
deduction by and seven cents, they're gonna have to have
analysis; forward; some pennies involved...and they...
outcome correct)

,VD$_{a5}$4, —————————— ...let "p" represent pennies...and p would
(notation intro- have to equal two, or p could equal seven.
duced; deduction by
analysis; forward;
outcome correct)

,D$_{s5}$4, —————————— OK, now, seven has to be ruled out, because
(deduction by they only had seven coins in all, and if they
synthesis; forward; only had seven pennies, all right, that would
outcome correct) take up all their coins and they certainly
would not have a dollar and seven cents.

,G4, —————————— So, they got two pennies, and that puts us
(establishes a down to a dollar and five cents, ah, with...
subgoal, or new five coins.
goal; outcome
correct)

,S, —————————— OK, five coins, dollar and five cents, ahm...
(summarizes and they have no nickels, they have absolutely
information) no nickels...

,T4, —————————— ...let's see...three quarters, that's seventy-
(trial combina- five, and two dimes will only make it ninety-
tion; outcome is five--I'm short a dime...
not incorrect,
furnishes infor-
mation about goal)

,PT1, —————————— All right, let's just try some possibilities,
(states a plan how about four quarters...uhm...one nickel,
without reference and two pennies...
to an expected
outcome; starts a
trial, but abandons)

,$C_{s12}4$, ————————— OK, I started the wrong way, I should have worked
down...I should have started with the dollar and
(looks back, seven cents and said they'd have to have either
condenses, seven or two pennies and then eliminate the seven
simplifies, cents right away and made it a simpler problem by
outcome correct) saying a dollar and five cents and five pennies,
or, and five coins.

,T?4, ————————— OK, if they had four quarters, one nickel, and two
(trial combina- pennies; let's see if these conditions satisfy
tion; $\underline{S}$ asks $\underline{E}$ the conditions of the problem. He needed change
question; outcome for a half-dollar...now if he had, if they had
incorrect, but four quarters, they could theoretically give him
furnishes infor- change for a half dollar...if that's what is meant
mation about goal) by change...can I ask you that? [Interviewer:
uh-huh] Would two quarters be reasonable to say
change for a half-dollar? [Interviewer: right]
OK, so the four quarters would be ruled out...
'cause if they had four quarters, they could
change a half-dollar, so that option is ruled out...

,i , ————————— [Interviewer: Could you say what you were think-
($\underline{E}$ asks $\underline{S}$ ing about now?]
question)

,S, ————————— Well, I'm just looking at the dollar and seven
cents, and to get the dollar and seven cents,
there's no other way about it except that they
could have two pennies or seven pennies...and
they can't have seven pennies, so they gotta
have two pennies...

,$C_{s12}4$, ————————— So, the problem is really now a dollar and five
cents with five coins, and one of my options did
(looks back, not work...
simplifies)

,$\underline{T}2$, ————————— OK...OK, I'm just trying one quarter now...that'll
leave me with eighty cents, and four coins..that
(trial combina- would be four twenty-cent pieces and they don't
tion; has make those things yet... A dollar and five cents
difficulty, with five coins...there can't be any nickels...
hesitations, well, maybe there's two nickels... Ah, these
leads to impasse) dumb problems!...

,$D_{s5}4$, ————————— Well, if they didn't have change for a quarter,
and they only got two pennies there, there cannot
(deduction by be any nickels...and the same reasoning if they
synthesis; for- didn't have change for a dime...uhm...
ward; outcome
correct)

,?, ————————— Am I interpreting the problem right that they have
($\underline{S}$ asks $\underline{E}$ exactly seven coins to start with and they total
question) to a dollar and seven cents? OK [Interviewer: uh-huh]

,S, ————————— OK, so now, there cannot, there's two pennies
(summarizes   and there are no nickels...or there could be
information)   one nickel and no dimes.

,T ⌐.1, ————————— and one dime--what if I have one nickel and
(trial combina-   one dime?...that's a possibility because that
tion, abandons   still would not give them enough, change for a
before comple-   quarter... OK, that takes up, uh...fifteen
tion)   cents, leaves me ninety cents with three coins
                     ...a half-dollar...

,T ⌐.1, ————————— OK, half-dollar...what if they had two half-
(trial on half-   dollars?
dollars; abandons)

,TS3, ————————— one half-dollar, one quarter...I'm just trying
(trial combina-   combinations...seems to be the best bet right
tion; summarizes   now...I'm trying to find combinations that give
information;   me five coins 'n dollar and five cents. A half-
obtains correct   dollar and one quarter, that's seventy-five cents
solution to   and I've got...three coins left... OK, there it
problem)   is...three dimes and two pennies, obviously...
                     trial and error...

,C_{11}. ————————— Just checking it out...fifty, seventy-five,
(checks result   three would be a dollar-five, a dollar-seven.
against condi-   Probably should have analyzed it something with
tions of problem)   algebra, but I didn't...OK?

Horizontal Coding Display

R, S_4, $D_{a5}5$, $RD_{a5}5$ $RD_{a5}5$, $RD_{a5}4$, $D_{a5}4$, $RD_{a5}4$, V, $RD_{a5}4$,

$VD_{a5}4$, $D_{s5}4$, G4, S, T4, PT1, $C_{s12}4$, T?4, ¿,   S,

$C_{s12}4$, $\underline{T}2$, $D_{s5}4$, ?, S, T⌐.1, T⌐.1, TS3, C_{11}.

The above problem solution took approximately ten minutes. However,
the analysis and coding obviously required several hours. The method is
quite demanding on the investigator. But there is a payoff, for the
investigator has an opportunity to observe the process of problem solving during its evolution. Information about the nature and frequency
of heuristic processes and even more importantly the effectiveness of
their application and their sequence in terms of problem-solving performance becomes clearer. One can examine such phenomena as the
relationship between goal-oriented planning and the appearance of key
heuristic processes, the interplay between backward and forward reasoning, the motivation for internal and/or terminal checking, the correspondence between modes of representation, the nature and frequency of

errors, the self-questions which evoke recognition of structural
similarities between problems, the variation between problem-solving
styles, and much more.

To illustrate some of these possibilities, consider the following examples. Goal-oriented planning is symbolized by P or P_{i}.
Heuristic processes such as deduction (D_s), pattern-search (T_7), or
general trial-and-error (T) are key processes in the production of
solutions. Suppose a given problem solver's codes across a variety
of problems frequently exhibited clusters of the form $P D_s E4$ near the
beginning of each problem, followed by clusters involving D_a or D_s,
but rarely, if ever, T_7 or T. This might suggest an organized deductive style, more formal than the "guess-and-test" orientation indicated
by successive T's. Moreover, if the deductive pattern were frequently
associated with the outcome symbols "1," "2," or "5," this might hint
at an attitudinal characteristic (inflexibility) of the problem solver,
perhaps an insistence that the "right" way to solve problems is via
a combination of straightforward deduction (D_s), the production of
equations (E_i) or expressions, and utilization of algorithms (A).

As another example, some problem solvers verbalize a rather
complete plan at the outset of a problem solution; others almost
never verbalize a plan; while for still others, the planning evolves
in stages as the solution unfolds. These characteristics may be
suggested by the presence, absence, and/or placement of planning
symbols (P). An analogous phenomenon exists with backward and
forward reasoning (D_s5, D_s6). Some problem solvers have a preference
for one or the other, while others vacillate from one to the other
during the solution. Still another analogous situation exists with
checking (C_{11}). Some check internally after each "step," some check
only at the end of the problem, and others do not check at all.

Is there a relationship between the structure of a problem and
the principal strategies used to solve it? For example, do "induction" problems tend to evoke pattern-search (T_7) and generalization
(I)? Is the generalization usually verified $(C_{11}, C_{a12}, C_{s12})$? Are
some problems, because of their structure or the nature of the question asked, more easily solved by working backward (D_s6) than by
working forward (D_s5)? Questions like these may have some light shed
on them by comparing coding strings within certain problems and across
problem solvers. Similarly, developmental differences in problem-
solving style, strategy, or presence of heuristics may be uncovered
by examining coding strings for the same problem across subjects
within and across developmental levels.

Finally, if a student learns to ask heuristic-oriented questions
of himself or herself during a problem solution (self-dialogue), is
there any effect on the production of "creative" ideas or the connection with related problems? To investigate this question, the
researcher might look into the codes for contiguous occurrences of
$\backsim L$, or $\backsim P_p$, or $\backsim$ followed by a major production heuristic $(D_s, D_a,$
T, I, C_{11} (error-search)).

As noted in the above examples, a process-sequence coding system can be a microscope through which we observe certain overt facets of the problem-solving process and gather a wealth of information. However, we must be certain, within reasonable limits of error, that different observers are seeing the same behaviors and interpreting them similarly. This raises the question of reliability, which is discussed next.

4. Reliability of the Coding System

The process-sequence code obtained from a problem-solving episode cannot avoid, at least to some degree, being a function of how an observer interprets a transcript or tape of the episode. This raises an important question. To what extent will trained coders, using the coding system described, differ in their coding of the same problem-solving episode? In an attempt to answer this question, the investigators devised a procedure for comparing the process-sequence codes produced by two coders from the same transcript. That procedure, its rationale, and a test by cross-comparison of the codes of four investigators will be described in this section. The reader should note that these results are preliminary, and that refinements of the coding system and greater experience with it should improve the present reliability.

In considering direct comparisons between different codings of the same problem-solving episode, the investigators found that it would be extremely difficult to proceed via a symbol-by-symbol approach. For example, suppose the transcript shows a subject repeating verbatim two consecutive sentences in a problem statement. It seems most reasonable to infer that part of the problem is being read, and this would be coded as "R." But what if the subject repeats verbatim a key phrase consisting of ten words from the original statement of the problem? Is this behavior rereading a portion of the problem (to be coded "R"), or is it recalling relevant data from memory (to be coded "S")? Either interpretation might be admissible.

As a first approach to resolve this ambiguity of interpretation, the investigators decided to group the coding symbols into "clusters," with each cluster containing closely related process symbols, and with disagreements within a cluster not being counted in coding comparisons. Thus, in the example just cited, the codes "R" (for reading) and "S" (for recalling) would be assigned to the same cluster, so that the disagreement hypothesized above would not be counted as such. In other words, subtle differences arising in the microscopic system tend to disappear as the system becomes more macroscopic, while the internal validity of the system remains generally intact.

To facilitate the counting of disagreements between coders, each cluster was assigned a Greek letter. The original process-sequence code for an episode, using Latin letters, could then be translated into a new code of Greek letters, in which disagreements would be counted as "true" disagreements in the sense of representing different process clusters.

Table 8B.3 shows the assignment of process-sequence codes to clusters, and also the Greek codes assigned to each cluster. For more specific information about the detailed processes within a cluster, the reader is directed to the *Dictionary* (Table 8B.2).

In addition to clustering coding symbols, the investigators agreed on certain other procedures to be followed in the coding of common transcripts for intercoder comparison. For each episode, each coder was provided with a copy of the audiotape of the episode, a copy of the verbatim transcript of the tape, and a copy of the subject's worksheet. To facilitate symbol-by-symbol comparisons, the transcript was arbitrarily divided into segments of approximately equal length. This was accomplished by counting and marking off a certain number of lines for each segment on the typed transcript. These segments were numbered sequentially. If a process overlapped two or more segments, it was coded as though it were contained in the last of the overlapped segments. For example, if a subject began a trial as part of a pattern search in Segment 9 and completed the trial correctly in Segment 11, the (Latin) coding would be:

Segment	Coding
10	--
11	$T_7 4$

As this example illustrates, it is possible for a segment to produce no code.

In translating from the original (Latin) coding to the clustered (Greek) coding, repetitions in the Greek code sequence within a segment may occur. If in a segment, for instance, a subject read part of the problem and then restated it in his or her own words, the Latin code sequence would be "R, Q." The clustered code corresponding to this is "$\alpha\alpha$." For the sake of simplicity, it was decided that repetitions of the Greek code would be collapsed. Therefore, in the latter example, the resulting Greek code was "α."

Symbols other than alphabetic process symbols (e.g., outcome, questions, error, and punctuation) were ignored in translating to the Greek code. Thus the sequence

$$?, TF_{d1}4, D_s5 3$$

was translated into Greek code as "$\theta \ \beta \ \epsilon$."

Once the translation from the microscopic Latin to the macroscopic Greek code was accomplished, the next task dealt with the assignment of a numerical coefficient of agreement for a given pair of Greek codings. It was decided that a percentage of agreement would be determined for each segment, and that these indices would be averaged across all segments to obtain a coefficient for the entire

Table 8B.3 *Cluster Definitions*

Cluster Code	Latin Correspondents	Description
α	R, S, S_3, S_4, Q	Analysis: Read, Summarize, Recall, Restate, Separate
β	F_{d1}, F_{d10}, F_a	Modeling Processes; Figurative; Visualization
γ	P, P_p, P_i, P_{p10}, P_{i10}, G, D_{a6}, D_{s6}	Planning Processes: Goal-Oriented
δ	L, L_8, L_9, U_t, U_o, O	Analogy: Processes Involving External Information
ϵ	D_a, D_s, D_{a5}, D_{s5}, I, D_{a10}, D_{s10}	Production Processes; Forward-Oriented
θ	T, T_2, T_7	Trial-Oriented Processes; Specialization; Pattern-Search
ν	V, E	Symbol-Introducing Processes
ω	C_{11}, C_{a12}, C_{s12}, C_n, B_{13}, B_{14}	Looking Back Processes; Checking, Studying
A	A	Algorithmic Process
X	X	Stops Work: Impasse

episode. Clearly, if one coder coded a given segment as "α ω γ ε" and another had "α θ γ ε," then the agreement for the episode should be .75. But what if one coder had "ω γ," while another had "ω γ ε"? Smith and Meux (1962) faced this problem in their coding of classroom behavior. They used an index

$$p = \frac{A(x,y)}{Max(S(x),S(y))}$$

where $A(x,y)$ represents the number of agreements in the two codings, and $Max(S(x),S(y))$ represents the greater of the number of code symbols used by the two coders. Using this convention, the agreement between the two coders for the example just given would be

$$p = 2/3 = .67$$

For the present work, the investigators decided to use the following modification of the formula:

$$p = \frac{A(x,y)}{Ave(S(x),S(y))}$$

where $Ave(S(x),S(y))$ represents the average of the number of code symbols used by the two coders, and $A(x,y)$ is the number of agreements. Thus in the example given,

$$p = 2/((2+3)/2) = .8$$

In examining several transcripts where coders disagreed on the number of symbols to be used, it was decided that $Ave(S(x),S(y))$ was a better index of agreement (or disagreement) than $Max(S(x),S(y))$.

Since individual segments were relatively short and occasionally contained behaviors which appeared to occur simultaneously, the investigators felt that the focus of concern for a given segment ought to be what processes occurred therein, not the order of those processes within the segment. Therefore, order was ignored in determining the number of agreements between two codings. It should be noted that such permutations were rarely observed (only two pairs of codings differed in order). Hence for the two codings "θ α ω" and "ω θ α," $A(x,y) = 3$ and $p = 1.00$.

Table 8B.4 shows two codings by different coders of the same episode with the index of agreement corresponding to each segment. The overall agreement between coders for this episode (the average of intercoder agreements for the fourteen segments) was 0.78.

Four of the investigators were recruited to participate in the test of intercoder agreement. For each problem-solving episode, six coefficients of agreement were calculated, one for each of the possible pairings of the four coders. Four problem-solving episodes were used in these comparisons, and each of the investigators coded all four episodes. The coefficients of agreement are exhibited in Table 8B.5.

Table 8B.4 *Intercoder Agreement (Two Coders)*

Segment	Code Coder 1	Coder 2	Agreement Index
1	α	α	1.00
2	α δ	α δ	1.00
3	β	β	1.00
4	θ	θ	1.00
5	ε	γ ε	.67
6	–	–	1.00
7	θ	θ	1.00
8	α	α	1.00
9	ε	ε	1.00
10	ω	α	0
11	δ	–	0
12	θ ε ν	θ	.50
13	ω γ	ω γ ν	.80
14	A	A	1.00

Coder pair average
.78

Table 8B.5 *Coefficients of Agreement, Coder Pair x Episode*

Coder Pair	Coefficient of Agreement for Episode				Coder Pair Average (4 episodes)
	1	2	3	4	
A–B	.83	.81	.76	.80	.80
A–C	.28	.76	.76	.51	.58
A–D	.60	.62	.78	.36	.59
B–C	.28	.67	.87	.50	.58
B–D	.57	.51	.63	.33	.51
C–D	.30	.63	.63	.52	.52

It is clearly evident from Table 8B.5 that one pair of coders--
pair A-B--is consistently more in agreement than the other
pairs. In three of the four episode codings, the A-B coefficient of
agreement is the highest. The average coefficient of agreement for
coder pair A-B over all four episodes exceeds the next highest coder
pair average by 0.20--a large margin. It is significant that coders
A and B had had more extensive practice using the coding system than
coders C and D, and also that their previous work had involved the
development and utilization of process-sequence coding. Moreover,
during the development of this coding system, Coders A and B provided
input and discussion about the difficulties and nuances of coding.
It appears that intensive practice with the coding system involving
research associates who are knowledgeable in mathematics and the
psychology of mathematical reasoning is a necessary condition for
high intercoder agreement.

While coder pair A-B reflected the greatest consistency, it
should be noted that many of the other coefficients of agreement
are also reasonable. Indeed, the highest coefficient of agreement
in the data is the B-C index on Episode 3. A further look at the
data suggests that much of the disagreement arises on Episodes 1
and 4, and that the overall agreement on Episodes 2 and 3 is rather
good. The averages of all coder pairs for Episodes 2 and 3 are 0.67
and 0.74, respectively, while those for Episodes 1 and 4 are 0.48
and 0.50.

Agreements to the extent indicated are modest but optimistic
for process-sequence coding of complex problem-solving behavior.
Some were higher than the investigators had expected, but most
reflected a need for intensive practice and discussion. One of
the future goals of this research team is continued practice and
dialogue aimed at improved systems for reporting and interpreting
problem-solving processes.

There are many unexplored questions in research on the process
of mathematical problem solving. To assist in this exploration,
researchers need tools and instruments which enable them to organize
observations of complex processes. The coding system given here is
an interim attempt at such instrumentation. It is hoped that it is
one step toward a meaningful connection between clinical research in
mathematics education and the teaching of mathematics in the classroom.

IX.

Syntax, Content, and Context Variables in Instruction

by

Janet H. Caldwell
Research for Better Schools, Inc.
Philadelphia, Pennsylvania

Task variables can be of use to the mathematics teacher as well as to the researcher. By examining the types of variables describing a problem task, the teacher can more clearly separate those effects which are due to the nature of the task itself from those due to other sources of variation. An analysis of the task variables pertaining to problems used in instruction helps teachers to be more effective in foreseeing difficulties, and in designing instruction to overcome these difficulties.

Task variables can also be of use to the textbook author and publisher in designing instruction in problem solving. For example, in most textbooks, word problems in an assignment are most often solved in the same way. Students seldom have an opportunity to solve a variety of problems; they can generally find the method for solving any problem by looking back a few pages. Analyzing task variables can help textbook authors and publishers to provide more variety and thus to provide more effective curriculum.

Two categories of task variables are discussed in this chapter: syntax task variables and content/context task variables. The uses of task variables in the classroom will be explored by considering how to design problems of varying difficulty levels, how to use task variables to create problems of isomorphic mathematical structure with varying syntax, content, and context, and how to use task variables in planning a unit.

1. Syntax, Content, and Context Variables as Indicators of Problem Difficulty

Some of the task variables affecting problem difficulty are outlined in Table 9.1. It is important for the teacher to recognize these variables for two purposes: (a) to identify the difficulty level and the reasons for the difficulty level of a given problem or set of problems; and (b) to create a set of problems of a given difficulty level where all problems are approximately equal in difficulty, or where problems are of increasing difficulty for specific reasons. It is also beneficial for *students* to be able to recognize changes in task

Table 9.1 *Some Task Variables Affecting Problem Difficulty*

Syntax Task Variables

Length	Total number of words
	Total number of sentences
	Number of words per sentence
Grammatical structure	Number of clauses
	Type of clauses
	Sentence depth
	Syntactic complexity
Numerals and mathematical symbols	Form (numeral, symbol, word)
	Magnitudes of numbers
	Type (fraction, decimal, etc.)
Question sentence	Placement of the question
Sequence	Order of the given data
Vocabulary	Difficulty level

Content Task Variables

Mathematical topic	Broad and narrow subject area classifications
	Traditional "problem types" (e.g., rate problems, age problems)
Field of application	Use of specific mathematical relationships which are presupposed
Mathematical equipment	Availability and required skills
Semantic content	Key words
	Mathematical vocabulary
Problem elements	Given information
	Goal information

(continued)

Table 9.1 *(continued)*

Context Task Variables

Problem embodiments or representations	Symbolic, pictorial, or manipulative
	Visual, oral, or written
Verbal context or setting	Familiar or unfamiliar
	Applied or theoretical
	Concrete or abstract
	Factual or hypothetical
	Conventional or imaginative
Information format	Presence or absence of hints
	Multiple-choice or free-answer

variables, and to note consequent effects on the problem solution. In this section, we will examine the effect on problem difficulty of changes in the task variables.

Varying Task Syntax

Syntax task variables may generally be altered without affecting a problem's mathematical structure. Familiarity with commonly occurring syntax task variables is to be encouraged; the kinds of changes involved in altering syntax task variables can be examined and similarities in the solutions of the problems can be noted.

The following problem is a familiar motion problem from first-year algebra. It uses simple vocabulary and short sentences. There are five sentences and 39 words (WRDNUM, as defined in Chapter II), with an average of 7.8 words per sentence. Each sentence contains just one main clause.

> *9.1(a)*   *Two cars start at the same place. They are going in opposite directions. The first car goes 30 miles per hour. The second car goes 45 miles per hour. In how many hours will they be 150 miles apart?*

The problem can be changed by varying the problem length. Lengthening the problem may tend to increase its difficulty; adding more words to the problem also changes some of the grammatical structures. The following problem still has five sentences, each of which has a single main clause, but it has 58 words (11.6 words per sentence), three more prepositional phrases, and two more adverbs than Problem *9.1(a)*.

> *9.1(b)*   *Two cars start at the same place at the same time. The two cars are going in opposite directions on a straight road. The first car goes east at 30 miles per hour. The second car goes west at 45 miles per hour. In how many hours will the two cars be 150 miles away from each other?*

The problem can also be altered by combining sentences. This tends to increase the problem difficulty, primarily because it produces a concomitant change in readability.

> *9.1(c)*   *Two cars going in opposite directions start at the same place. The first car goes 30 miles per hour, while the second car goes 45 miles per hour. In how many hours will they be 150 miles apart?*

This problem has 38 words, but only three sentences; the average sentence length, 12.7, is thus higher than in Problem *9.1(a)*. There are four main clauses, one compound sentence, and one participial phrase. The sentence depth and syntactic complexity are thus higher.

The problem can also be varied by using more difficult vocabulary. The following problem has five sentences, each containing one main clause, 39 words, and the same grammatical structure as Problem 9.1(a). But it has more difficult vocabulary and may therefore be a more difficult problem for some children.

> 9.1(d) *Two automobiles commence at the same location. They are traveling in opposite directions. The first automobile travels 30 miles per hour. The second automobile travels 45 miles per hour. In how many hours will they be 150 miles apart?*

Of course, for many children the kinds of changes made in Problems 9.1(a)-(d) will not affect their ability to solve the problem. Such a variation can assist the teacher in identifying the extent to which the readability of a problem is limiting a child's performance. It can also be instructive to the child to realize that all of these problems are "really the same," and that only the wording has changed.

Changing the problem from one which uses the English system of measurement to one using the metric system may also affect the difficulty level without changing the structure. This change in units of measurement is particularly important since many texts now use metric units.

> 9.1(e) *Two cars start at the same place. They are going in opposite directions. The first car goes 30 kilometers per hour. The second car goes 45 kilometers per hour. In how many hours will they be 150 kilometers apart?*

By simultaneously changing the grammatical structure, adding words, combining sentences, and making the vocabulary more difficult, we can create a much more complicated problem statement while leaving the problem structure intact.

> 9.1(f) *One automobile is traveling east, while another automobile is traveling west from the same initial point. The former of these travels at a rate of 30 miles per hour, while the latter travels at a higher rate of 45 miles per hour. How many hours will be required for the two automobiles to travel a distance sufficient to be 150 miles apart?*

This problem has three sentences, 62 words, an average of 20.7 words per sentence, five main clauses, two compound sentences, and many prepositional phrases and infinitives. It may be more difficult for many students to read and interpret this problem than Problem *9.1(a)*, but the algorithms used to solve the two problems are the same.

The same problem can be altered by effecting changes in the numerals and symbols used. Once again the difficulty may change, but the structure does not. The numerals may be written out in words, or symbols may be used in place of numerals.

> *9.1(g) Two cars start at the same place. They are going in opposite directions. The first car goes thirty miles per hour. The second car goes forty-five miles per hour. In how many hours will they be one hundred fifty miles apart?*

> *9.1(h) Two cars start at the same place. They are going in opposite directions. The first car goes 2x miles per hour. The second car goes 3x miles per hour. In how many hours will they be 10x miles apart?*

The magnitudes of the numbers may be altered with or without significantly changing the problem difficulty. The following problem might be used as a parallel test item to Problem *9.1(a)*.

> *9.1(i) Two cars start at the same place. They are going in opposite directions. The first car goes 60 miles per hour. The second car goes 90 miles per hour. In how many hours will they be 300 miles apart?*

Changing the numbers may also make the problem more difficult by changing the answer from a whole number to a fraction. This change causes a concomitant change in problem structure, in that the algorithm used to solve the problem now requires fractions as well as whole numbers.

> *9.1(j) Two cars start at the same place. They are going in opposite directions. The first car goes 40 miles per hour. The second car goes 50 miles per hour. In how many hours will they be 135 miles apart?*

Changing the numbers used in the problem to fractions or decimals may make the problem still more difficult.

> *9.1(k) Two cars start at the same place. They are going
> in opposite directions. The first car goes 32.5
> miles per hour. The second car goes 45.1 miles
> per hour. In how many hours will they be 145.2
> miles apart?*

The last syntax variables to be considered here involve the sequencing
of information. The question in a problem can be placed at the beginning or the end of the problem, or the order of the data can be
altered. Each of these changes may alter the problem difficulty
without changing the problem structure. The question in Problem
9.1(a) might be placed at the beginning:

> *9.1(l) In how many hours will two cars be 150 miles apart?
> They start at the same place. They are going in
> opposite directions. The first car goes 30 miles
> per hour. The second car goes 45 miles per hour.*

The order of the given information might be changed:

> *9.1(m) Two cars start at the same place. The first car
> goes 30 miles per hour. The second car goes 45
> miles per hour. In how many hours will they be
> 150 miles apart, if they are going in opposite
> directions?*

We have taken just one routine "word problem" and presented it in
thirteen different versions, in order to illustrate the ways in
which changes in syntax do and do not affect the problem. A child
who can immediately recognize all of these problems as "the same" is
a step ahead in solving verbal problems. Such recognition is not
automatic but must be taught.

In the following two versions of a multi-step problem, the data
have first been placed in the order in which they will be used to
solve the problem, and then have been resequenced so that they are
not in the order in which they are used to solve the problem.

> *9.2(a) Joe bought three shirts for $8.98 each and two
> ties for $6.95 each. How much did he spend all
> together?*

> *9.2(b) A shirt costs $8.98 and a tie costs $6.95. Joe
> bought three shirts and two ties. How much did
> he spend all together?*

The problems are identical with respect to content, context, and
structure, but the second problem is more complex than the first.

Because of the difference in syntax, the data must be reorganized as the student interprets the problem.

Thus, recognition of changes in syntax task variables enables one to simplify the interpretation of problem statements. A problem statement can be created parallel to the given statement which contains only the essential problem elements, and is thus easier to solve.

Varying Task Content and Context

Content task variables describe the subject matter of the problem. It is the content variables with which the teacher is primarily concerned in defining the scope and sequence of a course. Problems may be classified according to broad subject areas such as arithmetic, algebra, geometry, trigonometry, calculus, or logic, but the classification of a problem may also depend on the achievement level and mathematical background of the problem solver. Thus, the following problem might be solved differently by students at different levels of mathematics achievement.

> 9.3 *A young farmer has eight more hens than dogs. Since hens have two legs each, but dogs have four legs each, all together the animals have 118 legs. How many dogs does the young farmer own?*

A capable eighth-grade student might approach this problem with a trial-and-error strategy. The first-year algebra student who has just learned to solve linear equations in one variable may solve the problem by letting x = the number of dogs, x + 8 = the number of hens, and setting up the equation $2(x + 8) + 4x = 118$. The more advanced algebra student may use two variables to solve the problem, setting up the two equations $x + 8 = y$ and $2y + 4x = 118$. In determining the mathematical *content* of the problem, the teacher must consider the student's background.

We are interested in examining problems which have different content, but similar mathematical structure. Let us look at several examples. A problem may be classified according to traditional "problem types" (e.g., rate problems, mixture problems, age problems). This kind of classification is probably most familiar to teachers. The basis for the classification is found in the kinds of mathematical information needed to solve the problem but not specified in the problem statement. For example, in solving rate problems one must use the formula "distance equals rate times time," but that formula is seldom stated explicitly in the problem. Each different "problem type" has its own characteristic relationships of this sort, so that it is not always possible to maintain problem structure while changing "problem type." However, examples of problems with the same structure and syntax but of different "problem types" are the following:

9.4(a) Joan buys three pounds of candy at $1.25 a pound.
        How much does she spend in all?

                                                (Money problem)

9.4(b) Tom walks three hours at 1.25 kilometers an hour.
        How far does he walk?

                                                (Rate problem)

9.4(c) Mary worked three hours, earning $1.25 each hour.
        How much did she earn in all?

                                                (Work problem)

The non-mathematical context of these problems has changed along with
the "problem type."

In a much more advanced example, a geometry student may be asked
to prove that the diagonals of a parallelogram intersect at their
midpoints by using vectors (Problem 9.5(a)) or by using Cartesian
coordinates (Problem 9.5(b)). The given conditions and the goals
are the same for the two problems, but the acceptable procedure
(mathematical content) has been changed.

9.5(a) Let M denote the midpoint of
        $\overline{AC}$. $\overline{AC}$ and $\overline{BD}$ represent vectors
        α + β and β - α, respectively,
        the triangle law. Since δ is
        collinear with, equidirected
        with, and one-half the length
        of α + β, we have δ = (½)(α + β).
        By the triangle law, α + γ = δ =
        (½)(α + β) so γ = (½)(β - α).
        Therefore γ is collinear with,
        equidirected with, and one-half
        the length of β - α. Hence M is
        the midpoint of $\overline{BD}$. (Forbes, 1973, p. 357)

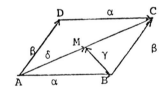

9.5(b) Since ABCD is a parallelogram,
        x = a + b and y = c. The coor-
        dinates of the midpoint of $\overline{AC}$
        are (x/2, y/2). But x/2 =
        (a + b)/2 and y/2 = c/2, so
        (x/2, y/2) = ((a + b)/2, c/2).
        Since ((a + b)/2, c/2) is the mid-
        point of $\overline{BD}$, the diagonals inter-
        sect at their midpoints.

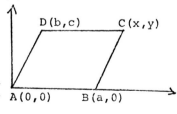

Mathematical characteristics such as the type of expression in
a problem (e.g., monomial, binomial, other polynomial) or the type
of operation used in the problem (e.g., addition, multiplication,
exponentiation) are also content task variables. An example of a

set of problems which varies the type of expression and type of operation systematically is the following set of algebraic computations (Krutetskii, 1976):

$9.6(a)$ $(a + b)^2$

$9.6(b)$ $(1 + \frac{1}{2}a^3b^2)^2$

$9.6(c)$ $(m + x + b)^2$

$9.6(d)$ 51^2

$9.6(e)$ $a^2 + b^2$

$9.6(f)$ $(\frac{1}{3} ab^3)^2 + (2a)^2$

$9.6(g)$ $2(m^2 + x^2 + b^2)$

$9.6(h)$ 98^3

The student must generalize across the problems from $9.6(a)$ to $9.6(d)$ and distinguish them from $9.6(e)$ through $9.6(h)$, which do not use the binomial formula. This becomes more difficult as the use of the formula becomes less obvious and the mathematical content of the problems varies.

Let us examine more closely the manner in which this series of problems was constructed. Problem $9.6(a)$ is a straightforward application of the formula $(a + b)^2 = a^2 + 2ab + b^2$. In Problem $9.6(b)$, there is still a binomial to be squared; but the first term is now a constant, while the second term includes a (fractional) coefficient and two variables with exponents. A trinomial is introduced in Problem $9.6(c)$, while in $9.6(d)$, the polynomial and the variables seem to have disappeared; the student must think of 51 as 50 + 1. The problems in the second half of the set *look* very similar to the ones in the first half, but are created so that the formula is *not* applicable. Problem $9.6(e)$ resembles $9.6(a)$, but it is the sum of two monomials of degree two rather than the square of a binomial; and so forth.

The presence or absence of key words, verbal clues to the operations to be performed in a word problem, may be varied easily from problem to problem, while maintaining the mathematical structure. Teachers often focus on such key words in teaching students to translate word problems into mathematical symbols. A list of some of these key words is given in Table 9.2. Let us consider the following basic problem:

$9.7(a)$ *Anthony has four balls. Jane has eight balls. How many balls do they have?*

Table 9.2 *Key Words*

Addition	Subtraction
sum	difference
in all	reduced (by)
together	less (than)
total	decreased
plus	minus
more (than)	fewer (than)
greater (than)	remain
increased	subtract
add	fall
rise	lost
gain(ed)	take away
earn	spend
save	change

Multiplication	Division
product	quotient
times	divide
multiply	per
each	each

The following problems add verbal clues.

> *9.7(b)   Anthony has four balls.   Jane has eight balls.*
> *How many balls do they have together?*

> *9.7(c)   Anthony has four balls.   Jane has eight balls.*
> *How many balls are there in all?*

Now consider the following problem and its variant. Both problems include key words, but *9.8(b)* includes a possibly misleading verbal clue whereas *9.8(a)* does not.

> *9.8(a)   Sam has fourteen dolls.   Ann has four more dolls*
> *than Sam.   How many dolls does Ann have?*

> *9.8(b)   Sam has fourteen dolls.   Sam has four more dolls*
> *than Ann.   How many dolls does Ann have?*

Problem variants may be constructed in which all of the key words are alternately included or omitted.

The use of specific mathematical vocabulary may also affect a problem's difficulty. For example, the following problem contains no technical mathematical words:

> *9.9(a)   Write a number in the box that makes the sentence*
> *true.   5 x ☐ = 50.*

On the other hand, this version of the same problem contains two technical mathematical words:

> *9.9(b)   Find the root of the equation 5x = 50.*

Problems having the same structure may also be varied by changing the given information, the number of conditions which are explicit or implied, the content of hints, and the goal information. A problem "to find" may often be recast as a problem "to show," implying a shift from direct to reverse thinking.

> *9.10(a)   Find the solution(s) of $3z^2 + 2z + 1 = 0$, where*
> *z is a complex number.*

> *9.10(b)   Show that the numbers $z = (-1 \pm i\sqrt{2})/3$ satisfy*
> *the equation $3z^2 + 2z + 1 = 0$ where z is a*
> *complex number.*

Context variables which describe the embodiment or representation of the problem may often be changed without affecting the problem structure. Such changes, of course, can substantially affect the problem difficulty. For example, as described in Chapter III, a problem may be symbolic, verbal, pictorial, or manipulative. A single task, such as adding two whole numbers, may be presented in any of these embodiments. The symbolic task simply asks:

9.11(a)   *2 + 3 = ?*

In a verbal embodiment, we have:

9.11(b)   Karen has two blocks. She buys three more blocks. How many blocks does she have all together?

The pictorial problem asks:

9.11(c)   How many blocks are there all together?

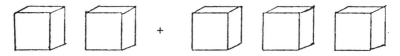

The manipulative mode problem presents sets of actual blocks, one set with two blocks and the other with three. The teacher then asks how many blocks there are all together.

The use of symbolic, verbal, pictorial, or manipulative embodiments may be geared to the developmental level of the child or to his or her familiarity with the mathematical operation(s) involved in the problem. It is generally believed that instruction in any specific concept should begin at a concrete manipulative level before progressing to the pictorial, the symbolic and the verbal levels. Of the examples given, then, a child would presumably first encounter the manipulative mode problem, then *9.11(c)*, *9.11(a)*, and finally *9.11(b)*.

Context task variables also describe the verbal setting of the problem. Some of the classifications which may be useful to the teacher include concrete versus abstract, familiar versus unfamiliar, conventional versus imaginative, and factual versus hypothetical problems (see Chapters III and VI). The familiar/unfamiliar dichotomy is, of course, dependent upon the problem-solvers themselves--their backgrounds and experiences. The classification of mathematical word problems as familiar or unfamiliar, and the issue of cross-cultural differences in standardized testing, are very closely allied. The following problem describes a situation familiar to most elementary school students:

9.12   *Tony has 47 marbles. He loses 12 marbles. How*
       many marbles does he have left?

The next problem describes a situation which may be unfamiliar to many
of the same students, but requires the same operation as *9.12.*

9.13(a)   *Mr. Jones took 55 pounds of raw cotton to the*
          gin. He got back 32 pounds of cotton fiber.
          How many pounds of seed did he get back?

An important task of the mathematics teacher is to encourage the
detection of the correct mathematical operations, even in unfamiliar
verbal contexts. A student skilled in problem solving will be able
to solve *9.13(a)* even without knowing what a cotton gin is, because
the student has a concept of problem structure which the problem
statement fits. By *explicitly* comparing problems in familiar and
unfamiliar contexts, the teacher may be able to develop this skill.
Nonsense words may help. For example,

9.13(b)   *Mr. Jones took 55 pounds of oozlop to the*
          geezenstack. He got back 32 pounds of oozlop
          meat. How many pounds of oozlop skin did he
          get back?

For the problem to *make sense*, it must be *assumed* that oozlop consists
only of meat and skin, just as in Problem *9.13(a)* it is assumed that
cotton consists only of fiber and seed. Students can profit from
specific instruction in stating such implicit assumptions.

The conventional/imaginative dichotomy provides similar opportunities to the teacher. A conventional problem is one similar to most
textbook problems, devoid of irrelevant information. It uses the
shortest, simplest, and most direct language possible. Thus, for
example, the following:

9.14(a)   *Tickets to a school play cost 25¢. The fifth grade*
          sold 120 tickets, and the sixth grade sold 132
          tickets. How much more money did the sixth grade
          make than the fifth?

An imaginative problem describes elements of the total situation which
are interesting and have imaginative appeal, but whose presence is not
necessary to understand the mathematical elements of the situation.

9.14(b)   *The boys and girls in the fifth and sixth grades at*
          the Grant School were trying to raise some money.
          They wanted to buy books for their library, and
          they wanted to give something to the Children's
          Hospital. They talked over many plans for raising

money and decided they would have a School Fair.
The two grades had a contest selling tickets. The
tickets were 25 cents each. The contest was close.
The fifth grade sold 120 tickets, and the sixth
grade sold 132 tickets. How much more money did
the sixth grade make than the fifth?
(Wheat, 1929, p. 36)

Variations in the content and context task variables can thus
provide the teacher with a diversity of problems of varying degrees
of difficulty. We stress the value of making such variations *explicit*
to the student in order to develop the general ability to solve word
problems.

2. Using Task Variables in Instruction

The classroom teacher pays attention, consciously or unconsciously,
to task variables each day in choosing problems as examples or counter-
examples. Conscious consideration of specific variables may improve
instruction by illuminating the sources of student difficulty. In the
next section two sample unit plans are presented which illustrate this
concept. Here we shall mention some additional dimensions of the use
of task variables.

Developing Equivalent Test Forms

One problem which arises frequently in the classroom is that of
developing equivalent test forms. These may be needed for review,
for make-up tests, to eliminate cheating, or for re-testing after
remedial instruction. The careful consideration of syntax, content,
and context task variables allows the teacher to create test forms
which are truly equivalent. Each problem in a test must be considered both individually and as an element in the test sequence.

Consider the following problem, which is similar to one discussed
in considerable detail in Chapter VI.

9.15(a) *Alan bought an equal number of books and flowerpots.*
Each book cost three dollars and each flowerpot cost
five dollars, so that he spent 48 dollars in all.
How many books did Alan buy?

First, the teacher might identify the task variables and the value of
each variable. The problem is a problem in arithmetic, or possibly
algebra (depending upon the student population). It describes the
cost of two objects with different prices. It is a concrete, applied,
factual, verbal, and familiar problem. It has 33 words in it and
three sentences. All of the vocabulary is appropriate for fourth

graders. The syntax is not excessively complex. There are some
standard "key words," the words "each" and "in all." The numbers
used are whole numbers, 3, 5, and 48, and the solution is a whole
number. The operations required to solve the problem are addition
(5 + 3) and division (48 ÷ 8) or (algebraically) the solution of the
equation 5x + 3x = 48.

One way to create an equivalent problem is to alter the numbers
used. An equivalent problem might be:

> 9.15(b)   Alan bought an equal number of books and flower-
> pots. Each book cost four dollars and each
> flowerpot cost three dollars, so that he spent
> 49 dollars in all. How many books did Alan buy?

Care must be taken in changing a problem in this way so that the computational solutions of both problems follow the same path through
the algorithm used. If the problem referred to nine-dollar books
and eight-dollar flowerpots, for example, the problem structure would
be different because the division operation would be more difficult
than in the given problem.

Another way of altering the problem is to change both the numbers
used and the objects purchased.

> 9.15(c)   Alan bought an equal number of plants and records.
> Each plant cost five dollars and each record cost
> four dollars, so that he spent 45 dollars in all.
> How many plants did Alan buy?

In doing this, we must be careful that the vocabulary remains at the
same grade level and that the computational algorithm remains the
same. We must also take care that the objects mentioned bear the
same relationship to each other as in the original problem. A problem about buying an equal number of plants and flowerpots, as we saw
in Chapter VI, is probably easier than one about buying an equal
number of books and flowerpots or plants and records, because it is
more natural to think of paying one price for the pair.

A more radical alteration of the problem changes the whole situation (content), but does not alter the vocabulary level, the syntactic
complexity, problem structure, or other task variables.

> 9.15(d)   A family has an equal number of brothers and
> sisters. Each brother has five books and each
> sister has two books, so that they have 42 books
> in all. How many brothers does the family have?

Notice, however, that the "key words" have been preserved, in order
not to affect the problem difficulty. Task variables can thus be
manipulated to produce equivalent test forms in the classroom with
a high degree of confidence (short of extensive statistical data on
the equivalence of the forms).

Varying Mathematical Structure

A second teaching application is to use task variables in creating problems with *varying* structures but with the syntax, content,
and context task variables held constant. This is in contrast to
the approach described in Section 1. Such sets of problems enable
the students to concentrate on differences in the mathematical structure of the problem solution rather than on the process of decoding
and translating the problem statement. Let us consider the following problem.

> 9.16 *The Student Council sold two kinds of nuts. Peanuts
> cost 25 cents a bag and almonds cost 45 cents a bag.
> They sold 30 bags of peanuts and 40 bags of almonds.
> How much money did they make all together?*

The next problem retains the same syntax, content, and context. The
structure, however, has changed.

> 9.17 *The Student Council sold two kinds of nuts. Peanuts
> cost 25 cents a bag and almonds cost 45 cents a bag.
> They sold 100 bags of nuts for $33.00 all together.
> How many bags of each kind of nut did they sell?*

The solution of this problem requires either the solution of an algebraic
equation or a trial-and-error process. Here are two more variants.

> 9.18 *The Student Council sold two kinds of nuts. Peanuts
> cost 25 cents a bag and almonds cost 45 cents a bag.
> They sold 50 bags of peanuts and made $48.50 all
> together. How many bags of almonds did they sell?*

> 9.19 *The Student Council sold two kinds of nuts. Peanuts
> cost 25 cents a bag and almonds cost 45 cents a bag.
> They used 160 bags of peanuts and sold mixed nuts
> for 40 cents a bag. How many bags of almonds did
> they use?*

In each of these problems the solution algorithm is different. The
similarity of syntax, content, and context makes it easier for students to detect and understand the reasons for the differences.

3. Unit Planning Using Task Variables

In this section two unit plans are described. The first involves
single-operation word problems, and is directed towards a sixth-grade
class; the second involves ratio and proportion, and is directed
towards a first-year algebra class. These unit plans are intended
to illustrate the systematic variation of selected syntax, content,
and context task variables, while other variables are held constant.
In addition, activities are provided which hold syntax, content, and
context variables constant, while structure variables are manipulated.
It is suggested that such intentional manipulation of selected task
variables can be a powerful pedagogical device in the teaching of
problem solving.

Solving Single-Operation Word Problems
(A 6th-Grade Sample Unit Plan)

The following unit is designed for a group of below-average sixth
graders. It deals with single-step, routine word problems employing
whole numbers. The broad subject area classification is arithmetic,
and the problem embodiments used in the unit are primarily verbal.
The problem statements are written with syntax and vocabulary appropriate for a fourth-grade level of reading ability.

Objectives

The objectives of this unit include:

1. Syntax variables

    a. Rearranging the information given and the question sentence
        without changing the nature of a problem.

    b. Recognizing two problems having different grammar and
        syntax as mathematically the same.

2. Content variables

    c. Recognizing "key words" and stating the arithmetic opera-
        tion with which they are most often associated.

    d. Writing number facts to accompany given word problems.

    e. Writing word problems to accompany given number facts.

3. Context variables

    f. Recognizing word problems that vary context while keeping
        syntax, content, and structure constant by identifying
        contextual information irrelevant to the problem's solution.

g. Recognizing two problems having different contextual embodiments (settings) as mathematically the same.

4. Structure variables

h. Recognizing the absence of information necessary to solve a problem, and stating what is missing.

i. Recognizing the presence of extraneous mathematical information in a routine word problem, and eliminating it from the problem.

j. Solving word problems using the correct whole number operations.

Activities

These activities are organized according to their association with one or more of the above objectives. The rationale for the sequencing of the activities is based on the hierarchy of task variables in Chapter I. That is, the students are in effect being led through Polya's stages of understanding the problem, devising a plan, and carrying out the plan.

Syntax Variables

Objective (a): Rearranging the information given and the question sentence without changing the nature of a problem.

The teacher first demonstrates how the information given in a problem can be rearranged without changing the nature of the problem itself. Examples which might be used include the following problems:

9.20(a) Ann has four cookies. James has six cookies. How many cookies do they have in all?

9.20(b) James has six cookies. Ann has four cookies. How many cookies do they have in all?

9.20(c) How many cookies do Ann and James have in all? Ann has four. James has six.

The students then rearrange the information given in a series of increasingly complex word problems, writing each problem in an alternative form.

Objective (b): *Recognizing two problems having different grammar and syntax as mathematically the same.*

The teacher demonstrates that two problems which are worded differently may represent the same mathematical situation. For example,

9.21(a) *Howard has 125 baseball cards. He buys 52 more cards. How many cards does he have now?*

9.21(b) *Howard already had 125 baseball cards, and today he bought 52 more. How many cards does he have now?*

The students are then given two sets of problems. The second set of problems consists of syntax variations on the first set; the grammar and/or syntax of each problem on the first list is changed without altering its solution. The problems in the second set are listed in random order. The students are asked to *match* each problem on the first list with the problem on the second list which is mathematically the same.

Finally, students are asked to rewrite a given word problem by using as *many* words as possible, or by using as *few* words as possible.

Content Variables

Objective (c): *Recognizing "key words" and stating the arithmetic operation with which they are most often associated.*

Students list words that are associated with each of the four arithmetic operations. For example, "What words or phrases make you think about adding?" A class list is compiled and posted as a bulletin board display. Possible answers can be found in the list of key words (Table 9.2).

The students then identify key words in word problems, and choose the correct operation for each problem. Sample problems are as follows, with key words underlined.

9.22 *Ray bought 325 baseball cards. He already had 518 baseball cards. How many baseball cards does he have in all?*

9.23 *Susan has 38 books. Harry has five less than Susan. How many books does Harry have?*

9.24   George *bought* 15 oranges. Ann *bought* three *times*
       as many oranges. *How many* oranges did Ann buy?

9.25   I am thinking of a number. My number is 82 *less*
       than 415. *What* is my number?

9.26   *Find* a number that is the *product* of 16 and 23.

9.27   Joe *has* 15 cookies. He wants to *divide* them *equally*
       among three friends. *How many* cookies does *each*
       friend get?

9.28   *Find* the number that is *equal* to the *quotient* when
       28 is *divided by* four.

The next day the students discuss problems with the key words
omitted. The missing words are varied, and the problems are interpreted. For example,

9.29   Oscar _____ 15 cookies. He _____ three cookies.
       How many cookies does he have _____?

9.30   Find a number that is the _____ of 8 and 4.

Next the students write problems using the key words on the class
list. The problems should use complete sentences. For example, a
suitable problem might be:

9.31   I have thirteen cookies. I eat five. How many
       cookies do I have *left*?

The underlined word is the key word from the list used in the problem.
Students may be asked to write on a specific topic, such as buying
groceries or going to the circus.

The class discusses how changing a few words can alter an entire
problem's meaning and solution. For example, the following sequence
of problems might be considered.

9.32(a)   John *has* five dollars. He *earns* three dollars.
          How much does he *have* now?

9.32(b)   John *has* five dollars. He *saves* three dollars.
          How much does he *have* now?

9.32(c)   John *has* five dollars. He *spends* three dollars.
          How much does he *have* now?

9.32(d) John _needs_ five dollars. He _has_ three dollars.
         How much does he _need_ now?

Another day the students may discuss the ambiguity of some verbal
clues. Those clues which may be misleading because they have alternate interpretations are so marked on the class list of key words
(DANGER! WATCH OUT!).

The students choose the correct operation for problems which
include possibly misleading key words. Sample problems follow.

9.33 Ann hit 16 homeruns this year. This is five more
      than she hit last year. How many homeruns did she
      hit last year?

9.34 The sixth grade went on a field trip. They went a
      total of 37 miles. They went six miles on a country
      road and the rest of the way on the highway. How
      many miles did they go on the highway?

9.35 What is my number? The sum of sixteen and my number
      is 25.

9.36 Our town has a large airport. There are 12 buildings.
      There are eight planes at each building. How many
      planes are there in all?

9.37 The cafeteria serves 180 people. There are two rolls
      per person. How many rolls are needed?

9.38 Fifteen times a number is 75. What is the number?

9.39 The difference between a number and seven is 33.
      What is the number?

This set of problems, designed to aid students in recognizing potentially misleading key words and reconciling conflicting verbal clues,
also varies the context task variables of problem setting and the
syntax task variables of problem length, readability, and sequencing.

Students may be asked to rewrite problems keeping certain key
word(s) and trying to change the operation used. For example, the
following problem might be considered initially:

9.40(a) Joseph and Tom have 40 marbles in all. Tom
         has 12 marbles. How many marbles does Joseph
         have?

This problem could be rewritten in several ways, and the meaning of "in all" discussed.

> *9.40(b)   Joseph has 40 marbles in all.   Tom has 12*
> *marbles.   How many marbles do they have?*

> *9.40(c)   Joseph has 40 marbles.   Tom has 12 marbles.*
> *How many marbles do they have in all?*

Objective (d):   Writing number facts to accompany given word problems.

The students practice writing number facts to accompany given situations depicted by the teacher using manipulatives, and to accompany pictures of mathematical situations.

The students write number facts to accompany given word problems, where the word problems have been designed to describe situations similar to the manipulative and pictorial situations.   The students match the different situations which are described by the same number facts.

Objective (e):   Writing word problems to accompany given number facts.

The students write word problems to accompany given number facts. For this activity, the teacher should provide a variety of possible contents (money, age, etc.) by introducing a set of characters and a situation (e.g., friends in a supermarket, a family having different ages).

Context Variables

Objective (f):   Recognizing word problems that vary context while
keeping syntax, content, and structure constant by
identifying contextual information irrelevant to the
problem's solution.

The teacher demonstrates how a problem setting may be changed without affecting the solution process for the problem.   For example, the following problems may be discussed.   (These problems were constructed so as to be as nearly identical as possible with respect to problem length, readability, and mathematical structure, as described in Chapter VI.)

> *9.41(a)   There is a number.   If this number were two times*
> *as large as it really is, then it would be equal*
> *to 28.   What is the number?*

9.41(b) Jenny is a girl. Jenny's father is three times
         as old as Jenny is, and he is 39 years old. How
         old is Jenny?

9.41(c) Eddie is a boy. If Eddie were four times as old
         as he really is, then he would be 48 years old.
         How old is Eddie?

9.41(d) There is a number. A second number is five times
         as large as the first number, and the second number
         is 55. What is the value of the first number?

For a second activity, the students may be asked to fill in missing words in problems so as to change the context. For example, the following problem may be concerned with "apples" or "gleeps."

9.42 I have 32 _____. I buy 71 _____. How many _____
      do I have in all?

Students may also be asked to fill in missing numbers in problems and then describe how to solve the problem.

Objective (g): Recognizing two problems having different contextual embodiments (settings) as mathematically the same.

The students state a word problem in pictures. Students use actual objects to act out similar word problems. The concrete, pictorial, and symbolic versions are compared and discussed. Examples of mathematical situations in everyday occurrences, and in newspapers and magazines, may provide the opportunity to make up word problems about the situations. These word problems can then be compared to other word problems which are mathematically the same. Word problems with varied contexts may be the focus of matching activities.

Structure Variables

Objective (h): Recognizing the absence of information necessary to solve a problem, and stating what is missing.

The students are given problems with missing information. They are asked to state what else is needed in order to solve the problem. Sample problems follow.

9.43 Mr. Hardy's bus ticket costs $4. How much will it
      cost in all for Mr. Hardy and his son to ride the bus?

9.44 *When the rain started, 208 people left the football game. How many people remained?*

9.45 *Ron Daly puts in telephones. He put in 60 phones. How many phones did he put in each day?*

9.46 *Joe bought a loaf of bread and a dozen eggs. The eggs were 78 cents. How much was the bread?*

9.47 *Find my number. It is five less than John's age.*

The problems are varied with regard to context task variables (abstract or concrete), syntax task variables (placement of the question, length), and content task variables (key words).

The students are then given problems in which every fifth word has been replaced by a blank. They will fill in the blanks and discuss their choices, to see if they make sense.

Objective (i): Recognizing the presence of extraneous mathematical information in a routine word problem, and eliminating it from the problem.

The students are given problems including irrelevant numerical information and asked to state what is unnecessary in the problem. They will then solve the problems. Some sample problems follow.

9.48 *Joe and Tom played marbles every day for three weeks. They have 50 marbles in all. Tom has 12 marbles. How many marbles does Joe have?*

9.49 *Our town has a large airport. It is 15 miles from my house. It has 11 buildings. There are seven planes at each building. How many planes are there in all?*

9.50 *What is my number? The sum of eight and my number is 32. The difference between 12 and my number is 12.*

9.51 *The cafeteria serves 210 people. Each person gets two pieces of chicken, milk, salad, vegetables, and five cookies. There are two rolls per person. How many rolls are needed?*

9.52 *Susan has 14 books. Harry has five less than Susan and Al has ten times as many as Susan. How many books does Harry have?*

The similarities between these problems and previous ones should be pointed out to the students; *9.48* is a revision of *9.40(a)*, *9.49* is a revision of *9.36*, *9.50* is a revision of *9.35*, and *9.51* is a revision of *9.37*. The problems were created by adding extra information to some of the problems from earlier sets.

Objective (j): Solving word problems using the correct whole number operations.

The students make up word problems and write them on index cards to be used as contest problems. Each contest problem is checked by the teacher for validity. They will then have a class competition, solving each others' problems. The rules must forbid problems with excessively large numbers or too many conditions.

The students may make up word problems to be put in a workbook for students in the fourth or fifth grades. Each student will be responsible for solving his or her own problems.

The students may then be given a word problem set as a culminating activity, providing practice in solving a variety of problems. Context, content, and syntax task variables describing problem length, vocabulary, key words (both helpful and misleading), problem setting, and sequencing of information should all be utilized in designing the problems.

Finally, the students may make a list of those characteristics of word problems which can change without changing the mathematics of the problem. For example, some things which can change include the order of the information, the actual words used, the number of words used, and the problem setting.

Solving Problems in Ratio and Proportion
(An Algebra I Sample Unit Plan)

Our second unit plan is designed for an average ninth-grade algebra class. The specific subject areas include ratio and proportion. The problem embodiments are symbolic: both equations and word problems are studied. It is assumed that the students have previously studied the simplification of rational expressions and routine computations with rational expressions.

Objectives

The objectives of this unit include:

1. Syntax variables

   a. Recognizing the various means of writing ratios (e.g., 4 to 5, 4/5, 4:5).

b. Recognizing the various means of writing proportions (e.g., 4/5 = x/10 and 4:5 = x:10).

c. Rearranging the information given and the question sentence without changing the nature of the problem.

d. Recognizing two problems having different grammar and syntax as mathematically the same.

2. Content variables

e. Recognizing that problems from specific fields of application may require the use of specific mathematical relationships understood to hold within the field of application (e.g., the definition of batting averages).

f. Recognizing and using key words for ratio and proportion.

g. Recognizing and interpreting specific mathematical vocabulary: ratio, proportion, means, extremes.

h. Identifying given information in a word problem involving proportions.

i. Identifying goals in word problems using proportions.

j. Writing equations to accompany given word problems.

k. Writing word problems to accompany given equations.

3. Context variables

l. Recognizing word problems that vary context while keeping syntax, content, and structure constant by identifying contextual information irrelevant to the problem's solution.

m. Recognizing two problems having different contextual embodiments (settings) as mathematically the same.

4. Structure variables

n. Stating a ratio as a fraction in lowest terms when given a situation described in a verbal problem.

o. Recognizing the absence of information necessary to solve a problem, and stating what is missing.

p. Recognizing the presence of extraneous mathematical information in a routine word problem, and eliminating it from the problem.

q. Solving word problems based on proportion.

Although the content areas of this unit plan and the preceding one are quite different, every objective in the sixth-grade unit also appears in this unit. The basic unit structure thus is relatively independent of content and can therefore be used for almost any content area.

Activities

The activities are again organized according to their association with one or more of the above objectives. Most activities are only sketched, however, requiring further elaboration by the teacher.

Syntax Variables

Objective (a): Recognizing the various means of writing ratios.

The class conducts an experiment, drawing several marbles, one at a time, from two bags containing red and blue marbles. Each marble is replaced after it has been selected and its color recorded. The class discusses estimating how many red marbles are in each bag, how many marbles in all are in each bag, and so forth. This leads to a discussion of the fraction of marbles in each bag that are red and thus to a definition of the term "ratio." Various ways of writing ratios are presented. Several examples are worked, and the students do some problems orally. Some of these use whole numbers:

9.53(a)   *16 to 20*

Some use fractions:

9.53(b) $1\frac{1}{2} : 6$

And some use algebraic expressions:

9.53(c) $(c - d)^3 \text{ to } (c - d)$

Objective (b): Recognizing various means of writing proportions.

The following problem is presented to the students:

9.54(a) $\frac{24}{50} = \frac{x}{20}$

Using their knowledge of various ways of writing ratios, the students generate as many different ways of writing this same problem as they can. Some alternative possibilities include:

9.54(b) $24/50 = \frac{x}{20}$

9.54(c) $24:50 = x:20$

9.54(d)   *24 to 50 = x to 20*

The advantages and disadvantages of each version should be discussed.

Objective (c): Rearranging the information given and the question sentence without changing the nature of the problem.

The teacher demonstrates how the given information can be rearranged without actually changing the problem itself. The following examples might be used:

9.55(a)   Five apples cost $1.00. I want to buy 12 apples. How much money do I need?

9.55(b)   I want to buy 12 apples. Five apples cost $1.00. How much money do I need?

9.55(c)   How much money do I need? I want to buy 12 apples. Five apples cost $1.00.

The students rearrange the information given in a series of increasingly complex word problems, writing each problem in an alternative form.

Objective (d): Recognizing two problems having different grammar and syntax as mathematically the same.

The teacher demonstrates that two problems which are worded differently may represent the same mathematical situation. The following examples may be used:

9.56(a)   The Record Shop sells three records for $15. Sally wants to buy four records. How much money will the records cost?

9.56(b)   Sally bought four records from the Record Shop where they were selling three records for $15. How much did the records cost?

The students match problems (to equivalent problems) having different
grammar and syntax. They then rewrite given problems by using as many
or as few words as possible.

Content Variables

*Objective (e): Recognizing that problems from specific fields of applica-
tion may require the use of specific mathematical relationships understood to hold within the field of application.*

Batting averages as examples of ratios are studied. Students learn
that batting averages are always expressed as the ratio of number of
hits to number of times at bat rounded to the nearest thousandth.

Profit-to-cost and profit-to-selling price ratios are discussed.
Students learn the basic assumed relationships between profit, cost,
and selling price. Problems are of different embodiments; concrete
personal examples (*9.57(a)*) are considered first, with more complex
symbolic problems (*9.57(b)*) considered later.

> *9.57(a)   You own a book store.   You buy the newest best
> seller for $5.   You sell it for $7.   What is your
> profit-to-cost ratio?*

> *9.57(b)   You own a book store.   You buy the newest best
> seller for x dollars.   You sell it for x + 2 dollars.
> What is your profit-to-cost ratio?*

Problem givens and goals should be varied so that students are
given profit and cost, profit and selling price, or cost and selling
price and are asked to find profit-to-cost or profit-to-selling price
ratios.

Ratios derived from the composition of chemical compounds are also
discussed, along with the necessary assumptions of mathematical relationships. For example, the ratio of hydrogen atoms to oxygen atoms
in water (H_2O) is 2:1.

Ratios comparing different units of measure also require the use
of implicit assumptions. For example, writing the ratio of seven
minutes to two hours first requires changing all units to minutes
(or hours). Students set up ratios comparing different units.

In addition to setting up ratios by using the implicit assumptions of a field of application, students may be asked to state
explicitly the assumptions made in a ratio or proportion word problem.

Objective (f): Recognizing and using key words for ratio and proportion.

Key words for ratios are identified by the students. Some examples are given in Table 9.3. Students write problems using the key words and set up the ratios involved. They may be asked to write several problems for a specific ratio, using the same key word(s) and different non-mathematical contexts.

Key words for proportions are identified and listed (Table 9.3). Students identify key words in textbook problems and then write their own problems using the key words.

Objective (g): Recognizing and interpreting specific mathematical
vocabulary: ratio, proportion, means, extremes.

Students give examples of ratios and proportions in both symbolic and verbal forms. The teacher defines the terms "means" and "extremes," explaining the solution of a proportion by developing symbolically the rule that the product of the means equals the product of the extremes. Students identify the means and extremes in problems from the text.

Objective (h): Identifying given information in a word problem
involving proportions.

Students identify the given information in word problems involving proportions. For example, the following problem is given:

9.58(a) Mr. Smith bought his house for $42,000 five years
ago. He is moving to another city and wants to
sell it for a profit that is 1/10 of his cost.
How much should he sell the house for?

The information given in the problem is identified: price of house originally and the profit-to-cost ratio.

Objective (i): Identifying goals in word problems using proportions.

Students identify goals of word problems involving proportions. For example, in Problem *9.58(a)*, the goal of the problem is identified as being the selling price of the house. Suggestions for the problem's solution are offered by the students; most set up the problem as a proportion,

9.58(b) $$\frac{1}{10} = \frac{x}{42,000}$$

and solve for x = 4,200. The students identify this as the profit rather than the selling price. Recalling the relationship cost +

Table 9.3 *Key Words: Ratio and Proportion*

<u>Ratio</u>	<u>Proportion</u>
out of	as
is to	at the same rate
per	ratio
each	rate
to	out of
	is to
	per
	each
	to

profit = selling price, they compute a selling price of $46,200.

Objective (j): Writing equations to accompany given word problems.

The students write equations to accompany given word problems involving proportion.

Objective (k): Writing word problems to accompany given equations.

The students write word problems to accompany given proportions. For this activity, the teacher may wish to provide a variety of possible contents (e.g., batting averages, chemical compounds).

Context Variables

Objective (l): Recognizing word problems that vary context while keeping syntax, content, and structure constant by identifying contextual information irrelevant to the problem's solution.

The teacher demonstrates how a problem setting may be changed without affecting the solution process for the problem. The following problems may be used as illustrations:

9.59(a) *I want to buy some books. I have fifteen dollars, and seven books cost 35 dollars. How many books can I buy?*

9.59(b) *I am thinking of a number. This number is related to fifteen, and seven is related to 35 in the same way. What is this number?*

The students may also be asked to fill in missing words in problems so as to change the context. For example, the following problem may deal with "records" or "gobbledygooks."

9.60 *Six _____ cost $15. How many _____ can I buy for $27.50?*

Students may also be asked to fill in missing numbers in problems and then describe how to solve the problem.

*Objective (m): Recognizing two problems having different contextual
embodiments (settings) as mathematically the same.*

Other problems using proportions and varying situations such as
batting averages, chemical compounds, and angles of a triangle, are
considered. Students identify similarities such as the presence of a
ratio in the given information. Assumptions peculiar to each application are identified, such as the definition of a batting average or
the theorem stating that the sum of the measures of the angles of a
triangle is 180°. Problems which have different embodiments but which
are mathematically equivalent are compared. An example follows:

9.61(a) *An alloy is composed of three parts nickel, two
parts aluminum, and one part zinc. How many
grams of zinc are there in 180 grams of the alloy?*

9.61(b) *One angle of a triangle is twice as large as the
smallest angle, and the third angle is three times
as large as the smallest angle. What is the
measure of the smallest angle?*

*Objective (n): Stating a ratio as a fraction in lowest terms when
given a situation described in a verbal problem.*

Structure Variables

Students examine various applications of ratios, stating similarities between them and setting up ratios for each. They study newspaper
advertisements for canned goods and determine the more economical buys
(e.g., four cans of soup for 89 cents or one can for 23 cents). Problems involving profit-to-cost ratios, profit-to-selling price ratios,
and ratios derived from chemical compounds are solved. Students may
also make up and solve their own word problems using ratios. These
student problems may be combined for a homework assignment, contest,
or class booklet.

*Objective (o): Recognizing the absence of information necessary to
solve a problem, and stating what is missing.*

The students are given problems with missing information. They
are asked to state what else is needed in order to solve the problem.
The problems are varied in regard to context, syntax, and content.

The students are given problems in which every fifth word has
been omitted. They are asked to fill in the omitted words and discuss their choices.

Objective (p): Recognizing the presence of extraneous mathematical information in a routine word problem, and eliminating it from the problem.

The students are given problems including irrelevant numerical information and asked to state what is unnecessary in the problem. They then write equations to accompany the problems and solve them.

Objective (q): Solving word problems based on proportion.

Students solve word problems using proportions. Students may also write their own problems.

4. Conclusion

We have considered syntax, content, and context task variables as indicators of problem difficulty, as tools enabling the teacher to create equivalent problems, and as a means of organizing instruction in problem solving. These variables, examined and analyzed in earlier chapters, have here been applied to instructional situations. Knowledge of the nature and effects of task variables has real utility. The teacher familiar with the vocabulary and the research is more effectively prepared to select and design appropriate problems, to foresee and overcome possible difficulties, to teach students the art of problem solving, to communicate his or her own experiences to other teachers, and to comprehend the experiences of other mathematics educators.

X.

Structure and Heuristic Behavior Variables in Teaching

A.

Applications of Problem Structure

by

George F. Luger*
University of Edinburgh
Edinburgh, Scotland

In this section two kinds of problems are discussed. First we look at "routine" problems, which can often be classified into standard "problem types," having content and/or structure characteristics in common. Secondly, we look at "non-routine" problems, and suggest the explicit analysis of problem structure as an effective means for teaching problem-solving skills. In both cases, teaching approaches are exemplified through short sample lesson plans.

1. Schema Driven Inferencing and Routine Problem Types

The word "schema" is used by Bartlett (1936) to refer to a structuring of information, a loose confederation of relationships, that represents the capacity to perform some task or function. In the terminology of Hinsley, Hayes, and Simon (1976) the "problem type" schema includes the semantic information contained in the general problem situation, and clues for using this information in solving the particular problem. In this section the word "schema" will refer to the structuring and storage of the semantic information necessary for problem solving.

Hinsley, Hayes, and Simon (1976) discuss schemata in relation to solving algebra word problems similar to those found in secondary school textbooks. They conclude the following:

a. Students categorize problems into "types." While problems are not *uniquely* categorizable, they fall broadly into groups such as "age," or "river travel," or "work" problems.

b. Students classify such problems even *before* they have assimilated all the important information, and before the problems have been formulated for solution.

---

*Current address: University of New Mexico, Albuquerque, N.M.

    c. Students possess a body of information about each problem type
which is potentially useful for formulating problems of that
type for solution. This information helps focus attention on
important facets of the problem.

    d. Students *use* this "category" or "problem type" information in
formulating problems for solution, not merely for classification.

The use of "problem type" information to focus on relevant facets of the
problem, or to recall and apply appropriate equations, are characteristics of *schema driven inferencing*.

To demonstrate what is meant by the semantic information associated
with a particular problem type, consider the following examples.

"River Problems":

10A.1 *If a boat takes 3 hours to go four miles up a river and
2 hours to return to the starting point, what is the
speed of the current?*

Some of the unstated assumptions in this type of problem are: (a) there
is no wind to affect the speed of the boat, (b) there are no obstructions
in the water, (c) the boat is not slowly taking on water, (d) the boat's
speed (in still water) as well as the speed of the river current is constant; and so forth. Equations associated with this problem type are:
Distance = Rate x *Time,* and *Speed (Net) = Speed (1)* $\pm$ *Speed (2),* where
Speed (1) and *Speed (2)* may refer to boat, wind, or current speed.

"Pulley Problems":

10A.2 *A man of 140 lbs. and a weight of 112 lbs. hang from a
rope over a pulley. Find the acceleration of the system.*

Here it is assumed that: (a) the man and the weight hang vertically
downward, (b) the rope does not stretch, (c) the pulley is fixed and
frictionless, etc. These facts, though not directly stated in the problem itself, must be understood to produce a correct solution. In addition, the problem solver must call on *Force = Mass* x *Acceleration,* the
value of the earth's gravitational force, and rules for obtaining a
resultant force.

"Money Problems":

10A.3 *If the value of 25 nickels and dimes in John's pocket
is $1.79, how many coins of each type does he have?*

An understanding of this problem statement must include the unstated
semantic information that the value of each nickel is 5 cents and the
value of each dime is 10 cents. In addition, "coins" must be interpreted as having both a *number* (the number of dimes) and a *value* (each

dime is worth 10 cents). This information must be *used by* students
to see that the problem statement is contradictory.

Thus, each problem type has its own semantic content. This content
should be considered carefully by the teacher before discussion of problems with the students. Lack of explicit discussion of problem-type
information is a major shortcoming of many secondary school textbooks,
which often assume that semantic content will be somehow "picked up"
during the process of problem solving. This assumption can be false,
especially for slower students. In fact, inadequate understanding of
the semantic content of a problem can be the major source of problem
difficulty not only for slow students but for students from different cultures.

It should be noted that semantic information, as we use the term,
refers both to problem *content* and problem *structure* (see Chapter I).
To the extent that it merely augments the problem statement with additional, unstated "givens," the semantic information may be considered
part of the problem "content." However, the underlying algebraic relationships (e.g., the equations associated with "river travel" or "pulley"
problems) are part of the problem "structure" and these too are included
in the "problem type" schema. The processes of equation instantiation
and the algorithmic solution of equations are structure-related.

These ideas will now be developed in a series of sample lesson plans
aimed toward assisting students in formulating problems for solution.

Lesson Plan 1: River Travel Problems

> *Objective: To enable the students to "set up" and solve river
> travel problems utilizing the semantic information
> associated with this "problem type."*

Select a set of six to eight "river travel" problems from algebra
textbooks. Once the problem type has been introduced with several problems, have students create "river travel" problems of their own.

Consider a simple example.

> 10A.4 *A boat that travels four miles per hour in still water
> goes downstream from pier A to pier B in two hours.
> If the return trip takes six hours, what is the speed
> of the current?*

Elicit, in discussion with the students, the semantic information indicated below:

(a) The forces that are acting on a boat traveling in the stream.
(Wind, current, bouyancy of the boat--is it slowly sinking;
does the engine or person rowing wear out?)

(b) An intuitive representation for describing boat speed up
and down the river; for example:

$$BSP + W + C + . . . = BSD$$
$$BSP - W - C + . . . = BSU$$

(where BSP is the boat speed, W is wind, C is current,
BSD is boat speed downstream, and BSU is boat speed
upstream).

(c) The quantities relevant to the situation, arriving at
answers to questions such as:

1. How is boat speed measured (in still water)? Is boat
speed constant in the "real world?" (No.) What is
done with boat speed in the problem? (It is idealized
and fixed.)

2. How is wind speed calculated? May it be ignored? May
this variable be ignored in ocean travel or air travel?

3. How is current measured? What is the difference
between "upstream and downstream"? Is the current in
a river constant? Are there places in the water where
the current changes? What happens where the river
bends?

Next, discuss appropriate equations for this problem type.

(a) 1. $BSP + C = BSD$

2. $BSP - C = BSU$

(b) Distance equals rate times time:

1. $D_1 = BSD \times T_1$

2. $D_2 = BSU \times T_2$

3. Are D_1 and D_2 different? Why?

(c) Proper equation instantiation.

1. $D = (BSP + C)T_1$ or $D = (4+C) \cdot 2$

2. $D = (BSP - C)T_2$ or $D = (4-C) \cdot 6$

(d) Proper operations to solve these equations.

Then present additional problems of the river travel category, with a repeat of the discussion above. Vary the problems systematically by:

(a) giving problems similar in structure to the problem above;

(b) making the problem statement more complex, but maintaining students' focus on the relevant equations;

(c) adding new relevant material such as a constant wind speed, or by introducing irrelevant information.

Finally, have the students make up and solve at least one river travel problem of their own.

Lesson Plan 2: Money Problems

> *Objective: To enable students to "set up" and solve coin problems utilizing the semantic information associated with this problem type.*

The teacher should select six to eight "money" problems. Problems should be ordered by difficulty for presentation, and the creation of additional problems by students should be encouraged. Consider the following example.

> *10A.5 Jon has $1.25 in nickels and dimes in his pocket. If the total number of nickels and dimes is twenty, how many nickels does Jon have?*

Elicit, in discussion with the students, the following semantic information:

(a) What coins could be used to make up $1.25 if pennies, nickels, dimes, quarters, and half-dollars are to be used? Make up several examples (5 quarters, 125 pennies, 4 quarters and 5 nickels, . . .).

(b) Formulate some intuitive representations, such as:

$$p + n + d + q + h = nc,$$

where p, n, d, q, and h refer, respectively, to pennies, nickels, dimes, quarters, and half-dollars, and nc is the number of coins.

(c) Which coins are actually used in this problem?

(d) Consider the value of the coins. Use examples such as: How many nickels make thirty cents? (.05n = .30) How many dimes make up $1.30? (.10d = 1.30)

In general, formulate possible value (v) combinations such as .01p + .05n + .10d + .25q + .50d = v.

Next, discuss appropriate equations for this problem type.

(a) n + d = x, where x is the number of coins.

(b) .05n + .10d = v, where v is the value of the coins.

(c) Determine the proper equation instantiation--.05n + .10d = 1.25 and n + d = 20.

(d) Be sure students can perform the correct operations to solve the equations.

Have the students solve several similar coin problems. Ask them to invent some problems; suggest making up an impossible coin problem.

Lesson plans similar to the two above may be constructed for teaching other problem types such as "mixture" problems, "work" problems, and so on.

Consider a final example, the teaching of "age" problems.

Lesson Plan 3: Age Problems

Objective: To enable students to "set up" and solve age problems through the use of semantic information associated with this problem type.

Review the idea of "variables" and how they may be used to represent changing values of numbers--such as the ages of people. Then represent specific "aging" conditions as algebraic expressions, using charts to represent the changes in ages. For example, if Jane is now 6, John 16, and their father 36, then their current and future ages and the relationships among them are:

	Jane	John	Father	
5 years ago	6 − 5	16 − 5	36 − 5	x − 5
current age	6	16	36	x
4 years from now	6 + 4	16 + 4	36 + 4	x + 4
10 years from now	6 + 10	16 + 10	36 + 10	x + 10

From a chart of this nature, it is easy to discern relationships between present and future ages. For example, "Jane's father is now six times Jane's age"; 6·(Jane's age) = (father's age) or "In four years, John will be half as old as his father": (John's age + 4) = 1/2·(father's age + 4).

Write "age problems" for *given* expressions such as x + 7 and 5 + y. Give assignments to groups or individuals that require:

(a) The representation of simple given age situations by algebraic expressions.

(b) The verbal description of simple age situations for which algebraic expressions are given.

(c) The verbal description of simple age situations and representation of the situations with appropriate expressions.

A point deserving particular attention is that of aging uniformity, which should be represented by a chart similar to that above. Discuss uniformity of aging by solving problems such as:

10A.6 *Martha is 12 years old and Bob is 15 years old. How much older than Martha will Bob be in 5 years?*

10A.7 *Tracy was 10 years old when Tony was 8 years old. Now, 5 years later, how much older is Tracy than Tony?*

10A.8 *Faith is 21 years old and Fred is 19 years old. Ten years from now, how much older than Fred will Faith be?*

Represent uniformity of aging with arithmetic or algebraic equations, and ask students individually or in small groups to illustrate uniform aging by writing and solving other similar problems. Require that the students produce a representation by means of arithmetic or algebraic equations.

Within the problem type referred to as "age problems," uniform aging is an example of unstated semantic information which must become part of the student's schema, and which may typically yield an equation. But it should also be noted that the algebraic relationships and algorithmic processes associated with age problems are not fixed: The problem structure may vary from arithmetic expressions to be computed, to single algebraic equations, to simultaneous algebraic equations. Thus, problem structure may vary considerably within the broad classification "problem type."

A notion often overlooked in traditional mathematics textbooks is that of *planning the solution*. Due to similarities in content and structure among problems of a given "type," plans may often be associated with problem types; and possible plans may be included in the schemata which we try to develop in students.

A plan for the "river travel" problem type above should include:

1. A drawing of the situation, presenting Pier A, Pier B, the river, the distance from A to B, the direction of the current, and so on.

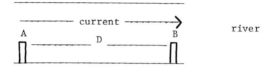

(Note that assumptions and/or idealizations are already being made: e.g., that the river is straight and the current is constant).

2. A statement of relevant quantities such as boat speed, current speed, distance, and time.

3. A statement of general equations relating relevant quantities and directions.

4. An instantiation of the equations with the relevant quantities, again with idealizations (ignoring wind or changeable current, etc.).

5. A solution plan for the equations (e.g., substitution).

6. A means of checking the answers.

Note that with the solution plan, particular *commitments* are made. These are essential to the success of this approach. Plans include commitments to the use of speeds, directions, or other material most important for each problem type. Plans must also include a commitment to the use of certain equations. Most important is correct equation instantiation, which relates the relevant quantities and ignores unnecessary values.

A lesson plan to develop classification and planning skills in problem solving follows. This plan, suggested by the Hinsley, Hayes, and Simon research, may be done in one class session, or preferably its methods may be regularly incorporated into class activities.

Lesson Plan 4: Developing Plans

Select a heterogeneous group of 20-30 word problems. Several problems that students have seen before and some entirely new ones should be included. Put each problem on an individual card.

Ask the students, individually or in small groups, to put the problems into classes by problem type, such as river travel, money, and so on. Check the problem classifications. Are there some problems that defy grouping? Put these in a separate category. Then ask the students, on new cards, to make *general plans* for solving each group of problems. These plans should include:

(a) Appropriate cartoons or drawings.

(b) Assumptions made in each group.

(c) Equations associated with each problem type.

(d) Any clues that might be helpful in equation instantiation.

(e) Any equation-solving information that might be helpful, and

(f) All appropriate checks for each problem type.

The students may then attempt to *use* their plans to solve the given problems.

2. Teaching Non-Routine Problem Solving through Analysis of Structure

The concept of problem structure discussed in Chapter IV is applied here to the teaching of problem-solving skills apart from the problem types of the previous section. The lesson plans in this section consist of games presented to students for *play* and *analysis*. The objectives are for the students (a) to discover the structure of the problems, (b) to relate sets of problems to each other when they have similar structure, and (c) to associate with each problem one or two heuristic processes that may be used in solving that problem. The selection of problems will generally be confined to games already presented in this book. The approach presented here is readily applicable to other games and puzzles.

Table 10A.1 summarizes the problem structures and associated heuristic processes for several selected tasks as they were developed in Chapter IV. From the table and the discussion that follows, clues for generalizable methods of associating problem-solving processes with problem structure are given. These clues suggest the necessity of carefully selecting and analyzing problem tasks prior to classroom presentation *and* the necessity of actual demonstration of the analysis process to the students. The view that experiencing the entire task environment (including false starts, loops, blind alleys, symmetries,

Table 10A.1 *Game Structure and Teaching Heuristic Processes*

Problem	State-Space Representation	Heuristic Process(es)
Pails of Water (cf. Problem 4.1)		
You are at the bank of a river with two pails. The first holds exactly three gallons of water, the second five gallons, and the pails are not marked for measurement in any other way. By filling and emptying pails, or by transferring water from pail to pail, find a way to carry exactly four gallons of water away from the river.	Figure 4.1	Subproblem Decomposition Working Backwards Trial & Error
Missionaries & Cannibals (cf. Problem 4.2)		
Three missionaries and three cannibals are on one bank of a river, with a rowboat that will hold at most two people. How can they cross to the other side of the river, in such a manner that missionaries are never outnumbered by cannibals on either riverbank?	Figure 4.2	Trial & Error Working Backwards (Utilization of Forward-Backward Symmetry) Subproblem Decomposition
Missionaries & Cannibals, One Rower (cf. Problem 4.3)		
(Same as above, with the additional condition that only one cannibal knows how to row.)	Figure 4.3	Trial & Error Working Backwards Related Problem
Jealous Husbands (cf. Problem 4.9)		
Three husbands and their wives are on one bank of a river, with a rowboat that will hold at most two people. How can they cross in such a manner that no wife is ever in the presence of a man other than her husband on either riverbank, unless her husband is also present?	Figure 4.8	Trial & Error Working Backwards Related Problem
Tick-tack-toe		
The opposing players alternately mark their choices of vacant positions in the 3x3 game diagram with X's and O's respectively. The goal is to obtain possession of three squares in a row, horizontally, vertically or diagonally.	Figure 4.9	Symmetry

continued

Table 10A.1 *(continued)*

Problem	State-Space Representation	Heuristic Process(es)
Number Scrabble (cf. Problem 4.6)		
The integers 1,2,...,9 are written on slips of paper. The opposing players take turns, each selecting one number at a time. Neither player may select a number already taken. The goal is to obtain exactly three numbers adding to fifteen.	Figure 4.6(a) [isomorphism]	Symmetry Related Problem
Jam (cf. Problem 4.7)		
The two players have different colored pencils. Each in turn colors a straight line in the given diagram along its entire length. The goal is to obtain three lines in ones own color intersecting at a single point.	Figure 4.6(b) [isomorphism]	Symmetry Related Problem

Tower of Hanoi (cf. Problem 4.11)

	State-Space Representation	Heuristic Process(es)
Four concentric rings are placed in order of size, the smallest at the top, on the first of three pegs. The goal is to transfer all of the rings from the first peg to the third in a minimum number of moves. Only one ring may be moved at a time, and no larger ring may be placed above a smaller one on any peg. (The problem generalizes to n rings.)	Figures 4.12 and 4.15.	Subproblem Decomposition Symmetry Generalization Recursion

Tower of Hanoi board

Tea Ceremony (cf. Problem 7C.1)

	State-Space Representation	Heuristic Process(es)
A host, an elder, and a youth participate in the ceremony. They perform four tasks, listed in ascending order of importance: feeding the fire, serving cakes, serving tea, and reading poetry. The host performs all the tasks at the outset; the tasks are transferred back and forth among the participants until they are all performed by the youth. Only one task--the least important a person is performing--may be moved at a time, and no one may receive a new task unless it is less important than any he is then performing. The goal is to transfer the tasks from host to youth in the fewest moves possible.	Same as Tower of Hanoi [isomorphism]	Subproblem Decomposition Symmetry Generalization Related Problem

and so on) is an essential part of learning problem-solving processes is implicit in the lesson plans. Explicit discussion of *which* heuristic processes are appropriate for a given problem, and *why*, is essential to this method.

Lesson Plan 5: Tick-tack-toe (I)

Divide the class into groups of four students. Give each group the task of analyzing tick-tack-toe (naughts and crosses). This will perhaps best be done by having each group play the game, two students against the other two. The object of the task is to discover winning and drawing strategies. This can be done by keeping fixed for one group the use of the symbol "X" and first move; the other group should throughout play use "0" and take the second move. Paper and pencil should be used to record and test different strategies. It can take more than half an hour for groups of students to analyze even a well-known game such as tick-tack-toe (Gardner, 1959a).

Ask each group of students to prepare a short analysis of the problem. They might break their analysis into (1) strategies for player with first move, and (2) strategies for player with second move.

Then ask several groups of students to present their strategies and analyses of tick-tack-toe. If help is needed, hint at the *symmetry* in the problem. Ask such questions as (1) How many different first moves are there? and (2) How many are *essentially* different? Strategies may take the form of rules such as: (1) "If I am second and first move takes the center, I must take a corner (any corner) to avoid losing," or (2) "If I am first, my best move is the center or the corner, because ..." Make a compilation of these rules from the students.

Answers to the following should be obtained by the end of the activity:

1. How many possible first moves are there in tick-tack-toe? (9) How many different (i.e., unique) first moves are there? (3; a corner, a side, and the center.)

2. How many unique second moves are there for each first move? For example, if first move is the center, there are only *two* different responses, a corner or a side.

The point should be made that strategies for winning (or not losing) are built on the previous two points. It is nearly impossible (for humans) to understand and successfully play tick-tack-toe without strategies built upon these. Discuss (1) and (2) above and the notion of *symmetries* in the problem. Describe how "different" states of the problem environment may be "equivalent" by symmetry.

Lesson Plan 6: Tick-tack-toe (II)

Divide the class into groups of four students each. Introduce "Number Scrabble" as presented in Table 10A.1. Let students oppose each other in the play of Number Scrabble; have them (as with tick-tack-toe) analyze this game and prepare sets of winning strategies.

Ask each group of students to write out a set of strategies for playing Number Scrabble. What should the first player do to win? Is a win guaranteed for either player? Are there strategies for drawing? If students have trouble analyzing Number Scrabble, have them proceed as follows:

1. Fix the first selected number (say 5).

2. What responses are there to this first selected number?

3. What responses are there to the combination of moves described above?

4. Can strategies be based on even numbers or odd numbers?

If students are having trouble analyzing Number Scrabble, ask them to figure out all of the different combinations of three numbers that add to 15. These are, after all, the *goal* combinations. They might get an array like this:

2 + 9 + 4	2 + 5 + 8	2 + 7 + 6	3 + 5 + 7
1 + 8 + 6	4 + 5 + 6	8 + 3 + 4	1 + 5 + 9

Have student try to arrange this array to show how many times or ways each number may be used to arrive at a goal. For example, if 5 is picked by the first player, only four possible sum combinations remain for the second player.

If the students cannot discover an arrangement of the array, suggest the "magic square" arrangement as presented in Figure 4.6(a). What patterns now emerge?

The following points should be made:

1. How many unique first moves are there? (three: an even number, 5, or an odd number excluding 5.)

2. How many unique responses to each different first move are there?

3. Discover the tick-tack-toe and Number Scrabble isomorphism. Use this relationship to help describe winning strategies.

4. Discuss hidden problem symmetry, and states equivalent by symmetry.

Lesson Plan 7: Tick-tack-toe (III)

Divide students into groups of four. Introduce "Jam" as presented in Table 10A.1, and let students oppose each other in the play of Jam. Again ask the students to discover winning strategies. "What is the best first move? Which line(s) go through the most points? How is the game related to tick-tack-toe?"

If students have trouble discovering winning strategies with Jam, suggest the procedures of the preceding lesson plans, and finally point out the isomorphism to tick-tack-toe (see Figure 4.6(b)). Ask the students to seek answers to questions such as: (1) How are the ways of winning in tick-tack-toe and the eight dots in Jam related? and (2) How do the nine (distinct) first moves in tick-tack-toe relate to the lines in Jam?

Lesson Plan 8: The Missionary-Cannibal Problem (I)

The students may work as individuals or within small groups. Give them the missionary-cannibal problem (Table 10A.1) to solve, and have each student use pencil and paper to record all moves.

Discuss problem *representation* and the missionary-cannibal problem. Have the students draw their own "map" of the situation. Perhaps it will take this form:

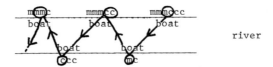

river

Eventually the students should describe and create for themselves the complete state-space representation of this problem (Figure 4.2).

Discuss the strategies which are helpful in solving the missionary-cannibal problem. Ask students to attempt each of the following strategies, and then discuss them: (1) divide the problem into subproblems; (2) work backwards from the goal; (3) trial and error (with and without backing up). Attempt to determine how appropriate each strategy is for the problem.

Lesson Plan 9: The Missionary-Cannibal Problem (II)

Give the students the missionary-cannibal problem for analysis, with the constraint that only one cannibal can row the boat. Have the students work in small groups or as individuals as they "play" and analyze the game.

Discuss the problem representation of this version of the problem. It is necessary to single out, by means of a special symbol, the one cannibal that can row.

Again have students construct, by trial-and-error, the complete state-space representation of the problem (Figure 4.3). Compare the state-space representation of this lesson with that developed in the immediately preceding lesson. Discuss again the three strategies mentioned above.

An additional lesson plan related to these problems can easily be developed using the "Jealous Husbands" problem (Table 10A.1). Then consider the missionary-cannibal problem again, and ask what would happen if the constraint that "missionaires are never outnumbered by cannibals on either riverbank (for fear of the missionaries being eaten)" is replaced by the constraint that "cannibals are never outnumbered by missionaries on either riverbank (for fear of the cannibals being converted)." How would this change affect the state-space representation? The solution strategies?

Ask students to create further isomorphs for the missionary-cannibal and the Jealous Husbands problems. Discuss the state-space representations and successful solution strategies for these new problems.

Lesson Plan 10: The Water Transfer Problem

Present students with the "Pails of Water" problem as given in Table 10A.1. Have them work in small groups or individually as they solve and analyze the problem.

Devise a representation for the sequence of steps in solving this problem. After the students have constructed their own state-space representation, let them compare it with that given in Chapter IV (Figure 4.1).

Discuss the following strategies for solving this problem: (1) the trial-and-error approach; (2) working backwards from the goal; (3) dividing the problem into subproblems.

Now change the problem so that the pails hold six and ten gallons. Can you get a measure of eight gallons? How does this problem relate to the first one? Will the same strategy work on each problem? How are the state-spaces of the two problems related?

Could pails of six and ten gallons be used to get a final pail of three gallons? If so, how? Is this problem related to the two problems discussed already in this lesson?

Lesson Plan 11: The Tower of Hanoi (I)

The objective for this lesson is the analysis of the four-ring Tower of Hanoi problem. The students may work as individuals or in small groups. If possible, give the students the Tower of Hanoi game boards for use during their analysis. Alternatively, students may easily make a Tower of Hanoi game by cutting four seriated circles of paper and placing them over three X's marking the posts.

Let the students play the Tower of Hanoi game and have them devise a sequence for transferring the four rings from peg A to peg C in the least number of moves. Then present the students with a state-space representation of the Tower puzzle (Figure 4.12). Have them verify the representation to their own satisfaction. Have them sketch their solution attempts as *paths* through the state-space representation.

Then analyze solution strategies for the four-ring Tower of Hanoi puzzle. How does trial-and-error work as a strategy? Can you work the problem backwards from the goal? How may the problem be divided usefully into subproblems? Is this an efficient method of solution? Are there any other strategies?

Lesson Plan 12: The Tower of Hanoi Problem (II)

Introduce the "Tea Ceremony" problem as shown in Table 10A.1. Have the students work individually or in small groups as they solve and analyze this problem. Have them devise a state-space representation for the Tea Ceremony problem. Suggestions should be given for labelling states and moves.

Compare the state-space representations of the Tower of Hanoi and the Tea Ceremony puzzles. How are they similar? The students should be able to establish that these two problems are themselves isomorphic. The solution strategies of either problem should be translated into equivalent strategies for the other.

Finally, the class should try to construct another isomorph of the Tower of Hanoi and the Tea Ceremony problems.

3. Conclusions

Two very different applications of the analysis of problem structure to classroom teaching have been developed. The first is based on the content and structure characteristics associated with the classification of routine problems into "types" (see also Chapter III). The second is based on the explicit (state-space) analysis of non-routine problems and games, as developed in Chapter IV. In both applications, we have observed how explicit attention to problem structure variables may assist in teaching insightful problem solving in the classroom.

X.

Structure and Heuristic Behavior Variables in Teaching

B.

Heuristic Behavior Variables in Instruction

by

Alan H. Schoenfeld
Mathematics Department
Hamilton College
Clinton, New York*

1. Introduction

As we have seen in Chapter V, there are quite a number of valuable heuristic approaches to problem solving in mathematics. There is also mounting evidence that careful instruction in problem solving *via* heuristic strategies can not only provide an opportunity for stimulating classroom discussion, but can demonstrably enhance students' problem-solving performance (Goldberg, 1975; Landa, 1974; Lucas, 1972; Schoenfeld, 1978). Unfortunately, the mastery of individual problem-solving techniques is not enough to make for good problem-solving performance; when there are a number of potentially useful heuristic processes to try on a problem and only one or two of them will help to solve it, the ability to select the right process will be a factor of critical importance in problem-solving performance.

We may make the following analogy. If we think of a problem as a "lock" and of the appropriate heuristic process as the "key" to that lock, the art of problem solving *via* heuristic processes is the art of finding the right "key" for a particular lock (and then using it, of course). If there were only a few keys, there would not be much of a problem; one could try all of them, until one that "fits" is discovered. Imagine, however, that there are a large number of keys. If there is no means for selecting the "right" key from among them, one might very easily squander an enormous amount of time trying the "wrong" keys. One might run out of time before finding the "right" one, or might give up in frustration over a series of unsuccessful attempts. In practical terms, then, the problem solver must

a) know how to use the right "keys," and

b) be able to select the "right key" efficiently.

---

*This work was supported by a Sloan Foundation Grant while the author was at The Group in Science and Mathematics Education, U. C., Berkeley.

This chapter is devoted to a discussion of these two goals. We shall address the following two major questions about problem solving in mathematics *via* heuristics approaches:

1) What instruction must the teacher provide, so that the student has the capacity to use an heuristic process correctly, when the student knows that it should be used?

2) How can the teacher help provide the student with information which will help the student select the appropriate heuristic approaches to particular problems or classes of problems?

As we saw in Chapters I and V, heuristic processes have two aspects. On the one hand, we find an heuristic process defined as "a general suggestion or strategy, independent of any particular topic or subject matter, which helps problem solvers approach, understand, and/or efficiently marshall their resources in solving problems" (Schoenfeld, in press). This would seem to make the application of heuristic processes independent of the nature of the problems to which they are applied. On the other hand, McClintock emphasizes in Chapter V that there often inheres in particular problems or classes of problems an amenability to approach by particular heuristic processes.

We shall see that these two perspectives on heuristic behavior give rise to two classes of heuristic processes, both of which can help the teacher to approach question (2) above. Those problems, or classes of problems, which give signs of being amenable to particular approaches may be said to "cue" the reader to the use of those processes; the approaches taken may then be called "cued heuristic processes." If the teacher can recognize these "cues" and pass them on to students, the students can then have a direct means for selecting the right "keys" for particular problems. This provides a direct and practical application of the themes discussed in Chapter V; we will discuss it at length, with examples, here. Now the question is: What about those tasks which do not cue specific heuristic processes? Is the student then left merely with a collection of potentially applicable heuristic processes from which to choose randomly? Fortunately, the answer is "no." We shall see that, in the absence of "cueing," heuristic processes often cluster consistently into groups which are usually applied at particular *stages* of problem solutions. There are "understanding the problem" heuristic processes, "checking the solution" processes, and many others.

Since the choice of these processes depends on the stage of the problem solution, we shall call these *stage heuristic processes*. At any stage of a problem solution, only a subset of potentially useful heuristic behaviors is likely to be appropriate; thus the result of focusing on stage processes is to allow for focusing on that set of processes most likely to be of assistance. In terms of our analogy, it allows for the selection of a reasonably-sized subset of "keys" having the greatest chance of "unlocking" a problem.

We shall provide a discussion of "stage" processes, and a framework for teaching them, at the conclusion of this chapter. We proceed with a discussion of question (1): What instruction must the teacher provide, so that the student has the capacity to use an individual heuristic process correctly, given that the student knows that it should be used?

2. Teaching Particular Heuristic Processes

It is easy to underestimate the complexity of individual heuristic processes, and to underestimate as well the amount of effort which must be invested in teaching any particular heuristic process before one can expect students to use it competently and reliably. In Sections 3 and 4 of this chapter, we discuss a variety of heuristic processes. In this section, we shall focus on one particular process at some length. Our purpose is to indicate some of the complexities which may be hidden in apparently simple statements of processes, and to point to the care which must be taken in teaching them. The heuristic process selected for this discussion is perhaps of "average" complexity. There are simpler ones, some of which are discussed in Section 3; but there are also many substantially more difficult heuristic processes.

The following heuristic process will henceforth be referred to as the *special cases* process:

If you do not feel that you have a solid grasp on what the problem asks of you, or of what the answer might be, consider a variety of special cases. You can often "discover" the answer, or see a pattern that suggests how to obtain it.

Each of the following five problems can be approached by use of the *special cases* process.

10B.1 *Find the sum of the series $S = 1 + 3 + 5 + 7 + \cdots + (2n-1)$ and prove that your answer is correct.*

10B.2 *Let $P(x) = ax^2 + bx + c$ and $Q(x) = cx^2 + bx + a$, where a, b, and c are non-zero. What is the relationship between the roots of $P(x) = 0$ and $Q(x) = 0$? Prove your answer.*

10B.3 *Two squares, each of length s on a side, are placed so that the corner of one square lies on the center of the other, as shown. Describe in terms of s the range of possible areas representing the intersection of the two squares.*

10B.4 *Prove that in a circle, the central angle which*
subtends a given arc is twice as large as any
inscribed angle which subtends the same arc. That
is, show that in the diagram, B = 2A.

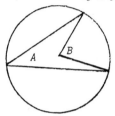

10B.5 *Of all the rectangles which have perimeter 40, which*
has the largest area?

Let us examine the way in which the *special cases* heuristic process is used in the solution of each of these five problems. In
Problem *10B.1*, to consider special cases means to compute the desired
sum for values of n = 1, 2, 3, 4, and so on until a pattern is dis-
cernible. The calculations appear as follows:

$$1 = 1,$$
$$1 + 3 = 4,$$
$$1 + 3 + 5 = 9,$$
$$1 + 3 + 5 + 7 = 16,$$

and at this point, the student might guess the next entry,

$$1 + 3 + 5 + 7 + 9 = 25,$$

as the pattern of squares on the right becomes clear. Having "discovered" that the sum of the first n odd numbers is n^2, the problem
solver can proceed to verify it by induction.

The application of the *special cases* process is quite different
in Problem *10B.2*. The initial temptation in this problem, prompted by
the phrase "the roots of P(x) = 0 and Q(x) = 0," is to look for a relationship between

$$\frac{-b \pm \sqrt{b^2 - 4ac}}{2a} \quad \text{and} \quad \frac{-b \pm \sqrt{b^2 - 4ac}}{2c},$$

a temptation to which the vast majority of problem solvers (both expert
and novice) examined by this author have succumbed. The relationship,
however, is obscure. If, on the other hand, one uses the *special cases*
process in the following way, the answer becomes apparent. Choosing
as special cases two or three polynomials which are easily factored,
one finds that:

the roots of $x^2 - 5x + 6 = 0$ are 2 and 3; those of $6x^2 - 5x + 1 = 0$ are $\frac{1}{2}$ and $\frac{1}{3}$;

the roots of $x^2 + 7x + 12 = 0$ are -4 and -3; those of $12x^2 + 7x + 1 = 0$ are $-\frac{1}{4}$ and $-\frac{1}{3}$."

the roots of $x^2 - 3x - 10 = 0$ are 5 and -2; those of $-10x^2 - 3x + 1 = 0$ are $\frac{1}{5}$ and $-\frac{1}{2}$.

It is not hard to see that the roots of $Q(x) = 0$ are the reciprocals of the roots of $P(x) = 0$ in each case. With a little more work, the argument can be completed. We shall return to this problem at the end of this section.

In Problem *10B.3*, one uses the *special cases* process to help one "suspect" the correct answer. There are two special cases which are easy to calculate: the case where the sides of the two squares are parallel, and the case where a side of the second square passes through a corner of the first. After examining these, one might suspect that the answer, as it is here, is always $s^2/4$. If one notices the symmetry of the two special cases, one might see that there is a symmetry argument to prove the general case (see Figure 10B.1).

In Problem *10B.4*, the application of *special cases* once again takes on a different form. The relationship between the angles A and B in Figure 10B.4 is elusive. If, however, one looks at a particular case, the case in which one side of the inscribed angle is a diameter of the circle, the relationship is clear (Figure 10B.2). Furthermore, it is easy to use the special case to establish the truth of the general case. A more complete discussion of this problem may be found on pages 104-106 of Polya's *Mathematical Discovery, Vol. I* (Polya, 1962).

Finally, in Problem *10B.5* a variety of special cases which range from short and wide rectangles (say 19 x 1) through "squarish" rectangles and then through tall and narrow ones (say 1 x 19), will provide students with an experiential basis for believing that the square is the answer. In later problem solving, this experiential foundation can provide a "real-world" check against some incorrect answers introduced by computational procedures.

We have seen, then, that the applications of the *special cases* heuristic process are many and varied. There is not nearly enough information in the given statement of the process to provide for all of these interpretations; rather, the statement is a convenient *label* for a set of similar procedures. If we expect students to be able to use the process, it will have to be illustrated by diverse examples, in much the way it has been here. In addition, students will have to be taught any heuristic process with the same degree of seriousness and attention that would be used with any other topic: the quadratic formula, for example. This means in particular that the heuristic

Figure 10B.1 *Diagrams for Problem 10B.3*

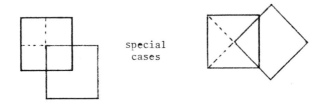

special
cases

the "general"
case

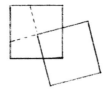

Figure 10B.2 *A Special Case for Problem 10B.4*

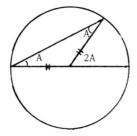

process should be explicitly *labeled* as an important technique
("Examining *special cases* is a valuable problem-solving technique.
You should consider it when..."); its description should be written
in full on the blackboard and stressed; examples of its use in various
ways should be provided and students should be given practice in applying it to problems; students should be reminded to use it whenever it
is appropriate on their homework and "scolded" when they do not; and
when the process is used to advantage in the classroom, its use should
be pointed out. With less training than this, we would not expect
students to become proficient in their use of the quadratic formula;
with less training, we cannot expect them to apply any heuristic process well.

Finally, we should stress the difference between the *process* and
the *product* of problem solving, and the different emphases to which
these lead in instruction. The *product* of mathematical thinking is
the *solution* to a problem, usually explained in logical and coherent
form. As such it can be elegant and mathematically correct, but show
little trace of the reasoning which produced it. For example, the
following might be a textbook proof that the roots of $P(x) = ax^2 + bx + c = 0$
and $Q(x) = cx^2 + bx + a = 0$ are reciprocals (see the discussion of Problem
10B.2):

"Suppose that x_0 is a root of $P(x) = 0$, or that $ax_0^2 + bx_0 + c = 0$
Since $c \neq 0$, $x_0 \neq 0$. Now

$$Q(\frac{1}{x_0}) = c(\frac{1}{x_0})^2 + b(\frac{1}{x_0}) + a = \frac{c}{x_0^2} + \frac{bx_0}{x_0^2} + \frac{ax_0^2}{x_0^2} =$$

$$\frac{ax_0^2 + bx_0 + c}{x_0^2} = \frac{0}{x_0^2} = 0,$$

since we know that $x_0 \neq 0$. Thus if x_0 is a root of $P(x) = 0$, $\frac{1}{x_0}$ is a root
of $Q(x) = 0$; and the roots of the two equations are reciprocals."

This algebraic *tour de force* is impressive and incontrovertibly
correct, but inaccessible to all but the few students who can figure
out where it comes from. If we expect students to be able to construct
an argument such as this, we will have to teach them the process that
leads up to the argument; even better, we should guide them to create
the argument themselves. For this problem, a classroom discussion might
begin with students factoring the special cases discussed for Problem
10B.2, and conjecturing that the roots of the equations are reciprocals.
At that point, the class and teacher can together translate the conjecture into an algebraic argument. Perhaps the idealized discussion would
proceed something like this:

Teacher: "We can have guessed that the roots of $P(x) = 0$ and $Q(x) = 0$
are reciprocals. Can someone put that into a form
that we can prove, such as, 'if something is true,
then something else is true?'"

Student: "How about 'If a number is a root of $P(x) = 0$, then its reciprocal is a root of $Q(x) = 0$'."

Teacher: "That's good, but working with words is difficult. Can you translate the words 'number' and 'reciprocal' into symbols we can use?"

Student: "Yes. We can try to prove that if x_0 is a root of $P(x) = 0$, then $1/x_0$ is a root of $Q(x) = 0$."

Teacher: "Very good. Now, what does it mean for x_0 to be a root of $P(x) = 0$?"

Student: "It means that $P(x_0) = 0$."

Teacher: "How can we use that in your last statement?"

Student: "We can try to prove that if $P(x_0) = 0$, then $Q(1/x_0) = 0$."

At this point the proof given above fits into a nice context, and "makes sense"; the student can understand where it came from and why one might think of it.

3. Cues Associated with Heuristic Processes in Problem Solving

In this section we shall discuss some "cued" heuristic processes. More precisely, we shall discuss certain classes of problems which are amenable to particular heuristic approaches, and contain indications of that amenability in their problem statements or problem structures. A recognition of such cues will enable the knowledgeable problem solver to select an appropriate approach to a problem with dispatch, thus making the entire problem-solving process more efficient. By systematically identifying such cues both in particular mathematical subject areas and problem solving in general, and passing the cues on to students with the kind of training that was discussed in Section 2, the teacher can substantially enhance students' problem-solving performance. Let us study some examples.

10B.6 *What is the sum of the series*

$$S = \frac{1}{1 \cdot 2} + \frac{1}{2 \cdot 3} + \ \cdots \ + \frac{1}{(n)(n+1)} \quad ?$$

Prove your answer.

10B.7 *Let S be a set which contains n elements. How many different subsets of S are there, including the empty set?*

The reader experienced at "exploiting similar problems" may immediately note the parallels between Problems *10B.6* and *10B.1*, and propose a similar heuristic approach. For students who see the problem out of context, however, it is not at all clear that mathematical induction is the appropriate means of approaching the problem. In a course recently given by the author, six of eight undergraduate mathematics and science majors failed to solve *10B.6* when it was assigned, and five of seven students with similar backgrounds failed to solve this problem in a problem-solving experiment conducted by the author (Schoenfeld, to appear). In that experiment, after working 20 problems, four of which were similar to *10B.6*, the seven students were given *10B.7*. None of the three "control" students solved it. All of the "experimental" students, who had had similar practice but in addition a list of heuristic processes including the one described below, solved *10B.7*. The problems just given all yield to the following *cued* heuristic process:

If there is an integer parameter, look for an inductive argument (Cued induction).

Is there an "n" or other parameter in the formula which takes on integer values? If so, this is the *cue* which should suggest the use of mathematical induction. To find a formula for f(n), one might try one of these:

A) Calculate f(1), f(2), f(3), f(4), f(5); list them in order, and see if there is a pattern. If there is, it might be verified by induction. (Note the use of *special cases.)*

B) See what happens as you pass from n objects to n + 1. If you can tell how to pass from f(n) to f(n +1), you may build up f(n) inductively.

Prototypic examples for the use of *cued induction* are easy to find; we have seen Problems *10B.1*, *10B.6*, *10B.7*, and can add these:

10B.8 How many different straight lines (at most) can be drawn through n points in the plane?

10B.9 Prove that the term $2^n 3^{2n} - 1$ is evenly divisible by 17, for any positive integer n.

This collection of five problems could serve as the basis for a class hour devoted to *cued induction*. The first three problems illustrate the use of technique (A). We have seen the pattern in *10B.1* and the inductive proof is easy; the pattern is almost as clear in *10B.6* (the answer is n/(n+1) and the argument by induction is straightforward; the answer to *10B.7*, 2^n, also emerges as a clear pattern. The argument by induction in Problem *10B.7* and the remaining two problems, can be used to illustrate the use of technique (B).

In Problem *10B.7*, assume that a set with n elements has 2^n subsets. Now we may ask what happens if we add an $(n+1)$st object, called X. For each subset we had before, we now have two: the subset by itself, and the subset augmented by X. Thus the number of subsets has doubled, giving us $2 \cdot 2^n = 2^{n+1}$, which is what we wanted to show.

In Problem *10B.8*, we can ask the following: suppose there are f(n) lines through n points. How many lines are added when the $(n+1)$st is added? The answer is easy to see (draw a diagram): there is one new line from the new point to each of the n points already there. Thus $f(n+1) = f(n) + n$. Since $f(2) = 1$, $f(3) = 1 + 2$, $f(4) = 1 + 2 + 3$, and in general $f(n+1) = 1 + 2 + 3 + \ldots + n$. Again by induction, the sum is $\frac{1}{2} n(n + 1)$.

The application of induction to Problem *10B.9* is slightly different. First, the problem is simplified if one recognizes that $2^n 3^{2n}$ can be written as $2^n \cdot 9^n = 18^n$; the problem can then be restated as "Prove that $18^n - 1$ is always divisible by 17." This can be proven without induction if one recalls that $x^n - 1$ always has a factor of $(x-1)$, but it is instructive to demonstrate the inductive proof. The problem, using (B), is: "If $18^n - 1$ is divisible by 17, how can we show that $18^{n+1} - 1$ is divisible by 17?" The latter term will be divisible by 17 if and only if the difference is; and since the difference is

$$(18^{n+1} - 1) - (18^n - 1) = 18^{n+1} - 18^n = 18^n (18 - 1) = 18^n(17),$$

we have the result that we want. Incidentally, it would be best to show students *both* of the arguments which solve Problem *10B.9*, and, in general, as many ways to view a problem as possible. One can never predict which method of solution to a problem will prove useful when one encounters a "similar related problem," and it is valuable to have both a large repertoire of techniques and the flexibility that one can derive from it. At the same time, however, we should be careful to note that "cued induction" does not always "work"; in spite of its similarity to Problem *10B.6*, there is no known simple expression for the sum

$$\frac{1}{1^2} + \frac{1}{2^2} + \ldots + \frac{1}{n^2} .$$

Our discussion of cued induction has been protracted in order to present a model of a classroom session for those who might consider devoting a day to it. The discussion of other cued heuristic processes will be more condensed. Whether or not one would actually choose to devote a class session to a discussion of cued induction would depend on a number of factors including the nature of the curriculum, time pressures, and so on. Even if one cannot take a day to discuss the process, it should be clear that, when problems such as these arise in the classroom, it is worth using them as prototypes and stressing the use of the process in general. The process is easily recognized and enhances student performance when used. With that, we turn to the next cued heuristic process.

Consider a similar problem with fewer variables.

If the problem has a large number of variables and is too confusing to deal with comfortably, construct and solve a similar problem with fewer variables. You may then be able to:

A) Adapt the method of solution to the more complex problem, or

B) Take the result of the simpler problem and build up from there.

Prototype examples for the *fewer variables* heuristic process are the following:

10B.10 *Prove that if* $a^2 + b^2 + c^2 + d^2 = ab + bc + cd + da$, *then*

$a = b = c = d$, *and*

10B.11 *Prove that for positive real numbers* x, y, z,

$$\frac{(x^2 + 1)(y^2 + 1)(z^2 + 1)}{xyz} \geq 8.$$

The *cue* for these processes is the presence of several variables, all of which enter symmetrically into the problem. In Problem *10B.10*, the profusion of symbols makes it difficult to see what is happening. The analogous two-variable problem, in view of the fact that the right-hand side of the equation is cyclic, is: Prove that if $a^2 + b^2 = ab + ba$, then $a = b$. This is easy, of course. Moving all the terms to the left and factoring, we obtain $(a - b)^2 = 0$, which gives us the desired result. Now the question is: how can this be exploited in the original problem? Since we will need that $a = b$, $b = c$, $c = d$ (and perhaps because the equation is cyclic, $d = a$ in good measure), and will need all of that information in *one* equation, our hope is that the method of the similar problem will work here and give us an equation like

$$(a - b)^2 + (b - c)^2 + (c - d)^2 + (d - a)^2 = 0.$$

Fortunately, it does.

In Problem *10B.11*, there is again a morass of symbols. Since x, y, and z all play the same role on the left and we have three similar products, it is reasonable to examine the one-variable problem "prove that $\frac{x^2 + 1}{x} \geq 2$." This is easy to prove--by algebra [$x^2 + 1 \geq 2x$ if and only if $(x - 1)^2 \geq 0$] or by calculus. Substituting y and z for x and taking the product gives the desired result.

One can build understanding in other ways as well. For example:

10B.12 Prove that for p, q, r, and s between 0 and 1

$$(1-p)(1-q)(1-r)(1-s) > 1-p-q-r-s.$$

The appropriate place to start is by showing that

$$(1-p)(1-q) > 1-p-q.$$

Multiplying both sides of this equation by $(1-r)$ and comparing terms will yield the three-variable version of the inequality, and multiplying both sides of that by $(1-s)$ and comparing terms will give the desired result.

Again, whether or not one has the time or desire to devote a class day to this process is an individual matter. But when problems such as these occur in the classroom, it is easy and beneficial for the teacher to point out to the students that what they are seeing is not an isolated "trick," but rather a coherent process which was "cued" by the form of the problem, and which the students themselves can learn to recognize and use.

Develop an argument by contradiction or contraposition (cued contraposition).

Consider argument by contradiction or contraposition, if:

(A) There is either an explicit or implicit "negative" conclusion in the problem statement, or

(B) The conclusion is not at all apparent from what is given, and one obtains more to "work with" by negating the conclusion, or

(C) The word *unique* appears in the conclusion.

Contradiction and contraposition are more than forms of argument. They are means of heuristic thinking which allow for the restructuring of problems in equivalent but sometimes more accessible formulations. Often (though certainly not always) there are cues in the problem statement which lead one to suspect that this type of argument might be appropriate.

The following problems are prototypes for the *cued contraposition* heuristic process:

10B.13 Prove that there is an infinite number of primes.

10B.14 Show that the roots of $P(x) = x^3 + 6x^2 + 11x + 2 = 0$ are all negative.

10B.15 Let P_1 and P_2 be <u>consecutive</u> prime numbers greater
than 2. If

$$Q = 1/2(P_1 + P_2),$$

prove that Q must be composite.

10B.16 Show that the identity element in a group is unique.

In Problems 10B.13-14 there are, respectively, implicit and explicit
negatives in the desired conclusions. In the first, "infinite" means
"not finite." If we turn the question around and ask, "What if there
were only a finite number of primes," we have the beginning of one of
the most famous proofs in mathematics. It appears in Euclid's *Elements*,
and is more than two thousand years old.* Similarly, we can turn the
question in 10B.14 around, and ask "What if we had a non-negative number
x which satisfied the equation?" Since any power of x is positive or
zero,

$$x^3 + 6x^2 + 11x + 2 = 0$$

means (a sum of non-negative terms, plus 2) = 0

   or
    (a number greater than or equal to 2) = 0,

which is impossible.

In Problem 10B.15, there is very little information to go on. We
want to show that Q is composite, meaning that we need to find a factor
of it. But where would a factor of Q possibly come from? Recognizing
this, we might ask: what if Q is *not* composite? Q is then a prime
number. Being the average of P_1 and P_2, Q is thus a prime which lies
between P_1 and P_2. Thus P_1 and P_2 cannot be consecutive primes.

We can *almost* formulate the response to Problem 10B.16 as part of a
general rule: "If one is asked to demonstrate that something with a
given property is unique, one should assume that there are two distinct
objects with that property and demonstrate that they must be identical
or that there is a contradiction." In this case, picking two distinct
identities e_1 and e_2 leads to the argument $e_1 = e_1(e_2) = (e_1)e_2 = e_2$.

The last problem in this section is the following:

10B.17 For what values of t does the system of simultaneous
equations
$$\left. \begin{array}{c} x^2 - y^2 = 0 \\ (x-t)^2 + y^2 = 1 \end{array} \right\}$$ *have either 0, 1, 2, 3, 4, or 5
solutions?*

---

*If there were only finitely many primes P_1, P_2, ..., P_n, then the number
$(P_1 P_2 P_3 \cdots P_n + 1)$, being larger than P_n, is composite, but none of the
primes $P_1, P_2, ... P_n$ are factors of it, a contradiction.

Figure 10B.3 *Graphs for Problem 10B.17*

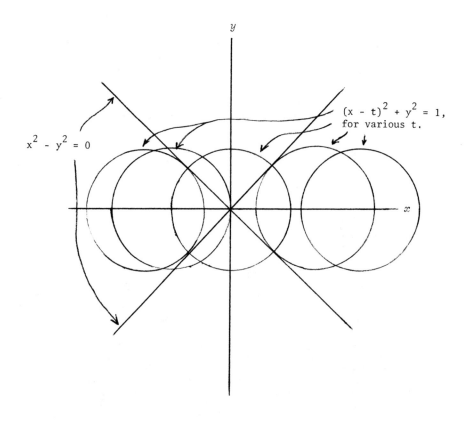

$(x - t)^2 + y^2 = 1$,
for various t.

$x^2 - y^2 = 0$

The algebraic solution to this problem is quite complex and often causes computational difficulties even for experienced mathematicians. The analysis is straightforward, however, if one thinks to use the following cued process.

Draw graphs of simple algebraic expressions (Cued Graphing)

(This is a special case of the general heuristic process *Draw a diagram if at all possible.*)

The graph of the first equation is a pair of straight lines passing through the origin at 45° angles to the x-axis; the graph of the second is a circle of radius 1 with center $(t,0)$. The only difficult point is in determining the value of t at which the circle is tangent to the two lines, $t = \sqrt{2}$ (see Fig. 10B.3).

The cue for graphing in this case is the presence of the equations, both of which can be interpreted graphically with ease. As is the case with other heuristic processes, the presence of the "cue" does not necessarily mean that recourse to the heuristic approach will "work," but merely that the approach should be considered. There are many problems for which graphing might be considered superfluous, but many like *10B.17* in which it is helpful.

Finally, we should point out that the above represent a sampling of the opportunities for classroom discussions about heuristic processes. There are a large number of "cues" to which we respond, sometimes unconsciously, while doing mathematics. If the teacher can keep an eye on his or her own problem solving, and try to recognize *why* he or she is doing what is being done and what stimulated it, this self-examination can yield valuable information to pass on to students.

4. "Stage" Heuristic Variables in Instruction

While there is a substantial class of "cued" heuristic behaviors, as we have seen in Section 3, there are a great many problems (the vast majority) for which there either are no such standard cues, or for which we have not discovered standard cues. In order to simplify the process of selecting appropriate heuristic approaches to problems, we introduce the notion of *"stage" heuristic processes.* The idea, in brief, is this:

All other factors being equal, certain families of heuristic processes are most likely to be of assistance in problem solving at particular stages in problem solution.

To develop this idea, we present an elaboration and clarification of the four-stage scheme (understanding the problem, devising a plan, carrying out the plan, looking back) presented by Polya and described in Figure 1.1. We examine some of the heuristic behaviors discussed in Chapters V and VIII.B, and array them in such a way as to be useful in instruction. The arrangement varies somewhat from that given in earlier chapters; this is a natural consequence of the fact that we are looking for applications for heuristic behavior variables to instruction, rather than an elucidation of them for research (compare with Figure 8B.1).

Figure 10B.4 presents a schematic overview of the problem-solving process, presented as a flow chart to indicate the dynamic nature of the process. The boxes in the left-hand side of the diagram represent "stages" of problem-solving activity, and the circles the results or outcomes of that activity. On the right-hand side of the diagram we have entered the four stages of Polya's description, and the relationship between that description and the flow chart.

Before we proceed to elaborate on the flow chart, however, we should stress that this organization is meant to be practical, and to be used by the teacher in the classroom (Schoenfeld, 1978). These points are meant to be discussed openly with students (although not necessarily in one sitting, and in language appropriate for their assimilation). For example, the student should be told about the processes in ANALYSIS, which we shall examine shortly. It should be made clear to students that "these are things you should be aware of when you *start* to work on a problem," and this theme should be repeated throughout the course. When a student is "stuck" after reading a problem, the heuristic processes in the ANALYSIS stage should be suggested as often being of assistance. On the other hand, if the student "jumps into" a method of solution without reflection, that student should be (gently) cautioned that such behavior often leads to misspent energy, and that it might be wise at least to consider some of the perspectives or heuristic approaches listed under ANALYSIS (see Table 10B.1).

The ANALYSIS stage begins, of course, with the reading of the problem, and may be said to be successfully completed when the problem solver has a useful formulation of the problem in a convenient representation, a sense of orientation and a mathematical context for the problem, and access to some mechanisms for a close examination of the workings of the problem. In a colloquial sense, the student has a "feel" for the problem and the beginnings of an understanding of what "makes it tick."

With the reading of the problem, there is an often underplayed (sometimes instantaneous and unnoticed) *categorization*, or establishment of a mathematical context for the problem (recognition of the "problem type"). If a problem can be categorized broadly, there may be access to a general framework within which it can be placed, and (a bonus!) access to a standard set of procedures, or a ready-made plan for solving the problem. Thus "this is a mixture problem" entails more than just recognition, for it may mean that one has a "mixture problem procedure" ready to apply. Similarly, recognizing that a problem is one of maximization in calculus tells the problem solver to look for an analytic representation of a variable quantity, and to use the first

Figure 10B.4 *A Schematic Overview of the Problem Solving Process*

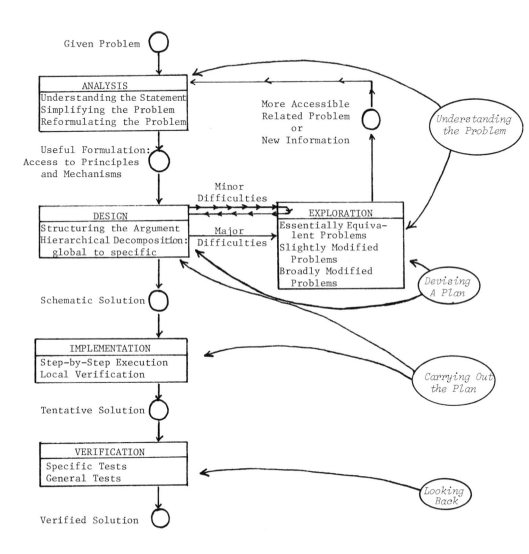

Table 10B.1 *Heuristic Processes Associated with ANALYSIS*

1. Classifying and establishing a context for the problem

2. Selecting a representation for the problem

3. Drawing a diagram if at all possible.

4. Exploring the conditions: "givens" and "goals".

5. Examining Special Cases:

    a) choosing special values to exemplify the problem and get a "feel" for it.

    b) examining limiting cases to see the range of possibilities

    c) setting integer parameters equal to 1,2,3,..., in sequence, and looking for patterns.

6. Looking for preliminary simplifications, through

    a) exploiting symmetry,

    b) "without loss of generality" arguments, including scaling.

Table 10B.2 *Heuristic Processes Associated with DESIGN*

1. Organizing the information from ANALYSIS (and EXPLORATION)

2. Structuring the argument

3. Serving as a "master control":

    a) keeping track of alternatives

    b) monitoring the success of particular approaches.

4. Enforcing an hierarchical (global to local) approach.

derivative to find its maximum. Such categorizations can also lead
one astray: witness the large number of problem solvers who try
analytic geometry or Heron's formula $A = \sqrt{s(s-a)(s-b)s-c}$, (where a,
b, c, are sides of the triangle and s = (1/2)(a + b + c)), to solve the
following problem:

> *10B.18 Find the area of a triangle whose sides are 25, 50,*
> *and 75.*

Yet such categorizations of problems into "types" are of great value
for the most part, and should be consciously exploited whenever
possible.

[handwritten marginalia: No triangle exists! what's this "thick" question!]

Concomitantly, we have within ANALYSIS the use of heuristic processes
to choose a convenient *representation* for the problem. This point can
be made briefly and powerfully to students, by asking them to multiply
the two numbers written in Roman numerals MCDLXVI and MMMDCCCLXXXVIII.
Students should be on the alert during this stage for what the givens
and the goals in a problem are, what one "usually" can obtain from the
givens and what their role in the problem seems to be, how they
relate to the goals, and whether the goals seem plausible in the light
of what is given. If possible, we should provide students with com-
pelling examples of the utility of diagrams. We have already seen two:
Figure 10B.3 provided for a simple analysis of the otherwise very complex Problem *10B.17*, and trying to draw a diagram of the "25,50,75"
triangle in Problem *10B.18* might well lead the student to the realization that the triangle "collapses." That problem serves as well as an
example for the utility of "scaling." If one thinks of the given
triangle as essentially a "1,2,3" triangle, the odds of seeing that
it "collapses" increase.

"Examining special cases" has already been described at length. We
have thus discussed the major heuristic processes associated with the
ANALYSIS stage. We should point out that these heuristic behaviors
may *not* occur in sequence; nor are all of them necessarily considered
for every problem or even most problems. Rather, they consist of a
set of behaviors *most likely* to prove of use and therefore worthy of
consideration at this stage of problem solving. A final example will
indicate the application of ANALYSIS to a problem.

> *10B.19 Find the largest area of any triangle which can be*
> *inscribed in a circle of radius R.*

After reading the problem, one may make a tentative classification
("This will probably involve calculus."), draw a diagram, and look for
a convenient analytic representation. For the sake of simplicity, one
might decide to look at the *unit* circle (scaling), and note (without
loss of generality) that the base of the triangle can be assumed horizontal. By examining a few special cases (and drawing more diagrams)
the problem solver may realize that, for any given horizontal base, the
isoceles triangle has the greatest height and thus the largest area.

The problem then reduces to that of finding the "right" horizontal base. At this point, a final choice of representation may be made. The "plan" is now known from context: one will express the area as a function of one variable and maximize using calculus.

The stage following ANALYSIS is called DESIGN, and its components are listed in Table 10B.2. DESIGN is of a somewhat different nature than the other stages of problem solving. It is not really an individual entity or phase, but rather pervades the entire problem-solving process. It is during the design phase that one plans a solution, but there is much, much more. DESIGN is, in a sense, the "master control" which monitors the entire problem-solving process and allocates problem-solving resources in as efficient a way as possible. Developing good DESIGN skills is critical for students. These behaviors, overall, are the consistent distinguishing marks of good problem solvers. By monitoring the way students work on problems and pointing out to them when they are or are not proceeding well, the teacher can have a tremendous impact on the students' problem solving.

In a sense, DESIGN is the most subtle and difficult of the aspects of problem solving to teach. It calls for a sensitivity on the part of the teacher to the way that students are proceeding through their work on problems, and a willingness to oversee the entire process. We shall limit ourselves here to a brief elaboration of the points listed above.

In its simplest form, DESIGN consists of "making a plan." At the very least, the student should be able to tell the teacher what he or she is thinking of doing, and why, at both *local* and *global* levels. That is, what will this particular operation result in (local level of design), and how does that result fit into the solution process as a whole (global level of design)? If one has a good idea of what should be done (for example, in a routine mixture problem), little more need be said. If the problem is complex or novel, however, DESIGN includes knowing how much ANALYSIS is necessary, and knowing when it is possible to begin outlining a plan. It means knowing when a plan is insufficient, and when to go to the next stage, EXPLORATION, for help. It keeps track of various options, so that there are "fail-safes" if one particular approach proves more troublesome than might have been expected. Equally important, it involves keeping track, globally, of the actions in which the problem solver is engaged, so that they are not wasted. This usually means maintaining some sort of hierarchical approach: for example, not getting involved in very complex computations on one part of a problem, if another part is hazy and unresolved. All too often we have seen a student solve a difficult equation only to discover that he or she did not know what to do with the answer once it was found. DESIGN should preclude this. The teacher should ask, and the student should be trained to ask, to what use any particular action in which the student is engaged will be put, and whether it is appropriate to be engaged in that action at that time.

Continuing our discussion of Figure 10B.4, we see that EXPLORATION is a very complex stage. It contains some of the most nebulous and difficult to apply of all the heuristic behaviors. An elaboration and exemplification of these would require a full volume. We shall limit ourselves to a few brief comments.

First, the reader should notice the similarity in organization between the phases of EXPLORATION which are listed in Table 10B.3, and the types of heuristic behavior variables described in Chapter V.

Second, *with all other factors being equal,* the three phases of EXPLORATION are such that (in general) success with a Phase 1 heuristic process is more likely to provide direct assistance in solving the original problem than a Phase 2 process; likewise, a Phase 2 process is likely to be of more immediate assistance than one from Phase 3. Of course, if an heuristic process from Phase 3 is "cued," one tries it as soon as it is appropriate (and does not wait until the "right" phase of the exploration stage). In general, these phases correspond to Polya's "rules of preference" (Polya, 1965).

Third and perhaps most important, all the work done in EXPLORATION must be subject to the intelligent management directions coming from DESIGN. If substantial progress is made with a particular exploration, the problem solver may return to DESIGN, decide that the plan for solving the problem is well-enough formulated, and proceed to implement it. If new insights are gained as to the mechanisms which "make the problem tick," the problem solver may decide to re-enter ANALYSIS with this new information and formulate another approach to the problem almost "from scratch." One should not be tempted by the separate boxes in Figure 10B.4 to think of the different stages of problem solving as disjoint entities, for they are interrelated in a variety of complex ways.

The next stage is IMPLEMENTATION. This stage needs little comment, save for an elaboration of the point that was just made. The alert problem solver monitors all phases of the problem-solving process. If a particular mode of IMPLEMENTATION is tedious, or tremendously involved, one may wish to retreat into DESIGN to select an alternative (even if the one being used is known to guarantee a solution); if there are "lessons to be learned" or generalizations that may be made, such decisions might profitably be made ("master control" will decide) before IMPLEMENTATION is finished.

Finally, we come to "looking back," or the stage of VERIFICATION (see Table 10B.4).

The VERIFICATION processes are straightforward, but they do need to be stressed with students. Checking over one's solution to a problem can return high profits for a small investment in time and energy. Yet students show consistently few signs of reliably checking over their work--and they pay the price. Of all the heuristic behaviors we have discussed in this chapter, "looking back" may be the easiest to teach and the most profitable.

Table 10B.3 *Heuristic Processes Associated with EXPLORATION*

Phase 1: Considering Essentially Equivalent Problems

    a) Replacing conditions by equivalent ones

    b) Recombining the elements of the problem in different ways

    c) Introducing auxiliary elements

    d) Re-formulating the problem, by

          i) a change of perspective or notation

         ii) considering argument by contradiction or contrapositive

       iii) assuming a solution and determining the properties it must have.

Phase 2: Considering Slightly Modified Problems

    a) Choosing subgoals (obtaining partial fulfillment of the goals in a directly useful way)

    b) Relaxing a condition and then trying to reimpose it

    c) Decomposing the domain of the problem and then working on it case by case.

Phase 3: Considering Broadly Modified Problems

    a) Constructing analogous problems with simplified structures, in the hope of exploiting

          i) the result of the analogous problem

         ii) the method used to solve the analogous problem

    b) Holding all but one variable fixed, in the hope of better understanding the role of that variable (or given)

    c) Examining *any* related problem, in the hope that the

          i) form,

         ii) givens, or

       iii) goals

    will provide information useful to the solution of this problem.

Table 10B.4 *Heuristic Processes Associated with* <u>VERIFICATION</u>

1. Checking to see that the solution passes these specific tests:

   a) Does it use all the pertinent data?

   b) Does it conform to reasonable estimates or predictions?

   c) Does it withstand tests of symmetry, dimension analysis, or scaling?

2. Checking to see that the solution passes these general tests:

   a) Can the solution be obtained differently?

   b) Can it be substantiated by special cases?

   c) Can it be reduced to known results?

   d) Can it be used to generate something which is known?

3. Checking to see if the whole process of solution can serve as a learning experience. Is there a lesson to be learned, and can one learn to be a better problem solver from this experience?

5. Conclusion

Perhaps it is appropriate at this point to return to Polya's words:

> the study of heuristic has practical aims; a better under-
> standing of the mental operations typically useful in
> solving problems could exert some good influence on
> teaching, especially on the teaching of mathematics.
> (Polya, 1957)

It can indeed. With proper attention to heuristic variables in instruction, the classroom can be more exciting and entertaining, and students
can learn to be better problem solvers. It is hoped that the discussion
of *cued heuristics* and *stage heuristics* in this chapter will assist in
achieving this goal.

REACTION PAPER 1

Task Variables in Mathematical Problem Solving

by

Max E. Jerman
Seattle Pacific University
Seattle, Washington

I am happy to see this work produced, for it brings together much
of the recent work on problem-solving task variables in mathematics.
Problem solving is a difficult area in which to do good research. I
commend the editors and contributors for the quality of their work and
for the effort expended in producing this volume. I trust there will
be additional volumes in future years as knowledge in this area
increases.

Clearly, this book is written for researchers. The objective is to
facilitate agreement on definitions of categories and tasks and to stan-
dardize vocabulary. This kind of thing should have been done years ago.
It will be a continuing effort for some time, I am sure, but unless
steps are taken toward standardization, no consensus will ever be
reached.

The opening chapter clearly indicates both the objectives and scope
of the work. Chapters I through V include reviews of the research literature on task variables, emphasizing the various categories of task
variables and their definitions. In Chapters VI through VIII experimental studies, in which the description or control of task variables
was the objective, are summarized. In Chapters IX and X, teaching applications with specific examples of unit plans are included.

The broad categories of variables identified and described by Kulm
in the opening chapter may be grouped as follows: (1) structural variables in the sense of the linear regression studies; namely those having
to do with syntax, content, and context; (2) heuristic variables; and
(3) problem representation variables. In Figure 1.1 a pictorial representation of a hierarchy of task variables is presented.

The chapter by Barnett provides a good review of syntax variables.
It traces the development of the quantification of syntactic variables
quite accurately.

The summary of studies on content and context variables is also
well done. I agree with Webb that a better definition is required of
how problems are alike or different (problem "types"). Classifying
problems according to their solution strategies is one way of proceeding. Perhaps teaching students the strategy required to solve a given
class or type of problems is the best procedure if such a single
strategy exists. However, it is often difficult if not impossible

to prepare problems in such a way that there is only one way in which to solve them. The variety of ways in which problems can and have been classified according to type is summarized in this chapter in considerable detail.

Chapter IV contains a fine review by Goldin of the literature on complexity variables, those variables which directly affect problem difficulty. Thinking ahead a bit, I am not sure that the artificial intelligence models discussed in this chapter have much to offer teachers in the way of specific suggestions for instruction (nor were they intended to do so). Researchers *have* found, however, that in trying to teach a computer to "learn," the essential ingredient is to provide relevant background relationships. Perhaps that finding has as much import for teachers as any that has come from the research to date.

The discussion of space-state symmetry groups in Chapter IV concerns me from the standpoint of being realistic enough to retain relevance. I believe that we, myself included, sometimes tend to be more detailed in our analyses of situations than may be warranted. Being mathematically oriented, it is easy to want to see some underlying structure, like a group, in what we are examining. I am not opposed to this, but I am concerned that our focus remain on problem-solving variables and instruction and that we do not, like Piaget, spend a great deal of effort in attempting to identify mathematical groups or other structures that do not exist. I am not saying that I believe the author of this chapter has fallen into such a trap; I am just expressing a concern that none of us do so.

Goldin poses several hypotheses in Chapter IV to be tested empirically. To be worthwhile educationally, the examination or testing of hypotheses such as those proposed should take place during initial instruction, not at some later time. This concern is similar to that which Brownell expressed in his review of studies on subtraction earlier than his own. We can *teach* students anything we choose. If as teachers we were more systematic and thorough in our approach to problem-solving instruction in the elementary grades, such research would be facilitated--students would then come to a problem-solving situation having had similar experiences, which would facilitate the study of transfer. The hypotheses are interesting and should be tested. The appropriate point for this is during initial learning, rather than later when a variety of heuristics may have been either rightly or wrongly learned.

In Chapter V the literature on heuristic processes as task variables is reviewed quite thoroughly by McClintock. The work of artificial intelligence researchers, and Wickelgren's methods, are also reviewed. Wickelgren's work is excellent in the sense that it presents a hierarchy of general problem-solving methods or strategies. I would like to see someone attempt to integrate the methods described by Wickelgren with the work of Piaget. Which strategies can be taught to and effectively used by children at the various developmental levels? Covington,

Crutchfield, and Davies (1974) demonstrate very clearly that fifth-grade students can be taught to use the decision-tree strategy very efficiently--the researchers were able to demonstrate significant transfer effects of the skills learned to areas such as English and mathematics. Students at earlier grades were not able to become as proficient with the decision-tree strategy as were fifth graders (Crutchfield, 1966).

The need to teach specific strategies or heuristics has been pointed out by many researchers. One such recommendation was made by Buswell (1956). He found a great variety of thinking patterns among the 499 college and high school students in his study. In fact, one of his conclusions was that variety rather than similarity was a striking characteristic of the problem-solving strategies used by students in the study (p. 136). Recommendations from this study included a call for increased emphasis on teaching critical reading skills and the teaching of specific strategies for problem solving (pp. 138-139).

The findings reported in Buswell's study seem to be consistent with the work recently reported by Bloom (1976). As students grow older, there will be a greater variety, spread, or range of achievement unless students are taught to a mastery level at each step along the way.

The task then, it seems to me, is to develop a well-defined task analysis for each problem-solving strategy, to arrange strategies in a hierarchical sequence, to develop teaching strategies for each step of the task analysis, and then to test hypotheses such as those recommended as learning occurs rather than at a later point.

When Wickelgren's strategies are sequenced according to the developmental stages Piaget has identified, the result might be as follows:

Number-conserving students whose ages range from 5 to 7 years:

1. Solve simple story problems

   a. Use manipulative aids to demonstrate solutions

   b. Draw pictures to show solutions

   c. Verbally give solutions

2. Discriminate between problem types

   a. State goals

   b. State context indicators of goals

   c. State context indicators of operations

   d. State context indicators of givens

        1) Explicit givens

        2) Implicit givens

    e. Discriminate between relevant mathematical terms

  3. Solve word problems

    a. Solve one-step problems involving addition and subtraction

    b. Identify extra or unneeded information

Students whose ages range from 8 to 12 years can:

  4. Do all of the above

  5. Solve one-step problems using multiplication and division

  6. Use the following problem-solving strategies:

    a. Systematic trial and error

    b. Classificatory trial and error

    c. Decision trees

  7. Solve two-step problems

  8. Write mathematical sentences for each problem

  9. Find alternate ways to solve many problems

Students whose ages range from 13 years up can:

  10. Do all of the above

  11. Use the following specific strategies:

    a. Subgoals

    b. State evaluation or hill climbing

    c. Contradiction

  12. Generalize or solve the general case for a given problem

The developmental sequence of strategies and steps proposed above is certainly tentative, but it seems to be consistent with the current literature. Much work remains to be done, to be sure. Perhaps jointly we can determine the optimal sequence.

Another aspect of development that may be important to problem solving is the development of linguistic structures in human speech. Linguistic complexity may be a relative thing rather than an absolute. The use of scales such as the Schmidt-Kettel Scale of Linguistic Complexity (Schmidt, 1977) or the Miscue Analysis by Goodman (1967) may shed some additional light on the nature of linguistic depth and complexity. The interrelationship between the development of cognitive skills and language may provide important information.

Memory is also an important variable to be considered in problem solving. Scandura (1977) provides an extensive review of the litera-ture on memory and its relationship to the problem-solving process. Perhaps more work might be expended profitably on determining the extent of the memory load required by various types of problems, or by the various types of heuristics. Why are some heuristic processes apparently easier to recall and use than others? In what ways can problem types or heuristics be chunked to facilitate their accurate recall and use in particular situations? In what ways can manipulative materials be used to improve the teaching and learning of heuristics?

The coding systems suggested in Chapter V are quite detailed. Per-haps if enough work is done with such systems, a clearer picture of the problem-solving process will emerge. The effort in doing research of this type will be well spent if it succeeds in providing clues to cognitive processes.

The study reported by Goldin and Caldwell in Chapter VI is quite interesting. The problem set seems well designed and representative of the desired categories. The translation modeled after Bobrow's STUDENT is clear, and a very interesting method of determining syntactic complexity is presented. The difficulties with the system of experimen-tal problems are fairly acknowledged. Overall the results of the study are most interesting. I hope that this study will be replicated in the near future. It would be interesting to see if the problem categories are significant predictors in a regression analysis.

The study on concept acquisition by Waters (Chapter VII.A) is also interesting. The task involved the use of attribute cards, and it was found that slight variations in problem embodiment tended to induce subjects to vary their solution strategies. I certainly agree with this conclusion. The report by Goldin and Caldwell also contained a similar statement. From all the research that I have read, it seems clear that problem format as well as problem structure is a most power-ful influence on the choice of solution strategy. It may be some time before all the subtleties are clearly understood; however, the work needs to be done.

The study by Days (Chapter VII.B) was intended to examine the relationship between problem complexity and the cognitive level of the subjects. Eighth graders were asked to think aloud while solving problems. The protocols were scored, and task variables defined and quantified. Again it was found that strategies varied as structure varied, with a wider variety of strategies or processes being used on problems with more complex structures. The finding that "systematic trial and error" was most frequently used on complex problems is most interesting. This finding would seem to lend support to the findings of studies in which linguistic variables were better predictors of problem difficulty for older subjects than were computational variables. Complexity of sentence structure is probably not affected as much in a trial-and-error situation as are mathematical variable counts. The classification procedure used in the study seems to be well thought out, and useful for further research.

Chapter VII.C contains a review of studies on state-space analysis and transfer. The chapter is well done. I agree with Luger that transfer must be specifically taught. If we expect transfer to take place, we must teach in a way that will bring it about. Similarities and differences between problems must be pointed out. Students ought to spend some time categorizing problems according to type in some sense, in order to facilitate transfer. These points are further developed by Luger in Chapter X.A.

In Chapter VIII.A, Harik presents an analysis of the heuristic process of trial and error. As was expected, the largest percentage of the students used a trial-and-error strategy to solve the problems. One cannot help but wonder if the result could have been anticipated due to the age of the subjects and their previous training.

In Chapter VIII.B a process-sequence coding system is presented. The process is quite detailed and complex. A considerable amount of training will be required of anyone who wishes to use the system reliably.

The last chapters contain examples by Caldwell, Luger, and Schoenfeld, of teaching methods in which task variables play an important role. Outlines of several sample instructional units are presented. The objectives for the lessons are explicitly given and the sample lessons are designed to teach to the objectives. In all they are well done, and several are appropriate for improving learning transfer.

In summary, the book will be a valuable source of ideas and methods for future research. Allowing for the few omissions mentioned above, I believe that significant steps have been taken toward a better understanding of human problem solving, particularly in mathematics. I believe the objectives for the work have largely been met. Nevertheless, we have just begun what may prove to be a long journey. Perhaps work such as that by Paul Torrance, on cultural influences on problem-solving slumps at various age levels, and by Madeline Hunter, on teaching skills, can be synthesized with the above-mentioned studies to provide guidance on our journey.

In addition, some of the techniques used by earlier researchers, such as Buswell, may be helpful to us today in studying problem solving. Buswell had students solve problems, and then arrange cards on which numerals and operation signs were written to show the order in which they had been used. This approach, in addition to verbalization, gave the researcher a very clear picture of the sequential process used. It also provided students with more concrete referents for their solution strategies. Perhaps a companion volume to this current book could be one in which the experimental techniques used by many researchers were reviewed and compared. Such a volume might prove useful to all of us, since we tend to forget rather quickly what has been done in previous years.

REACTION PAPER 2

Task Variables in Mathematical Problem Solving

by

Jeremy Kilpatrick
University of Georgia
Athens, Georgia

While reading the papers contained in this volume, I wrote down three questions that seemed especially pertinent to the topic of task variables in research on problem solving in mathematics:

1. To what does the word "problem" refer?

2. What do we mean when we talk about "problem structure"?

3. What is meant by "problem space"?

My answers to these questions agree with some statements in the volume and conflict with others.

Regarding the first question, I am not so much concerned with a definition of the term "problem" as with understanding what we mean when we say two problems are "the same" or "different." The distinction, introduced in the first chapter and maintained throughout the volume, between a statement of a problem and a representation of a problem is useful in this connection. We think of the same problem as capable of expression by means of various statements and as capable of representation in different ways. "The problem" somehow exists in our thought in a fashion separate from its expression and its representation. The distinction, shown in the hierarchy of task variables in Figure 1.1, between syntax, context, and content variables can be used to explore the notion of problem identity. Syntax variables are those whose manipulation preserves problem identity: it is the same problem whether expressed in English or in French and whether expressed in the first person, active voice or the third person, passive voice. Context variables are those whose manipulation preserves problem structure: the missionary and cannibal problem discussed in Chapter IV and its variant expressed in terms of "hobbits and orcs" are not the same problem, but they are isomorphic; they differ only in their context. Content variables are those whose manipulation preserves problem similarity but not isomorphism: addition of the condition "only one cannibal knows how to row" to the missionary and cannibal problem yields a similar, but not identical or isomorphic, problem; changing the number of rings in the Tower of Hanoi problem produces similar problems, and so does changing the number of towers. One of the relatively unexplored issues in task variable research, as noted in several chapters, is the characterization of dimensions of similarity between problems. The syntax, context, and content variable distinction seems to be a valuable first step in beginning this exploration.

It may be useful to think of a problem as a kind of equivalence class of problem statements in which syntax and context are allowed to vary, but content is not. Under this interpretation, the answer to the second question above is that "problem structure" refers to the common property of problem statements in the same equivalence class. Problems that are in different equivalence classes have different structures. Similarity of problems is really similarity of structure. As noted in several chapters, we teachers of mathematics need to help our students learn to distinguish similarity of problem statements from similarity of problem structures.

Now we come to the third question, which deals with representation. According to Newell and Simon (1972), the "problem space" is the space in which a person's problem-solving activities take place. Consequently, it should be understood as dependent upon the particular representation of the problem that the solver has constructed. In order to understand how people solve problems, researchers need to study the problem spaces they construct and the activities they perform in these spaces. State-space analysis, as portrayed in Chapter IV, seems to offer a way of approaching the question of problem spaces, at least for certain kinds of problems. Goldin makes the important point that the same problem can have different state-spaces, depending on its representation. This observation suggests that, just as it is helpful to distinguish problem statement from problem representation and state-space from problem space, so it might be helpful to distinguish the structure of a problem from the structure of its representation. The structure of a problem is, as Newell and Simon suggest in discussing explicit representation of the task environment, not open to veridical description. The structure of various "official" or "canonical" representations of a problem is dealt with by state-space analysis, among other techniques. The structure of a person's idiosyncratic representation of a problem is dealt with by analyzing the individual's problem space, which includes more than a state-space. Problem spaces encompass not only the person's knowledge of the problem but also errors made when the problem's conditions are violated. One of the dangers of a heavy reliance on state-space analyses of puzzle problems to investigate problem solving in mathematics is that puzzle problems are distinctive precisely because their conditions are easily understood and used. In much problem solving in mathematics, understanding the conditions is a major source of difficulty and violations of the conditions are common.

From the point of view of the problem as a task environment, content variables *determine* the structure of the problem. Change them and you have changed the problem's structure. Consequently, I would argue that the "key words" discussed in Chapter III should not be considered to refer to content, but to syntax. In my view, for example, Problems *3.25* and *3.26* are the same problem stated differently:

> *3.25   The milkman brought on Sunday 4 bottles of milk more*
> *than on Monday. On Monday he brought 7 bottles. How*
> *many bottles did he bring on Sunday?*

*3.26   The milkman brought on Monday 7 bottles of milk.   That
         was 4 bottles less than he brought on Sunday.   How
         many bottles did he bring on Sunday?*

The problem is obviously capable of different representations, but the
two statements refer to the same problem because they have the same
data, the same unknown, and the same relation between data and unknown.
On the other hand, Problems *3.38* and *3.39* differ not only in context
but also in content:

*3.38   Find the smallest set of whole numbers such that every
         integer from 1 to 7 is either an element of the set or
         a sum of the elements in a subset.*

*3.39   A woman has a chain with seven gold links.   She would
         like to take a seven-day trip by carriage.   The driver
         has agreed to take her for one link of the golden chain
         for each day, payable at the end of the day.   If it
         costs the woman five dollars to have a jeweler open one
         link, what is the least amount of money she would have
         to spend to open links so the driver can have one link
         the first day, two links the second day, and so on?*

Problem *3.38* does not require determination of the number of cuts
necessary to yield subsets of the appropriate numbers of elements,
nor does it require calculation of the cost of the cuts.

The argument is made in this volume that content and structure
variables are to be distinguished on the basis that structure
variables require a mathematical analysis of the problem and content
variables do not. I find this argument unconvincing. The situation
becomes especially cloudy when one considers what is meant by problem
"type." Webb asserts in Chapter III that problem type is a content
variable if it can be identified from the problem statement "without
mathematical processing;" otherwise, it is a structure variable. How
can one decide when mathematical processing begins in problem solving?
The remarks above suggest that problem type is best thought of as a
context variable. "Related rates" problems share common features of
embodiment; they need not be stated in the same syntax, and they need
not have the same structure--although problem types are usually identified in the expectation that problems of the same type will be
similar in structure and representation.

In line with the position I have expressed above, content and
structure variables can be distinguished as follows: "content
variables" refer to the *structure of the problem*, and "structure
variables" refer to the *structure of a representation of the problem*.

Goldin makes the nice observations that the valid representations
of a problem fall into isomorphism classes and also that distinct problems may have isomorphic representations. The latter observation, by

the way, supports the contention that problems are better characterized
in terms of their statements than in terms of their representations.
I part company with Goldin, however, when he asserts that "by any
reasonable definitions" Problems *4.4a*, *4.4b*, and *4.4c* do not differ in
syntax, context, or content. (Problem *4.4a* involves two nickels and
two dimes in a row with a space between, the object being to exchange
the positions by a series of legal moves; Problem *4.4b* involves three
nickels and three dimes, with the same rules and the same object; and
Problem *4.4c* involves four nickels and four dimes, with the same rules
and the same object.) By what I consider a reasonable meaning of
"content variable," the three problems *do* differ in content. The statements of the problems are clearly different, and the use of different
number words has a nontrivial effect. Most people would agree, I think,
that the three problems are different. Of course, the problems also
have non-isomorphic representations, and consequently so-called
"structure" variables are needed to characterize this difference.

I suggest that the hierarchy of task variables ought to be amended
so that Newell and Simon's distinction between the structure of the task
environment and the structure of the problem space is maintained; that
is, so that both "content" and "structure" variables are viewed as
describing structure. I also suggest that both algorithmic and heuristic processes be viewed as operating within the person's problem space
and that strategies be viewed as combinations of such processes. And
finally, I suggest that one not attempt to link Polya's four phases of
problem solving to the categories of task variables. I find the proposed linkage arbitrary, strained, and--to coin a term--unheuristic.

The volume as a whole is eloquent testimony to the value of an
explicit treatment of task variables in research on problem solving.
Many of the research studies cited have been reviewed elsewhere, but
different facets emerge when the studies are considered in terms of
the task variables involved. The hierarchy of task variables and the
accompanying types of task analysis that are presented in Chapter I,
despite the areas of disagreement described above, represent real
progress in the conceptualization of problem-solving research.

Barnett's discussion of syntax variables in Chapter II is an
impressive contribution, and the information-processing model he uses
to organize the discussion is especially helpful. Consideration of
the information-processing activities of a problem solver in reading
the statement of a problem leads one to consider the role of irrelevant
information in the statement. According to the analysis provided above,
the presence or absence of irrelevant information ought to be considered a syntax variable, since such information by definition does
not change the problem. But of course it may have a profound effect
on the solver's representation of the problem. Robinson and Hayes
(1978) have shown how one can study the processes by which problem
solvers judge the relevance of information in the problem statement.
In their technique students read a problem twice, a section at a time,
each time judging whether or not the information in the section is
relevant to the solution. Differences in reaction time depending on

whether the problem's question is at the beginning or end of the statement are used to test a model of attention to various types of information.

Reaction time data, although popular in psychological research, have rarely been used in research on problem solving in mathematics. Such data seem especially promising for testing models of problem-solving processes. For example, Malin (1979) demonstrated that the efficiency of strategies such as working backward depends on both the structure of the problem and the information-processing demands made on the problem solver by the strategy. Perhaps the heavy dependence on correctness of solution as a dependent variable, and the corresponding avoidance of reaction time data, accounts for some of the failure of researchers in mathematics education to observe much effect when syntax, context, and content variables are manipulated.

Most of the attempts to study the effects of variations in syntax by means of regression analysis have used correctness of the solution as the dependent variable. The emphasis has been on problem difficulty. Barnett recommends attention to process variables such as the form of the equations used in a solution. Since there are so many ways for final solutions to go wrong that do not depend on problem syntax, intermediate product variables, such as the correctness of the operations selected or the equations written, might also be taken as dependent variables. For example, an early and little known regression analysis study (Kilpatrick, 1960) attempted to predict both correct equations and correct solutions from syntax variables.

Barnett cites some weaknesses of the linear regression model, but he does not sufficiently stress the most serious faults of the research studies he cites that have used the model: the lack of a theory to guide the selection of variables, the crude measures used for many of the variables, and the high ratio of variables to problems (which all but guarantees good prediction).

Webb presents a discussion of content and context variables in Chapter III that, despite his use of terms in a different sense than I would, nicely sets out some important dimensions of task difference. "Mathematical topic" and "field of application" are useful categories for classifying problems, although neither category fits the characterizations I have given of content and context variables. These categories seem to refer not to variables that can be manipulated to yield different problems, but to classes of problems characterized by various values of content and context variables, as well as by the mathematics used to solve the problems and the uses to which the problems are put. I would take small exception to the generalization Webb makes at the end of the chapter, to the effect that most context variables do not greatly affect problem difficulty, by noting that problems in logical reasoning, and syllogistic reasoning problems in particular, seem to be highly susceptible to context variation. Mayer (1978) has shown how manipulating the meaningfulness of a problem's context can have profound effects on inference processes.

My earlier remarks have suggested some of my admiration for Goldin's analysis, in Chapter IV, of problem structure and complexity. Despite our disagreement on some details, his explication of state-space homorphisms and isomorphisms provides a solid and original framework for viewing the structure of problem representations. I am less happy with his implication that nonroutine problems are especially open to state-space analysis--what makes them good candidates is not that they are nonroutine, but that they are essentially puzzle problems in which the number of choices of moves is restricted. These, however, are minor quibbles in view of the outstanding contribution the chapter makes.

McClintock argues at the beginning of Chapter V that heuristic processes are inherent in certain problems. His use of the subproblem decomposition of the Tower of Hanoi problem to illustrate this point highlights an important distinction. Solution of the four-disc problem entails solution of the three-disc problem, but the solver of the four-disc problem need not have used the heuristic process of subproblem decomposition. Thus the distinction between solving a problem in which a heuristic process would be helpful, and actually using the heuristic process to solve the problem, is important. In the case of a computer programmed to solve the problem, one would want to know whether the machine was identifying and solving subproblems as part of the solution. In the case of a human solver, one would like some evidence that the solver is aware of the heuristic process--whether or not he or she was aware of applying it in solving the problem. Use of heuristic processes seems to require some degree of consciousness in their use, but the implied possibility of subconscious or accidental use suggests that further exploration of this issue would be worthwhile. In this connection, McClintock's characterization (in his discussion of Krutetskii) of heuristic processes as volitionally controllable or initiatable, as opposed to the more involuntary and synthetic mathematical abilities, is provocative. I have trouble seeing abilities as processes or as combinations of processes, but I am challenged by McClintock's formulation.

In the first part of Chapter VIII, Harik gives a slightly different twist to the notion of inherency of heuristic reasoning processes, defining it with respect to both the problem itself and a population of solvers. Whether or not "inherent" is the best word to use to refer to a process used by most people in solving a particular problem, it does seem useful to characterize problems in terms of both the potential utility of various heuristic processes in yielding a solution and the actual use of these processes by a given set of problem solvers. Harik's work provides an interesting example of the use of the state-space concept to analyze algebraic tasks, but one should note that the analysis assumes that the problem solvers have incorporated the unstated assumption in the problems she uses that the solution values will be positive integers. Harik does not give sufficient attention to the knowledge that the solver brings to the task and that is used both in constructing the problem space and in deciding how to move through it. For example, she characterizes guesses as totally or partially random, ignoring the fact that even the wildest guesses are constrained by various problem conditions and, in the case of numerical answers, are almost always round numbers to simplify calculations. Harik's discussion of problem reduction is interesting, but one should distinguish between her use of the term and Polya's advice to reduce the problem to a simpler one. Again, a process is not a heuristic process unless it is undertaken deliberately and with some degree of conscious intention. Reduction to a simpler problem is a way of transforming a problem so that the solution of the simpler version may be of use in the solution of the original problem. Someone who solves part of a problem so that only a simpler subproblem remains should not be automatically credited with reduction to a simpler problem. Otherwise, everyone who solves a complex problem is using the heuristic processes of reduction to a simpler problem and subproblem decomposition. Harik's use of graphical means to portray patterns of guessing is a valuable device that is likely to prove fruitful in subsequent research studies.

The Goldin and Caldwell study reported in Chapter VI is notable for the careful attempt to control syntax, context, and content variables. The difficulty of controlling one variable at a time is illustrated by the contrast between "factual" and "hypothetical" versions of the same problem: in attempting to manipulate context, the investigators found that they had to manipulate syntax as well. As an aside, I was struck by how closely the behavior of the STUDENT computer program used in the study resembles the advice to problem solvers given by Dahmus (1970). In effect, Dahmus attempts to program students to solve routine word problems, so perhaps one should not be surprised that this computer program incorporates some of his advice.

Two of the studies, those reported by Waters and Luger reported in Chapter VII, refer to the "deep end" hypothesis of Dienes and Jeeves (1965, 1970). As Goldin observes in Chapter IV, one needs to consider the performance on both tasks in testing this hypothesis, and the real question is whether task order affects *total* performance. It is wrong to argue from differences in significance levels, but the authors do not make this clear. The "deep end" notion has some subtle aspects; it should not be interpreted indiscriminately.

Waters' use of structured questions to get at problem solvers' intentions is an interesting approach. Other researchers have obtained retrospective evaluations and have tried to match them to strategies as defined by sequences of moves, but few researchers have been bold enough to interrupt the solver to ask why a given move had been made. In setting up his tasks, Waters attempted to manipulate context while holding content constant. Although the tasks were isomorphic, their state-space representations, as Waters notes, were not. In other words (using my terminology), the structure of the problem was the same, but the structure of the problem's representation was not the same.

The study by Days in Chapter VII shows that his distinction between simple and complex problems apparently has some implications, but since there are so many dimensions of distinction, one cannot know which ones are most important. Some obvious follow-up work is called for. Days' distinction between explicit and implicit reference to problem elements in the statement of the problem seems to have some promise for predicting problem difficulty, although in another study (Kilpatrick, 1960) a measure of implicitness predicted correctness of equations, but not correctness of solutions.

The process-sequence coding system presented by the research team in the second part of Chapter VIII is a tool that, although somewhat cumbersome to apply, can be used to illuminate some features of problem solving. The discussion of the communication between problem solver and coder shows some of the points where "noise" can enter the system, but insufficient attention has been given to difficulties at both ends of the communication channel. At the problem solver's end, the authors appear to assume that the solver is aware of all of his or her thoughts, or more precisely, that the thoughts exist in a form that can be grasped, if not necessarily reported accurately, by the solver. The phrases "genuine process behavior" and "what actually happened during problem solving" suggest that the authors view thinking as an object open to discovery rather than as a construct approached through various fallible methods. At the coder's end of the communication channel, the discussion overlooks the arbitrary nature of the code. Coding systems are devised to serve particular purposes, and no system can do everything. Any system highlights some features at the expense of others. The system presented in Chapter VIII can be used with a large set of problems to provide information on a large set of "processes," but one needs to ask whether sufficient attention has been given to the context and content dimensions along which problems can vary. One should also ask whether the calculation of intercoder agreement for the system has not made too many compromises; if protocols are to be coded symbol-to-symbol, then an estimate of symbol-by-symbol agreement between coders is essential. The important point, however, is that rather than pushing toward a comprehensive coding system, researchers need to step back and ask what purpose is to be served by a system and then design it accordingly.

Caldwell's advice to teachers in Chapter IX regarding the use of syntax, content, and context variables demonstrates clearly the value of explicating task variables. Although she and I appear to differ in what we mean by content and structure variables, the examples she provides are excellent. One could have a profitable discussion in a mathematics class (or among a group of researchers) by asking which of the 13 versions of the routine word problem that she presents at the beginning of the chapter really refer to "the same" problem. I liked the unit plans for teaching about task variables. The first plan probably attempts to do too many different things, but I thought the ideas for showing students how syntax and context might vary were quite good. In discussing context variation, I think it would be especially helpful for students to see that the same numbers in the same relationship can be provided with different "cover stories," and I would place more emphasis on the students actually working up the cover stories themselves.

In the first part of Chapter X, Luger makes some important points about problem structure variables in teaching. In particular, I thought

his discussion of the semantic content that machines (and therefore
students) need in order to "understand" a problem ought to be pondered
by every teacher. Many of the suggestions he gives for teaching, such
as the representation of "uniform aging," are first-rate. I do feel
that the topic of "problem type" needs to be handled with care by
teachers. Experience in both the United States and the Soviet Union
shows how unproductive a heavy emphasis on identifying problem types
can be. I think teachers who want students to classify problems by
type should give some examples, perhaps borrowed from Krutetskii (1976),
of problems that superficially appear to be of the same type but are not.

In the second part of Chapter X, Schoenfeld also discusses problem
types, but within the context of getting students to see when certain
heuristic processes might aid problem solving. Schoenfeld is probably
right in terming problem categorization an "underplayed" process, but
again one needs to avoid too rigid a stance. The whole question of how
problems are to be sequenced during instruction in heuristic processes
needs further thought and research. One needs to orchestrate instruction so there is a good balance between intensive experience with a
given heuristic process and problems of a given "type" and extensive
experience in which identification of the appropriate process is the
chief goal. Schoenfeld has provided some thoughts relating to this
issue, but much more needs to be done. I am not convinced that his
partition of heuristic processes into "cued" and "stage" processes is
worth pushing too far.

One reason problem solving is such a popular topic among teachers
and researchers is that people can read many alternative meanings into
the term "problem." When problems range all the way from sterile textbook exercises to real-life situations waiting to be given a mathematical
formulation, the topic obviously provides something for everyone--and the
opportunity for considerable confusion when people discuss the topic.
The present volume has attempted to organize some of this confusion and,
consequently, has taken a step toward a theory of problem solving. As
Shulman and Elstein (1975) astutely note, "a theory of problem solving
must be, first, a description of how different kinds of problems are
solved and, second, a taxonomic or logical analysis of the interrelations
among problem types" (p. 14). Both of these components have been
addressed thoughtfully and fruitfully in this volume.

REFERENCES

Aiken, L. R. Language factors in learning mathematics. *Mathematics Education Reports*. Columbus, Ohio, 1967. (ERIC Document Reproduction Service No. ED 068 340)

Arbib, M. A. *Algebraic theory of machines, languages, and semigroups*. New York: Academic Press, 1969.

Ashton, M. R. *Heuristic methods in problem solving in ninth grade algebra*. Unpublished doctoral dissertation, Stanford University, 1962.

Banerji, R. *Theory of problem solving: an approach to artificial intelligence*. New York: American Elsevier Publishing, 1969.

Barnett, J. C. Toward a theory of sequencing: study 3-7: an investigation of the relationships of structural variables, instruction, and difficulty in verbal, arithmetic problem solving (Doctoral dissertation, Pennsylvania State University, 1974). *Dissertation Abstracts International*, 1975, *36*, 99-100A. (University Microfilms No. 75-15787)

Barnett, J. C. Heuristic emphases in the instruction of mathematical problem solving. *Mathematics Teacher*, 1976, *69*, 613-614.

Bartlett, F. D. *Remembering*. Cambridge: Cambridge University Press, 1936.

Beardslee, E., & Jerman, M. *Linguistic variables in verbal arithmetic problems*. Columbus, Ohio, 1973a. (ERIC Document Reproduction Service No. ED 073 926)

Beardslee, E., & Jerman, M. *Syntactic variables in word problems solved by students in grades 4-8*. A paper presented at the National Council of Teachers of Mathematics annual meeting, Houston, 1973b.

Beardslee, E., & Jerman, M. *Structural, linguistic, and topic variables in verbal and computational problems in elementary mathematics*. A paper presented at the AERA annual meeting, Chicago, 1974.

Binet, A. *L'etude experimentale de l'intelligence*. Paris: Schleicher Freres, 1903.

Blake, R. N. *The effect of problem context upon the problem solving processes used by field dependent and independent students: a clinical study*. Unpublished doctoral dissertation, University of British Columbia, 1976.

Bloom, B. *Characteristics and school learning*. New York: McGraw Hill, 1976.

Bobrow, D. Natural language input for a computer problem-solving system. In M. Minsky (Ed.), *Semantic information processing*. Cambridge, Mass.: MIT Press, 1968.

Botel, M., Dawkins, J., & Granowsky, A. A syntactic complexity formula. In W. MacGinitic (Ed.), *Assessment problems in reading*. Newark, DL: International Reading Assoc., 1973.

Bourbaki, N. *Elements of mathematics series* (English Translations), Vol. I (Theory of Sets, 1968), Vol. II (Algebra, Part I, 1974), and other volumes. Reading, Mass.: Addison-Wesley.

Branca, N. & Kilpatrick, J. The consistency of strategies in the learning of mathematical structures. *Journal for Research in Mathematics Education*, 1972, *3*, 132-140.

Brennan, C. *Problem solving variables*. Unpublished mimeographed paper, Pennsylvania State University, 1972.

Brownell, W. A., & Stretch, L. B. The effect of unfamiliar settings on problem-solving. *Duke University Research Studies in Education*, Durham, N.C.: Duke University, 1931 (1).

Bruner, J. *Toward a theory of instruction*. Cambridge, Massachusetts: Belknap Press, 1966.

Bruner, J. S. *The relevance of education*. New York: W. W. Norton, 1973.

Bruner, J., Goodnow, J. J., & Austin, G. A. *A study of thinking*. New York: John Wiley & Sons, 1956.

Burns, P. & Yonally, J. Does the order of presentation of numerical data in multi-step arithmetic problems affect their order of difficulty? *School Science and Mathematics*, 1964, *64*, 267-270.

Buswell, G. *Patterns of thinking in problem solving*. (University of California Publications in Education, No. 2). Berkeley: University of California Press, 1956.

Caldwell, J. *The effects of abstract and hypothetical factors on word problem difficulty in school mathematics*. Unpublished doctoral dissertation, University of Pennsylvania, 1977.

Caldwell, J. and Goldin, G. A. Variables affecting word problem difficulty in school mathematics. *Journal for Research in Mathematics Education*, 1979, *10* (5), 323-336.

Charosh, M. *Mathematical challenges*. Reston, Va.: National Council of Teachers of Mathematics, 1965.

Chartoff, B. T. An exploratory investigation utilizing a multidimensional scaling procedure to discover classification criteria for algebra word problems used by students in grades 7-13 (Doctoral dissertation, Northwestern University, 1976). *Dissertation Abstracts International*, 1977, *37*, 7006A.

Cohen, M. P. Interest and its relationship to problem solving ability among secondary school mathematics students (Doctoral dissertation, University of Texas, 1976). *Dissertation Abstracts International*, 1977, *37*, 4929A.

Cook, B. *An analysis of arithmetic, linguistic, and algebraic structural variables that contribute to problem solving difficulty in algebra word problems.* A paper presented at the AERA annual meeting, New Orleans, 1973a.

Cook, B. *Structural variables in algebra word problems.* Unpublished mimeographed paper, Pennsylvania State University, 1973b.

Covington, M., Crutchfield, R., & Davies, L. *The productive thinking program.* Columbus, Ohio: Charles E. Merrill, 1974.

Crutchfield, R. Sensitization and activation of cognitive skills. In J. Bruner (Ed.), *Learning about learning: a conference report.* Washington, D.C.: U.S. Office of Education, 1966.

Dahmus, M. E. How to teach verbal problems. *School Science and Mathematics*, 1970, *70*, 121-138.

Dale, E. & Chall, J. S. A formula for predicting readability. *Educational Research Bulletin*, 1948, *27*, 11-20.

Days, H. C. *The effect of problem structure on the processes used by concrete- and formal-operational students to solve verbal mathematics problems.* Unpublished doctoral dissertation, Purdue University, 1977.

Denholm, R. A., Hankins, D. D., Herrick, M. C., & Vojtko, G. R. *Mathematics for individual achievement* (Books 7-8). Boston: Houghton Mifflin, 1975.

Dienes, Z. P., & Jeeves, M. A. *Thinking in structures.* London: Hutchinson Educational, 1965.

Dienes, Z. P., & Jeeves, M. A. *The effects of structural relations on transfer.* London: Hutchinson Educational, 1970.

Dolciani, M., Berman, S., & Wooton, W. *Modern algebra and trigonometry: structure and method* (Book 2). Boston: Houghton Mifflin, 1973.

Dolciani, M., & Wooton, W. *Modern algebra structure and method* (Book 1). Boston: Houghton Mifflin, 1973.

Dresher, R. Training in mathematics vocabulary. *Educational Research Bulletin*, 1934, *13*, 201-204.

Duncan, E. R., Capps, L. R., Dolciani, M. P., Quast, W. G., & Zweng, M. *Modern school mathematics: structure and use, K-6.* Boston: Houghton Mifflin, 1972.

Duncker, K. On problem solving. *Psychological Monographs,* 1945, *58,* (5, Whole No. 270).

Durell, C. V. *A new geometry for schools.* London: G. Bell & Sons, 1960.

Durnin, J. *Assessing behavior potential: a comparison of three methods.* Unpublished doctoral dissertation, University of Pennsylvania, 1971.

Earp, N. W. *Reading in mathematics.* Columbus, Ohio, 1969. (ERIC Document Reproduction Service No. ED 036 397)

Earp, N. W. Procedures for teaching reading in mathematics. *Arithmetic Teacher,* 1970, *17,* 575-579.

Ernst, G. W., & Newell, A. *GPS: a case study in generality and problem solving.* New York: Academic Press, 1969.

Fehr, H. F., Fey, J. T., & Hill, T. J. *Unified mathematics: course 1.* Menlo Park, CA: Addison-Wesley, 1972.

Feigenbaum, E. A. & Feldman, J. *Computers and thought.* New York: McGraw-Hill, 1963.

Ferguson, R. L. *Computer-assisted criterion-referenced measurement.* Unpublished manuscript, University of Pittsburgh: Learning Research and Development Center, 1969.

Forbes, J. E. An eclectic program in geometry. In K. B. Henderson (Ed.), *Geometry in the mathematics curriculum. Thirty-sixth yearbook of the national council of teachers of mathematics.* Reston, VA: NCTM, 1973.

Frandsen, A., & Holden, J. Spatial visualization in solving complex verbal problems. *Journal of Psychology,* 1969, *73,* 229-233.

Gardner, M. *Mathematical puzzles and diversions.* New York: Simon & Schuster, 1959a.

Gardner, M. (Ed.) *Mathematical puzzles of Sam Loyd.* New York: Dover Publications, 1959b.

Gardner, M. *New rathematical diversions from Scientific American.* New York: Simon & Schuster, 1966.

Gelernter, H. A note on syntactic symmetry and the manipulation of formal systems by machine. *Information and Control,* 1959, *2,* 80-89.

Gelernter, H. Realization of a geometry theorem-proving machine. *Proceedings of an International Conference on Information Processing.* Paris: UNESCO House, 1959. Reprinted in Edward A. Feigenbaum & Julian Feldman (Eds.), *Computers and thought.* New York: McGraw-Hill, 1963, 134-152.

Gelernter, H. & Rochester, N. Intelligent behavior in problem-solving machines. *IBM Journal of Research and Development,* 1958, *2*(4), 336-345.

Gibb, E. G. et al. *Mathematics around us* (Book 6). Glenview, Ill.: Scott Foresman, 1975.

Gilmary, Sister. Training effects of reading remediation to arithemtic computation when intelligence is controlled and all other school factors are eliminated. *Arithmetic Teacher*, 1967, *14*, 17-20.

Gimmestad, B. J. *Mathematical problem solving inventory for community college students*. National Collection of Research Instruments for Mathematical Problem Solving, Department of Mathematical Sciences, Purdue University, 1977.

Goldin, G. A. Critical commentary I, the psychology of mathematical abilities in schoolchildren (V. A. Krutetskii). *Investigations in Mathematics Education*, 1977, *10*(2), 48-52

Goldin, G. A., & Luger, G. F. *Artificial intelligence models for human problem solving*. Technical Report, Graduate School of Education, University of Pennsylvania, 1973.

Goldin, G. A., & Luger, G. F. *Problem structure and problem solving behavior*. Proceedings of International Joint Conference on Artificial Intelligence, 1975, Tbilisi, USSR. Cambridge, Mass.: MIT-AI Press.

Goldin, G. A., & Luger, G. F. *State-space representations in problem solving research*. Unpublished manuscript, 1979.

Goldin, G. A., & McClintock, C. E. The theme of problem symmetry. *Problem solving in school mathematics. National council of teachers of mathematics 1980 yearbook*. Reston, VA: NCTM, in press.

Goldberg, D. *The effect of training in heuristic methods on the ability to write proofs in number theory*. Unpublished doctoral dissertation, Columbia University, 1973.

Goodman, K. What we know about reading. In P. D. Allen & D. J. Watson (Eds.), *Findings of research in miscue analysis: classroom implications*. Urbana, Ill.: National Council of Teachers of English, 1967.

Gramick, J. *Should algorithms be taught to conform to observed behaviors?* Unpublished doctoral dissertation, Univerity of Pennsylvania, 1975.

Greeno, J. G. Hobbits and orcs: acquisition of a sequential concept. *Cognitive Psychology*, 1974, *6*, 270-292.

Hadamard, J. *An essay on the psychology of invention in the mathematical field*. Princeton, N. J.: Princeton University Press, 1945.

Harris, Z. S. *Structural linguistics*. Chicago: University of Chicago Press, 1951.

Hater, M. A., & Kane, R. B. *The cloze procedure as a measure of the reading comprehensibility and difficulty of mathematical English*. Columbus, Ohio, 1970. (ERIC Document Reproduction Service No. ED 040 881)

Hatfield, L. L. Heuristical emphases in the instruction of mathematical problem solving: rationale and research. In L. L. Hatfield (Ed.), *Mathematical problem solving: papers from a research workshop*, ERIC, 1978.

Hayes, J. R. & Simon, H. A. Understanding written problem instruction. In L. W. Gregg (Ed.), *Knowledge and cognition*. Potomac, Md.: Erlbaum, 1974.

Hayes, J. R. & Simon, H. A. *Psychological differences among problem isomorphs*. Pittsburgh: Carnegie-Mellon University (CIP # 303 Psychology Department), 1975.

Henderson, K. B. & Pingry, R. E. Problem solving in mathematics. *The learning of mathematics, its theory and practice. Thirty-first yearbook of the National Council of Teachers of Mathematics*. Washington, D.C.: NCTM, 1953.

Henney, M. A. The relative impact of mathematics reading skills instruction and supervised study upon fourth graders' ability to solve verbal problems in mathematics (Doctoral dissertation, Kent State University, 1968). *Dissertation Abstracts International*, 1969, *29*, 4377A. (University Microfilms No. 69-9556)

Henney, M. A. Improving mathematics verbal problem-solving ability through reading instruction. *Arithmetic Teacher*, 1971, *18*, 223-229.

Hill, T. J. *Mathematical challenges II, plus six*. Reston, VA: National Council of Teachers of Mathematics, 1974.

Hinsley, D., Hayes, J., & Simon, H. From words to equations: meaning and representation in algebra word problems. In M. A. Just & P. A. Carpenter (Eds.), *Cognitive processes in comprehension*. Hillsdale, N.J.: Erlbaum, 1977.

Hively, W., II, Patterson, H. L., & Page, S. H. A universe-defined system of arithmetic tests, *Journal of Educational Measurements*, 1968, *5*, 275-295.

Houtz, J. C. Problem solving ability of advantaged and disadvantaged elementary school children with concrete and abstract item representation (Doctoral dissertation, Purdue University, 1973). *Dissertation Abstracts International*, 1974, *34*, 5717A.

Hunt, E. G. *Artificial Intelligence*. New York: Academic Press, 1975.

Ingle, J. A. Prediction of word problem difficulty on the basis of problem characteristics (Doctoral dissertation, George Peabody College for Teachers, 1975). *Dissertation Abstracts International*, 1975, *36*, 2157A. (University Microfilms No. 75-22, 273)

Jansson, L. C. *Structural and linguistic variables that contribute to difficulty in the judgment of simple deductive arguments*. A paper presented at the AERA annual meeting, Chicago, 1974.

Jerman, M. *Instruction in problem solving and an analysis of structural variables that contribute to problem-solving difficulty* (Technical Report No. 180). Stanford University: Institute for Mathematical Studies in the Social Sciences, November 1971.

Jerman, M. *Structural variables in arithmetic problems.* Mimeographed paper, Pennsylvania State University, 1972.

Jerman, M. Individualized instruction in problem solving in elementary school mathematics. *Journal for Research in Mathematics Education,* 1973, *4*, 6-19.

Jerman, M., & Mirman, S. *Structural and linguistic variables in problem solving.* Pennsylvania State University, 1973. (ERIC Document Reproduction Service No. ED 081 285).

Jerman, M., & Mirman, S. Linguistic and computational variables in problem solving in elementary mathematics. *Educational Studies in Mathematics,* 1974, *5*, 317-362.

Jerman, M., & Rees, R. Predicting the relative difficulty of verbal arithmetic problems. *Educational Studies in Mathematics,* 1972, *4*, 306-323.

Johannot, L. *Recherches sur le raisonnement mathematique de l'adolescent.* Geneva: Neuchatel, Delachaux, et Niestle, S. A., 1947.

Johnson, D. M. *The psychology of thought and judgment.* New York: Harper, 1955.

Johnson, E. S. An information processing model of one kind of problem solving. *Psychological Monographs,* 1964, *78*, 4.

Johnson, H. C. Problem solving in arithmetic: a review of the literature. *Elementary School Journal,* 1944, *44*, 396-403.

Johnson, J. T. On the nature of problem solving in arithmetic. *Journal of Educational Research,* 1949, *43*, 110-115.

Kane, R. B. The readability of mathematical English. *Journal of Research in Science Teaching,* 1968, *5*, 296-298.

Kane, R. B. The readability of mathematical textbooks: revisited. *Mathematics Teacher,* 1970, *63*, 579-581.

Kantowski, E. L. Processes involved in mathematical problem solving (Doctoral dissertation, University of Georgia, 1974). *Dissertation Abstracts International,* 1975, *36*, 2734A. (University Microfilms No. 75-23764)

Kantowski, E. L. The teaching experiment and soviet studies of problem solving. In L. L. Hatfield (Ed.), *Mathematical problem solving: papers from a research workshop,* ERIC, 1978.

Kennedy, G., Eliot, J., & Krulee, G. Error patterns in problem solving formulations. *Psychology in the Schools,* 1970, *7*(1), 93-99.

Kilpatrick, J. *Formulas for predicting readability and solvability of verbal algebra problems.* Unpublished master's thesis, University of California, Berkeley, 1960.

Kilpatrick, J. *Analyzing the solution of word problems in mathematics: an exploratory study.* Unpublished doctoral dissertation, Stanford University, 1967.

Kilpatrick, J. Problem solving in mathematics. *Review of Educational Research,* 1969, *39,* 523-534.

Kilpatrick, J. *Research in the teaching and learning of mathematics.* A paper presented at the Mathematics Association of America meeting, Dallas, 1973.

Kilpatrick, J. *Variables and methodologies in research on problem solving.* A paper presented at the Research Workshop on Problem Solving, University of Georgia, 1975. Reprinted in L. L. Hatfield (Ed.), *Mathematical problem solving: papers from a research workshop,* ERIC, 1978.

Kinsella, J. Problem solving. In *The teaching of secondary school mathematics. Thirty-third Yearbook of the National Council of Teachers of Mathematics.* Reston, VA: NCTM, 1970.

Kleinmuntz, B. (Ed.) *Problem solving: research, method, and theory.* New York: John Wiley & Sons, 1966.

Knifong, J. D., & Holton, B. An analysis of children's written solutions to word problems. *Journal for Research in Mathematics Education,* 1976, *7,* 106-112.

Krushinski, J. *An analysis of linguistic structural variables that contribute to problem solving difficulty.* Unpublished master's thesis, Pennsylvania State University, 1973.

Krutetskii, V. A. An investigation of mathematical abilities in schoolchildren. In J. Kilpatrick & I. Wirszup (Eds.), *Soviet studies in the psychology of learning and teaching mathematics* (Vol. 2). Stanford, CA: School Mathematics Study Group, 1969.

Krutetskii, V. A. *The psychology of mathematical abilities in schoolchildren.* Chicago: University of Chicago Press, 1976.

Kulm, G. Teaching problem-solving heuristics: a critique of two studies. *Journal for Research in Mathematics Education,* 1977, *8,* 153-155.

Kulm, G., Lewis, J. F., Omari, I., & Cook, H. *The effectiveness of textbooks, student generated, and pictorial versions of presenting mathematical problems.* Columbia University, 1972. (ERIC Document Reproduction Service No. ED 062 139).

Landa, L. N. *Algorithmization of learning and instruction.* Englewood Cliffs, N. J.: Educational Technology Publications, 1974.

Landa, L. N. The ability to think--how can it be taught? *Soviet Education,* 1976a, *5,* 4-66.

Landa, L. N. *Instructional regulation and control: Cybernetics, algorithmization and heuristics in education.* Englewood Cliffs, New Jersey: Educational Technology Publications, Inc., 1976.

Lane, M. (Ed.) *Introduction to structuralism.* New York: Basic Books, 1970.

Laughlin, P. R. ·Selection strategies in concept attainment as a function of number of persons and stimulus display. *Journal of Experimental Psychology,* 1965, *70,* 323-327.

Laughlin, P. R. Selection strategies in concept attainment. In R. L. Solso (Ed.), *Contemporary issues in cognitive psychology.* Washington, D. C.: Winston, 1973.

Lazerte, M. E. *The development of problem-solving ability in arithmetic.* Toronto: Clark, Irwin, 1933.

Levi-Strauss, C. *Structural anthropology.* New York: Basic Books, 1963.

Levi-Strauss, C. *Elementary structures of kinship.* Boston: Beacon, 1969.

Linville, W. J. The effects of syntax and vocabulary upon the difficulty of verbal arithmetic problems with fourth grade students (Doctoral dissertation, Indiana University, 1970). *Dissertation Abstracts International,* 1970, *29,* 4310A. (University Microfilms No. 70-7957)

Loftus, E. J. *An analysis of the structural variables that determine problem solving difficulty on a computer-based teletype.* (Technical Report No. 162) Stanford, CA: Institute for Mathematical Studies in the Social Sciences, Stanford University, 1970.

Longeot, F. Analyse statistique de trois tests genetiques collectifs. *Bulletin de l'institute national d'etude du travail et orientation professionelle,* 1964, *20,* 219-237.

Lucas, J. F. An exploratory study in the diagnostic teaching of elementary calculus (Doctoral dissertation, University of Wisconsin-Madison, 1972). *Dissertation Abstracts International,* 1972, *32,* 6825A. (University Microfilms No. 72-15,368)

Luger, G. F. *The use of 'artificial intelligence' techniques for the study of problem solving behavior.* Unpublished doctoral dissertation, University of Pennsylvania, 1973.

Luger, G. F. The use of the state-space to record the behavioural effects of subproblems and symmetries in the Tower of Hanoi problem. *International Journal of Man-machine Studies,* 1976, *8.*

Luger, G. F. & Bauer, M. Transfer effects of isomorphic problem situations. *Acta Psychologica,* 1978, *42,* 121-131.

Lyda, W. J., & Duncan, R. N. Quantitative vocabulary and problem solving. *Arithmetic Teacher,* 1967, *14,* 289-291.

Maki, D. P., & Thompson, M. *Mathematical models and applications.* Englewood Cliffs, N. J.: Prentice-Hall, 1973.

Malin, J. T. Information-processing load in problem solving by network search. *Journal of Experimental Psychology: Human Perception and Performance,* 1979, *5,* 379-390.

Martin, M. D. Reading comprehension, abstract verbal reasoning, and computation as factors in arithmetic problem solving (Doctoral dissertation, State University of Iowa, 1964). *Dissertation Abstracts International*, 1964, *24*, 4547-4548A. (University Microfilms No. 64-3395)

Mayer, R. E. Effects of meaningfulness on the representation of knowledge and the process of inference for mathematical problem solving. In R. Revlin & R. E. Mayer (Eds.), *Human reasoning*. Washington, D. C.: V. H. Winston, 1978.

Miller, G. A., Galanter, E., & Pribram, K. H. *Plans and the structure of behavior*. New York: Holt, Rinehart & Winston, 1960.

Minsky, M. & Papert, S. *Progress report of the MIT artificial intelligence laboratory*. Cambridge, Mass.: MIT Press, 1972.

Monroe, W., & Englehart, M. A critical summary of research relating to the teaching of arithmetic. *Bureau of Educational Research Bulletin No. 58*, Urbana, Illinois: University of Illinois, 1931.

Moses, B. E. The nature of spatial ability and its relationship to mathematical problem solving (Doctoral dissertation, Indiana University, 1977). *Dissertation Abstracts International*, 1978, *38*, 4640A.

Nesher, P., & Teubal, E. Verbal cues as an interfering factor in verbal problem solving. *Educational Studies in Mathematics*, 1975, *6*(1), 41-51.

Newell, A., Shaw, J. C., & Simon, H. A. Elements of a theory of human problem solving. *Psychological Review*, 1958, *65*, 151-166.

Newell, A., Shaw, J. C., & Simon, H. A. *The processes of creative thinking*. Paper P-1320, Santa Monica: Rand Corporation, 1959a.

Newell, A., Shaw, J. C., & Simon, H. A. *Report on a general problem-solving program*. Paper P-1584, Santa Monica: Rand Corporation, 1959b.

Newell, A., Shaw, J. C., & Simon, H. A. Empirical explorations with the logic theory machine: a case study in heuristics. In E. A. Feigenbaum & J. Feldman (Eds.), *Computers and thought*. New York: McGraw-Hill, 1963.

Newell, A., & Simon, H. A. *The simulation of human thought*. Paper P-1734, Santa Monica: Rand Corporation, 1959.

Newell, A., & Simon, H. A. Human problem solving: the state of the theory in 1970. *American Psychologists*, 1971, *26*(2), 145-159.

Newell, A., & Simon, H. A. *Human problem solving*. Englewood Cliffs: N. J.: Prentice-Hall, 1972.

Nilssen, N. J. *Problem-solving methods in artificial intelligence*. New York: McGraw-Hill, 1971.

Nisbett, R. E., & Wilson, T. D. Telling more than we can know: verbal reports on mental processes. *Psychological Review*, 1977, *84*, 231-279.

Paige, J., & Simon, H. A. Cognitive processes in solving algebra word problems. In B. Kleinmuntz (Ed.), *Problem solving: research, method, and theory.* New York: John Wiley & Sons, 1966.

Perfetti, C. A. Lexical density and phrase structure depth as variables in sentence retention. *Journal of Verbal Learning and Verbal Behavior,* 1969, *8,* 719-724.

Piaget, J. [*Six psychological studies.*] (D. Elkind, Ed.). New York: Vintage Books, 1968.

Piaget, J. [*Structuralism*] (C. Maschler, Trans.). New York: Basic Books, 1970.

Piaget, J., & Inhelder, B. *The psychology of the child.* New York: Basic Books, 1969.

Poincare, H. L'invention mathematizue. *Revue de mois,* 1908, *6.*

Pollak, H. O. On mathematics applications and real problem solving. *School Science and Mathematics,* 1978, *78*(3), 232-239.

Polya, G. *How to solve it* (2nd Ed.). New York: Doubleday, 1957.

Polya, G. *Mathematical discovery.* Vols. 1 & 2. *On understanding, learning, and teaching problem solving.* New York: John Wiley & Sons, 1962, 1965.

Polya, G., & Kilpatrick, J. *The Stanford mathematics problem book with hints and solutions.* New York: Teachers College Press, 1974.

Posamentier, A. S., & Salkind, C. T. *Challenging problems in algebra 1.* London: Macmillan, 1970.

Reed, S. K., Ernst, G. W., & Banerji, R. The role of analogy in transfer between similar problem states. *Cognitive Psychology,* 1974, *6,* 436-450.

Rising, G. Some comments on a simple puzzle. *Mathematics Teacher,* 1956, *49,* 267-269.

Robinson, C. S., & Hayes, J. R. Making inferences about relevance in understanding problems. In R. Revlin & R. E. Mayer (Eds.), *Human reasoning.* Washington, D. C.: V. H. Winston, 1978.

Rohrman, N. L. The role of syntactic structure in the recall of English normalizations. *Journal of Verbal Learning and Verbal Behavior,* 1968, *7,* 904-912.

Roman, R. A., & Laudata, N. C. *Computer assisted instruction in word problems rationale and design.* Pittsburgh: Learning Research and Development Center, University of Pittsburgh, 1974.

Rosenthal, D. J., & Resnick, L. B. *The sequence of information in arithmetic work problems.* A paper presented at the annual meeting of AERA, New York, 1971.

Ruddell, R. B. The effect of oral and written patterns of language structure on reading comprehension. *Reading Teacher,* 1964, *18,* 270-275.

Sax, G., & Ottina, J. R. The arithmetic achievement of pupils differing in school experience. *California Journal of Educational Research,* 1958, *9,* 15-19.

Scandura, J. *Problem solving: a structural process approach with instructional implications.* New York: Academic Press, 1977.

Schmidt, E. *What makes reading difficult and the complexity of structures.* A paper presented at the annual convention of the National Reading Conference, New Orleans, 1977.

Schoenfeld, A. *Can heuristics be taught?* Unpublished manuscript (SESAME Project), University of California, Berkeley, 1976.

Schoenfeld, A. Can heuristics be taught? In *Cognitive process instruction.* Philadelphia, Penn.: Franklin Institute Press, 1979.

Schonberger, A. K. The interrelationship of sex, visual spatial abilities, and mathematical problem solving ability in grade seven (Doctoral dissertation, University of Wisconsin, 1976). *Dissertation Abstracts International,* 1976, *37,* 3536A.

Scott, R., & Lighthall, F. Relationship between context, sex, grade, and degree of disadvantage in arithmetic problem solving. *Journal of School Psychology,* 1967, *6,* 67.

Segalla, A. *Using structural variables to predict word problem solving difficulty for junior college arithmetic students.* Paper presented at the American Educational Research Association annual meeting, New Orleans, 1973.

Sheehan, D. J. The effectiveness of concrete and formal instructional procedures with concrete- and formal-operational students (Doctoral dissertation, State University of New York at Albany, 1970). *Dissertation Abstracts International,* 1970, *31,* 2738A. (University Microfilms No. 70-25, 479)

Sherrill, J. M. The effects of different presentations on mathematical word problems upon the achievement of tenth grade students. *School Science and Mathematics,* 1973, *73,* 277-282.

Shklarsky, D. O., Chentzou, N. N., & Yaglom, I. M. *The USSR Olympiad problem book.* San Francisco: W. H. Freeman, 1962.

Shulman, L. S., & Elstein, A. S. Studies of problem solving, judgment, and decision making: implications for educational research. In F. N. Kerlinger (Ed.), *Review of Research in Education* (Vol. 3). Itasca, Il: F. E. Peacock, 1975.

Siegel, S. *Non-parametric statistics for the behavioral sciences.* New York, McGraw-Hill, 1956.

Silver, E. A. *An examination of student perceptions of relatedness among mathematical word problems.* A paper presented at the National Council of Teachers of Mathematics annual meeting, San Diego, 1978.

Simon, H. A. *The science of the artificial.* New York: Wiley, 1969.

Slagle, R. *Artificial intelligence: the heuristic programming approach*. New York: McGraw Hill, 1971.

Smith, B. & Meux, M. *A study of the logic of teaching*. Urbana, Ill.: University of Illinois Press, 1962.

Smith, F. The readability of sixth grade word problems. *School Science and Mathematics*, 1971, *71*, 559-562.

Smith, J. P. *The effects of general versus specific heuristics in mathematical problem solving tasks*. Unpublished doctoral dissertation, Teachers' College, Columbia University, 1973.

Spache, G. D. New readability formula for primary-grade reading materials. *Elementary School Journal*, 1953, *53*, 410-413.

Spencer, P., & Russell, D. Reading in arithmetic. *National Council of Teachers of Mathematics Yearbook*, 1960, *25*, 202-223.

Suppes, P., Hyman, L., & Jerman, M. *Linear structural model for response and latency performance in arithmetic* (Technical Report No. 100). Stanford, CA.: Institute for Mathematical Studies in the Social Sciences, Stanford University, 1966.

Suppes, P., Jerman, M., & Brian, D. *Computer-assisted instruction: the 1965-1966 Stanford arithemtic program*. New York: Academic Press, 1968.

Suppes, P., Loftus, E. J., & Jerman, M. Problem solving on a computer-based teletype. *Educational Studies in Mathematics*, 1969, *2*, 1-15.

Taschow, H. G. Reading improvement in mathematics. *Reading Improvement*, 1969, *6*, 63-67.

Taylor, D. W. Discussion of papers by Adriaan D. de Groot and by Jeffrey M. Paige and Herbert Simon. In B. Kleinmutz (Ed.), *Problem solving: Research, method, and theory*. New York: John Wiley and Sons, Inc., 1966.

Taylor, W. L. Cloze procedures: A new tool for measuring readability. *Journalism Quarterly*, 1953, *30*, 414-438.

Thomas, G. B. Jr. *Calculus and Analytic Geometry* (4th Ed.). Reading, Mass.: Addison-Wesley, 1969.

Thomas, J. C. An analysis of behavior in the hobbits-orcs problem. *Cognitive Psychology*, 1974, *6*, 257-269.

Thompson, E. N. Readability and accessory remarks: Factors in problem solving in arithmetic (Doctoral dissertation, Stanford University, 1968). *Dissertation Abstracts International*, 1968, *28*, 2464A-2465A. (University Microfilms No. 67-17547)

Travers, K. J. A test of pupil preference of problem-solving situations in junior high school mathematics. *Journal of Experimental Education*, 1967, *35*, 9-18.

Tripp, L. *Structural variable definitions for verbal arithmetic problems*. Unpublished mimeographed paper, The Pennsylvania State University, 1972.

Usiskin, Z. *Algebra through applications with probability and statistics*, Chicago: The University of Chicago Press, 1976.

Usiskin, Z. Six nontrivial equivalent problems. *The Mathematics Teacher*, 1968, *4*, 388-390.

VanderLinde, L. F. Does the study of quantitative vocabulary improve problem solving? *The Elementary Science Journal*, 1964, *65*, 143-152.

Waters, W. M. The use and efficiency of a scanning strategy in conjuctive concept attainment (Doctoral dissertation, University of Pennsylvania, 1979). *Dissertation Abstracts International*, 1979, *40*, 1331A.

Webb, L. F., & Sherrill, J. M. The effects of differing presentations of mathematical word problems upon the achievement of preservice elementary teachers. *School Science and Mathematics*, 1974, *74*, 559-565.

Webb, N. L. *An exploration of mathematical problem-solving processes.* Unpublished doctoral dissertation, Stanford University, 1975.

Webb, N. L. *Problem-solving inventory for exploring processes used by upper high school students.* National Collection of Research Instruments for Mathematical Problem Solving, Department of Mathematical Sciences, Purdue University, 1976.

Wertheimer, M. *Productive thinking.* New York: Harper, 1959.

Wheat, H. G. The relative merits of conventional and imaginative types of problems in arithmetic. *Contributions to Education, No. 359.* New York: Columbia University Teachers' College, Bureau of Publications, 1929.

Wickelgren, W. *How to solve problems.* San Francisco: W. H. Freeman, 1974.

Willmon, B. Reading in the content area: A 'new math' terminology list for the primary grades. *Elementary English*, 1971, *48*, 463-471.

Wilson, J. W. *Generality of heuristics as an instructional variable.* Unpublished doctoral dissertation, Stanford University, 1967.

Wilson, K. A distribution-free test of analysis of variance hypotheses. *Psychological Bulletin*, 1956, *53*, 96-101.

Winer, B. J. *Statistical principles in experimental design.* New York: McGraw-Hill, 1962.

Winer, B. J. *Statistical principles in experimental design* (2nd Ed.) New York: McGraw-Hill, 1971.

Yngve, V. H. A model and a hypothesis for language structure. *Proceedings of the American Philosophical Society*, 1960, *104*, 444-466.

Index